To My Mother

Glory Road

THE BLOODY ROUTE FROM
FREDERICKSBURG TO GETTYSBURG

BRUCE CATTON

WHITE LION PUBLISHERS LIMITED
London, Sydney and Toronto

First published in The United States of America

Copyright 1952 by Bruce Catton
All rights reserved

White Lion edition 1977

ISBN 7274 0335 4

Made and printed in Great Britain
for White Lion Publishers Limited,
138 Park Lane, London, W1Y 3DD
by Hendington Limited,
Lion House, North Town, Aldershot, Hampshire.

Glory Road

Contents

FIVE

Lincoln Comin' Wid His Chariot

SIX

End and Beginning

ONE

Deep River

1. For What There Was in It

Returning to his regiment in the fall of 1862 after a furlough in his home city of York, the chaplain of the 102nd Pennsylvania Infantry looked at the ravaged Virginia countryside and noted in his diary that war was very mysterious. It destroyed and wasted, and wherever the armies had gone "the desolation has become almost complete," but back home it was not like that at all. Pennsylvania had put 150,000 men into uniform, and by now a good many of them had gone under the sod, whether with or without appropriate graveside ceremonies. Yet what one actually saw in that state was the hustle and excitement of boom times. Never (to all appearances) had the country been so well off.

"What a marvel is here!" wrote the chaplain. "Something new under the sun! A nation, from internal resources alone, carrying on for over eighteen months the most gigantic war of modern times, ever increasing in its magnitude, yet all this while growing richer and more prosperous!"[1]

As a summary of the effects of war on the national well-being this was neither complete nor wholly accurate, and it might have been bitterly disputed by some of the chaplain's own fellow Pennsylvanians. In the town of Berkeley, in Luzerne County, little more than one hundred miles from boom-town York, insurgent citizens

recently had rioted in protest against the military draft and had subsided only after the militia had fired upon them, with four or five
insurgents left dead in the streets. Nor was this spirit of dissent confined entirely to Pennsylvania, where it was noted that the anthracite
fields were filled with unrest. Similar riots had taken place in the
West, notably in the picturesque lakeside town of Port Washington,
Wisconsin, and if the country was in fact benefiting by the war, the
benefits seemed to be highly uneven and the distribution of them most
inequitable.[2]

Yet in a sense the good chaplain was quite correct. He had put
his finger on something which contained the germ of much history.
Whether he was in fact commenting on an effect of the war or on
a strange, elusive symptom of something which had actually helped
to cause the war may be another matter. At the very least he had
spotted something important, and he was justified in using exclama-
tion points. He had seen one side of the war very clearly.

The trouble in that autumn of 1862 was that there were so many
sides to see. Lord Lyons, British Minister to the United States, was
being given a glimpse of quite a different side, and in mid-November
he was reporting on it to Her Majesty's Foreign Secretary, Lord
Russell. The Federal government had finally nerved itself, once and
for all, to remove General McClellan from command of the Army
of the Potomac, and the deep significance of this act had not been
lost on various Northern leaders of the Democracy. They had seen
it clearly enough as an indication that the administration was now
determined to crush the rebellion completely. The last chance for
compromise had ridden out of the war on the special train that carried McClellan out of the Virginia theater to his home at Trenton,
New Jersey; and these Northern Democrats were dismayed, since a
ruthless war to the bitter end might not be a war which they could
enthusiastically support.

In his dispatch to Lord Russell, Lord Lyons tried to analyze the attitude of the leaders of the Democratic party, North.

"At bottom," he wrote, "I thought I perceived a desire to put an
end to the war, even at the risk of losing the Southern states altogether; but it was plain that it was not thought prudent to avow this
desire."

Nothing would come of this immediately, his lordship believed; but
the Democrats who quietly confided in him—cautious men who talked

obliquely, stopping short of flat commitments, letting inferences and gestures speak for them—had implied that if their party came into power in the North "they would be disposed to accept an offer of mediation, if it appeared to be the only means of putting a stop to hostilities."[3]

Thus a great deal depended on the point of view, for war's different sides had different meanings. To one point of view war meant boom times, intense activities, and good money in the pocket; to another it meant slow death for sacred American ideals. And to still another it meant personal opportunity, with sure advantage coming to him who was canny enough to play the angles correctly. For it was becoming clearer and clearer that the profound changes which were being wrought by this war were in effect creating a new country here, with all of the opportunities that are usually to be found in a new country. There was a folk saying which followed the expanding frontier: "It's good to be shifty in a new country." In 1862 there were any number of openings for the shifty.

As witness the case of Major General Joseph Hooker.

General Hooker that fall had been enjoying a slow recuperation from a light wound received at Antietam. He spent his convalescence in Washington, where he found comfortable quarters in the national insane asylum—a fact of which, luckily, nobody bothered to make anything in particular—and as a wounded hero and a man undeniably gifted with charm he had been lionized to a degree; most especially by certain people who could do an ambitious general a great deal of good.

There had been, for instance, the Secretary of the Treasury, Mr. Salmon Portland Chase, who came to see the general bearing a large basket of fruit and accompanied by his daughter, the beautiful Katherine Chase. Pictorially, the meeting was indubitably a success—handsome general, pink and clean-shaven, bandaged foot resting elegantly on a cushioned stool; stalwart cabinet minister looking almost unutterably dignified and distinguished, inclining his head and saying: "General, if my advice had been followed, you would have commanded after the retreat to James River, if not before"; and Katherine, young and tall and altogether lovely, devoted to her father, the most talked-about and ultimately the most tragically unfortunate young woman in wartime Washington. . . . The American album would be richer if a cameraman had been present.

General and Secretary sparred gently, each one devoting his not inconsiderable talents to the job of finding out where the other stood and just how he could be useful. It seems that they came finally, in this and in later meetings, to an unspoken understanding. Each one was inordinately ambitious, but their ambitions did not conflict—one wanted to lead the country's armies, the other wanted to live in the White House, and it might be that they could rise together. Chase confided to his diary that Hooker struck him as "a frank, manly, brave and energetic soldier, of somewhat less breadth of intellect than I had expected, however, though not of less quickness, clearness and activity"—which was not too bad an appraisal. Hooker, being no diarist, did not record his impression of Mr. Chase. He did, however, shortly after the meeting, issue a public statement strongly supporting the Emancipation Proclamation.[4]

For if Hooker had no great breadth of intellect, he was at least shrewd; shrewd enough, in any event, to perceive the trend of the tide that was setting in just then and to place himself in proper relationship to it. Beginning with the fall of 1862, it was obvious that the great war for reunion was also to be a war against slavery, and the implications of that fact were there for any man to read. What Lord Lyons's confidants had made out, Joe Hooker had made out also. Final control of things was very likely to rest in the hands of men who could forgive any sin to him whose heart was right on the matter of the Negro. If a belief in emancipation were essential to salvation, henceforward General Hooker would have such a belief.

Sign and symbol of his conversion could be seen in his new friendship for the Vice-President, Mr. Hannibal Hamlin of Maine. Mr. Hamlin had no more actual authority than any other vice-president of the United States, and yet he was a man worth cultivating. He was a stalwart among the abolitionists, and if he lacked power he did not lack influence. The group in Congress which was visibly and with apparent success moving to make this war its own personal possession was close to him; it would hear a word spoken in his ear, it would probably show gratitude for any favors which he might receive. So when Vice-President Hamlin visited Hooker's sickroom accompanied by Brigadier General Hiram Berry, seeking a favor, he got an excellent reception.

Hooker and Berry were well acquainted already, of course. Berry had led a brigade in Phil Kearny's division on the peninsula and was by that fact alone marked as a good soldier: in the brief time he had before a Confederate bullet found him, Kearny had made his Red Diamond Division famous, and one of his brigadiers was bound to carry some of that fame with him. Furthermore, Berry reflected some of the glory that had been glimpsed and lost that gloomy June night in front of Richmond, when Kearny and Hooker had gone to McClellan to demand that orders for retreat be canceled. They themselves would lead their troops in a wild assault on the Rebel lines, swords flashing in the smoky dusk along the pine flats, triumph snatched from defeat by a victory-or-death charge at the desperate eleventh hour, destruction for all traitors and everlasting fame for the soldiers who had dared so nobly. Berry had been present when that demand was made, had heard McClellan's icy refusal and Kearny's furious reply that risked a court-martial, and—as a citizen of Maine and a good friend of Mr. Hamlin—had written to the Vice-President some highly informative letters about the whole business, helping thereby to improve Hooker's standing with what was now the dominant group in Washington.[5]

Hooker greeted his callers with warmth. Stretched out on a lounge with his wounded foot on a cushion (the foot now was just about healed), he swung into a breezy discussion of the battle of Antietam. The Vice-President was known to be no admirer of McClellan, and Hooker rose to the occasion, explaining just where and how McClellan's generalship fell short on that bloody field. The subject was a congenial one—Hooker seldom was in better voice than when he was pointing out the defects of his superior officer—and a good deal of time passed. Then at last there was a pause and the inevitable question: Well, gentlemen, what can I do for you?

What he could do, it developed, was to recommend General Berry for promotion. Berry was now a brigadier and wanted to be a major general, and Hooker's recommendation would help. Hooker replied with enthusiasm. The promotion was richly deserved, he declared, and he would do everything in his power to help bring it about. He added that he would even like to see Berry given command of the division which he, Hooker, once had led—a solid testimonial, this last, going beyond mere politics, for it was a crack outfit and still called itself Hooker's division, and a soldier like Hooker was certain to be proud and touchy about such things. It was perfectly characteristic

of Hooker to embed one flash of genuine feeling in the middle of a
calculated political stroke.

True to his word, when the guests left Hooker at once wrote to
Henry Wager Halleck, general-in-chief of the nation's armies. He
was quite aware that as far as Halleck was concerned the word of
Joe Hooker might not carry too much weight. Halleck had seen a
good deal of Hooker in his pre-war California phase, when the dashing army officer had descended almost to the level of beachcomber,
and Halleck definitely did not admire him. Indeed, the best surviving
evidence that Halleck really did have some of the acumen he was then
supposed to have may consist in the fact that from the very beginning
he was firmly convinced that sooner or later the flawed character
which he had observed along the Sacramento would get General
Hooker into serious trouble. Hooker assumed, possibly with some
justification, that it was principally Halleck who had kept him from
getting command of the Army of the Potomac when McClellan was
relieved.

Yet if Halleck was distrustful, he was not opposing Hooker in all
things. If the battle of Antietam had had an individual hero, that
hero was probably Hooker; and McClellan, either not knowing or
not caring that Hooker was one of his bitterest critics, had recom-
mended, before his own removal from command, that Major General
Hooker, U. S. Volunteers, be commissioned also as Brigadier General
Hooker, U. S. Army—a recommendation which the War Department
had accepted and acted upon, so that by the time he returned to active
duty Hooker had the new commission in his possession. This was the
best possible evidence that Hooker stood well with the administration,
for promotion in the regular ranks was the greatest reward the War
Department could offer to a professional soldier. Every regular-army
officer was at all times conscious that this war, be it nobly won or
miserably lost, was in any event going to *end* someday; and when it
ended all of the fine volunteer commissions, with the various per-
quisites and the increased pay and allowances that went with them,
would at once evaporate. Upon that day a regular who had gone to
bed a major general might wake up to find himself a mere captain
once more, responsible only for one flea-bitten battery of artillery and
possessing no more than a captain's pay and prospects. Promotion in
the regular ranks represented security. No matter what happened,
Hooker would be a general the rest of his life; he could retire as a gen-

eral and he would infallibly be buried as a general, with a starred flag to mark his gravestone.[6]

From a cold and calculating viewpoint, therefore, Joe Hooker had already made a success out of the war. Yet even though the army contained very few officers who were more completely capable of taking a cold and calculating view of things, Hooker was no man to be satisfied with a partial achievement. As Secretary Chase had seen, his ambition was great. Also, a good part of Joe Hooker was perfectly genuine, and a great deal of the criticism which he so freely bestowed on his superiors came simply because his professional competence was outraged by the blunders he had had to witness. He felt that he could handle things better himself, and he had reason for thinking so. If such blunders continued—and it seemed very likely that they would —it was as certain as anything could be that the high command would someday be groping desperately for a man with military abilities like those owned by General Hooker. When that day came, Hooker proposed to be standing where the high command could not help reaching him.

It was good to be shifty in a new country. The Secretary of War, Edwin M. Stanton, with his hot little eyes, and the fire-breathing abolitionist from Michigan, Senator Zachariah Chandler, followed Secretary Chase's lead, dropping in to sound the general out and to size him up. At the same time obscurer men came in to do what General Berry had done: to seek favors and simultaneously to exhibit political backing. One of these was an Indiana colonel named Solomon J. Meredith, who very much wished to be a brigadier general. He was not especially noteworthy in his own right, but he had political connections as good as the very best.

Meredith was a breezy giant of a man in his early fifties. A North Carolinian by birth, he had moved to Indiana as a young man, settling in Wayne County, near the Ohio line, and getting a firm foothold in county politics. He had a gift for it. During the next two decades, while he developed a prosperous farm, he was twice elected sheriff of his county, was sent to the state legislature for several terms, and finally won appointment as United States marshal for the district of Indiana—the kind of political plum that goes only to a man with first-rate credentials. In addition to a record of loyal service with the new Republican party, Meredith's assets included a firm personal and political friendship with one of the Midwest's most remarkable men, Oliver P. Morton, the famous war governor of Indiana.

No general who was properly mindful of his own chances for advancement was going to overlook any claims that might be supported by Governor Morton. As far as the Midwest was concerned, Morton *was* the Union cause incarnate—a man without whom (to the certain knowledge of Abraham Lincoln and others) war west of the Alleghenies could not successfully be carried on. He was a man of savage driving force, and in his code the only binding rule in war was that you had to win. He struck with equal fury at those disloyal to the sacred cause and those who got across the political path of Oliver P. Morton. In sum, he was a man of influence, and if General Hooker had had any doubts about it the recent experience of Major General Don Carlos Buell might have enlightened him.

General Buell had had the command in eastern Kentucky and Tennessee, charged with quieting the troubled border region while Grant, farther west and south, groped down the Mississippi Valley toward Vicksburg. Buell was a West Pointer, a close friend of Mc-Clellan, a grave and serious man of considerable ability. He had had many difficulties in recent months, one of the worst of them being a complete inability to get along with Governor Morton. Buell had many Indiana regiments in his command, and Morton, as the governor who had raised and equipped those troops, always tried to retain some control over them even after they had gone on active service far outside Indiana. General and governor had bickered about this off and on for some time.

The matter had come to a head, apparently, at the end of September, when Confederate armies led by Braxton Bragg and Kirby Smith slipped through the loose Federal cordons and came driving up through Kentucky toward the Ohio River, raising Middle Western temperatures to a high pitch, especially Governor Morton's. Morton rushed a number of green Indiana regiments to Kentucky to help meet the invasion, and they had bad luck. One Confederate invading wing caught a column of these men near the town of Richmond, southeast of Lexington, and broke it to pieces, inflicting a thousand casualties and capturing upward of four thousand men. The other invading wing seized a Union fort at Munfordville a fortnight later, capturing four Indiana regiments entire. The Confederates seemed on the verge of making a complete conquest of Kentucky, and Morton hurried

there in person, bitterly blaming Buell for the disasters. At the end
of September, accompanied by a Union brigadier general bearing the
unlikely name of Jefferson Davis, Morton stalked into the Galt Hotel
at Louisville looking for trouble.

It seemed likely that he would find it. Davis was Indiana-born and
-bred, a regular-army officer who had been in the Fort Sumter garrison in the spring of 1861 and who, coming north after the fort fell,
had taken leave of absence and had gone to Indiana to raise and
become first colonel of the 22nd Indiana Infantry. Just now he was
under a cloud. He had quarreled bitterly with Major General William
Nelson, one of Buell's corps commanders, and had been sent north
of the Ohio with an official rebuke spattered across his service record.
As a good Hoosier, he had gone at once to Indianapolis to see Governor Morton. Morton was already denouncing Nelson, whom he
held largely responsible for the defeat at Richmond, so when he went
to Louisville he had Davis come along, and if an Indiana general who
was rebuked could stay rebuked they would find out about it. In the
hotel lobby they encountered Nelson himself.

Nelson was a huge ox of a man—three hundred muscular pounds
on a frame six feet four, a man who alternately glowed with hail-
fellow geniality and stormed with titanic rage. A former navy lieutenant turned soldier, he had raised and trained many Union troops
in Kentucky. He had a breezy way in battle; in one fight he comforted green troops by telling them: "If they don't hit me you needn't
be a bit afraid, for if they can't hit me they can't hit the side of a barn."
Buell considered him one of the Union's most valuable officers.

Now he and Davis immediately began to bristle at each other. From
bristling they went to snarling, passing profanities hotly, and presently it was the back of Nelson's great hand across Davis's face.
Then Nelson stalked majestically away. Davis hesitated, borrowed
a revolver from an aide, strode after Nelson, called to him, and when
he turned around shot him dead. He then surrendered his revolver
and submitted quietly enough to military arrest.

So here was a sensation and a clear case for the sternest military
discipline: Buell's most trusted lieutenant shot dead (before a hotel
full of witnesses) by a subordinate, in Buell's own headquarters city,
on the eve of a fateful battle. And yet somehow nothing whatever
came of it.

The fateful battle was fought and the Confederates retreated—not

so much because of anything Buell's troops had done to them as
because of the strange caution of the Rebel commander, General
Bragg. Shortly thereafter Buell was relieved of his command, and
the Civil War knew him no more. And Brigadier General Jefferson
C. Davis received not so much as a slap on the wrist for killing a
major general. Instead he presently returned to duty, ultimately to
advancement.[7]

Before he was relieved from duty Buell requested General Halleck to appoint a military court to try Davis for murder. The subject
was considered at Washington, and late in October Secretary of the
Navy Welles noted that the case was discussed by the Cabinet. But in
the end Davis was released to the civil authorities, a grand jury refused
to vote an indictment, and any Union general who meditated upon
the matter was bound to conclude that this Governor Morton was a
man of very solid and far-reaching influence.

So when Colonel Meredith of the 19th Indiana came asking for
preferment and displayed himself as an intimate friend of Governor
Morton, Joe Hooker was going to listen very attentively and he was
going to be obliging if he could. Meredith did want quite a lot, to be
sure—a brigadier's commission, to begin with, plus command of the
most famous fighting brigade in the army, General John Gibbon's
magnificent Iron Brigade, of which the colonel's 19th Indiana was a
part.

Command of the brigade was vacant just then, Gibbon having
been promoted to divisional command. The only trouble was that
Meredith was by no means the logical person to take the brigade.
He had been in the brigade's first battle—at Groveton, on August 28,
when the four green regiments had stood off Stonewall Jackson's entire
corps and had lost 33 per cent of the numbers engaged—and had
conducted himself well enough there, suffering a minor injury and
rejoining his regiment on the march up through Maryland. But at
Antietam, where the brigade had spearheaded Hooker's furious attack on Lee's left, Meredith had not even been present. He had
reported himself unfit for duty a day or so earlier because of the hurt
received at Groveton and the fatigue of the marching since and had
gone off to Washington to recuperate and to angle for promotion. In
the stern code of John Gibbon this was about enough to write him
off the army roster, especially since the lieutenant colonel who led the
regiment in Meredith's absence was killed in action. It was Gibbon's

feeling that either Colonel Fairchild of the 2nd Wisconsin or Colonel Cutler of the 6th Wisconsin fully deserved promotion to brigade command and that Meredith did not deserve it at all.

General Gibbon's advice was not asked, however. Hooker took counsel, one supposes, with his own ambition and meditated on the strong long arm of the governor of Indiana, then wrote out the requested recommendation. And so Meredith, early in December, with a brigadier's star on either shoulder, took command of the Iron Brigade, while Gibbon stormed fruitlessly and wrote Hooker down as a man who "sacrificed his soldierly principles whenever such sacrifice could gain him political influence to further his own ends."[8]

Which is as it may be; bearing in mind that everything, or nearly everything, depends on the point of view, and that the reality of the Civil War was different for different people. The war meant boom times for canny civilians, as a chaplain had noted, and it meant high danger for sacred ideals, as leading Democrats had confided to the British minister; and to a General Hooker it meant infinite alluring possibilities, with personal advancement coming surely to the man who was shifty enough to play his cards skillfully. Yet these points of view were not the only ones valid in that fall of 1862. There was also the point of view of the private soldier, whose outlook upon the war was necessarily narrow but who at least stood, as he made his own personal survey of things, a little closer to the ultimate realities of life and death.

There was the point of view, to be more specific, of this same Iron Brigade, to whose command the swanky new brigadier from Indiana was just now ascending.

The brigade had been whittled thin these last few months. In mid-August it had mustered in its fouɪ regiments close to twenty-four hundred men. Three battles and five weeks later it stood at less than a thousand, and just before Antietam, General Gibbon had appealed to the high command to give him a new regiment—a Western regiment, if possible, since the Iron Brigade men came from Wisconsin and Indiana and would get on better with men from their own part of the country. A few weeks after Antietam his request was granted, and on October 9 the brigade was drawn up on the parade ground to give formal welcome to its new comrades, the brand-new soldiers of the 24th Michigan Volunteer Infantry.

The welcome was of the coldest, and the ceremony seems to have pleased no one. On one side of the parade stood the four regiments of veterans—19th Indiana and 2nd, 6th, and 7th Wisconsin: rangy, sun-tanned men in worn and dusty uniforms, who lounged in the ranks with that indefinable easy looseness which only veterans possess and who wore the black slouch hats which were the distinguishing headgear of this brigade as if they were badges of great honor—which, as a matter of fact, they were. The veterans looked across the open ground at the newcomers with complete and unconcealed skepticism and hostility. In every line of their bearing—in the set of their jaws, the tilt of their heads, the look about their eyes peering out from under those valued hatbrims—they expressed for all to see the age-old, impersonal, unformulated feeling of the veteran for the recruit: We have had it and you have not, and until you have been where we have been and have done what we have done we do not admit you to any kind of fellowship.

The boys from Michigan got the message perfectly. They came up to line nervously that morning, thoroughly aware that the newness and neatness of their uniforms proclaimed them rookies with the test of manhood still ahead of them. Their very numbers were a count against them. Here they were, one regiment, with nearly as many men present for duty, armed and equipped, as were present in all four of the regiments across the parade. With their arrival the brigade had nearly doubled in size. And with the inexorable illogic of the soldier, it was somehow just then the fault of these boys from Michigan, and a just ground for shame to them, that they brought 900 to the field instead of the veterans' 250.

In addition to which they wore the regulation forage caps instead of the black hats which the brigade had made famous.

Yet this mere matter of being new and green and clumsy would not, of itself, have caused real estrangement between the four veteran regiments and the one new one. The veterans would have been wary, of course, reserving judgment until they had seen these newcomers under fire, treating them with a lofty but not really malicious contempt until after their first battle, and then either outlawing them entirely or receiving them to full brotherhood without reservation. But they would not have given them a cold and savage hostility, which was what even the least sensitive mental antennae were picking up on this field today. For a damning word had come to camp ahead of this new regiment. Here, said camp rumor—unsubstantiated, but accepted as gospel—here were *bounty men*.[9]

The bounty man was comparatively a new addition to the Army of the Potomac. For the most part, the army was still made up of what even then were beginning to be called "the old 1861 regiments": volunteers in the purest sense of the word, men who had enlisted for no earthly reason except that they wanted to go to war, moved by that strange and deceiving light which can lie upon the world very briefly when one is young and innocent. That light was leaving the landscape rapidly in 1862, and volunteering was much slower. To stimulate it, various states, cities, and counties were offering cash bounties to recruits: solid rolls of greenbacks, adding up, in some cases, to as much as a thousand dollars, and in all cases to several hundreds.

Now this business of the bounty somehow summed up all of the contrasting truths about the war—boom times, noble ideals becoming sullied, great opportunities for the calculating; plus the fact, beginning to be visible to private soldiers, that the man who was moved by pure patriotism and by nothing else was quite likely to get the worst of it. For while the bounties were enabling local units of government to fill their quotas, they were also bringing into the army a great many men whose primary concern in enlisting had been neither the saving of the Union nor the satisfaction of some sacred and indefinable inner instinct, but solely the acquisition of sudden wealth. Some of these men, having taken the money, might earn their wages by becoming good and faithful soldiers. Others would slack and skulk and beyond any question would desert the first time occasion offered— going off to some other state to enlist for another bounty, as likely as not. All of the confusion and contradiction of war were mixed up in this bounty system, in the way it worked and in the fact that it had been adopted at all.

The old volunteer regiments of the army were, conceivably, the last reservoir of the original hope, enthusiasm, and incredible lightness of spirit with which the war had begun. Beyond the scheming and the driving and the solid achieving of the governors and the generals and all the others, the war finally would come down to this spirit that lived in the breasts of the enlisted men. It was what the war was ultimately about, and if the war was finally going to be won it was what would win it, the men who had carried the spirit being killed, the spirit somehow surviving. The veteran inevitably drew a sharp distinction between the man who volunteered because this spirit moved him and the bounty boy who joined up for what there was in it; and here, in the Iron Brigade itself, proudest and hardest of the army's warriors, there was a bounty regiment!

Actually, there was nothing of the kind. Camp rumor once again had outrun the truth. Like every one of the thousands of regiments in the Civil War armies, this 24th Michigan had its own history, different from all of the others, just as each soldier had his individual biography, unwritten but unique. In plain fact, instead of being one of the first of the bounty regiments, this outfit was one of the last of the old rally-round-the-flag groups of simon-pure volunteers.

In July 1862 the mayor of Detroit had called an open-air mass meeting of patriotic citizens to consider how Detroit would provide recruits under the most recent call for 300,000 volunteers. The meeting had been a failure—had, indeed, broken up in an actual row. There had been hissings, catcalls, fisticuffs, until finally the speechmaking dissolved in a free-for-all fight, with Southern sympathizers tearing down the speakers' rostrum and manhandling the speakers, and the sheriff and his deputies coming on the scene with drawn revolvers to restore order and send everybody home. Good citizens felt this as a shame and a disgrace. The rowdies who broke up the meeting, they declared, were not native Copperheads but secessionists-in-exile from Canadian Windsor, across the river. Detroit must redeem its good name; it did so, finally, by holding a new, better-policed citizens' meeting at which it was agreed that Wayne County should raise an extra regiment in addition to the six called for by the new quota.

A rousing campaign for recruits was put on. Judge Henry A. Morrow, who had seen some service in the war with Mexico, was made colonel of this extra regiment, and Sheriff Mark Flanigan—he who had led the flying wedge of deputies to subdue secession at the lamentable first mass meeting—was announced as lieutenant colonel; and by the end of August the regiment had been fully recruited. Many of the recruits were wage earners with families, and it would be some time before the army paymaster would make his rounds. To avert hardships, Detroit businessmen raised a relief fund and some of the men drew money from it—whence came the report that the 24th was a bounty regiment.

The 24th took off for the East just before the Army of the Potomac fought at Antietam, and it left Detroit in a fine glow of patriotic sentiment. Nearly all of its officers carried presentation swords—Colonel Morrow's the gift of the Detroit bar, Lieutenant Colonel Flanigan's the gift of the deputy sheriffs of Wayne County, while one of the company officers carried one given by the printers of the Detroit *Free Press,* of whose composing room he had been foreman. The regiment was feted along the road en route east: there is mention of an elaborate banquet at Pittsburgh, where every man was presented with a bouquet by a pretty girl and where, as a veteran wrote later, "a portion of the regiment was in a fair way of being captured." The regiment got to Maryland just in time to see the dusty files of the Army of the Potomac marching up to the shattering fight at Antietam. After that battle was over the 24th was moved up to join the army, and it camped on the battlefield in dismaying closeness to a huge pile of amputated arms and legs.

Then came the ceremony by which the 24th joined the Iron Brigade. Colonel Morrow unfortunately felt that the occasion called for a speech and made one, pulling out all the stops to let the brigade know how glad the 24th was to be here. He drew for his pains a dead silence, not a cheer or a ripple to show that anybody had heard him. A diarist in the 24th wrote glumly: "A pretty cool reception, we thought. We had come out to reinforce them, and supposed they would be glad to see us."[10]

The camp comradeship which these recruits had heard so much about would apparently have to be earned. It could be earned only in battle. Meanwhile, the regiment might as well get ready. It was drilled prodigiously; Colonel Morrow gave the boys battalion drill for six hours every day, with an additional four and one half hours of "other evolutions of the school of the soldier." When General Gibbon left the brigade for divisional command early in November, he told Morrow and the other field officers they had the best-drilled regiment he had ever seen for a rookie regiment.

This was heartening as word trickled down through the ranks. But it was not enough. There were those four veteran regiments which refused to warm up. The brigade broke camp and began a long march from the upper Potomac to the Rappahannock as the Army of the Potomac moved glacially southeast in a well-meant effort to get around Robert E. Lee's flank. As it moved it outmarched the wagon trains and the men went hungry. The 24th, which was living those days under an almost unendurable tension anyway, waiting for the chance to fight its way into the brigade's fellowship, set up a chant one rationless morning of "Bread! Bread! Bread!" The veteran regiments, equally unfed and for that matter equally capable of kicking up a noisy row over it, looked at them coldly and refused to join in the clamor. Once more the 24th had been put in its place.[11]

December came, and the Iron Brigade, along with most of the rest of the army, went into camp near a little town called Falmouth, a mile or so upstream from the charming colonial city of Fredericksburg. There were flurries of snow and there was a good deal of cold rain, with abominable mud underfoot, and for the 24th Michigan there began that endless process of attrition which, for some regiments, was even more deadly than battle itself. Boys began to get sick, and many of the sick ones died. Like all new regiments, the 24th held formal military funerals in such cases, until one day a rookie soldier on the firing squad mistakenly loaded his musket with ball cartridge and shot a comrade through the body.[12] This might have caused the veterans to jeer—clumsy soldiers who shot each other at a military funeral!—but it did not happen. The veterans were not even admitting the 24th to the implied comradeship of derision. They were simply cold and aloof.

This new regiment would have only one chance at salvation. Before long, by signs which even the private soldiers could read, the army would go across the Rappahannock to fight. When that day came, the 24th would have to prove itself. Its salvation, like so many other values in this strange and terrible war, would in the end have to be bought by the stand-up valor of the private soldier.

2. Jordan Water, Rise over Me

A desolate wasteland of war, as bleak and comfortless as what the last man will see when he takes his last look around, lay between Fredericksburg and the Potomac River landings. It had been pleasant enough in that other geological epoch before the war: nice rolling country marked off into plantations and small farms, well timbered between the pastures and the tilled fields, with great houses on the hilltops and small cabins placed at intervals along the meandering roads. Men had lived here for two centuries and they had given the region a look of order and prosperity. But the armies had come, and everything had been swept away.

The railroad line that ran from Fredericksburg to the riverside terminus at Aquia Creek, where travelers from the south in the old days had left the cars to go aboard the waddling river steamers for the last leg of the leisurely trip to Washington—this line with its bridges, culverts, and docks had been destroyed, rebuilt, destroyed again, and rebuilt anew. All of the timber had been cut down to make trestles and crossties, to corduroy the unpaved roads, to build wharves and piers and stockades and sheds and huts, to provide fuel for locomotives and steamboats and firewood for the stoves and campfires of the soldiers. Colonel Herman Haupt, superintendent of military railroads, complained that the locomotives of his construction trains now had to haul all their own fuel up from the landing, to which place it came down-river in barges. Along the road from the landing up to Fredericksburg there remained now not so much as a stick.

Most of the houses had fared as the wood lots had fared. Some had been torn down for building material, some had been burned by accident, and some had simply been destroyed. A newspaper correspondent saw "tall chimneys standing, monuments of departed peace, in the midst of wastes that had been farms." Nothing else remained. The livestock was all gone, the fences had vanished, every bit of household furniture or farm equipment that could be carried away had disappeared. The desolation was complete.[1]

Much of this was just the inevitable wastage of war. The Army of the Potomac sprawled over a wide strip of land to the north and east of Fredericksburg, close to the Rappahannock River, and its main lines of supply ran back to the Potomac River landings, Aquia Creek and Belle Plain. Over the fifteen or twenty miles of atrocious roads which crossed this country, all of the food, clothing, ammunition, and other supplies for 130,000 men had to be carried—of grain and hay alone the quartermasters had to move 800 tons a day—and the endless wagon trains that lumbered back and forth over the cramped roadways, drivers shouting and swearing and fighting one another for the right of way, were a destroying force that rolled over the landscape and mashed it flat. If a culvert collapsed on a road near somebody's house, the house was torn down to provide timber for a new culvert, and that was that. Moving or standing still, the army could not help creating its own wasteland.

But there was beginning to be more to it than that. The army had grown lawless, although it had not been lawless earlier. It had marched the length of the Virginia peninsula the preceding spring, it had spent many weeks in front of Richmond, it had maneuvered for a time near this same Fredericksburg, and there had been a long hike up to western Maryland. In all of it the foraging, pillaging, and wrecking which took place had been of minor consequence. But during the last few weeks the soldiers seemed to be turning into unabashed thieves. What had been done before had been furtive, a matter of individual soldiers sneaking away from their commands, grabbing what they wanted, and then running for cover. Now it was being done quite openly, with soldiers sweeping up chickens, hogs, cattle, sheep, and everything else that they could carry off. Some of the men, it is recorded, had learned how to steal beehives without being hurt. Houses were invaded and ransacked, fruit cellars and corncribs were despoiled, and the disorderly skein of stragglers that raveled out around the army knew very few restraints when desirable rebel property was encountered.

Indeed, the job could not be blamed entirely on stragglers. If much foraging was done in defiance of officers, much of it also was done with their hearty encouragement. Some men of the 6th Wisconsin complained to their colonel that they were short of rations. The colonel pointed to a clump of farmhouses on a hill and said: "I'm going to take a short nap. Don't let me see or hear of your foraging on this march. I think I see a smokehouse near that white residence." The 5th New Hampshire raided a well-stocked hen house and its Colonel Cross scolded the men sharply—because they let one hen escape. Later, after a sheepfold had been raided, when General Hancock wanted to search the camp of the 5th for traces of stolen sheep, Cross stalled him off until his men were able to plant the bloody pelts in the adjacent camp of the 7th New York. That evening Cross enjoyed roast mutton with the rest of the regiment.[2]

A Pennsylvania recruit in General Andrew Humphreys's division recalled that as many as two hundred men from one regiment in his division were arrested on the march with stolen goods in their possession. Yet they were not punished, aside from being confined overnight, and the stolen property was not confiscated. This soldier wrote that the men were convinced that "it was their bounden duty to forage upon all inhabitants of the enemy's country."[3]

Other explanation there was none. And yet this was a curious business. These outbreaks were not coming from rookies or from third-rate troops. There were no better regiments in the army than the 6th Wisconsin and the 5th New Hampshire, and there were no better colonels than theirs. Humphreys's division, commanded by one of the best men in the army, belonged to the V Corps, where regular-army discipline prevailed. If these men were suddenly getting the notion that it was right to spoil the Egyptians, the army was changing and the change deserved study.

But the high command had more pressing things to think about.

The high command just then was Major General Ambrose E. Burnside, to whom the administration seemed to have given the Army of the Potomac in a mood of sheer desperation. In some ways Burnside was about as incompetent a general as Abraham Lincoln ever commissioned, and he comes down in history looking stiff and stuffy with frock coat and incredible whiskers, a man who moved from disaster to disaster with an uncomprehending and wholly unimaginative dignity. Yet there must once have been a warm, rather lively human being somewhere back of the major general's trappings. Burnside was gay and frisky as a West Point cadet, and when he was commissioned a second lieutenant in 1847 and was sent off to Mexico he gambled away his passage money on an Ohio River steamer and had to borrow from a Louisville merchant in order to make the trip. Later, in Mexico City, he played cards so enthusiastically and unskillfully that his pay was in hock for six months in advance, and he would have had to resign in disgrace if a senior officer had not loaned him enough to pay up. He fought Apaches in New Mexico after the war, acquiring a wound and some modest distinction. Transferred east, he wooed a Kentucky belle and took her to the altar, only to be flabbergasted when she returned a firm "No!" to the officiating minister's climactic question. (The same girl later became engaged to an Ohio lawyer, who apparently had heard about Burnside's experience. When the wedding date arrived this man displayed to her a revolver and a marriage license, telling her that it had to be one or the other and she could take her pick. This time she went through with the ceremony.)[4]

In 1852 Burnside invented a breech-loading rifle, resigned from the army to build a factory and manufacture it, and went broke when he lost a War Department contract which had seemed to be certain. George B. McClellan, then vice-president of the Illinois Central Railroad, bailed him out by giving him a job in the railroad's land office, and when the outbreak of the war called him back into military service Burnside had become treasurer of the road.

It must be admitted that the tradition of failure thus seems to have been fairly well established before he ever became a general; yet it also seems that the man who put that record together was at least not a stodgy person. Something essential in his make-up must have got bleached out in the long years since he got into the history books. He was never anything resembling a great general, yet he apparently was an interesting sort of human being.

The soldiers themselves, in this fall of 1862, were beginning to warm up to him. For the most part they were taking their cue from the IX Corps, which had invaded the Carolina islands with him earlier that year and which felt that "Old Burny" was as good as the best. The IX Corps recalled that under Burnside in Carolina the rations had always been good. The general had forever been poking his nose into the mess shacks, sampling the food, checking on the supplies issued by the commissary. A veteran in the 48th Pennsylvania, applauding him for that remembered care, wrote sententiously that "the nearest way to a soldier's heart lays right through his haversack," and a V Corps private agreed that the men were always willing to cheer when they saw Burnside's "manly countenance, bald head, and unmistakable whiskers."[5]

With his new duties as army commander, Burnside was spending no time looking into company kitchens or harassing the commissaries. This was a little oversight for which he was to pay a high price a bit later, and in its small way it illustrated his whole problem. He needed to be a good strategist and an able tactician, to be sure—after all, he had to lead his troops into action against Robert E. Lee—and yet in some ways it was almost more important for the commander of the Army of the Potomac at that time to be a good housekeeper. This army lived and moved under the weight of a peculiar curse. So many incompetents wore shoulder straps, and there was so much lost motion between orders and their execution, that unless the commanding general did spend part of his time looking into the matter of his soldiers' rations, those rations were going to deteriorate very swiftly.[6]

As with rations, so with weightier things. As a sample, there was the relationship between pontoon boats and high strategy.

The high strategy by which Burnside was moving in mid-November of 1862 was not too bad. Burnside had inherited the army in the general vicinity of Warrenton, with an advance in progress down the line of the Orange and Alexandria Railway. To continue that advance as McClellan had begun it struck Burnside as unwise. The farther the army got, the more it would expose its communications. To General John Pope, some three months earlier, Lee and Stonewall Jackson had demonstrated the evil things that could befall Yankee supply lines that were rashly exposed in that part of the country, and the lesson had not been forgotten.

So Burnside had decided to swing the whole army over to tidewater. There would be wide rivers to cross that way, but the lines of supply would be short and pestilent Rebel raiders could not easily get at them. He would have his advance guard wade the Rappahannock at the fords a little way upstream from Fredericksburg to drive off the Confederate outposts. Then he would lay pontoon bridges at Fredericksburg and cross the rest of the army and the supply trains before Lee's army could reach the vicinity to contest the crossing. He must have, he calculated, twelve days' rations in the wagons, together with a big drove of beef cattle, and Colonel Haupt was assembling workers and material to rebuild the railroad bridge once the town had been secured. All of this done, the army would move southward, and somewhere below the Rappahannock it would meet and fight the Army of Northern Virginia.

On November 12, a few days after he had taken command, Burnside submitted this plan to higher authority. General Halleck was not in favor of it. He was rarely in favor of any plan devised by a subordinate, and he knew perfectly how to qualify any approval he did express so that if disaster came his own record would contain no stain. President Lincoln, who was beginning to catch onto this trait of the general-in-chief, examined Burnside's proposal for himself and on November 14 he telegraphed his approval, remarking that the plan would succeed if Burnside moved fast—otherwise not. On the next day Burnside put the army in motion.

By the morning of November 17 Burnside's advance reached the

Rappahannock River fords, and Yankee patrols went prowling down to the bank to exchange gibes with the Confederate sentries across the river. The advance was styled the Right Grand Division and constituted a third of the army, the II Corps under Darius N. Couch and the IX Corps under Orlando Willcox. Commander of the whole was Major General Edwin V. Sumner—Bull Sumner of the white whiskers and the tremendous parade-ground voice, the ramrod-backed old regular who had been commissioned a second lieutenant away back in 1819 and who, in more than forty years of service, had become the very embodiment of the code by which the old-time professional soldier lived. The code was simple. One automatically gave complete loyalty to all persons in superior authority, one obeyed all lawful orders without question, and one never, under any circumstances, was afraid of anything. Made incarnate in the person of an aging major general, the code had its limitations. It did not necessarily produce a man fitted to command a third of an invading army. It did, however, produce a man you could count on, and if the old man's virtues were limited, they were solid. Worse men have worn a major general's stars.

Sumner got his two corps up to the river, and the rest of the army went into bivouac not far behind him, within easy marching distance of the Fredericksburg crossing where the pontoon bridges were to be made. So far the movement had been remarkably deft and speedy— a point that is often overlooked when the dreary mistakes of the Fredericksburg campaign are recounted. Across the river Lee had hardly more than a corporal's guard—a couple of batteries of field artillery, a skimpy regiment of cavalry, and a few hundred infantrymen. Far upstream Jeb Stuart was scouting to learn whether the Yankees had in fact left Warrenton. A division from James Longstreet's corps, plus the army artillery reserve, was under orders to march from Culpeper to Fredericksburg, but it would not show up for several days. Jackson and his half of the army had not yet left the Shenandoah Valley. The way was open. Sumner's men could wade the river, the rest of the army could cross the river on the pontoon bridges at Fredericksburg, ample supplies could be carried across in the wagons, and Lee's army would find itself neatly outflanked.

Thus it was not at all a bad program which Burnside had mapped out. Its execution, however, depended on the immediate appearance, on the Yankee side of the river opposite Fredericksburg, of several dozens of the clumsy wooden scows with which the army built its pontoon bridges. And these scows were not there, nor did it appear that they were anywhere else where a harassed army commander could quickly get hold of them. In the entire military hierarchy, from general-in-chief down to humblest private, nobody seemed to know exactly where these scows were, except for a weary regiment of volunteer engineer troops, and these lads—wrestling personally with the ungainly things scores of miles from the spot where Burnside's army was waiting—had no idea that anybody in particular wanted them or that there was any especial hurry about anything.

No pontoons, no bridges; no bridges, no crossing of the river. The equation, to Burnside, seemed complete. A gambler might have felt otherwise, might have sent Sumner and his advance guard across at once, trusting that the old man could hold his position and feed his men until the missing pontoons did show up. But it would have taken a gambler to order it. It was beginning to rain. A late November rain is apt to be a long one, and the Rappahannock is quite capable of rising six feet in twenty-four hours when the rain comes down. If Sumner's forty thousand crossed and the Rappahannock did rise, the fords would cease to be fords, Sumner could neither be supplied, reinforced, nor withdrawn, and Lee might well find himself in position to destroy a solid third of the Union Army. It seemed to Burnside that, having moved his army here in lawful expectation of pontoons, he could do nothing now but sit down by the waters as hopefully as might be and wait for them.[7]

In which posture, then, he paused by the river, not looking his best but definitely more sinned against than sinning. He waited because other men had failed and because he himself, decent, amiable man, could not conjure up the storm that would blow slackness and incompetence out of the channels of command. The general waited and the army waited, and on the opposite shore the Army of Northern Virginia began to assemble in all of its strength, and it waited likewise. What could once have been done with ease became presently a matter of great danger and difficulty. The overdue pontoon train which was the cause of all of this delay moved down from the upper Potomac like a bewildered snail, the men who were directly responsible for it doing their best but making little progress.

These bridge tenders belonged to the 50th New York Engineers, one of the few volunteer sapper regiments in the army. The 50th New York had had the boats, balks, planks, wagons, and other equipment

some fifty miles northwest of Washington, and just now it was this
regiment's singular fate to epitomize the way in which things went
wrong in this army.

The engineers had had a bridge across the Potomac at Berlin,
Maryland, ever since early October, and when McClellan moved his
army down from western Maryland to the Warrenton area this had
been the principal crossing. There was another pontoon bridge six
miles upstream at Harper's Ferry, with a subsidiary bridge there over
the Shenandoah as well. At Berlin, in addition to the bridge, there
were fifty-six additional boats in the Chesapeake and Ohio Canal,
plus a land train of twenty boats stacked up, ready to go, on ponderous wagons, together with other wagons full of supplementary equipment. The army had gone on south and the engineers sat idly and
happily by their unused bridges and spare boats and waited for orders.

When orders finally came they were six days late: first in the series
of blunders which the army was eventually to pay for at Fredericksburg. GHQ had decided on November 6 to move the pontoon train
down to Washington so that it could quickly be brought down into
Virginia in case of need, but some functionary at GHQ forgot that
there was such a thing as a military telegraph line and simply put
the orders in the mail. As a result, it was November 12 before the
orders got to Berlin and were opened by Major Ira Spaulding, commander of the 50th New York Engineers. Six days behind schedule,
then, Major Spaulding learned what he was supposed to do.

GHQ wanted to keep the bridges at Harper's Ferry, so Spaulding
was to detail a company to take charge up there, sending with that
company certain additional boats and planking for maintenance.
The Berlin bridge was to be dismantled and its component parts were
to be taken to Washington, along with all of the spare boats, wagons,
and odds and ends of surplus equipment which were at Berlin. When
Major Spaulding had got his regiment and all of this equipment to
the Volunteer Engineer Brigade depot in Washington, his instructions
said that he was to make up a pontoon train on wheels as rapidly as
possible and stand by ready to move on a moment's notice.

The major went to work promptly. By evening he had his bridge
disassembled and a train of thirty-six boats was in the canal moving
down toward Washington. Next morning another train of forty boats
and matériel got off and the wagons were made ready to begin the
journey overland. The company which had been detailed to stay at

Harper's Ferry was made responsible for getting the last odds and ends rounded up and shipped; the rest of the regiment was on the way, either floating down the canal with the water-borne scows or slogging along overland with the great wagons. After making a final checkup Spaulding himself went to Washington by railroad, and late that night he reported to his boss, Brigadier General Daniel P. Woodbury. Woodbury looked at Spaulding's orders, and thus himself learned for the first time that a pontoon train was to be prepared for possible service with the army. The hour being late, he told Spaulding to come back next morning and they would see what new orders there might be.

Next morning was November 14: the same day President Lincoln was telling Burnside that his plan of action was approved but that if he moved he had better move fast. While Spaulding waited at Woodbury's headquarters, Woodbury went off to see Halleck, who by now knew that Burnside had permission to move via Fredericksburg and who had previously been warned that if this move were made Burnside would have to have the pontoons immediately. Just what Halleck had on his mind that morning nobody ever quite made out, but in any case, Woodbury finally returned to his own office and told Spaulding to put his boats and wagons in depot as fast as they reached town and to put his men into camp. This, of course, countermanded the original orders to make up a new train and stand by.

The first lot of boats came in that evening and more arrived next morning, November 15, as did a telegram from an engineer officer on Burnside's staff asking how about those pontoons. By night all of the men and matériel which had been at Berlin were in Washington. The matériel was stowed away in the engineer depot on the Anacostia River just above the navy yard, and the 50th Engineers were in camp nearby. That evening General Woodbury gave Spaulding a new set of orders: make up two pontoon trains of twenty-four boats each to go down to Belle Plain by water, the boats being made up in rafts, each boat to be loaded with its own allotment of planking, timbers, ropes, and other gear. As far as General Woodbury knew, the boats were wanted at Belle Plain, not elsewhere. Consequently, no wagons were sent with them, which meant that when they did reach Belle Plain there would be no way to carry them over to the Rappahannock.

Getting these boat-rafts together was a chore, but the engineers kept at it smartly and next morning the steamer *Hero* showed up, took the rafts in tow, and went off downstream. This done, Spaulding was ordered to make up a train of twenty more boats, with transportation for forty, to go down to the Fredericksburg area by land. It took much longer to get this ready. First the major had to go to the quartermaster depot and draw two hundred horses. Then he had to indent for two hundred sets of harness, which were delivered at the engineer depot in their original boxes and so had to be unboxed and fitted together before they could be put on the horses—many of which, it then developed, had never been in any kind of harness before and had strong objections to being harnessed now. While this was going on, the major had to get teamsters detailed from the casuals' camp at Alexandria, had to draw rations and forage, and had to keep his own men busy loading the cumbersome boats and their equipment on wagons. All in all, it was the afternoon of November 19 before the train finally went creaking down from the engineer depot, rumbled across Long Bridge, crept on through Alexandria, and at last camped for the night in a pelting rain half a dozen miles from its starting point.

Now Major Spaulding and his men had been working very hard, and they had even harder work ahead of them, but they were men who toiled in a gray nightmare and all that they did was vanity and a mockery. For while they were making up their train, and while the paddle-boat *Hero* with its ungainly rafts was chugging down the Potomac—to go hard aground, at last, and wait some hours for release—while all of this was happening, General Burnside and General Sumner were waiting by the Rappahannock fords with forty thousand good soldiers who could either cross the river free now or cross it at a dreadful price a little later on, and who were barred from doing it now because Major Spaulding, his engineers, and the pontoons were still many miles away.

The nightmare was to get worse. The next day was November 20, and Sumner still waited at Falmouth with his forty thousand men, while Joe Hooker moved in close behind him with forty thousand more. Across the river the leading elements of Longstreet's corps were beginning to dig themselves in on the range of low hills that runs north and south behind the town of Fredericksburg. The time left to the Army of the Potomac was beginning to be very short indeed. And on the Telegraph Road south from Alexandria the rain was continuous and the road was turning to clinging, bottomless mud. The wagons mired down—there were few heavier, unhandier things on wheels in those days than an army wagon carrying a pontoon boat—and in places the soldiers had to lift them along by sheer muscle. The steamer *Hero* docked her pontoons at Belle Plain, but there was no good way to get them to Falmouth; the men in charge of them did not know that anyone over at Falmouth wanted them, and anyway, no one seems to have notified Burnside that they had reached Belle Plain.

The rain continued to fall. Major Spaulding wrote plaintively that "the roads are in such a shocking condition that I find I cannot make over five miles a day with my bridge train, and to do even this much I am obliged to haul many of my wagons for miles by hand and work my men half the night."[8] The engineers were struggling knee-deep in mud in a perpetual cold rain, and the worst part of the whole route—the notoriously boggy bottom lands along Chopawamsic Creek—lay ahead of them. Major Spaulding decided that something would have to be done.

It must be remembered that, as far as the major knew, time was no particular object. General Woodbury wrote later that "no one ever informed me that the success of any important movement depended in the slightest degree upon a pontoon train to leave Washington by land." Both he and Major Spaulding supposed that this was simply a routine movement involving no especial reason for hurry.[9] Even so, a conscientious engineer officer was apt to balk at a routine movement which took all winter, which was what this trip down the Telegraph Road was beginning to look like. So Spaulding at last gave in and sent an officer back to Washington to get a steamboat and bring it down to the mouth of Occoquan Creek. At that point they would make their boats up into rafts, load the dismantled wagons and the rest of the matériel aboard, have the steamboat tow them down to Belle Plain, and send the horses along by land.

They did it that way in the end, having a prodigious amount of trouble rafting their boats through the shallows at the mouth of the Occoquan. By November 24 they had everything afloat and were on their way, and late that night they reached the sprawling wharves at Belle Plain. The horses had not arrived yet—even without any wagons to pull, it was weary plugging down that muddy highway—but Spaulding was able to draw other horses from the base quartermaster, and he kept his men working most of the night. The following afternoon he was able to report at Burnside's headquarters with the long-lost pontoons close behind him.[10]

Apparently he got meager thanks for his effort. He had obeyed orders and he and his men had worked very hard to do it, but by now the situation had developed in such a way that everybody concerned would have been much better off if the engineers and their boats had remained stuck in the mud all winter. All of Longstreet's corps was in position across the river now, and Lee was there with it. Jackson had begun to pull his troops out of the Shenandoah Valley, where he had been hoping against hope that the misguided Yankees would try to attack him, and was en route to Fredericksburg.

So Burnside's plan, which had been good enough a week ago, was no good at all any more. He had never had any idea of fighting his way across the river here. He just wanted to get across and then do his fighting somewhere farther to the south, and this had seemed like a good place to do the crossing. Yet now, when a crossing right here was looking more and more inadvisable, Burnside and his army waited stolidly on the riverbanks, and the charming little colonial town began, in spite of logic, to take on more and more military importance, as if something in its atmosphere had from the beginning been fated to draw the charge of lightning from the gathering storm clouds.

The railroad from Aquia Creek to Richmond crossed the river at Fredericksburg—or at least it had done so in the old days, before war smashed the bridge—and it was much on Burnside's mind. He was suggesting now to Colonel Haupt that a supply of railroad iron had better be floated up the Rappahannock under navy convoy for use in relaying the track south once Lee had been driven away. Haupt was objecting to this, pointing out that they could not rebuild the line south until they had first rebuilt the bridge, and that once the bridge had been rebuilt they could bring the new rails in by train and save a laborious transshipment at the riverside. Still, Burnside was boss, and "it shall be done if you desire it."[11]

Haupt had found Burnside a good man to deal with. To a subordinate about this time he wrote that "General Burnside is one of the most reasonable and practical men I have ever met." Haupt was a man of many expedients, and he had invented a species of car ferry which was saving much time and labor in the supply of this army. At Alexandria, Haupt had assembled a number of Schuylkill River coal barges. These had been lined up in pairs, side by side, each pair bound firmly together with long timbers bolted transversely, railroad tracks laid lengthwise on top. Each pair of barges thus treated made one serviceable car float capable of carrying the sixteen loaded freight cars which made up a military supply train. The trains, then, as they came down from the north to Alexandria, were simply run on the floats there and were towed down to the railroad docks at Aquia Creek. It took about an hour to transfer a train to the float, six hours for towage, and another hour to get the train back on the tracks again. Without breaking carloadings, a freight train of supplies for the army could get from Washington to Falmouth between dawn and dusk.[12]

A capable operator, this Haupt. The Northland may have had trouble finding competent generals just then, but when it sent up an industrial technician it invariably sent up a good one. Just now Haupt rather doubted that there would be much new track to lay once the army got possession of Fredericksburg. The line south from Fredericksburg was still intact, and if a battle were fought and the Rebels were driven off, it seemed improbable that in their retreat they would have time to destroy much track. However, to play safe he agreed that he would order an extra ten miles of rails, just in case.

Haupt's letter was significant on a couple of points. The casual reference to the purchase of ten miles of railroad rails as a form of insurance demonstrated that the United States was an industrialized nation waging industrial warfare, even though that fact was not yet understood. A great deal of industrial muscle was available if ten miles of railroad iron were the small change of the latest military offensive. (In the South the progressive deterioration of the railroads was already a serious problem, and there were not ten miles of spare rails in all the Confederacy.)[13] More immediately, Haupt's unemotional calculation that Lee would probably be driven out of Fredericksburg too abruptly to leave time for railroad destruction was an indication that the high command was already accepting as inevitable what it had not even dreamed of a fortnight earlier: a bloody battle for mere possession of the opposite bank of the Rappahannock.

The high command, of course, was of several minds. Burnside was toying with ideas of feints downstream to draw off the bulk of Lee's strength, feints upstream to draw it in the opposite direction, feints right here to make possible an unopposed crossing elsewhere. Exactly what all of this would amount to was never clear, but the ideas were at least stirring in his mind. Sumner, who had the great virtue of loyalty, stoutly supported Burnside's plan even though he did not quite understand it. Joe Hooker had more than enough military intelligence to perceive the folly of an attempt to force a crossing here, and he left none of the army's ranking commanders in doubt about his feelings. Nor, for that matter, did he leave Washington in doubt. As early as November 19 he had sent a private letter to Secretary Stanton, putting on record his own criticism of his commanding officer. When Hooker wrote he had just come up behind Sumner, and he had his two army corps camped close to United States Ford on the Rappahannock. He told Stanton that, boats or no boats, he ought to be allowed to take his men across the river and go driving south without worrying about pontoon bridges or anything else. He could live off the country; he would be entering, he said, a rich agricultural district unspoiled by war, and the foraging would be good. In general, he could smash things up so thoroughly that the enemy would have to hurry back to protect Richmond and would not be able to defend the Rappahannock crossings here or anywhere else.[14]

In many ways Hooker's idea was perfectly sound. But Hooker—was Hooker; strange mixture of the conniver and the sincere patriot. In sending to the Secretary of War a pointed criticism of his own commander, he was violating both military law and military etiquette, not to mention the canons of ordinary civilized behavior. And since there was obviously no chance whatever that the Secretary of War, getting Hooker's letter, would promptly reverse Burnside and order the movement which Hooker suggested, what Hooker was really trying to do with all of this irregularity was to get his own rightness and Burnside's wrongness on record in advance of the catastrophe which Hooker scented on the wind. Burnside, Hooker felt, was not going to last long. After Burnside?

Yet the important thing about this army was never the rivalry of its generals, nor, for that matter, the generals themselves. For this was an army that had to operate strictly on its own. From beginning to end, at one level or another, its command was either erratic or beset with slackness and incompetence. Something like this business of the pontoons was always happening, something was always going irretrievably wrong, owing less to any single shortcoming than to a general failure on the part of someone in shoulder straps. It is impossible to disagree with the historian who remarked that the army was cursed "by a line of brave and patriotic officers whom some good fairy ought to have knocked on the head."[15] What the army finally was to do, if indeed it was to do anything, would at last depend almost entirely on the men in the ranks. Individual leaders who were worthy of them, these men did indeed have here and there, at varying levels of command from company to army corps. But leadership which, as a whole, came even close to being good enough for them —that, from the day the war began to the day it ended, these men never got.

In addition, they had suffered lately a psychic wound, having lost McClellan, the one commander for whom they felt affection and with whom they felt at ease. They had no light to follow now but the light they might find in their own spirits, and that light was guttering very low as they waited by the riverbank with the weather growing colder and the muddy bivouac becoming more and more cheerless. It seems that they began to get a premonition of disaster, a premonition that was less the result of a conscious appraisal of their chances than the product of many small failures and minor irritants, aggravated by the fact that the indecision at general headquarters was too obvious for the most heedless private to miss. They had cheers for Old Burny when they saw him by the roadside, but the cheers were growing perfunctory. The soldiers were a glum crowd now and they rarely felt like cheering anyone.

For one thing, they had not been paid for months. For another, in this movement down from Warrenton a great many units had somehow been marched away from their equipment and were now enduring the sleet and snow without tents or blankets. For still another, the quality and quantity of the rations were visibly deteriorating. Fights broke out as regiments which the commissaries had missed tried to raid the supplies of better-nourished outfits. A diarist in the 9th Massachusetts recalled later: "Never were we any worse off for supplies." A veteran in the 22nd Massachusetts wrote feelingly of their bivouac, from which 588 men of the regiment were absent because of sickness: "This plain became a wallow-hole; the clay surface freezing at night and thawing by day, trampled by thousands of men, made a vast sea of mud. . . . It had to be scraped and washed off to prevent our tents from becoming hog pens." The rookie

146th New York, which had just joined up, learned that army life was not quite as it had been imagined, and its historian recalled: "Many of the older regiments around us were tired of the service and anxious to return home, and the infection spread among the new regiments."[16]

Often enough, spirits went up or down with the quality of the food. For six mortal weeks the 79th New York had had nothing to eat but hardtack and salt meat. One day, by great good luck, a captain in this regiment got some potatoes. He sliced them and fried a huge panful and sat down with his tent mate, the regimental chaplain, to eat them. In blissful silence the two men ate fried potatoes, emptying the pan to the last crinkly slice, carefully dividing and eating that, and then leaning back to light their pipes, feeling that life might be joyous after all. The chaplain had said grace over their meal, and after that the two had spoken not a word; but at last the captain took his pipe from his mouth and said gravely: "Chaplain, those potatoes needed *salt*." The chaplain thought it over, then nodded judicially, and the two men resumed their contented silent smoking.[17]

However, it is quite clear that, taking the army as a whole, something more was wrong than a mere shortage of rations. What was going on was not just the normal grousing of soldiers who have begun to see that war is not quite as much fun as they had expected it to be. This army was beginning to understand its own handicaps, and it was beginning to lose confidence. Most of the rank and file knew no more about what the high command had in mind than the rank and file usually knows, but the rank and file was not in the least stupid and it could read the omens as well as anybody. What lay back of these myriad complaints about mud, bad food, and poor leadership comes out in a letter written just at this time by one soldier who happened to be completely articulate—Captain Oliver Wendell Holmes, Jr., of the 20th Massachusetts, a twice-wounded man of proven valor from a stout, battle-tried regiment. On November 19 Holmes wrote:

"I've pretty much made up my mind that the South have achieved their independence & I am almost ready to hope spring will see an end. . . . The army is tired with its hard and its terrible experience & still more with its mismanagement & I think before long the majority will say that we are vainly working to effect what never happens—the subjugation (for that is it) of a great civilized nation. We shan't do it—at least the army can't."[18]

What Holmes could put into words in a letter to his own kin, other soldiers could only think—or, more likely, feel, leaving the thought unformulated and being conscious only of a deep depression. Yet the depression and what lay back of it were hidden if possible. Like the two officers who found uplift in a pan of fried potatoes, the soldiers kept their spirits up with such devices as were available, which included, for the men on picket duty along the river, the exchange of not wholly ill-natured insults with the Confederate pickets across the river. As, for instance:

"Oh, Yank! How did you like Bull Run?"

"Better bury your dead on South Mountain."

"What do you think of the New York election?" (Democrats had just made Horatio Seymour, suspected of strong Copperhead tendencies, governor of New York, roundly defeating the Unionist candidate, General James Wadsworth, and the Confederates were inclined to make much of it.)

"What do *you* think of Ben Butler?"

"Oh, the Louisiana Tigers will bring him to Richmond."

"The Louisiana Tigers? There's none of them left—the last died running."[19]

And so on, very like the catcalling of schoolboy gangs on the playground, except that these gangs unaccountably carried rifles and might at any moment quit yelling and start shooting at each other. The exchange had a sharp edge now and then. The whole army chuckled over the answer one brash Federal got when, observing that the Confederate on the opposite bank was exceedingly ragged, he called across to know if Rebels did not have any decent clothes. The Reb looked him over for a minute, then called back: "We-uns don't put on our good clothes to butcher hogs."

But whether it approached the event with grousing, with despairing letters home, or with jeers at the enemy's pickets, the army knew that it was drifting steadily toward a battle. It drifted with fatalism. In fact, so contradictory is the spirit of man that the soldiers even displayed a febrile enthusiasm, for although all the signs were bad, yet action was action, the battle might possibly be won, and a great battle won would bring the war near an end. A newspaper correspondent in early December wrote that "the Army of the Potomac never felt

better" than it did when the long blue columns at last began to draw
out of the scattered camps and head toward the banks of the deep
unbridged river.[20]

For Burnside, after sitting there bemused for three weeks, had
finally come to a decision. It seemed to him now that the enemy
would be more surprised by a crossing right at Fredericksburg than
by a crossing at any other place, and in a way he was right. Probably
nothing in all the war surprised Lee quite as much as the discovery
that his enemy would move up for a frontal assault at Fredericksburg,
although this was not a surprise that gave the Federals any military
advantage. In any case, on December 9 Burnside called the Grand
Division commanders to headquarters and instructed them to have
their commands ready to move at daylight of December 11, each man
carrying three days' rations and sixty rounds of ammunition, battery
and ammunition wagons to carry three days' forage for their horses.
To Major Spaulding, Burnside sent word to stand by: the army was
at last ready to use those pontoons.

There is record of a party given by officers of a New England regiment in a riverside hut the night the orders came out. Some twenty
men who had no illusions about the kind of reception they were going
to get when they crossed the river met to sing songs and to drink
whisky punch. At the end, just before the party broke up, someone
lifted his glass and cried: "To the health of Little Mac!"

The hut rocked with cheers and the glasses went bottoms up, and
a man who was present wrote that the soldiers were sustained that
night by a positive faith that McClellan would yet return and lead
the army to victory.[21]

With that faith, or such other faith as they could muster, the men
marched up to the river. As the 16th Maine marched through deserted camps the men could hear the high soft voice of a contraband
camp servant lifted in the song, "Jordan Water, Rise over Me."[22]

3. Big Stars Are Busting

It was three o'clock on a cold December morning, and there was a
heavy wet fog along the river and many strange noises in the night:
a creaking and a thumping and a scrabbling, the sound of wagons
and horses and men getting great hollow weights down a steep bumpy

road where no one could see three feet beyond the end of his nose. There was this river, and beyond it there was a silent lifeless town, and beyond the town there was an open plain bordered by low hills, and in this bleak three-in-the-morning chill all of these lay invisible, and the shadow of death rested upon them and could be felt there in the dark by the riverside. The 50th New York Engineers were going to throw pontoon bridges across the Rappahannock to Fredericksburg.

Major Spaulding had his orders, and he was building three bridges: one of them opposite the dock at the lower end of town, where steamboats used to receive passengers and freight in the days when Fredericksburg had a normal life to live, and the other two a bit farther upstream, opposite the center of town. He had chosen his spots by daylight, and now the men were extending the bridges into a void, building for a farther shore which they had to take on faith, anchoring their scows in the chuckling black water and binding them together with long timbers and fastening planking on top of the timbers, trying to do it silently, but knowing perfectly well that whatever faith might say about the farther shore there were alert enemies over there somewhere, hearing these sounds and cannily interpreting them and preparing to act as soon as the light should come. For a few hours the darkness was a protecting cloak.

The darkness did not last nearly long enough. By six o'clock it had thinned, and although the fog remained there was a dim gray light along the river. From the Confederate side there came a measured boom-boom of two fieldpieces, the signal by which the Rebel commander on the water front notified his army that the Yankees were coming across. Presently the engineers could see the water-front buildings of Fredericksburg in the mist not far off. There were many Confederates hidden in and about those buildings, and as the slow light grew these looked at the bridgebuilders over the sights of their rifles. There was a crackling snap-snap of infantry fire all along the water front, and the engineers ran back off their half-finished bridges to take cover, leaving dead and wounded men along the wet planking.

The Yankee water front along here belonged to General Couch, who commanded the II Corps, and as soon as the firing began he spread a line of infantry along the bank to return the fire. This did no good. It was so dark and misty that the Federals could not see any targets across the river, and although they did a good deal of

shooting they killed no Rebels. The firing died down after a while
and the engineers ran out on the bridges again, thus getting close
enough to the Fredericksburg shore to be perfectly visible to the waiting Confederates, who zestfully reopened fire and again drove the
men to cover.

When it got lighter things were not much better. The Confederates
in the town were Mississippians, and they hid in basements and behind low barricades and in rifle pits dug in the lee of brick buildings,
and the Federals across the river had very little chance to hit any
of them. The men who tried to complete the bridges had to do their
work less than a hundred feet from the Confederate shore, and they
were sitting ducks to be shot. Time and again the engineers ran out
to finish the job; each time, with very little delay, the waiting Confederates drove them back; each time the supporting Federal infantry
fired completely ineffective volleys.[1]

General Burnside had certain plans, and they called for the building
of two sets of bridges: this group of three, opposite the town itself,
where he proposed to cross the right wing of his army, and another
set a mile or more downstream, where the left wing was to cross. The
downstream-bridge gang had it easy. The Confederate shore there
was open and could quickly be swept clear, and by midmorning the
downstream bridges were finished and ready for use. But upstream it
was obvious that no bridges could be completed until the Rebels had
been driven out of Fredericksburg, and they were never going to be
dislodged by any long-range infantry fire.

The Federal army that morning contained 120,000 men, and most
of them were lined up on the high ground overlooking Fredericksburg, waiting for a chance to get across, and here they were, stopped
cold by a solitary Confederate brigade, 1,500 men at the most—an
unwelcome modern version of Horatius at the bridge. It was intolerable, and Burnside at last called in his chief artillerist, Brigadier
General Henry J. Hunt, and told him to blast Fredericksburg off the
face of the earth if he had to—anything, just so he pulverized that
Mississippi brigade and made it possible for the New York engineers
to finish their job.

This Hunt was a notable gunner, one of the most useful officers the
Union Army possessed, a good organizer and solid fighting man,
keen student of the new science of gunnery, a man who believed in
great massed sheaves of gunfire but who also insisted that each indi-

vidual gun crew must take the time to get on the target before it
fired. He had lately taken the Federal gunners over the coals about
this latter point, decreeing that except when they were firing canister
at close range they must not, even in red-hot action, fire at a rate
faster than one round per gun in two minutes. To fire faster, he remarked, was to fire wildly, which did no good. Furthermore, an
officer who shot up all his battery's ammunition in a hurry was
probably an officer who wanted a good excuse to take his guns back
out of action. He would be treated as such henceforth, in any case,
and no battery hereafter would be allowed to withdraw from action
just because it was out of ammunition. It would send for more ammunition, and while it waited it would remain under fire, officers and
men at their posts, unless higher authority ordered it to withdraw.[2]

Hunt had been spending a week or more getting his batteries posted
on Stafford Heights, as the high ground above the river was called.
He had more than 140 guns in line—Rodman three-inch rifles, ten-
and twenty-pounder Parrotts, and a handful of four-and-one-half-
inch siege guns, long monsters too cumbersome for field maneuver
but useful in a spot like this. Rather more than one hundred of these
guns would bear on the water front opposite the frustrated bridgebuilders, and he gave the gunners their orders—fifty rounds per gun,
pick your targets, and remember what the regulations say about firing
deliberately.

So the guns opened, and a tremendous cloud of smoke came
rolling down from Stafford Heights to cover the river and the open
plain and the tormented town, and presently tall columns of blacker
smoke from burning buildings went up to the blue sky, and the
waiting Federals saw walls and roofs collapse and bricks and timbers
fly through the air, while men who had lived through Malvern Hill
and Antietam said this was the most thunderous cannonade they
had ever heard. Most of the inhabitants of Fredericksburg had left
town, so that to an extent Hunt was shelling a deserted town; even
so, soldiers recorded that it was not pleasant to see the whole might
of their artillery turned upon human habitations.[8]

The bombardment ended at last, and there were many wrecked
buildings along the water front. The engineers trotted out on the
bridges again, but the ominous pin points of flame sputtered around
basement windows and low barricades, and more engineers were shot
down, and once again it was too hot to build bridges. General Hunt

had wrecked Fredericksburg, but he had not driven out the Mississippians. Huddling under cover, they had had a hard time of it, but they had not had more than they could take, and as soon as the gunfire ceased they were ready to fight again. They were teaching Hunt the lesson which artillerists have to learn anew in each generation—that a bombardment which will destroy buildings will not necessarily keep brave defenders from fighting on amid the wreckage.

The solution to the problem was at last accomplished by the infantry under Colonel Norman J. Hall, who had one of General Oliver Otis Howard's brigades in the II Corps and to whom General Hunt suggested that the way to get the Rebels out of Fredericksburg was to go over and push them out personally. Colonel Hall took his 7th Michigan down to the water front, borrowed some of Major Spaulding's pontoons to use as assault boats, got some of the engineers detailed as oarsmen, and sent landing parties across the river despite losses. The Michigan men got a foothold along the far bank, the 19th and 20th Massachusetts were sent over as support waves, and the three regiments finally combed the last Confederates out of the waterside gun pits and went driving on to secure the town.[4]

This fight was rough while it lasted. There was a swirl of door-to-door fighting, and the 20th Massachusetts lost ninety-seven officers and men in a street-fighting advance of fifty yards. Colonel Hall, a regular-army officer who admired nonchalance in action, recalled later how very Bostonian and unemotional the New England soldiers were during this fight. There was the 20th's colonel quietly telling a company commander: "Mr. Abbott, you will take your first platoon forward." Platoon advances and is almost instantly knocked out by rifle fire. "You'll have to put in the second," says the colonel; and the captain, acting slightly bored by the whole affair, goes forward with the second platoon in the best old-world style. In his official report Colonel Hall said he could not presume to say all that ought to be said about "the unflinching bravery and splendid discipline" of these Yankees. Privately, in conversation with one of the regimental officers, he remarked that the 20th, like the regulars, did its fighting without bothering to strike heroic attitudes. Groping for the expression he wanted, he hit upon an odd one: "The 20th has no poetry in a fight."[5]

In the end, the soldiers got the town secured and went on to skirmish with Rebels on the outskirts. The bridges were finished, the rest of Colonel Hall's brigade came across, and from Stafford Heights the Federal gunners looked for targets beyond the town, firing furiously whenever they found one.

So the long day ended, and men remembered afterward that a strange golden dusk lay upon the plain and the surrounding hills, as if a belated Indian-summer evening had come bewildered out of peacetime autumn into wintry wartime. There was a haze on the horizon, and the western sky was scarlet and purple as the sun went down, and most of Fredericksburg seemed to be burning. A chaplain in the 33rd New York wrote that the smoke "rolled gently upward in dark columns, or, whirling aloft, chased itself in graceful rings like a thing of beauty." As it grew darker, these smoke clouds glowed red when the shell exploded, and the gun pits on Stafford Heights were picked out by stabbing flames as the guns were fired. A newspaper correspondent wrote: "Towering between us and the western sky, which was still showing its faded scarlet lining, was the huge somber pillar of grimy smoke that marked the burning of Fredericksburg. Ascending to a vast height, it bore away northward, shaped like a plume bowed in the wind."[6]

Attended by whatever beauties of nature and burning homes, the Federals now had a foothold on the southern bank of the Rappahannock—which at Fredericksburg is actually the western bank, the river running nearly north to south just there—and Burnside could put his troops across as he pleased. There may have been some reason for haste. Lee was still unable to believe that Burnside planned to make his main assault here, for the hills behind Fredericksburg, where Lee's army had been entrenching for weeks, made an ideal defensive line, and to the last moment the Confederates thought this crossing at Fredericksburg must be a ponderous feint. As a result, Jackson's corps was still watching possible crossings a dozen miles downstream. When Colonel Hall's men secured the town Lee had only half of his army on hand. But Burnside frittered away the next day with a deal of marching and countermarching, and Lee had plenty of time to call in Jackson and assemble the seventy-eight thousand men of the Army of Northern Virginia on the high ground west of the Fredericksburg plain.

That ground actually is not so very high, the hills for the most part rising only forty or fifty feet above the plain. For Lee's purposes, however, the ground was exactly right—high enough to offer an impregnable defensive line, but not high enough to scare the Federals and keep them from attacking at all. Directly west of the town, and a little less than half a mile away, rose the modest ridge known as Marye's Heights, with a white-pillared Virginia mansion picturesquely sited on the crest. To the north, slightly higher hills slanted off to the river, offering Lee's left flank a position that could not be taken. (It could be turned, to be sure, if the Yankees cared to march eight or ten miles upstream, but the field of Burnside's vision had narrowed so that he could see nothing but what was immediately in front of him.) To the south, the high ground pulled farther and farther away from the river, ending, nearly four air-line miles from Marye's Heights, in a wooded knoll that overlooked a weedy grade crossing on the Richmond railroad, a spot known locally as Hamilton's Crossing. From the protected left-flank position to the hill by Hamilton's Crossing, the Confederates were well dug in, all set to kill as many Yankees as might come at them.

Burnside was a trained soldier who presumably knew the folly of smashing head-on into a perfect defensive position, and he had evolved a plan which might just possibly have worked if everything had gone exactly right. The left wing of his army, styled the Left Grand Division, was commanded by Major General William B. Franklin, who had demonstrated in the Antietam campaign that he would not drive ahead any faster than his commander forced him to do, but who, that limitation aside, was a solid and capable soldier. Franklin had under him two excellent army corps, the I Corps under John F. Reynolds and the VI Corps of William F. Smith— "Baldy" Smith, that staunch friend of the departed McClellan who seems to have had the stamina once to tell McClellan to his face that his dealings with Copperhead leaders looked like treason.

Franklin was to take his men across by the downstream bridges, and Sumner was to cross his Grand Division by the upper bridges. Hooker, with the remaining third of the army, was to stand by ready to support either or both. Burnside's general idea appears to have been for Franklin to drive through past Hamilton's Crossing, out-flanking Lee's right and rolling his line up to the northward. Once this had begun, Sumner was to break through at Marye's Heights, Lee would then have to retreat in great haste, the jubilant Federals could despoil and slay in his wake, and the war would come to a close.

That, at any rate, is what Burnside later said that he had planned and directed before the battle began. His written orders appear to have called for something rather different: a simple reconnaissance in force by Franklin, an advance by Sumner to a providentially unoccupied hill, the intervention of a fortunate army between two separated retreating bodies of Confederate troops. One of Burnside's notions, apparently, was that the Rebels would withdraw as soon as they were pushed a little, and he was careful to warn Franklin and Sumner not to let their men fire into each other when they got up on top of the line of hills.

Burnside's planning, in brief, was very foggy; and as a crowning misfortune it developed that one of the worst of his failings was a simple inability to use the English language clearly. None of his subordinates understood just what he wanted them to do, and under the circumstances the battle could become nothing but a simple exercise in the killing of Union soldiers. Some of the soldiers appear to have been aware of this. A newspaper correspondent going about the camps that day asked various officers what the Confederate Army was up to. There it was, with scores of guns on commanding hills and with more and more of the Union Army parading into town under the very muzzles of those silent guns; why didn't the Rebels open fire? He got a variety of explanations: the Rebels were low on ammunition, Lee did not wish to bombard a Virginia town, the Southern army was in retreat, and so on. Finally the reporter tagged an enlisted man, who looked over toward the silent, ominous hills and remarked: "They want us to get in. Getting out won't be quite so smart and easy. You'll see."[7]

Whatever the Rebels may have wanted, the twelfth of December was a mild sunny day, and during the whole of it the Army of the Potomac assembled its hosts on the heights east of the river and sent them slanting down to the water in endless blue columns bright with flags and polished muskets, their crossing announced by the unceasing route-step tramp of tens of thousands of men on the hollow swaying bridges. Some of the Rebel guns on the western hills might have reached these bridges and the approaches. Mostly they did not try, except for one of Jackson's batteries which possessed an English-made Whitworth rifle, a breechloader with a range longer than the artillerists of that day quite knew how to use. These gunners fired a few rounds at Franklin's downstream crossing, putting one bolt through a paymaster's tent on the Yankee side of the river just as the paymaster had spread his greenbacks out on a barrel-and-plank table. The bills went whirling and dancing up about the wrecked tent like a green blizzard, and the ensuing scramble by stragglers and orderlies was something the army long remembered.[8] Otherwise the crossing was peaceful enough. If the deluded Yankees were indeed going to make their fight here, no Confederate commander wanted to keep them from trying it.

Yet the Federal strength was great, and this unending muster of the troops was so impressive that even stolid, impassive Longstreet began to worry at last, and he asked his chief of artillery if he had not better get some more guns to defend Marye's Heights. The gunner laughed at him; once he opened fire, he said, not even a chicken could live on the plain between the hills and the town. Longstreet looked again and was reassured. Later, when Lee asked him if the overpowering weight of Federals might not be too heavy for him, Longstreet promised to kill every man in the Union Army, provided his ammunition held out.[9] The Yankees were with power, but in all the war the Southerners never had to worry as little about a battle as about this one.

Sumner sent his entire command into Fredericksburg, but he did not go with it. Burnside kept him on the home side of the river, feeling that if the old man once got over the bridges he would be unable to keep from getting up into the front line of attack, which was no place for a Grand Division commander. There was a day-long sputter of rifle fire on the skirmish lines outside of town as Federals and Confederates bickered over the approaches; and inside the town there was a prodigious amount of looting of the empty houses, so that Couch finally put a provost guard at the bridges to keep the looters from getting their plunder across the river. By nightfall, he wrote, the guards had collected "an enormous pile of booty."

Franklin put in the day getting his divisions across by the lower bridges, and by evening he had them posted on a north-and-south line facing the Confederate hills, with Abner Doubleday's division acting as flank guard on the left. As the men took their places the Iron Brigade, by chance, found itself quartered on the Bernard plantation, some three miles below Fredericksburg, and Company C of the 6th Wisconsin had a contraband cook who until comparatively recently had been held in servitude on this very estate. This one was highly pleased to be back, a free man protected by Lincoln's soldiers, on the plantation where he was born and bred. Yet when he saw some of his soldiers chopping down a fine shade tree to get firewood he ran up to them, pointing toward the manor house and pleading earnestly: "You break dat ol' man's heart if you cut down dat tree! His grandfather planted dat tree!"[10]

Night came at last and army movements ceased, and this great host of Federal soldiers, put down here so deliberately and so ostentatiously, waited for the action which the morning was sure to bring. The generals at the downstream end of the line were nervous. Franklin and his two corps commanders, Reynolds and Smith, interpreted Burnside's orders as calling simply for an armed observation of enemy strength. In a chat with Smith, Burnside had agreed that a good deal more than that was needed, and he had promised to send over supplementary orders. The generals sat up until three in the morning waiting for them, but they never came, either then or thereafter. Franklin, who was prepared to go by the script though the heavens fell, told Reynolds his original instructions stood: send out one division when day came, to seize the hill at Hamilton's Crossing, hold another division ready to support it, and if all goes well, which is not likely, someone will doubtless order something additional.

Dawn came in cold and foggy, with a slow wind in the leafless trees. As the brigades moved out to take their places they could hear the innumerable army noises, but they could see neither their own ranks nor the enemy's, and George Meade spread out his Pennsylvania division in a gray watery light facing west along the edge of a muddy road that led south. Doubleday took his men in on Meade's left, and Gibbon, going into action as a division commander for the first time, lined his men up on the other side. Everybody lounged in the ranks and waited for the fog to lift.

It lifted at about eleven o'clock, and when it went up it went up dramatically, like the curtain of a theater. The Federals were spread out all across the plain south of Fredericksburg, rank upon long rank, with national and regimental banners bright in the morning breeze, guns drawn up at intervals between the brigades, everything looking very martial and splendid, as if war were some sort of pageant. The Rebels were hardly visible. The hills which sheltered them were heavily wooded, and a low railway embankment that ran across the plain in front of the hills was fringed with a stubbly second growth where some advanced lines were concealed. They had a mass of guns planted on the knoll by Hamilton's Crossing, and a mile farther north they had another big bank of guns half hidden in a rising grove. Stonewall Jackson was an old artillerist himself, and he always made good use of his guns. As the last wisps of fog blew away, the Southern gunners stared at the limitless target that lay in front of them, trotted up to their pieces, pulled at trail handspikes and spun elevating screws, and opened fire. Gibbon's and Meade's men, drawn up along the highway, had to stay there and take it, while the Federal batteries rolled forward to make reply and a great turbulence of boiling smoke and heavy sound went tumbling up the sky.

Holding still to be shelled is about as unpleasant a job as infantry gets, and the Yankees in the open plain found it especially hard because they could very easily see the cannoneers who were firing at them. Naturally, they hated them; one soldier wrote that the Rebel gunners, visibly busy around their pieces, looked "like fiends who stirred infernal fires." An indignant general routed one straggler out of a ditch and ordered him to rejoin his command. The straggler saluted and said: "General, I will, jest as soon as them fellers quit throwin' railroad iron at us." And back on the far side of the Rappahannock the chaplain of a Pennsylvania regiment, returning to camp with some wounded men, told the contraband cook of the regimental officers' mess to take some hot coffee over to the embattled regiment. The contraband, looking wide-eyed at the flashing shells that were exploding all over the plain, shook his head emphatically. "I'se not gwine up dar whar so many big stars are busting!"[11]

It was at times like this that the Civil War officer was supposed to display a dramatic disregard of danger. To keep his troops steady he had to expose his own person; he had to do it with an air, as if to show that he simply was not aware that there was any danger. The boys of the 16th Maine, growing restive under the cannonade, presently found themselves gaping at Captain James Hall, who had his 2nd Maine battery drawn up in action beside them and who was blithely sitting his horse, carrying on a conversation with the 16th's commander, Lieutenant Colonel Charles W. Tilden, and the brigadier, Colonel Adrian Root, who were on their horses a dozen yards away from him. Since the air was full of truly deafening noise, the three officers had to shout at the top of their lungs to make themselves heard, but aside from that they might have been three civilian horsemen who had met on a bridle path in a park on a pleasant May morning and were stopping to pass the time of day.

While the soldiers hugged the ground and watched admiringly, a Rebel shell came whistling in between Captain Hall and the two colonels, narrowly missing the colonels and going on to crash into a caisson in the rear, exploding it with an earth-rocking crash. Captain Hall looked faintly annoyed. Very deliberately he dismounted, walked over to one of his guns, and painstakingly sighted it at the Rebel battery which had fired the shot. Satisfied, he stepped back and waved his hand to the gun crew. The gun was fired and landed a direct hit, dismounting a Rebel gun amid a cloud of torn earth and flying splinters. The battery commander walked back to his horse, mounted, and resumed the interrupted conversation as if nothing had happened.[12]

Such dramatics might help to make shell fire endurable, but in the end the battle would be decided by what the infantry did. By noon or thereabouts the Federal gunners had beaten the Confederate gunfire down just enough so that the infantry could go forward. Meade took his division into a ragged patch of woodland along the edge of the railroad track, Gibbon went into the fringe of the same woodland a little later and a little farther north, and the artillerists let their guns cool while the foot soldiers fought in the swampy underbrush. Meade's division by good fortune stumbled into a gap in Jackson's lines and for a short time made great headway, crumpling up a couple of A. P. Hill's brigades, killing one of his brigadiers, taking prisoners, and just for a moment making it look as if Burnside's battle plan might make sense after all. But although there were more than sixty thousand armed Federals on this plain south of Fredericksburg (one of Hooker's two corps had been sent down here as insurance), these two divisions seemed to be all that Franklin could get into action. The Army of the Potomac was up against its old, old difficulty: visibly outnumbering its enemy, it nevertheless was put into action in such a way that where the actual fighting was going on there were more Rebels present than Yankees. Stonewall Jackson sent in fresh troops, and the Federal assault columns were smashed and came running back into the open, hotly pursued. Across the open plain, shaken by the blast of many guns, there rose the high unearthly keen of the Rebel yell.

That yell—"that hellish yell," a Michigan soldier called it—appears to have been an actual power in battle, worth many regiments to the

Confederacy. A Federal surgeon wrote after the war: "I have never, since I was born, heard so fearful a noise as a Rebel yell. It is nothing like a hurrah, but rather a regular wildcat screech." And lest that be thought the nervous reaction of a timid noncombatant, here is the verdict of a front-line veteran from the 6th Wisconsin:

"There is nothing like it this side of the infernal region, and the peculiar corkscrew sensation that it sends down your backbone under these circumstances can never be told. You have to feel it, and if you say you did not feel it, and heard the yell, you have *never* been there."[18]

A spine-chilling thing, the Rebel yell. Not for nothing did old Stonewall himself, grimmest of all America's soldiers, call it "the sweetest music I ever heard."

Yelling like fiends, then, and inspired equally by hatred of the Yankee invader and the desire to plunder the invader's camp and person of good boots, blankets, and coffee, the Rebels came storming across the railroad and down into the plain as if they would shove the last Federals into the river. But Franklin's supply of support troops was practically limitless, and the Federal artillery was ready and waiting. The battery commanders held their men in until the Confederates were within point-blank range, and then they hit them hard with canister and slammed in additional salvos as fast as they could load their pieces, this being one occasion when General Hunt's one-round-in-two-minutes rule did not apply. The Confederate fighting lines were cut and broken and the men withdrew to their trenches on the wooded hillsides, and all of the important fighting on this part of the battlefield was over.

It remained, however, for the Iron Brigade to carry out a little assignment which had no effect on the battle itself but which at least restored internal harmony to the brigade.

This brigade was down at the extreme left of the army, and while the serious fighting was going on elsewhere, Jeb Stuart's horse artillery and dismounted cavalry had been making pests of themselves in some broken country near the river. The Iron Brigade was ordered to go out and put a stop to it. So Solomon Meredith, wearing his general's stars in action for the first time, sent the rookie 24th Michigan into a tangled bit of woodland where Rebel snipers lurked, with the 7th Wisconsin in immediate support and the rest of the brigade following after.

Despite all the fine things the generals and the war correspondents wrote about troops being eager to get into battle, Civil War soldiers were as sensible as any others and went into action usually because they had to and not because they liked it. But this was one of the times when some men really wanted to fight. This 24th Michigan had been ostracized for two solid months and it had had all it could take. If it did not soon redeem itself under fire its life simply was not going to be worth living any longer, and nothing the Rebels could do to it was half as bad as the cold contempt it was getting from the rest of the brigade. So when orders came through the men went forward with a grim determination that might have taken them straight through the middle of Jackson's main line if anyone had thought to point them that way. The brigade rolled forward, the four veteran regiments happy enough to let someone else go in the front line, watching the straw-feet with the half-amused, critical eyes of old-timers.

Into the wood went the 24th, and Stuart's gunners fired at them with cold accuracy. One man was beheaded by the first shot, and then a shell tore an arm off a file closer, and another man was mashed and still another was beheaded—all dreadfully unnerving for green soldiers. But Colonel Morrow halted them, and while unseen snipers fired at them and shell came crashing through the trees to inflict more casualties, he dressed the regiment's lines with elaborate care and coolly put the men through the manual of arms. The soldiers had been drilled within an inch of their lives that dreary fall, and now they went through all of this with regular-army precision. They were not killing any Rebels just then, but they were demonstrating to one and all that they could take it, and the veterans, some distance in the rear, looked on with dawning approval. Then the 24th went ahead again, taking great pains with its alignment, marching through that woodland like the West Point corps of cadets. General Doubleday admired them hugely but disliked the way Meredith was handling the brigade and deposed him and gave the command to Lysander Cutler, colonel of the 6th Wisconsin. The wood was cleared at last and Cutler flung a skirmish line out on the far side, and the shooting ended.

That evening the 2nd Wisconsin had the picket line, and as battle-wise veterans they quickly made a deal with the Rebels in their front by which neither side would do any shooting without giving due warning in advance, so that nobody had to stay under cover. But in the

morning the Michigan regiment relieved the 2nd Wisconsin. Being
very ardent and trigger-happy, they opened fire at once without waiting to be told about the agreement, and although the Wisconsin boys
yelled a frantic last-minute warning, a good many Rebels were shot
and a furious little fire fight raged up and down the picket lines, almost
bringing on a general engagement. Toward the end of the day there
came one of those odd incidents which were perfectly characteristic
of that strange war, although it is hard to imagine them happening
in any other war known to history. In all of this firing and sniping, a
certain Confederate private and one of the Wisconsin soldiers began
to develop a personal enmity toward each other, so that between shots
they yelled bitter insults, and finally they got so angry that just shooting at one another would not answer. The thing went too deep for
killing, and it had to be settled with fists. So the other soldiers called
an informal truce, and the two men laid down their weapons and
went out into the clearing and had a furious, emotion-releasing fist
fight—these two boys who had been perfectly satisfied to try to kill
each other up to the moment when their enmity became personal.

The rest of the soldiers cheered them on, agreed in the end that the
fight was a draw, and worked it out so that there was no more firing
on the picket line. Rebels and Yanks got together and traded coffee
for tobacco and agreed not to fight any more unless the higher-ups
actually ordered an advance. The two pugilists, presumably, washed
the blood off their faces, and the 24th Michigan sat down by its
campfires to count its losses.

These had not actually been very heavy—a total of thirty-six, as
the regiment's historian remembered it, of whom only seven were
dead; the fighting in the wood and along the picket line had not been
very severe after all. But somehow the way the regiment had handled
itself under fire thawed out the veterans. From enlisted men up to
commanding officers they agreed that these Michigan boys would do,
and there was no more talk about "bounty boys" after Fredericksburg. An officer in the 6th Wisconsin wrote grandiloquently: "They
showed themselves of a fibre worthy to be woven into the woof of the
Iron Brigade." The enlisted men used no fancy language, but they
did begin dropping into the 24th's camp at the close of day to borrow
tobacco and swap yarns, just as members of friendly regiments always did, and the historian of the 24th noted that "the greatest cor-
diality ever after prevailed."[14]

So the great battle of Fredericksburg accomplished this much, if nothing more; it enabled a new regiment to come out of Coventry and join the brotherhood of proven fighters. In that brotherhood it would appear that the boys had plenty of company.

4. Burnished Rows of Steel

The men of the II Army Corps were veterans and they knew a bad spot when they saw it. From the moment they crossed the river they disliked the looks of this Fredericksburg setup. They had had one laugh, coming over, when the Rebels began to shell the road right where the band of a nine-month regiment had posted itself. The musicians all ran for cover except the bass drummer, who simply cowered in the dust behind his big bass drum and fancied himself secure.[1] Other laughs were few. The heights west of town looked dangerous, and those heights were obviously where the high command intended the II Corps to go.

There was something eerie about the morning of the battle. Stragglers were on the prowl in alleys and back yards between the ruined looted houses, some of the men capering grotesquely in women's chemises stolen from ransacked bedroom closets. Sidewalks and gutters were littered with smashed furniture, crockery, wearing apparel, and other odds and ends carried out of homes by aimless marauders. Generals and generals' aides went cantering up and down the crowded streets, very busy, while the regiments dressed their ranks on the side streets to a thin spatter of bugle calls and shouted commands. Heavy cold mist filled the air, so that every down-street vista was like an open window into nothingness. In the air, too, palpable as the December fog itself, was the chill suspicion that cruel disaster lay just out of town to the west.

By midmorning the ranks were lined up in the proper order, and the sun burned away the fog. From the south the men could hear the crash of gunfire as Franklin's men made their unavailing assault on Jackson's lines. (On the Stafford Heights a green company cook asked what that noise was. Rebel guns, they told him. He listened and shook his head and said: "You fellers needn't think you can fool me. I've heard that noise too often in Philadelphia; they're unloading boards somewhere.")[2] There was a final flurry of galloping aides with orders, and then burly General William H. French sent his skirmish line trotting across the yards and around the outbuildings on the fringe of town and out into the open plain. The Rebel outposts fired a few shots and leisurely fell back toward the chain of hills to the west. General Darius N. Couch, commanding the II Corps, climbed to the cupola of the courthouse to look things over. The main body of French's division began to march out of town, and all the cannon in the Rebel army seemed to come to life at once, flashing along the hilltops from left to right as far as the men could see.

If the army had tried, it could not have found a worse place to make an attack. Between Fredericksburg and Marye's Heights there was a hollow plain perhaps half a mile wide. The town itself was on a little plateau; leaving it and advancing toward the heights, one went down a little slope and came presently to a wide ditch carrying the spillway of a canal from a paper mill a mile to the north. There was not much water in this canal, but the ditch itself was deep and its banks were steep. A spry individual could cross it anywhere, but a formal column of attack could cross only where it was bridged, and it was bridged in just two places.

To make an attack, therefore, the troops had to come out in solid columns of fours—of all formations, the one most vulnerable to enemy fire, with the men all bunched together in a cohesive target and nobody able to use his own weapon in reply. Reaching the open, these dense helpless columns must march straight ahead for two hundred yards within easy range of the Confederate artillery, which could smite them from in front and on both flanks. (Rebel sharpshooters on the heights also had them within range.) Then the columns must cross the ditch by the two bottleneck bridges, one of which had been partly destroyed, so that the men had to walk on the stringers; and after they were across, the columns had to turn right and left and spread out into the long lines of battle, two ranks deep, by which the actual assault would be made. Fortunately the ground rose sharply just beyond the ditch, so that the men would be under cover while they deployed. But as soon as the lines were formed they must climb the little slope and come out in the open and tramp forward for four hundred yards to reach Marye's Heights, at the foot of which there was a wide sunken road with a four-foot stone wall on the Fredericksburg side, as invulnerable a trench as the Rebels could have found in the whole state of Virginia.

In this sunken road and behind this wall Longstreet had put four ranks of riflemen, with abundant reinforcements nearby. Above them, on the hill slopes, were more infantry. Still higher, and extending far to the right and left so that they could lay down a horrible crisscross of fire, were the guns. The artillerist had not exaggerated very much: once all of these people commenced to fire, a chicken would have had a hard time getting across that plain.

French's men started off bravely enough. Nathan Kimball's brigade was in the lead, and he had a couple of new regiments which had never before been under fire. Kimball sat his horse by the roadside as these green regiments came by, noticed the white-lipped tension in the ranks, and cried out: "Cheer up, my hearties, cheer up! This is something we must all get used to! Remember, this brigade has never been whipped—don't let it get whipped today!" The rookies felt that this helped a little, but not much, and when the veteran regiments in the brigade raised a cheer the two new regiments could not quite find their voices.[3]

Kimball brought his two parallel columns out of town in fine order, flags gay in the breeze, weapons at the right shoulder, field officers tramping along with drawn swords and turning as they tramped to shout commands. Longstreet's gunners began hitting the marching columns before they were fairly outside the town, but they kept coming on. They got across the canal at last and swung into line and then came up over the bank, four regiments abreast, rookies and veterans together. One hundred yards behind them there was another brigade, with a third brigade coming up behind that one. The Rebel guns fired faster and faster, and the files shifted to right and left as the men closed up the gaps that were made by the shell. It was more comforting to march elbow to elbow, and as long as a man could feel his comrades immediately beside him he was willing to keep going.

From the far side of the Rappahannock, General Hunt's massed artillery opened fire furiously, striking at Longstreet's guns, trying to beat down the Rebel fire and give the infantry a chance. The earth seemed to rock and a choking mist lay on the plain. Hunt's gunners found that they could not silence the Confederate batteries. The range was long, the Southern guns were protected by earthworks, and the fuses for the long-range shell were worthless. Sometimes the missiles exploded over Federal troops instead of over Rebels; more often they simply did not explode at all. One exasperated gunner reported afterward that "as solid shot, the ordnance shrapnel was serviceable."[4]

About one hundred yards short of the sunken road there was an almost imperceptible rise in the open ground, a little swell which would not be noticed ordinarily but which today was like a high mountain ridge swept by great storms. If they lay flat on the ground just before they got to this rise, attacking troops might be protected from the fire of the Confederate infantry; but once they got on this insignificant crest, the fight had to be to a finish. There could be no more hiding—a man lying down could be shot as casily as a man standing erect—and it was precisely here, where they made a perfect target at shotgun range, that the assaulting troops must halt to deliver their own fire. An infantry attack in that war rarely implied an uninterrupted advance with the bayonet. It usually meant getting the attackers to close quarters so that they could break the defensive line with their own fire. This little rise was where the Federals must stand to deliver the fire that would break the Rebel line—unless, indeed, it should develop that this particular Rebel line could not be broken by any weight of fire whatsoever, in which case this was where the boys would stand while they found out.

Kimball's men had lost heavily crossing the plain, but they were still in formation, and as the long brigade lines wavered to a halt on this low crest the men set up a cheer. Nobody could hear it in the tremendous tumult. The stone wall seemed to blaze from end to end with one crackling sheet of flame, the guns on the heights crashed and thundered, and if Kimball's brigade had not been whipped before, it was whipped now. The men had never run into anything like this. Standing four ranks deep behind perfect protection, the Southern riflemen could keep up an almost continuous fire. The attacking brigade got off an unsteady volley or two, a few men irresolutely stumbled forward a few steps, and then the brigade fell completely apart. Some of the men ran for the rear, some huddled behind a square brick house which stood in the middle of this last rise in the ground, and others found shelter amid a few shacks by the main highway, a couple of hundred yards to the right. Most of the men simply dropped back a few yards, lay on the ground amid the dead and wounded, kept their tattered flags flying, and maintained as much of a fire as they could.

Up came the second brigade, a double line of blue more than a

quarter of a mile from end to end, swinging up over the bank by the
canal and rolling forward into the battle smoke. It reached the last
fiery crest and halted there to open fire, and the Rebel musketry overwhelmed it. When it broke, the third brigade came marching up to
take its place, and the third brigade, too, was smashed and French's
entire division had been put out of action. The survivors clung desperately to the bare ground and to moderately protected spots behind
the scattered buildings, firing pluckily but without much effect. To
General Couch, aloft in his cupola, peering down through the blanketing smoke, it looked as if the division had simply vanished. One
of the men who cowered behind the brick house wrote afterward
that although the Southern artillery was firing as fast as ever, the
musketry was so continuous and so intense that he could not recall
hearing the reports of any cannon.[5]

Winfield Scott Hancock had been ordered to follow French into
action, and he had his men moving out of town as soon as the last of
French's brigades crossed the canal. Hancock formed his division
as French had done, in three successive brigade lines, he himself riding personally back and forth along the outskirts of the city to gouge
the stragglers out of alleys and fence corners, driving his men in. His
leading brigade dressed its ranks carefully when it mounted the high
ground beyond the canal, and then it went ahead bravely, the battle-
tested veterans crouching low as they walked forward.

From the open field where no man stood erect there rose a wan,
scattered cheer, prostrate men shouting their greeting. Hancock's men
made a fine sight coming up, and a wounded man was seen to prop
himself on one elbow and swing his cap in welcome. Some of the men
who had been lying down scrambled to their feet to go forward with
this new charge. The Confederate gunners knocked great holes in the
wide blue lines, and the stone wall blazed out as wickedly as ever.
When the leading regiments tried to tear down a fence just beyond
the final rise in the ground, the fire from the sunken road broke them
all to bits. The men who were not shot ran back through the swirling
smoke, or stumbled over to the lee of the brick house, or lay on the
ground amid the dead and wounded. To the Confederates on the
heights, when the smoke drifted away, it looked as if all the plain
had turned blue.

Second wave now—General Thomas F. Meagher's Irish Brigade,
Meagher himself magnificent in a tailored uniform coat of darkest

green, silver stars embroidered on black shoulder knots, a yellow silk scarf across his breast—"a picture of unusual grace and majesty," a Pennsylvania soldier wrote. The Irishmen had only one of their green flags this day, the others having grown too tattered for use and the replacement flags not having arrived, and this one green flag was borne by the 28th Massachusetts, a regiment of Bay State Irish specially recruited for this brigade. Every man in the brigade wore in his cap a sprig of evergreen, and Meagher sent them down Hanover Street and out toward the canal, 69th New York in the lead.[6]

Like the others, the brigade formed beyond the canal and went swinging ahead, and the men who lay on the ground raised their heads and cheered as they saw them coming. The men tramped on, past the dead and the wounded and the beaten-out men of the other commands, and got up to that deadly, insignificant little high place in the flat plain, and the smoke rolled down on them like a killing cloud. The men could see very little and they could hear nothing at all but the unending racket of the firing. It was all but impossible for officers to pass an order in the choking, confused tumult. Now and then men got a glimpse of a few officers farther forward trying to tear down an obstructing fence. The 88th New York knelt behind another fence and opened its own fire, and the whole field was a pandemonium of smoke and flame and shouting men. Captain Condon of the 63rd New York learned that he was in command of the regiment, and when he tried to get the men together he could find only nine of them. As he was lining up this remnant of a command he saw a slightly larger fragment drifting up out of the smoke, a green flag at its head: the colonel of the 28th Massachusetts, who had a dozen men with him. The two officers shook hands and agreed that the brigade had been cut to pieces,[7] and in the end they got their men back to the riverbank and found General Meagher rallying other survivors. By evening he was able to assemble 250 men out of the 1,400 the brigade had taken into action.

The plain was covered with smoke, and men on each side saw the fighting only in glimpses, and what they saw was always the same. Up in front, in that last deadly zone between fifty and one hundred yards from the stone wall, one firing line would be crumbling and going to pieces under the fearful Confederate fire; farther back, while this was happening, the broad blue lines of a new brigade would be coming up into view on the high ground near the canal; and back by the town, compact columns would be marching down the parallel highways, making their way toward the canal. There never seemed to be any end to it, and the Confederates lost all track of the number of separate assaults they had repelled. While the Irish officers were plucking their men out of the smoke fog, Hancock's third brigade was coming over the plain—Brigadier General John Caldwell's men, who had broken the Rebel line at Bloody Lane above the Antietam, going in now as then on the heels of the Irish.

What had been done by the Antietam could not be done here. Caldwell got part of his brigade up to the high-water mark—his valiant 5th New Hampshire, Colonel Cross and three successors all down with wounds, the regiment under its fifth commander in ten minutes; part of his 81st Pennsylvania, with the combined 61st and 64th New York beside them. They could advance no farther. The very endurance and determination of the survivors of the earlier attacks were a handicap. These men lay by the hundreds all across the front in a ragged belt two hundred yards deep, keeping up such fire as they could manage, and in the blanketing smoke they shot wildly, hitting their own comrades in the front lines.[8] Meanwhile, the fire from the sunken road and from the heights came without a moment's letup. No man who stood upright in the open plain could hope to live long.

Yet there were men who wanted to try. Up to Caldwell came the slim, handsome young colonel who commanded the two New York regiments, a dandy of a man with pointed mustaches, the name of him Nelson Miles. He wanted permission to take his two regiments and make a bayonet charge straight up the road for the stone wall. It needed just one spirited dash to clear that wall, he argued, and if two regiments started, men all over the plain would jump up and follow them. But Caldwell refused. There were no supports; if the men did breach the Rebel line they could not stay there, the thing was just impossible. . . . And then Caldwell was wounded and was carried off the field, and Miles took a bullet in the throat and went to the rear with blood dripping through the fingers which he held pressed against the wound. There was nothing for the survivors to do but hug the ground and hope for the best.[9]

From his perch in the cupola General Couch had seen some of this —not much, for the smoke was very heavy, and from the rear one could make out little but the dim forms of blue-clad men swaying uncertainly in a terrible haze that glowed and sparked with deadly fire. (One man who watched the attackers from the heights beyond the river found himself amazed that the heavy fire "did not absolutely sweep them from the face of the earth.") General Howard, who stood beside Couch for a time, heard him gasp as the smoke lifted briefly: "Oh, great God! See how our men, our poor fellows, are falling!"[10]

Couch decided that enough of them had fallen in front of the stone wall, so he told Howard to lead his division farther to the right, where the Rebel line looked a bit softer. If this impregnable line could not be stormed, perhaps it might be flanked, and Howard must try. There were plenty of troops available to follow him in if his men won any success, and Howard rode off to put his division into action.

Couch's idea was a good one, but the shape of the ground was against it. Although no one seems to have realized it at the time, it simply was not possible for an attack issuing from Fredericksburg to hit the Rebel line anywhere except along that impassable sunken road. It looked as if Howard could cross the ditch where the others had crossed and could then shift to his right until he was half a mile or more north of Marye's Heights; but when his men tried it they found that they could edge to the right only a little way before striking impassable ground. A long slough, known locally as Gordon's Marsh, ran to the north on the western side of the ditch: an unobtrusive dike which forced every Federal assault on this part of the field to drift to the left and go crashing up against the one front that could not be broken.[11]

Howard's men drifted and instead of flanking the stone wall they came in, at last, over the wreckage of the other two divisions, fared as they had fared, and reached the outer boundaries of human endurance on that same little rise of ground in front of the wall. Survivors hid out behind houses or face-down on the earth as the others had done, and it seemed that no one could live out in the open. Howard wrote that he had "a feeling akin to terror" whenever he had to send an aide or a mounted orderly forward with a dispatch.[12]

The men who lay in the open used what poor cover they could get. One officer saw three men sheltering behind a dead horse. Here and there a man would be able to get two or three rocks which he would pile up in a pitiful little barricade. Many a soldier lay behind the corpse of a comrade while he loaded and fired. In the brick house and in other houses back on the edge of town sharpshooters found vantage points from which they could fight effectively. They and the men in the field kept up a fire which now and then stung the Southerners painfully. The Confederate brigadier who commanded the troops back of the stone wall was killed, various guns in the upper pits were put out of action from time to time, and it was made risky for any Confederate to pass from one level to another of the defenses on the smoking hillside. But there was nothing in this fire that could possibly drive the defenders away. One Federal who remembered how effectively the Rebels were hidden behind the wall remarked that "no doubt for every Johnny hit a ton of lead was expended," and the men could hear their bullets spattering harmlessly on the stones and knew they were killing very few of the enemy.[13]

Somewhere far to the rear, beyond the deep river, insulated from reality by distance, by the trappings of command, and by sheer mental confusion, there was a guiding intelligence for this army, and to it there came dimly the news of this great fight. It sluggishly sent back repeated and unvarying orders to attack and to keep on attacking. Divisions from the III, V, and IX Corps came over to join in the fight, and always the story was the same. The men who went into action were mostly veterans, and as they marched out into the range of the Confederate gunners they were able to assay with complete accuracy the exact measure of their chances on this smoking plain; yet it is not recorded that any of them turned away or refused to go forward, and each brigade went in with a cheer, however it might be fated to come out.

A brigade from the V Corps tried to come in through an unfinished railway cut at the left. The Rebel gunners, vigilant above the battle smoke, saw the brigade coming and swung their guns over and waited for it, and when it came out on the level ground they racked it. The men who were not hit were blinded by the dirt and gravel kicked up by the flying canister, and the brigade drifted back and took refuge in a stretch of low ground near the railway and found to its horror that it was huddling in a spot which had been a sink for a Rebel camp. In the 22nd Massachusetts it was recalled that while the men cowered in this unpleasant spot the quavering voice of a very proper ex-schoolteacher in the ranks was lifted in inquiry: "Who is in command of Company H?" A sergeant growled a reply: who wanted to know, and why? And the ex-schoolteacher—primly, as if the village debating society had convened here in front of the stone wall—made his answer: "I move that we be taken out of here by some responsible officer." The regiment's historian wrote that this drew an unfeeling reply from the sergeant.[14]

Most of the soldiers on the plain would have seconded the motion if they could have heard it. But the high command kept putting more people in instead of taking them out, and the Rebels methodically shot them down as fast as they came in, and the rifle fire rose to an unheard-of intensity. General Caldwell, up by the brick house, wrote that it was "the hottest I have ever seen," and a private soldier said the men in an attack "stood as though they were breasting a storm of rain and sleet, their faces and bodies being only half turned to the storm, with their shoulders shrugged."[15] Finally, in desperation, Couch ordered field artillery out into the open. His chief of staff protested that no battery could live in that field, and Couch agreed that that was probably true but said the gunners would have to go out there anyway: something had to be done to cut down the Confederate fire, and anyway, it was better to lose guns than men.

So the artillery went in at a gallop, clattering across the ditch and swinging into battery on the higher ground just beyond—a Rhode Island and a New York battery from the II Corps and a battery of regulars from the IX Corps. They were in trouble from the very start. Sharpshooters were hitting the regulars before they even had their guns unlimbered, and the Rebel artillerists quickly found the exact range and began exploding their shells right over the battery. Within twenty minutes the battery commander and a dozen men had been knocked out, most of the horses had been killed, and the survivors had been driven away from the guns three times. Never had they been in so hot a spot.

It was the same with the others. The Rhode Island battery lost men so fast that its skipper, Captain John G. Hazard, went back to the ditch, rounded up infantry stragglers, and brought them up to help work his guns. General Howard, who saw it all, wrote that his conduct was "equal to anything I ever saw on a field of battle." And presently young Lieutenant Adams, commanding the right section of this battery, limbered up one of his guns and went galloping madly forward with it until he was less than 150 yards away from the stone wall, where he unlimbered in the open road. This looked like nothing in the world but a spectacular way to commit suicide, and three cannoneers in succession were killed at the gun's muzzle before the first charge could be rammed home. But the gun and its crew stayed there, pounding at close range at the stone wall, firing, as one of Hancock's staff reported, as coolly as if they had been firing blank cartridges on a review.[16]

The winter twilight came, and Couch rode forward to the brick house and found the smoke and dusk so heavy that he could not see the enemy and supposed that the enemy could not see him, although, as he wrote later, he was "aware of the fact that somebody in our front was doing a great deal of shooting." It seems that he rode from one end of his prostrate battle line to the other, chatting with Lieutenant Adams and his gunners for a while and then riding slowly to the other flank. Except for the gunners and the men who were sheltering behind the brick house, he was the only man in the field who was not lying down taking cover. At length, cool and unhurried, he rode back to town, and if there was anything about the plight of his troops which he did not know it was not because he had failed to go out and see for himself.[17]

And still the high command had not had enough. It kept sending fresh troops in as resolutely as a butcher pushing raw material into a mincing machine. General Andrew Humphreys from the V Corps brought forward his two untried brigades of Pennsylvanians—nine-month troops enlisted the previous summer, hurried down to Antietam just too late to get into the fighting there, somewhat looked down upon by the long-term troops, but drilled and disciplined by one of the sharpest taskmasters in the army. Humphreys was tall and slim; he had been born without nerves and was decidedly a martinet, and as he took his regiments in he left no one behind. The colonel of one outfit had detailed half a dozen of the youngest, frailest soldiers to guard the regiment's knapsacks which had been piled in a side street, but Humphreys made harsh remarks about stragglers and relentlessly drove the boys on with the rest.

He got his soldiers across the canal and formed them into two lines in the murk of the fading day, and it seemed to him that the only possible chance was to keep going without a halt. If the men ever stopped to fire they were lost, best make a straight bayonet charge out of it. He issued his orders accordingly, his rookies fixed bayonets, and forward they went. As they came up through the human debris of all the previous charges, the unwounded men on the ground reached up and tried to hold them back, telling them that it was no use to go on. It was nearly dark, the field was very muddy, and the men stumbled on through the dead and wounded and the clutching hands of the unwounded, and their lines grew disordered. A staff officer galloped up, sword swinging in the dim light, yelling to the men to close and dress their ranks; and just then a great sweep of fire lit up the entire length of the stone wall, and farther up the hill and far off to right and left there were incessant quick flashings from the Rebel cannon, and the staff officer was shot down and so was nearly half of the division. The men staggered to a halt—as close to the wall, Humphreys noted proudly, as anyone got that day, and it simply was not in them or in any men to get any closer—and they fired a ragged volley or two. Then they gave way as all the others had done and went streaming back toward the town.

The 9th Massachusetts, coming up to this inferno of a field on the heels of this repulse, saw Humphreys sitting his horse all alone, looking out across the plain, bullets cutting the air all around him, and the men spontaneously set up a cheer. They were standing in the same fire themselves, but something about the way the general was taking it pleased them, and they cheered. Humphreys looked over, surprised, waved his cap to them with a grim smile, and then went cantering forward into the deadly twilight.[18]

It was almost entirely dark when Rush Hawkins's brigade from the IX Corps made one final assault, coming up from the railway cut and swinging out into the open ground comparatively undamaged, and then getting the worst of it in one tremendous blast that seemed to shake whole regiments apart. The colonel of the 13th New Hampshire wrote that "with one startling crash, with one simultaneous sheet of fire and flame, they hurled on our advancing lines the whole terrible force of their infantry and artillery." Others who saw that charge said that the whole field was lit up as if by sheet lightning when the Rebels opened fire. For a few moments there was a wild melee as the broken lines swayed back and forth; some of the men, unhurt by the Rebel fire, were injured simply by being knocked down and tramped on in the unendurable confusion, and Colonel Hawkins noted that "everybody, from the smallest drummer boy on up, seemed to be shouting to the full extent of his capacity." Part of the brigade overlapped the left of the II Corps line and was shot by Federal bullets, and finally what was left of it sagged back into the shelter of the railway cut, and it was too dark to fight any more that day.[19]

Around midnight Joe Hooker had the V Corps move up to relieve the exhausted survivors of the afternoon's assaults, and a couple of brigades of regulars were sent out into the plain to form a strange belly-to-earth line of battle in the pitch-darkness in front of the stone wall. When light came the regulars found their situation extremely uncomfortable. In the darkness they had stretched out just before reaching the flat summit of that final, invisible little ridge. The ground sloped just enough so that they could not be hit by the Rebel marksmen if they lay absolutely flat. The man who sat up or even lifted his head was almost certain to get hit, for the Confederates, standing at ease behind their stone wall or being equally easy in the rifle pits and gun emplacements farther up the hill, had nothing to do and were very much on the alert. As one soldier wrote, "The Confederate gunners seemed to follow the rule of Donnybrook Fair and whenever they saw a Yankee head they tried to hit it with a solid shot or shell." A regular officer recalled that from dawn to dusk the men were "unable to eat, drink, or attend to the calls of nature, for so relentless were the enemy that not even a wounded man or our own stretcher-bearers were exempted from their fire." Not until night could the men be withdrawn. One brigade, which had accomplished nothing whatever during its all-day vigil and had not fired a shot, reported that it had suffered 140 casualties.[20]

The 24th New Jersey, one of the greenhorn regiments in Kimball's brigade, could find only thirty-six men when it called the roll after the fighting stopped. During the night several scores of lost men and bewildered stragglers rejoined, but the regiment was still skimpy and the men were very blue next day when word came to fall in: there was going to be another attack on that stone wall. Obediently, but without a trace of enthusiasm, the 24th fell in—under a captain, all of the field officers having fallen. The captain stood before the regiment, noted that the color-bearers had not survived the action, and called out: "Who will carry the flags?" There was a dead silence. Then two non-coms quietly stepped forward and took up the state and national colors. The captain quietly shook hands with them, and the regiment dressed its ranks. And after a bit news came that orders had been changed, the attack was off, and the men relaxed.[21]

The story of Fredericksburg comes down at last to a simple account of the bravery which men can display and the price that can be exacted of them because they do display it; and if the men gain anything at all by any part of it, there is a transcendental scale of values in operation somewhere which it would be nice to know about. One of Humphreys's colonels remarked that the battle had been a great defeat "owing to the heavy fire in front and an excess of enthusiasm in the rear." The correspondent of the Cincinnati *Commercial* disgustedly wired his paper: "It can hardly be in human nature for men to show more valor, or generals to manifest less judgment, than were perceptible on our side that day."[22]

And yet this disastrous fight, as barren of concrete results as any battle the Army of the Potomac ever fought, was nevertheless in its own tragic way a dim beacon light for the future—a dull smoky flame burning reddish-black deep in the night, a glow rather than a blaze, shedding a very patchy and imperfect light, yet nevertheless keeping the winter dark from becoming absolute.

For the significant thing about that endless succession of doomed assaults across the plain was not, after all, the fact that a stupid general ordered them, but the fact that the army which had to make them had never once faltered.

Over and over, hour after agonizing hour, the story had been the same: up front a column of attack being hammered to a bloody wreck, in the rear a new column forming, going in with a cheer even though everyone from file closers to brigadier knew just what was going to happen. Each new column moved up and was broken and another one formed in its rear and came on without any hesitation, long ranks of polished rifle barrels gleaming in the December sunlight. Here they were, moving forward endlessly, those burnished rows of steel in which the poet of the battle hymn had seen the unanswerable writ of a fiery gospel. They were borne by an army that was uninspired and badly led, an army which by its own account of things had lost all its morale but which somehow kept coming on.

TWO

All Played Out

1. A Long Talk with Robert

The Secretary of the Navy was familiar with the omens, and on December 14 they were very bad. It was generally known in Washington that a great battle had been fought at Fredericksburg, and while the War Department had nothing whatever to say about it, Mr. Welles felt that it was giving the show away by the very manner in which it kept silent. He had found, Mr. Welles noted in his diary, that whenever the War Department had unwelcome news which it would greatly prefer not to publish, it managed to perform the purely negative act of not publishing "with a great deal of fuss and mystery, a shuffling over of papers and maps, and a far-reaching vacant gaze at something undefined and indescribable."[1]

This entry reflects in part the extreme irritation which Secretary Stanton and General Halleck always seemed able to arouse in Mr. Welles, who was very articulate when irritated. But it also reflects the fact that the department had very good reason for shuffling its papers and looking off into space. The country was not believed in condition to absorb any more really bad news—as hardy a patriot as Governor Morton of Indiana had recently warned Lincoln that "nothing but success, speedy and decided, will save our cause from utter destruction"[2]—and the department had the worst of news for it. What was likely to happen next was more than the Secretary of War or the general-in-chief had any idea.

General Burnside at least had his army back on his own side of the river. For a time he had nourished the wild notion of making one more great assault on the stone wall. He would lead his own IX Corps, which still loved him, in a wild charge that might puncture and destroy that defensive line which the rest of the army had been unable even to reach. This idea he had settled upon in the desolate night hours following the disastrous attacks on December 13, and his subordinate generals, after some argument about who should bell the cat, had finally been able to make him see that no one in the entire army, aside from himself, had the faintest notion that such a charge could possibly succeed. Indeed, it may be that Burnside himself felt the same way about it. General Couch, talking to him in the ruined town that evening, "could see that he wished his body was also lying in front of Marye's Heights," and the whole project may have been an unreasoned groping on Burnside's part for a dramatic and honorable exit from the mess into which he had blundered.[3]

Dissuaded from this insane venture, Burnside ordered a retreat. Here again his subordinates disagreed with him, and Hooker and Couch argued strongly that the town at least should be held as a bridgehead to make possible a new offensive thrust later on. Their advice may have been sound, but Burnside had had all the Fredericksburg he wanted and he would not listen. On a wild, windy night two days after the battle the army went back to the eastern bank, pulling its bridges behind it, and the men assumed that they were going to go into winter quarters and began to build canvas-roofed huts for warmth and comfort.

Yet Burnside was not through. The streak of obstinacy which had kept him ordering his brigades up to Marye's Heights long after everyone else had seen that it was hopeless was still in him. He had no intention of giving up his plans for an offensive—believing, apparently correctly, that an offensive before midwinter was what the administration wanted—and he quietly began to formulate new plans while the army licked its wounds and counted up the costs of the great battle.

Put down on paper, those costs were just as dreadful as they had seemed likely to be in the heat of action. In killed, wounded, and missing the army had lost more than 12,600 men, of whom almost exactly 10 per cent had been killed in action. The great bulk of the casualties had been incurred in front of the stone wall, where more than 900 Federal corpses had been counted, and there had been nothing whatever to show for them. Confederate losses on that part of the field had been very light, and there had not been at any time the slightest chance that the Federals could break through there. In the fight made by Franklin's men near Hamilton's Crossing the terms had been more nearly equal. Confederate losses there had been at least comparable to the Union losses, and the Confederate grip on the line of higher ground had been shaken briefly, even if not seriously threatened.[4] Yet if that was the most that could be said—and it was —the battle as a whole had to be written down as a dismal failure. Lee's army had lost only 5,300 men, and much the greater part of it had not been in action at all.

If Lee's army had not suffered much, the town of Fredericksburg had suffered dreadfully. In plain English, the town had been sacked, and the destruction which General Hunt's guns had caused had been the least of its woes. Both before, during, and after the actual fighting, the Army of the Potomac had unleashed upon this historic town the spirit of unrestrained rowdyism. The very divisions which had mustered the incredible heroism to make the repeated attacks on the stone wall had also put on display the very essence of jackbooted vandalism. A veteran of the 118th Pennsylvania left a description:

"The city had been rudely sacked; household furniture lined the streets. Books and battered pictures, bureaus, lounges, feather beds, clocks, and every conceivable article of goods, chattels, and apparel had been savagely torn from the houses and lay about in wanton confusion in all directions. Fires were made, both for warmth and cooking, with fragments of broken furniture. Pianos, their harmonious strings displaced, were utilized as horse troughs, and amid all the dangers animals quietly ate from them." A soldier in another Pennsylvania regiment noted "great scenes of vandalism and useless destruction of books, furniture, carpets, pianos, pictures, etc.," and reported a grotesque carnival aspect in streets still swept by Confederate shell as Union soldiers cavorted about in women's dresses and underwear. "Some of these characters," he added, "might be seen with musical instruments, with big horns, violins, accordions, and banjos"; and he noted that his own regiment took several hundred bottles of wine out of someone's cellar, a part of this wine appearing later on the colonel's own mess table. One illiterate private rifled an express office and carried off a huge bundle of receipts and canceled checks under the impression that he was robbing a bank and getting money.[5]

Brigadier General Alfred Sully, from Howard's division, took over a handsome house for his headquarters and told members of the 1st Minnesota, of which he had previously been colonel, to go through it and take anything they wanted. It belonged to his brother-in-law, who, he said, was a damned Rebel. Perversely, the Minnesota boys took nothing whatever from it and even established a guard there so that nobody else could loot it either. The regimental historian, maintaining that the sack of Fredericksburg was justified by the laws of war, added regretfully that "it would be pleasanter to remember Fredericksburg had there been no looting."[6]

Some of the higher officers, indeed, looking back on it, did argue that by the ancient rules of warfare Fredericksburg was properly open to pillage. An inhabited town, it had been called on to surrender before the battle and it had refused, and the troops had then taken it by storm. Since time immemorial, a town taken under such conditions was fair prey for the men who had captured it. But the men who looted Fredericksburg were not going by the books. The Army of the Potomac behaved there as it had never behaved before, and none of the explanations commonly advanced for lawless behavior by Union troops in this war holds good in this case.

Looting, pillaging, and illegal foraging by Federal soldiers are usually blamed on loosely disciplined Western troops, or on the riffraff bounty men, or on the German regiments brought up in the European tradition, or on the excesses natural to an army which is supplying itself from the enemy's country, or on the studied policy of commanders like Sherman and Sheridan who were frankly out to make Southern civilians tired of the war. But not one of these reasons is any good here. Fredericksburg was ransacked, not by free-and-easy Westerners but chiefly by Easterners of the II Corps and the V Corps, crack outfits with excellent discipline. The army contained no bounty men to speak of, and the German regiments were not in Fredericksburg. The army was not living off the enemy's country but was solidly planted on its own supply lines, and it was under the direction of a general who, however breath-taking some of his deficiencies may have been, was at least a good, amiable man who tried not to make war on civilians. If the usual explanations are good, Fredericksburg should have survived the occupation with minor damage. Actually, the army all but took it apart.

It seems that a new spirit was taking possession of this army. It had been visible before the battle; there had been that wild epidemic of sheep stealing and general lawlessness on the march down from Maryland, which was obviously the prelude to the spoiling of a taken town. A soldier in the 24th New Jersey had written that his conscience bothered him when he saw his fellow soldiers "robbing the poor families of all the little they possessed." At breakfast-time campfires, he said, it was common to hear men tell how "helpless women cried to see their small stock of poultry carried away."[7] A man from the 8th Ohio was heard arguing with a man from the 19th Indiana as to which regiment had managed to collect and send home the greater amount of plunder, and an officer in the 79th New York noted sadly that "wanton destruction of property and all the probable results of a successful siege develop only the most devilish propensities of humanity."[8]

This officer considered that misbehavior by Northern troops simply strengthened Southerners in their desire for independence. He argued, logically enough: "I think, were low ignorant ruffians to visit my home while I was away fighting, burn my house, lay waste my property, insult mother and sisters, beggar the little children I might love, taunt the gray hairs I might respect, leave starvation in the place of plenty, I should feel singularly strengthened in my early delusion." He blamed the whole trouble on "the accursed conduct of the press with its clamor for a vigorous prosecution of the war," and he spoke bitterly of "the effect of the savage appeals of our journals at home."

The New York soldier was beginning to see it. The war was changing, and it was no longer being looked upon as a species of tournament between unstained chivalrous knights. It had reached a point now where the fighting of it was turning loose some unpleasant emotional drives. It had become a war *against*—against slavery, perhaps against the men who owned slaves, by inevitable extension against that man and his family and his goods and chattels who by living with the hated institution seemed to have made war necessary and who in any case were standing in the road when the avengers came. The people here in Virginia had become aliens, and their land was strange and foreign, and therefore subject to hate. The 14th Vermont came down from the North and went into camp in Alexandria, the very first Southern city the regiment had ever seen, and a member of the regiment promptly commented that "the dirty, filthy condition of the streets in Alexandria is not only discoverable in all Southern cities but exhibits very plainly the blighting effects of slavery." A soldier in the equally green 33rd Massachusetts took his first look at Virginia, found its sleepy hamlets unlike New England's trim villages, and wrote caustically: "Let me say here that the towns of Virginia are composed of a barn, one outhouse, and a haystack."⁹ Behind such sentences, obviously, lay a feeling of being among the infidels. If the war must be carried on with greater vigor, as all the spokesmen of government were saying, then these infidels were not to be treated too gently, and if bad things happened to them it did not matter very much.

It was not a genteel, restrained, orderly country that was feeling this changed emotional current. It was a nation with the infinite raw strength of graceless youth, moving with gigantic careless energy into a future that was not known to have any bounds whatever. It was feeling its oats and it was flexing muscles bigger than anybody else ever had, and if people got hurt along the way it was not even going to notice. It had been like that from the beginning and it had not yet grown mellow and thoughtful, and it was not for nothing that its national air was a little tune called "Yankee Doodle," which has no words to speak of and expresses no sentiment on earth but sheer perky impudence.

This was the country of the boisterous forty-niner, the hell-roaring lumberjack, and the riverman who was half horse and half alligator. Without rancor (and also without the slightest hesitation) it annihilated Indian tribes so that it could people a wilderness, asserting that the only good Indian was a dead Indian and remarking casually of its own pioneers that the cowards never started and the weak died along the road. As it faced the cathedral aisles of endless virgin forests it shouted for immediate daylight in the swamp, even if whole generations must be brutalized for it. It was the country that invented the bucko mate and the Shanghai passage, and if the skysails of its incredible clippers gleamed on the farthest magic horizon they were taken there by men under the daily rule of clubs and brass knuckles. This nation accepted boiler explosions as the price of steamboat travel and it would boast presently of a dead gandy-dancer for every cross-tie on the transcontinental railroad. It wore seven-league boots and scorned to look where it planted them, and each of its immense strides was made at immense human cost. And the army of this country, buckling down to it at last in a fight which had to go to a finish, was going to be very rough on enemy civilians, not because it had anything against them but simply because they were there.

Of genuine hatred this army had practically none. The wild young men who ruined ancestral portraits and pranced in the smoky streets wearing the embroidered undergarments of gentlewomen were expressing nothing but plain hooliganism, which somehow was the obverse side of the medal that had laid nine hundred corpses in front of the stone wall west of town. Both sides of the medal bespoke raw youth which cheered and guffawed by turns, whose noble best forever went arm in arm with its ugly worst.

Before Burnside pulled his men back across the river there was a truce, and details from both armies went out to relieve such wounded as still lived and to bury the dead. In front of that stone wall, where all the dead men were Yankees, the lifeless bodies were nearly all naked. During the cold night needy Rebels had come out to help themselves to the warm coats and pants and the good Yankee shoes which the dead men would no longer need. An officer from the 48th Pennsylvania, supervising the work of one detail, fell into conversation with a Confederate officer, and the Confederate told him: "You Yankees don't know how to hate—you don't hate us near as much as we hate you." The Confederate gestured toward the pitiful naked rows of despoiled corpses and asked in effect: Do you think we could ever treat your dead that way if we didn't hate you?[10]

Whether that Confederate hatred was real or whether the casual stripping of Yankee corpses was simply one moré manifestation of the brutally realistic American spirit may be a story in itself. The point is that others besides that one Rebel officer felt the Federals to be lacking in hatred: among them, none other than Burnside himself. Congressman George W. Julian of Indiana, one of the sternest of the abolitionist leaders, had a chat with Burnside not long after the battle and wrote:

"General Burnside told me our men did not feel toward the Rebels as they felt toward us, and he assured me that this was the grand obstacle to our success. Our soldiers, he said, were not sufficiently fired by resentment, and he exhorted me, if I could, to breathe into

our people at home the same spirit toward our enemies which inspired them toward us."

Burnside's soldiers might have explained things a little differently
if anyone had asked them about the grand obstacle to success. As a
matter of fact, they did put it differently—quite differently—and without being asked. A soldier in the 5th Wisconsin wrote after this battle: "Was there ever an army so cruelly handicapped as the Army of
the Potomac? Is there, in military annals, any record of men pre-
serving their discipline, patriotism, courage, in spite of such adverse
circumstances as beset these men of the North?"[11]

However, Congressman Julian had been talking to the commanding general, not to the enlisted man, and no leader of the abolitionists ever needed to be told twice to go out and stir up more hatred.
Julian later recounted that in the political campaign of the following
summer "I fully entered into the spirit of General Burnside's advice
. . . to breathe into the hearts of the people a feeling of animosity
against the Rebels."[12] The wind was being sown and the whirlwind
would soon be ready for reaping.

Yet it seems that the soldiers who would have to be around when
the reaping took place had small part in the sowing. This army was
doubly deficient—in leadership and in vindictiveness—and the men do
not appear even to have tried to hate their enemies. On the contrary,
they exercised a good deal of ingenuity in order to open a highly
illegal but quite friendly trade with them, with the wide Rappahannock as the bearer of their peaceful cargoes. The classical essentials
for a thriving peacetime trade were present; that is, each side had a
surplus of goods greatly in demand by the other side, the Federals
having plenty of coffee and the Confederates having an excess of
tobacco. And as the pickets walked their posts by the river it soon
occurred to Northerners and Southerners alike that the war would
get on just as well and would be a good deal less onerous to the
individual if some of that coffee could be swapped for some of that
tobacco.

It is probable that every regiment which was stationed on the
river took part in this trade at one time or another, and the routine
was always much the same. The following appears to have been
typical:

Sunny winter day: 17th Mississippi on picket on the Rebel side of
the stream, 24th New Jersey guarding the shore just opposite. Shouted

conversation over the water reveals a mutual desire to trade. Jersey men presently get a small board, whittle it into something resembling the shape of a boat, put in a mast, use an old letter for a sail, put a load of coffee aboard, point it for the Confederate shore, and let it go. The intention is good, but the performance is poor: the home-made craft capsizes in a mid-river gust of wind and floats off downstream, bottom up, its cargo a total loss.

Among the Mississippians there seem to have been men who knew a bit more about the design and construction of sailing vessels, and they presently brought a much more practical craft down to the water—a little boat two feet long or thereabouts and five or six inches wide, carefully hollowed out to provide cargo space and equipped with rudder and sails that would actually work. This boat made a successful passage. The Jersey soldiers who received it took from its hold a note reading:

"Gents U. S. Army: We send you some tobacco by our packet. Send us some coffee in return. Also a deck of cards, if you have them, and we will send you more tobacco. Send us any late papers if you have them." The letter was signed by "Jas. O. Parker, Co. H., 17th Mississippi Vols."

The vessel's lading was as stated in the manifest, and in addition there was a small book, *Questions on the Gospels,* by the Reverend R. Bethell Claxton, D.D., which one of the Federals kept with him through the rest of the war. And the Jersey men sent coffee and hardtack over on the little boat's return trip, with a note promising that there would be a deck of cards the next time the outfit came on picket. The boat made a number of round trips and became quite famous—so much so that the better part of each regiment would come down to the shore to greet it.[13]

This tendency on the part of the soldiers to forget that there was a war on worried the high command, and stern orders were issued, to which the soldiers paid no more attention than they had to. Now and then the thing went farther than toy boats loaded with coffee and playing cards. Men crossed the river at times to get together personally with their enemies, and a Confederate general left a half-scandalized, half-amused account of how he nabbed a few Yankee soldiers visiting his own men and prepared to send them off to Richmond as prisoners of war, only to have his men plead almost tearfully that he just couldn't do it—they had given the Yankees their

word of honor that if they came over to visit they would be allowed
to go back again. In the end the general relented on a stern don't-
let-it-happen-again basis.[14] The elements in this war were mixed
and contradictory. If one side robbed corpses and the other side
robbed housewives, there was on both sides, deep in the bones and
the spirit, this strange absence of rancor, which may, in the end, explain why it was that the two sections were finally able to reunite after
a war which would seem to have left scars too deep for any healing.

It does not appear that this willingness to fraternize ever appre-
ciably dulled the fighting edge of either army, but it undoubtedly
led to a good many security leaks. Armies whose outposts spend
much of their time exchanging gossip are not likely to keep their
secrets very well. This probably hampered Burnside more than it
hampered Lee, for the Confederates just then did not need to make
many plans and hence had few secrets to keep. Their job was just
to stand by and keep the Yankees from doing whatever they proposed
to do next. Burnside was supposed to be aggressive, and he did his
best to live up to the role. But to the end of his career as commander
of the army he seems to have kept very few secrets from his opponents.

Since nothing came of the plans which he laid after Fredericksburg,
the fact that Lee quickly found out about them did no particular
harm. What really made trouble for Burnside was the fact that he
could not keep his plans hidden from his own subordinates, who
learned about them long before they were supposed to and, learning,
made much trouble for him.

Burnside bestirred himself on the day after Christmas, nearly a
fortnight after the battle. All of the wounded had been removed
from the field hospitals to the general hospitals farther to the rear,
many of them having been transferred by steamer all the way back
to Washington. The unwounded survivors of the battle were making
themselves tolerably comfortable in the camps near Falmouth—camps
which, as a historian of Hancock's division wrote, now had "room
enough and to spare," a full two thousand of Hancock's five thousand
men having been shot.[15]

As before, Burnside's first problem was to get across the river.
This time he would leave the Fredericksburg crossing strictly alone.
He would make an elaborate feint at crossing by the fords upstream,
and then he would throw the bulk of his army across at Muddy

Creek, some seven miles below Fredericksburg. Artillery positions to protect the crossings were selected, and access roads were corduroyed. In addition, Burnside decided to try to make some sort of effective use of his cavalry.

Army of the Potomac cavalry had been very poorly handled thus far in the war. It operated under many handicaps, the initial one being that it was almost uniformly recruited from among ardent young men who thought that it would be fine to be dashing troopers but who had never in their lives been on horseback before enlisting. As a result, a Yankee cavalry regiment needed a lot of training. Before it could even begin to amount to anything as cavalry, everybody from the company officers on down had first to learn how to get on a horse and how to stay on once the brute began to move. Since practically all of the Confederate cavalrymen were superb horsemen to begin with, their squadrons started with an enormous advantage. Worse yet, the Yankee high command in the first part of the war does not appear to have understood exactly what cavalry was for. All too often the cavalry commands were split up and attached to separate infantry units, and there was a common tendency to employ them largely for routine picket and courier duty. Hardly anyone ever tried to use them the way Stuart used his mounted brigades. One result of this was that cavalry's standing in the army was not high. A cavalry officer recalled ruefully that "it was a byword in our army that a reward would be paid for a *dead* cavalryman."[16] A disgruntled foot soldier remembered:

"Our cavalry had lost caste altogether with the infantry. Their reported skirmishes with the enemy, and 'driving in the Rebel pickets,' were received with incredulous smiles and jeers until they became mum as oysters. When hailed for information . . . they would gaze at the infantry in stupid wonder at such questions, then would laugh among themselves at some remark of one of theirs about 'doughboys'; the laugh would then change to sullen anger as some shrill-voiced infantry veteran would inquire, loud enough to be heard a mile away, 'Did you see any dead cavalrymen out there?' This pertinent question had the effect of making every rider drive spurs into his horse and briskly move forward, while the sounds of laughter and jeers long and loud of their tormentors the 'doughboys' followed them."[17]

Cavalry's status was not going to improve until somebody made effective use of the mounted arm, and this Burnside set out to do. He detailed fifteen hundred mounted troops to ride upstream in connection with the army's projected move. Five hundred of these, to deceive the Rebels, were to make a feint toward Warrenton and Culpeper, as if the army planned a sally in that direction, and then were to return to Falmouth as ostentatiously as possible. The remainder—picked men, chosen from eight of the army's best cavalry regiments—were to cross the Rappahannock at Kelly's Ford, speed over to the Rapidan and cross it at Raccoon Ford, and then strike boldly south, breaking both the Virginia Central and the Fredericksburg railroads, swinging clear west of Richmond, and then plunging south all the way to the coastal point of Suffolk, where the Federals had a small garrison under General John Peck. At Suffolk transports would be waiting to bring the troopers back to Aquia Creek.

Whether even a picked body of Federal cavalry could at that time have performed a risky maneuver like that under the noses of Stuart's sharp-eyed, hard-riding patrols is probably open to serious question. The mere fact that the venture was to be tried, however, indicated that Burnside was prepared to use the mounted arm with boldness and imagination, and it raised cavalry morale immensely. Major Henry Lee Higginson of the 1st Massachusetts Cavalry called the project "a risky expedition but a buster," and felt that it was "a brilliant plan," and when the squadrons trotted upstream it looked as if a new day was about to dawn.[18]

But these moments of bright hope never seemed to last very long in this army. The cavalry made a brisk thirty-mile march and went into bivouac just inshore from Kelly's Ford, full of enthusiasm, and never got any farther. For just as they were making their camp Burnside got a cryptic telegram from Abraham Lincoln saying, "I have good reason for saying you must not make a general movement without letting me know of it," and the cavalry had to be told to stop and await further orders. Major Higginson wrote angrily that "we could and would have done anything," adding that "such checks destroy the enthusiasm of any army."

Lincoln's telegram was a stunner. As far as Burnside was aware, no one in the army aside from a couple of his most trusted staff officers knew that a general movement was in the cards. He concluded hopefully that something special, to which the movements of his own army had to conform, must be going on in some other mili-

tary theater, so he went up to Washington to see the President and find
out what was up.

What was up was the kind of intrigue which had become standard
operating procedure for the officer corps of the Army of the Potomac.

Just before New Year's Day two brigadiers in Baldy Smith's VI
Corps had taken leaves of absence. These officers were John Newton,
commanding Smith's 3rd Division and John Cochrane, who had the
1st Brigade of that division. Having taken Smith and the Grand Division commander, Franklin, into their confidence, these generals
quickly left for Washington to indulge the perennial recourse of the
unhappy army officer; viz., to See Their Congressmen. Specifically,
they intended to see Senator Henry Wilson of Massachusetts, chairman
of the Senate Military Committee, and Congressman Moses F. Odell
of New York, a member of the powerful Joint Committee on the Conduct of the War. As so often happened in the Army of the Potomac,
however, their military planning was deficient because of a failure of
intelligence; that is, they had neglected to note that Congress was in
recess over the holidays, which meant that both of these statesmen
were out of the city. Cochrane, however, had been an important
Republican congressman himself back in 1861, and he had connections, so presently the two generals were talking with Secretary of
State Seward, and before the day was over Seward took them to the
White House and got them in to Lincoln's study.

Newton was senior officer and he spoke up first, doing a good
deal of clumsy beating around the bush and almost defeating his own
purpose. He tried to tell Lincoln that the army was in a bad way
and would come to pieces if Burnside tried to maneuver it again,
but he said it poorly. Later Newton explained that "I could not say
directly to the President that the whole trouble was that the privates
had no confidence in General Burnside," although it is hard to see
why he could not. That was what he and Cochrane had come to
Washington for, and somewhere along the line a little frankness might
have helped. As it was, he gave Lincoln the idea that here were two
self-promoting officers who simply wanted to get their commander's
job, and Lincoln spoke up with a good deal of heat—no doubt, in
one way and another, having had about all of that sort of thing he
cared to take in his twenty-one months as President. Cochrane, who
was a little more outspoken, assured Lincoln that they were moved
solely by patriotism and were just trying to give the President informa-

tion which he needed to have. This got Newton back on the rails, and he went on to say that in his opinion the condition of the army was such that if it were again led into defeat along the Rappahannock it would be utterly destroyed. The two generals wagged their heads to corroborate themselves, suggested that the President might want to look into things for himself, and at last took their leave.

And this was what lay back of Lincoln's telegram, as Burnside learned when he reached the White House. Halleck and Stanton sat in with him, while Lincoln gave the gist of the complaint, withholding the names of the two talebearers. Burnside angrily demanded that the two men be cashiered, and for once Halleck supported him, but after all, that was a side issue. The big question was the intricate relationships existing among Burnside, his generals, the enlisted men in his army, the War Department, and the President, and nobody quite seemed to know what the next step ought to be.[19]

A bit later Burnside had a private talk with Lincoln in which he had some remarks of his own to make about lack of confidence. Secretary Stanton, he said bluntly, "has not the confidence of the officers and soldiers" and probably lacked the confidence of the country also, and the same went for Halleck. There was likewise a gulf between Burnside and his own generals; Burnside was convinced that the army ought to drive forward for another river crossing, "but I am not sustained in this by a single Grand Division commander in my command." It was his belief, he added, that he himself ought to resign, not merely from the command of the army, but from his commission as a general, becoming a civilian once more. Meanwhile, since it was vital for the President to have about him officials whom the country and the army believed in and would support, the President might want to give some thought to the idea of replacing Stanton and Halleck too.[20]

After Burnside left the White House the President tried desperately to get a little help out of Halleck. Brushing aside the question of resignations, Lincoln put it up to Halleck bluntly: Burnside wanted to renew the offensive, but his top commanders disagreed, and wasn't this a spot where the general-in-chief ought to go into action? Lincoln wanted Halleck to go down to Fredericksburg, look the ground over, talk with the various generals, and then either tell Burnside to go ahead or have him call the whole thing off. With that tartness that he could use when he had to, Lincoln told Halleck: "If in such a difficulty as this you do not help, you fail me precisely in the point for which I sought your assistance."

This hurt Halleck's feelings. He wrote to Stanton, offering his resignation, and the sounds of his grief reached the White House. In the files Lincoln's letter to him acquired the notation in Lincoln's handwriting, "Withdrawn, because considered harsh by General Halleck." More than this Halleck did not do, until a few days later he got a letter from Burnside stating that officer's belief that he was entitled at least to some general directions as to the advisability of crossing the Rappahannock. This finally roused Halleck a little, and on January 7 he wrote to Burnside saying in effect that he had always been in favor of a forward movement, that the object was to defeat Lee's army rather than to capture Richmond, and that since Lee's army lay beyond the river it would be necessary for Burnside to cross the river if he proposed to fight. The big idea, Halleck went on solemnly, was "to injure him all you can with the least injury to yourself." But Halleck made it clear that it was entirely up to Burnside to decide when, where, and how to get across the river.

Beyond this Halleck would not go. With the whole machinery of government thrown into action, he had at last been put on record as believing that the commander of the army ought to do something. If between the army commander and the generals who would have to make his strategy effective there was such paralyzing doubt and distrust that any campaign was foredoomed to failure, Halleck was going to keep his hands out of the whole mess. Lincoln had brought him to Washington to handle just such tangles as this, but when Halleck had told the army commander that in any fight it was advisable to inflict more injury than he received, he had reached his limit. Lincoln dropped Burnside a line saying that he had seen Halleck's letter and that he endorsed the idea of a forward movement, although Burnside must understand that the government was not trying to drive him. Meanwhile, Lincoln did not see how it would help any just now to accept Burnside's resignation. Burnside would have to take it from there and do the best he could with it.[21]

This Burnside would do. His soldiers and the country might have been better off if Burnside had been more of a quitter, but that was one defect which he lacked. He had a responsibility which he knew was too big for him, but as long as he had it he would go ahead with it. The man seems to have felt the lonely isolation of his position very keenly. General Baldy Smith dropped in on him one evening, and Burnside was very frank about it. Everybody he ever talked to, said Burnside, had some personal interest to serve. The commander of the army could never be sure that what was said to him was motivated by either loyalty or friendship. Therefore, Burnside continued, it was his custom every night, after everything had quieted down, to send for Robert and have a long talk with him.

Robert was an aged and devoted colored servant who had been with Burnside for many years and who had charge of the cooking at army headquarters. Every night in the big Virginia mansion which had been taken over for army headquarters, with the trim patrols from the crack cavalry squadron which acted as headquarters guard standing on the alert outside, and the dapper staff officers in sashes and epaulets ornamenting the anterooms within, Robert and the general sat down by the fire for a long talk. Only then, said Burnside, could he feel that he was talking with someone who really had his interests at heart. And Baldy Smith wondered irreverently if that was how the Fredericksburg battle plan had been drawn up.[22]

2. *The Fools That Bring Disaster*

The authorities had not said anything about going into winter quarters, because there was this plan of Burnside's for a winter campaign, and sooner or later something was likely to come of it. But the soldiers figured that nothing more was going to happen until spring, which was quite reasonable of them, and in the five weeks that followed the battle of Fredericksburg they went to work to provide themselves with all-weather houses in place of the pup tents that were government issue for times like these.

This army carried thousands of axes in its wagons, and the soldiers took them and swarmed over the hills and ravines that bordered the Rappahannock, felling trees and trimming them into logs, until the land for miles around was bleak and naked under the January sky.[1] It would appear that some of the men were handy with axes and that some of them were not. There is a reminiscence in one of the old books about a regiment of backwoodsmen from Wisconsin which watched one day while a detail of city-bred New Yorkers labored mightily to cut up a pile of logs into ties for Colonel Haupt's railroad. The Wisconsin men stood it as long as they could, and finally they sent over a delegation: Give us those axes before somebody kills himself, and we'll cut the ties![2]

Every regiment took its turn with the axes, and not long after the first of the year the great sprawling camp of the army began to look like a crude but permanent city. The log-and-canvas huts which covered hills and plains were ranged in orderly fashion along company and regimental streets, with broad main-traffic arteries going past division and corps headquarters. The city even had its own barren parks—open fields, the earth packed down like concrete, where brigade and battalion drills were held. A few genuine civilian houses survived here and there, serving as quarters for high-ranking officers and their staffs. Most of the houses were simply torn down for their lumber.

The huts in which the army lived were much of a pattern. The usual course was for four men to club together to make and occupy one hut. They would lay up pine logs to a height of three or four feet, in a rectangle twelve feet long by a little more than six feet wide, and there would be a ridgepole running from end to end of the enclosure six feet off the ground. Four shelter-tent halves (each of which measured approximately six feet by four) were then buttoned together, thrown over the ridgepole, and brought down to the logs at the sides and made secure. The logs were carefully chinked with mud, and the gable ends were filled with whatever was available—with woodwork if the men could shape it easily, with extra shelter tents if such could be stolen, sometimes with rubber blankets if the men happened to own them. A door was cut in one end and a fireplace was built beside it with a mud-and-stick chimney which usually was somewhat defective. (A favorite trick at night, one soldier remembered, was to lay a flat board across the top of the nearest smoking chimney and then run before the resulting smudge sent the occupants out looking for a fight.) At the far end of the hut there generally would be two double bunks running from wall to wall. The theory was that two men sleeping together and sharing their blankets could keep warmer than if each man had a bunk to himself.

Styles in bunks varied, however. A New York soldier wrote that in his outfit the men took planks and made oblong frames on the ground inside their hut, "like onion beds in a garden," filling the frames with dead leaves or pine boughs. If the planks were wide enough to make the bed-place fairly deep, and if enough leaves or boughs were gathered, he said, the bed was as snug as anyone could wish. A Massachusetts soldier remarked that on cold nights the rookie would put on all of his clothing, overcoat included, before he went to bed, but that the old-timer would undress and then use his discarded clothing as extra covers on top of his blankets. It was much warmer that way, the veteran said.[3]

But even though its camp was snug enough, this army was very dispirited as the new year began. It was not well, for one thing. There was much sickness and there were many deaths, and never a day passed without the sound of firing squads discharging their farewell volleys over new graves in the cheerless hills. The rookie regiments in particular lost men from disease, but there were deaths among the veteran regiments too, and it seemed that these losses somehow were much more depressing than the deaths that occurred in battle. One soldier wrote that death in a military camp was just as moving, and caused just as much grief to be felt and shown, as death in time of peace in one's own home town.[4] These young men were far from their families, and if they had the rude strength of youth, they also had youth's terrible capacity for loneliness, and when a man fell ill that loneliness took hold of him very hard. Then his comrades did their best to take a little of his loneliness away by visiting his sickbed, bringing him camp gossip and any dainties which they might have, writing letters for him and showing other little attentions. If he died, they inherited his loneliness (it would be quite unendurable to suppose that he took it with him) and the mourners who went about the streets of this military city were desperately unhappy.

Yet death and loneliness visit the camp of a victorious army of high morale also. Men fell ill and died that winter, and were sincerely mourned, among the high-spirited Confederates across the river, and yet no Southerner remembered the winter afterward as a time of unrelieved gloom. The trouble on the Yankee side of the river was that there did not appear to be any sensible reason for anything. There had been many deaths and it looked as if they had all been wasted. It was as certain as anything could be that there would be more deaths in future, and it seemed likely that they would be wasted too. The soldiers were left with nothing to believe in. A thoughtful chaplain recorded:

"The phrensy of soldiers rushing during an engagement to glory or death has, as our boys amusingly affirm, *been played out.* Our battle-worn veterans go into danger, when ordered, remain as a stern duty so long as directed, and leave as soon as honor and duty allow. Camp followers, and one third of our armies may now be classed in that category, keep out of the range of shell and minnie." When illustrated magazines came to camp, the padre continued, the soldiers would look at the pictures showing mounted officers with drawn swords nobly leading their heroic troops into action and would jeer loudly and repeat: "All played out!"[5]

The eminent Bostonian cavalryman, Major Higginson, wrote that "stupidity and wickedness" ruled the army, and concluded: "We are getting on to perdition. If the people at home do not take the mismanagement of this war and this government to heart, we shall have a disgraceful peace before summer." A less distinguished Bay Stater in the 33rd Massachusetts wrote that "our poppycorn generals kill men as Herod killed the innocents," and even stouthearted Major Rufus Dawes of the 6th Wisconsin wrote home that "this army seems to be overburdened with second-rate men in high positions, from General Burnside down. . . . This winter is, indeed, the Valley Forge of the war."[6] William Thompson Lusk, a former medical student who was gloomily serving in the 79th New York, gave way to despairing anger in a letter which indicates that President Lincoln himself was not out of the reach of a soldier's resentment just then:

"Alas my poor country! It has strong limbs to march and meet the foe, stout arms to strike heavy blows, brave hearts to dare—but the brains, the brains—have we no brains to use the arms and limbs and eager hearts with cunning? Perhaps Old Abe has some funny story to tell, appropriate to the occasion." A week later this same soldier wrote, in another letter: "Mother, do not wonder that my loyalty is growing weak. . . . I am sick and tired of disaster and the fools that bring disaster upon us."[7]

Thus the army, apparently. And yet there are few ventures which offer as many chances for error as this business of trying to determine exactly how an army feels and what it proposes to do about it. Private soldiers have hidden emotional reserves which neither they nor anyone else can bring out for inspection and analysis, and the very men who declare that loyalty is for fools and courage a delusion may be precisely the ones who, when ordered, will lift a cheer and tramp across a fire-blasted meadow to attack a stone wall which they know full well is death to approach. They can sometimes take a good deal more than one thinks, and when they finally approach the point at which they will flatly refuse to take any more they are not likely to do very much talking about it. The thing to watch then is what they do and what they fail to do, and not what they say.

In this, oddly enough, the private soldier most closely resembles the private civilian, which indeed he is in another incarnation. Those who fancy that he would not go anywhere if they themselves were not there, heaven-sent, to lead and inspire him, can do a great deal of fruitless worrying about him, and early in this winter of 1863 this worrying was reaching its high point for the whole war.

Among those who worried was the Union quartermaster general, Montgomery C. Meigs, a grave and estimable man who deserves just a little better of posterity than he seems likely ever to get. Meigs had a hard job to do and he did it extremely well, and yet he is remembered today principally because an impish Confederate cavalryman hung the barb of a practical joke upon him. Confederate cavalry raided deep behind the Yankee lines that winter and seized a telegraph office, from which there presently came a dispatch to General Meigs in his office at Washington protesting bitterly about the poor quality of the mules which the Confederacy was getting via its captures of Yankee wagon trains. The wire was signed with the mighty name of Jeb Stuart, which has kept it from being forgotten, and it tends to be the only thing one thinks about when Meigs's name comes up.

As 1862 ended and 1863 began, Meigs sat down to send a friendly unofficial letter to General Burnside, and the general tenor of it was that if the army did not soon win a victory the country would be too discouraged to go on with the war any longer. The army was very expensive (said Meigs, who had to purchase much of its matériel and equipment) and it was consuming the country's resources:

"I begin to apprehend a catastrophe. . . . Exhaustion steals over the country. Confidence and hope are dying. . . . I begin to doubt the possibility of maintaining the contest beyond this winter, unless the popular heart is encouraged by victory on the Rappahannock."

In broad and somewhat hasty strokes Meigs then sketched a plan of campaign, which seemed chiefly to call on Burnside to get his army in between the Confederate Army and Richmond—sound advice, unquestionably, if there were just a way to carry it out. Meigs mentioned rapid marches of the kind made by Napoleon at Jena and Robert E. Lee at Second Bull Run, and then ascended to high rhetoric with a demand for speedy action: "Rest at Falmouth is death to our nation —is defeat, border warfare, hollow truce, barbarism, ruin for ages, chaos!"[8]

Which might possibly be so. Yet the whole case is a bit curious, and the anxiety of General Meigs comes down from the long ago as the deathless symbol of the reluctance of important folk to trust the courage and endurance of their less distinguished fellow citizens. This army had fought for different reasons at different times—to capture Richmond, to repel invasion, to save itself from destruction, and so on. Now, apparently, it must fight to encourage the civilians; or, more accurately, to encourage government officials who believed that the civilian needed to be encouraged. Never before had the army been asked to fight for a reason so inadequate.

Nor was the moment propitious. The weather had been clear and mild ever since the battle of Fredericksburg, which meant that the roads were dry and consequently passable. But the calendar said that midwinter was arriving, and sooner or later midwinter would bring a good deal of rain and snow. To begin a campaign now would be to gamble that more than 100,000 men, plus many thousands of very heavy wheeled vehicles, would be able to move swiftly over a network of totally unpaved roads which would become literally impassable once normal winter weather set in. The dismayed populace which was looking anxiously for victory along the Rappahannock might very easily, instead, see its principal army stuck hopelessly in the mud. The soldiers who had built winter quarters without waiting to be told had things sized up: warfare was just impossible at this time of year, and no sensible man would try it.

Sensible men, however, really had very little to do with it. The war itself did not make very much sense, which may have affected the way it was directed. It was being fought because emotion had been evoked to deal with a crisis that called for intelligence. There had been the great argument between men and sections, with many old values endangered, and on each side there had arisen men with blazing eyes and hot hearts to arouse their fellows to imminent peril. Fear had been called forth (because it is thought that men are most surely to be aroused by fear), and then came the anger that goes with fear, and finally the great unreason that goes with both had come out to take control of things—a situation deeply lamented by all who had created it.

So it might be quite true that a sensible man would not try to begin a campaign in roadless Virginia in mid-January, and yet a mid-January campaign could be ordered for all of that. The young men who were on the march had to walk in the glare cast by all of those frightened yesterdays, which could light both the wise and the foolish in but one direction. Just now the army was being asked to outmarch and outfight Robert E. Lee for the sake of the emotional uplift which such a victory would provide for the people back home: people who themselves neither marched nor fought but simply paid the bills and endured and were therefore believed to be in dire need of emotional uplift, and who, since emotional ties could not easily be dissolved, would be obliged to mourn such men as were destroyed by the marching and the fighting. None of this made any sense. The winter campaign was a complete triumph of unreason, and it would be useless to judge it by the standards of sensible men.

After his fashion Burnside had learned something by experience. He was not going to try to cross the river at Fredericksburg, and instead of going headlong over those deadly entrenchments on the low hills he would attempt to go bloodlessly around them. The plans that he now laid called for a swift march upriver with pontoon bridges put across the Rappahannock at United States Ford. The army would cross there, Lee would be outflanked, and the Fredericksburg line would be evacuated; and while General Meigs's rosy dream of actual interposition between Lee and Richmond might fail, it should at least be possible to force a battle in the open country, where superior Federal muscle could make itself felt. It would be tried, in any case, and the orders went out.

They were no sooner out than they had to be changed slightly. Lee was just as much aware as was Burnside that the crossing at United States Ford led straight to his rear, and it developed presently that he had a force dug in there to contest the crossing. So Burnside made Banks Ford, near Falmouth, the objective, and directed that pontoons and other equipment for five bridges be on the bank there by dawn of Wednesday, January 21. General Hunt was to line the hills with guns to deal with any Confederates who tried again to obstruct Yankee bridgebuilders. Hooker and Franklin were to set their grand divisions in motion on Tuesday morning, January 20. Sumner was to wait at Falmouth and put his men over the river after these two had crossed. All in all, here was a new campaign, and maybe it would have an outside chance to work if the weather would just hold.

The weather had been very good so far. January was more than half gone and the ground was dry and firm and the air was balmy—the men had played baseball in the open drill fields, and there had been a big match between a team from the 19th Massachusetts and one from the 7th Michigan for a sixty-dollar side bet, with Howard's entire division looking on. (It was won by the 19th Massachusetts; irritatingly enough, the scribe who recorded the event forgot to say what the score was.)[9] Burnside issued a general order announcing that "the auspicious moment seems to have arrived to strike a great and mortal blow to the rebellion," and the rookie 33rd Massachusetts was drawn up and harangued by its colonel, who announced that no Massachusetts regiment had yet lost a flag and added that they would be in action with the enemy "tomorrow morning at 6 o'clock." The regiment cheered and the band struck up "Yankee Doodle" and the army got under way.[10]

It took bugles and drums and flags—these last held aloft by men who bought the privilege of carrying them by taking extra risks in all battles—to get an army started in those days. On this twentieth of January the Army of the Potomac moved out of its unhappy camps near Falmouth under the thin January sunlight with hope and doubt riding invisible, of equal status, at the head of the column. After breakfast, by way of starting things off, the buglers in each brigade sounded a call known as "the general," which alerted everyone. (All bugle calls had names: breakfast call was "peas on a trencher," dinner was "roast beef," and the call which summoned men to advance against the enemy was known for some reason as "Tommy Totten.") The men struck their tents and packed their knapsacks and loaded the regimental wagons, and then they fell into their places by squads. Half an hour later the bugles blew "assembly" and the squads formed into companies—tall men at the right, short men at the left, everybody jostling elbows and passing wisecracks as the lines stiffened across the field, company officers out in front barking little orders and being important. Then, with all the companies formed, the colonels and the brigadiers came out and the bugles sounded "colors," the national and regimental flags were unfurled, and the companies moved in to right and left of them to form regimental front, each regimental adjutant carefully noting which company was last to come into line and assigning that company to the rear of the regimental column during the march.[11]

One after another the regiments swung and wheeled into column and went down through the emptying camps—bands playing, drums rolling and crashing, feet hitting the ground all together, nobody lapsing into the informal route step until camp had been left behind. Maybe the road ahead was going to be smooth and dry and easy to walk on, with a pleasant campground at the end of it in the cool of a clear twilight, and maybe it was going to lead through mud to some soggy cold swamp, and indeed, for all anyone knew, it would perhaps for some of the men be the last of all the roads on earth, curling over a far-off horizon from which nobody could take a backward glance. There were always those possibilities every time the army broke camp and took to the road; and this day the army set out glad for the winter sunlight and doubtless hoping for the little favors which a soldier is permitted to expect—dry ground, pleasant sun, clear skies at night.

If the army hoped for these things it did not get them. The sky clouded over during the afternoon, even though the air remained warm for a while, and by evening it was raining; a slow drizzle at first that soon became a steady downpour, with a howling wind whipping the rain down the country roads, setting in like a winter storm that has no intention of stopping. Up in Washington, fifty miles to the north, Secretary of the Navy Welles looked out of his snug office into a "furious storm" and worried over the safety of two of Navy's most prized ships, monitors *Weehawken* and *Nahant,* cruising coastwise down the Atlantic in the trough of this nor'easter. Their skippers, he hoped, would have the caution to take shelter behind Delaware breakwater. (*Nahant* did put in, Welles found out later; *Weehawken* rode out the storm, being more seaworthy than the secretary dared hope.)[12] And the army, launched on a campaign which involved using unpaved roads to get at an unwhipped enemy who lay beyond an unbridged river, took what shelter it could in the tangled second growth back from the river crossings and wondered what was in the cards for tomorrow.

What was going to happen tomorrow was more of the same, only a great deal worse, and there was a very uncomfortable night to endure first. The men pitched their pup tents for covering from the icy rain, and they tried to build fires under the dripping branches. The air seemed too heavy to carry the smoke away and the wood was too wet to burn decently anyway, and the smoldering useless camp-fires made a monstrous smudge miles across and indescribably thick, and the men blinked smarting eyes and lay flat on the soaked ground to get a little air. All wagon trains were lost somewhere in the water-logged rear, and if a man had food in his haversack he ate.[13] He did not eat a hot meal, in most cases, because it was very hard to kindle the wet wood into enough of a blaze to boil coffee or frizzle salt pork.

Morning came and the rain grew worse. The New York *Times* correspondent, surveying the situation with the dispassionate reserve proper to his station, wrote to his paper that "the nature of the upper geologic deposits of this region affords unequaled elements for bad roads." Virginia soil, he explained, was a mixture of clay and sand which, when wet, became very soft, practically bottomless, and exceedingly sticky.[14]

This was putting it mildly. The rainy dawn lightened reluctantly to a dripping daylight, and the troops floundered out into the roads and tried to resume the march. Someone got the orders mixed, and two army corps presently met at a muddy crossroad, committed by unalterable military decree to march squarely across each other. They moved sluggishly but inexorably, the men plodding on with bowed heads, big gobs of mud clinging to each heavy foot. In some fantastic manner the two blind columns did manage to get partly across each other, and everybody was cursing his neighbor, the Virginia mud, the cold rain, and the whole idea of having a war at all. In the end the two corps came to a helpless standstill, having got into a tangle which half a day of dry weather on an unimpeded drill ground would not have straightened out.[15]

But that was a minor problem, the way things were going. The ponderous pontoon trains which were supposed to lead the way to the river had got off to a very late start. Once again headquarters had forgotten to tell the engineers that their boats were going to be needed. When word finally got through the roads were bad, and the tardy trains moved more and more slowly and at last ceased to move at all, axles and wagon beds flat against the tenacious mud. Mixed in with them, and coming down parallel roads and plantation lanes, were the guns and caissons which were also wanted at the riverbank. There were also many quartermaster wagons and ambulances and battery wagons and all of the other wheeled vehicles proper to a moving army, and by ten in the morning every last one of them was utterly mired, animals belly-deep in mud.[16]

The high command made convulsive efforts to hitch along. Infantry was ordered out into the fields on either side of the road so that it might march past these stalled trains—*somebody* ought to be moving somewhere—and the columns quickly churned the fields into sloughs in which a man went to his knees at every step. A soldier in the 37th Massachusetts told what came next:

"Finally, after we had advanced only two or three miles, we filed into a woods and details were made of men to help pull the wheeled conveyances of the army out of the mire. At this we made very little progress. They seemed to be sinking deeper and deeper, and the rain showed little inclination to cease. Sixteen horses could not move one pontoon with men to help."[17]

The man from the *Times* noted that double and triple teams of horses and mules were harnessed to each pontoon, and wrote: "It was in vain. Long powerful ropes were then attached to the teams, and 150 men were put to the task on each boat. The effort was but little more successful. They would flounder through the mire for a few feet—the gang of Lilliputians with their huge-ribbed Gulliver—and then give up breathlessly."[18]

A New York soldier noted that guns normally pulled by six-horse teams would remain motionless with twelve horses in harness. In some cases the teams were unhitched and long ropes were fastened to the gun carriages, and a whole regiment would be put to work to yank one gun along. When a horse or a mule collapsed in the mud, this soldier added, it was simply cut out of its harness and trodden underfoot and out of sight in the bottomless mud.[19] Another veteran recorded:

"The army was accustomed to mud in its varied forms, knee-deep, hub-deep; but to have it so despairingly deep as to check the discordant, unmusical braying of the mules, as if they feared their mouths would fill, to have it so deep that their ears, wafted above the waste of mud, were the only symbol of animal life, were depths to which the army had now descended for the first time."[20]

The day wore on and the rain came down harder and colder than ever. A cannon might be inched along for a few yards with triple teams or three hundred men on the draglines; when there was a breather and it came to a halt, it would sink out of sight unless men quickly thrust logs and fence rails under it. Some guns sank so deeply that only their muzzles were visible, and no conceivable amount of mere pulling would get them out—they would have to be dug out with shovels. All around this helpless army there was a swarm of stragglers, more of them than the army had ever had before, men who had got lost or displaced in the insane traffic jams, men who had simply given up and were wandering aimlessly along, completely bewildered. A private in the 63rd Pennsylvania wrote that "the whole country was an ocean of mud, the roads were rivers of deep mire, and the heavy rain had made the ground a vast mortar bed."[21]

The situation grew so bad that the men finally began to laugh—at themselves, at the army, at the incredible folly which had brought them out into this mess. One soldier remembered: "Over all the sounds might be heard the dauntless laughter of brave men who summon humor as a reinforcement to their aid and as a brace to their energies," which doubtless was one way to put it. The impression gathered from most of the accounts is that it was the thoroughly daunted laughter of men who had simply got punch-drunk. Men working with the pontoons offered to get in the boats and row to their destination. One sweating soldier remarked that the army was a funeral procession stuck in the mud, and a buddy replied that if they were indeed a funeral procession they would never get out in time for the resurrection. Luckless Burnside came spattering along once, and the teamster of a mired wagon, recalling the general's pronunciamento which had begun this march, called out with blithe impudence: "General, the auspicious moment has arrived."[22]

Most of this was taking place close to the river, and the Rebels on the far side saw what was going on and got into the spirit of things, enjoying themselves hugely at the sight of so many Yankees in such a mess. They shouted all sorts of helpful advice across the stream, offered to come over and help, asked if the Yankees wanted to borrow any mules, and put up hastily lettered signs pointing out the proper road to Richmond and announcing that the Yankee army was stuck in the mud.

Night came and brought no improvement, except that the pretense of making a movement could be abandoned for a while. Many of the soldiers found the ground too soggy to permit any attempt at sleep and huddled all night about inadequate campfires. The supply wagons

were heaven knew where, and the rain had soaked the men's haversacks, ruining hardtack and sugar and leaving cold salt pork as the
only food. Once again a vast smudge drifted across the country. An
engineer officer on duty at Banks Ford wrote that the army's campfires
presented "the appearance of a large sea of fire" and added that the
smoke covered the entire countryside and even blanketed the Rebs on
their side of the Rappahannock.

The smoke was the only Yankee creation that did cross the river.
This engineer officer wrote to Burnside, earnestly urging that the enterprise be abandoned. The Confederates were waiting for them, he
said; they had a plank road on their side of the river by which they
could easily wheel up all the guns they needed. The Army of the
Potomac, which had planned to build five bridges, would do very
well to get up enough pontoons for two, "but if we could build a
dozen I think it would be better to abandon the enterprise."[23]

Burnside was a hard man to convince, and next morning the old
orders stood: get down to the river, make bridges, go across, and lick
the Rebels. The *Times* man wrote that the dawn came "struggling
through an opaque envelope of mist," and recorded that the rain
showed no signs of stopping. Looking out at the sodden countryside,
he continued: "One might fancy that some new geologic cataclysm
had overtaken the world, and that he saw around him the elemental
wrecks left by another Deluge. An indescribable chaos of pontoons,
wagons, and artillery encumbered the road down to the river—supply
wagons upset by the roadside—artillery 'stalled' in the mud—ammunition trains mired by the way." In a brief morning's ride, he said, he
had counted 150 dead horses and mules. The chaplain of the 24th
Michigan wrote: "The scenes on the march defy description. Here a
wagon mired and abandoned; there a team of six mules stalled, with
the driver hallooing and cursing; dead mules and horses on either
hand; ten, twelve, and even twenty-six horses vainly trying to drag
a twelve-pounder through the mire."[24]

Somehow, that morning, the high command did get a few wagons
forward, and some commands received a whisky ration. In Barnes's
brigade of the V Corps the officers who had charge of the issue seem
to have been overgenerous, and since the whisky went down into
empty stomachs—for the men had had no breakfasts—there was presently a great deal of trouble, with the whole brigade roaring drunk.
There were in this brigade two regiments which did not get along

too well, the 118th Pennsylvania, known as the Corn Exchange Regiment, and the 22nd Massachusetts. Just after the battle of the Antietam the brigade had been thrust across the Potomac in an ineffectual stab at Lee's retreating army and it had been rather badly mauled. Most of the mauling had been suffered by the Pennsylvanians (it was their first fight and they carried defective muskets), and somehow they had got the notion that the Massachusetts regiment had failed to support them as it should. This morning, in the dismal rain by the river, with all the woes of the world coming down to encompass them round about, the Pennsylvanians recalled this ancient grudge and decided to make complaint about it. In no time the two regiments were tangling, and when some of the 2nd Maine came over and tried to make peace, the argument became three-sided. Before long there was a tremendous free-for-all going on, the men dropping their rifles and going at one another with their fists, Maine and Massachusetts and Pennsylvania tangling indiscriminately, inspired by whisky and an all-inclusive, slow-burning anger which made hitting someone an absolute necessity. The thing nearly took an ugly turn when a Pennsylvania major drew a revolver and made ready to use it, but somebody knocked him down before he could shoot, and in the end the fighters drifted apart with no great damage done.[25]

By noon even Burnside could see that the army was helpless, and all thought of getting across the river was abandoned. One private wrote afterward that "it was no longer a question of how to go forward, but how to get back," and that sized it up. Slowly, and with infinite difficulty, the army managed to reverse its direction and began to drag itself wearily back to the camps around Falmouth.

The home-coming was cheerless enough. Before the march began the men had been ordered to dispose of all surplus baggage and camp equipment, which meant that they had to destroy all of the improvised chairs, tables, desks, and other bits of furniture which they had made for their comfort, since there was no way to ship these things to the rear. They returned, therefore, to camps which had been systematically made bleaker and more barren than they had been before. (Here and there the regimental officers had evaded these orders. The colonel of the 9th Massachusetts had told his men to destroy nothing, as they would probably be back soon enough—he apparently had little faith that any march of Burnside's was going to lead to anything—and when they set out on the march he left the regimental quartermaster and a detail to look out for things. As a result, the 9th still had all of its little extras.) There were occasional mix-ups and quarrels. The 6th Wisconsin found the 55th Ohio in what it considered its own camp and prepared to fight. The Ohio colonel made peace by explaining that his men had been ordered there by corps command, by inviting the Wisconsin men to share the supper which his Ohioans had just cooked, and by pointing out that the ground was roomy enough for both regiments anyhow.[26]

Very few of the regiments came back as compact, well-organized bodies. They came trailing and straggling in, many of the men at the point of complete exhaustion, and it took days to get everyone reassembled. A good many soldiers, in fact, never did get back. Some of them just quietly wandered away, disgustedly leaving an army which could do no better than wade up to its thighs in winter mud, and these elusive waifs were hard to catch. The 24th Michigan found it had thirty absentees when it returned, and its lieutenant colonel was Mark Flanigan, who used to be sheriff of Wayne County, owned a sword presented by the county's deputy sheriffs, and had had much experience at catching defaulters and fugitives. Sheriff Flanigan took a military posse and backtracked up the river looking for his wandering soldiers. He returned after some days with a baker's dozen of them, plus a few civilians whom he had arrested for helping deserters to escape. He reported that the trail of the other soldiers was too dim to follow.[27]

Some of the men indeed had gone beyond the reach of any sheriff. Spending forty-eight hours in the cold rain and mud without warm food or dry clothing was just as hard on the ordinary human constitution in 1863 as it would be now, and there was a dreadful toll of sickness and deaths as a result of this march. In some cases men who became too exhausted to walk back to camp simply lay down in the swampy fields and died, their bodies remaining by the roadside for days afterward. Many more managed to get back to camp but went off to the hospital tents with pneumonia or other maladies. Altogether, it is probable that this mud march killed and disabled as many soldiers as were lost in some of the army's regular battles. The men settled back into camp with gloom thick and heavy. A diarist in the 3rd Michigan wrote: "I never knew so much discontent in the army before. A great many say that they 'don't care whether school keeps or not,' for they think there is a destructive fate hovering over our army."[28]

There exists an informal history of one of the New York regiments in this army, a book in which the military career of every member of the regiment is briefly summarized. The regiment had an eventful career and suffered numerous losses, and after many of the names in its roster are entries like "Killed in the Wilderness," "Died in Andersonville Prison," and so on. But the commonest one of the lot is the simple "Died at Falmouth."[29] The Wisconsin officer who said that this winter was the army's Valley Forge was hardly exaggerating.

Yet there was a hard indestructible core in the army somewhere, a grimly humorous acceptance of the worst that could happen. A staff officer in the II Corps, which did not make the mud march, wrote that during the week following this disaster the roads around Falmouth were covered with disorderly wandering parties of returning soldiers, bedraggled, unhappy-looking, weapons and uniforms encased in mud, faces lean and glum and unshaven, the men looking like the tattered ends of some Falstaff's army that had come completely unraveled. The staff officer encountered such a group one day: twenty men, or thereabouts, plodding through the mud. The sight offended him, and he barked out the starchy demand of the staff officer: "Who *are* these men?"

He got his answer from a non-com, who spoke up as promptly and as proudly as if he were announcing the arrival for inspection of the most polished and pipeclayed regiment in the army's dandiest corps:

"Stragglers of the 17th Maine, sir!"[30]

3. The Third That Remained

Someone had sent to army headquarters a boned turkey as a gift for the commanding general, and Robert, the faithful retainer, who alternately cooked for the general and soothed his tired spirit with a rare and complete selflessness, was serving it up for lunch. General Burnside seemed to have regained his poise. During the mud march, as he confessed to a friend, the strain had driven him almost frantic. Now the mud march was over, and that part of the army which maintained its organization had extricated itself from the villainous roads and was back in its camps. The general was more easy, and today he had guests at the luncheon table.

They may have been oddly chosen, all things considered. They came out of the past, when it had been possible for General Burnside to have friends in the army. It did not seem possible now. The weight of command made him suspect the motives of all around him. It would appear, too, that his strange, unmilitary humility did have its limits. It had been broad enough immediately after Fredericksburg to make him write to Halleck, "For the failure of the attack I am responsible"; broad enough to make him declare both before and after that battle that he knew he was not competent to command an army.[1] But a good deal of time had passed. The battle was fought on December 13 and it was now January 23, and Burnside was no longer able to accept the responsibility for all of the terrible things that had happened. He had had black nights after Fredericksburg, when he repeated over and over, "Oh, those men! Those men over there!" as if the frozen, blue-carpeted field in front of the stone wall remained constantly before his eyes.[2] One gathers that he had to prove to himself that it was not entirely his fault that all of those bodies had been flung there. Someone else must be at fault too.

He had with him as his luncheon guests General Franklin and General Smith, and the two found him somewhat moody. Understandably so: for although they did not know it, he was just then convincing himself that these two friends, among others, had helped to bring about defeat in battle. He did not seem able to tell them about it at this lunch where they ate delicate boned turkey, but blame was taking shape in his mind. He was talkative and morose by turns. Once, after a spell of silence, he burst out: "You will presently hear of something that will astonish you all!"[3]

More than that he would not say, and his visitors at length took their leave, well fed but somewhat puzzled. After they left, Burnside wrote a document which was to be the vehicle of the promised astonishment. It bore the heading, "General Order Number 8," and it contained the substance of his confused analysis of the disaster at Fredericksburg, together with an expression of his dim feeling that he who had not deserved high command had at least deserved better subordinates than he had been given. Brooding upon these things, he had distilled a bitter fury, the exquisite rage of pure impotence, and he gave full vent to it.

When fury and rage are turned loose they have to have a target, and Burnside's target was principally Joe Hooker.

General Order Number 8 had a great deal to say about Hooker, most of it quite true. It alleged that he habitually uttered "unjust and unnecessary criticisms of the actions of his superior officers," that he tried "to create distrust" in the minds of fellow officers, that he said and wrote things designed to create false impressions, and that he was much given to "speaking in disparaging terms of other officers." It climaxed these variously phrased allegations by asserting that, as a man unfit to hold an important commission, Hooker "is hereby dismissed the service of the United States."

Almost by afterthought, as if he had suddenly realized that it took authority higher than that of an army commander to cashier a general, Burnside added that this order was issued "subject to the approval of the President of the United States."

Having unburdened himself about Hooker, Burnside then went on, apparently, to take in everybody else whose habits or actions had bothered him.

A second paragraph announced that Brigadier General W. T. H. Brooks, a division commander in the VI Corps, had been complaining of the policy of the government and had been using language tending to demoralize his command. Brooks, like Hooker, was dismissed from the service—subject, again, to the approval of the President.

A third paragraph took care of General Newton and General Cochrane, who had made that hurried end-of-the-year trip to Washington with a tale to tell, and whose identities had at last become known to Burnside. "For going to the President of the United States with criticisms of the plans of their commanding officer," these two were to meet the fate of Hooker and Brooks.

A final paragraph wrapped up the odds and ends. It undertook to relieve certain officers from duty, "it being evident that they can be of no further service to this army." Among them were the recent luncheon guests, Franklin and Smith. Franklin, Burnside felt, had done less than he might have done in the attack at Hamilton's Crossing, and Smith—blameless enough so far as Fredericksburg went—lacked faith in the success of an overland move toward Richmond; they must go, along with Franklin's assistant adjutant general, a Lieutenant Colonel Taylor. Burnside was swinging blindly by now.

Into this proscription list he put one of his own favorites, Brigadier General Ferrero of the IX Corps; someone had told him that Ferrero had recently overstayed a leave of absence. He also got Cochrane into this list of those who were to suffer the lesser punishment of losing their commands but not their commissions—apparently forgetting that a few sentences earlier he had ordered him cashiered outright.[4]

With all of this committed to writing, Burnside took off for Washington to show it to the President and, if possible, to get his approval. There was no way to undo defeat. The Angel of the Resurrection could not be summoned down to the ghastly field below Marye's Heights to restore the fallen to life, but it might at least be possible to revive the modest self-esteem of the commanding general. If this army's great handicap had been a clogging of the channels of command by enmity and distrust toward the commander, here was a purge to set everything straight. If nothing else could be said for it, the paper would at least make interesting reading for all ranks. As Burnside had promised his guests at luncheon, it was a stunner.

It was not, in the end, anything more than that. Like most presidents, Lincoln was forever being given dramatic compositions by men in high positions with the assurance that his signature at the foot of the paper, his nod of approval to the man who had written it, would solve everything and enable him to sleep quietly of nights. Seward had offered to run the White House for him back in the early days when the war was hardly begun, presenting him with a cunning letter which survives as a historical curio. A year later General McClellan had written down his own solution for the nation's ills and had handed it to the President in order that the country might be saved. Now Burnside, and this; while the army sickened in a dirty camp by the cold river and by every sign an army can give indicated that it had at last made up its mind about things.

Lincoln presumably could read the signs. They had rarely been any worse.

General Hooker himself, focusing the sharpest of eyes upon the opportunities which defeat and disaster were opening for an energetic man at the top of the heap, was contemptuously telling a New York *Times* correspondent that President and Administration were "played out" and that there ought to be a dictator. General Howard, pious soldier and unyielding anti-slavery man, was noting that he had just been obliged to bring to trial two officers "for disloyal language directed against the President and the general commanding." He stopped their mouths, but he wrote that "discontent had taken deep root" and he himself felt "a want of confidence in the army itself."[5] And just when Burnside was writing his screed, German-born Carl Schurz, a devoted but slightly inexpert major general in the XI Corps, was saying in a letter to Lincoln:

"I am convinced that the spirit of the men is systematically demoralized and the confidence in their chief systematically broken by several of the commanding generals. I have heard generals, subordinate officers, and men say that they expect to be whipped anyhow, that 'all these fatigues and hardships are for nothing, and that they might as well go home.' Add to this that the immense army is closely packed together in the mud, that sickness is spreading at a frightful rate, that in consequence of all these causes of discouragement desertion increases every day—and you will not be surprised if you see the army melt away with distressing rapidity."[6]

But those, after all, were the comments of the generals—three generals as completely dissimilar, by the way, as could be found in all the army—and generals are often mistaken about what their men are thinking. The really ominous signs in those days were coming from the enlisted men themselves, and it was what the men were doing, not what they were saying, that was ominous.

They were not, as a matter of fact, saying anything at all, which in some ways was the worst sign of the lot.

There had been a big review of the II Corps not long since, and Burnside and Sumner had ridden down the lines together, gold-braided staff officers clanking at their heels. Ordinarily this would have brought cheers, regardless of the identity or personal popularity of the generals; the men liked to cheer at such times and were quite ready to accept any decent excuse to start. But this time a sullen, unnatural silence lay across the field. White-haired old Sumner was outraged. Some sort of cheer at a review was as much the commanding general's due as a salute, and this was shameful flouting of military etiquette. He told General Couch, commander of the corps, to make the men do their duty.

So, on order, corps and division and brigade commanders and their aides rode up and down the lines, swinging their hats and swords and earnestly calling for three cheers. Not a cheer did they get. The

silence lay unbroken upon the wintry field save for their own piping
exhortations and, here and there, a single derisive cry in response:
as embarrassing a moment, one would suppose, as a commanding
general could well experience.[7]

They had made up their minds about things, those soldiers, and
they were expressing themselves unmistakably. They were saying nothing where normally they would have been noisy. Also, in steadily
increasing numbers, they were simply laying down their weapons and
going home, quietly piling up the enlisted man's ultimate vote of no
confidence in the war and in the men who were running it.

A veteran in the Iron Brigade wrote that desertions from the Army
of the Potomac after the mud march were averaging two hundred a
day, stimulated to some extent, no doubt, by a flood of letters from
anti-war people in the North, who seemed to be engaged in an organized letter-writing campaign to encourage desertion. If a soldier
yielded to such pleas, things were usually made as easy for him as
possible. His best course was simply to write to his family or to his
friends, saying that he wanted to come home. They would send to
him by express a box containing civilian clothing. (Such boxes were
coming in that winter almost literally in carload lots.) The soldier
would put on the civilian clothing, slip quietly out of camp, and,
usually, that would be that.[8]

In Washington the provost marshal had his patrols watching every
road and every bridge, for the tide of deserters was flowing north
in full spate. Detachments of troops held all three of the bridges
over the Potomac—Chain Bridge, well upstream, Aqueduct Bridge
at Georgetown, and Long Bridge at the foot of Seventh Street. A
string of pickets guarded every road leading from the city to the open
country, and there was an especially heavy guard over the Anacostia
Bridge near the navy yard. This bridge led to roads for Baltimore and
Annapolis, gave access to other roads leading to the shore of Chesapeake Bay, and communicated also with the road south via Port Tobacco, which was the principal route for contraband trade with the
South. Cavalry patrolled all of the country roads near Washington,
and there was a navy patrol along the water front. Provost guards
were stationed at every dock and pier and rode the ferries to Alexandria. A chain of pickets surrounded Baltimore.[9]

Every train that left Washington bound north was examined by the
provost guard as it pulled out of the station. In addition, other guards

came aboard to search the cars afresh when the train reached Annapolis Junction, twenty-five miles out. Enlisted men legitimately traveling north on furlough were infuriated by all of this, especially since part of the function of the provost guards seemed to be to keep private soldiers out of the first-class carriages. "This is what makes a soldier hate himself and all others, for he thinks a dog is thought more of than he is," wrote a Michigan veteran savagely. Not until one passed Harrisburg, said this soldier, did he escape from the interfering vigilance of the guards.[10]

Yet all of this did very little good. There were many ways by which a soldier who wanted to desert could be helped on his way. The Confederates circulated handbills through the Federal camps, offering free transportation to practically any spot on earth to all who would come through the Rebel lines and give themselves up. Many men accepted these offers. A few—foreign-born mechanics and artisans, for the most part—tried to remain in the South and earn a living, their skills being in much demand. More often, the men who surrendered simply gave their paroles as prisoners of war and presently were shipped back through the lines to Annapolis, where the Federals maintained a camp for paroled men who were awaiting formal exchange.

In theory a soldier at this camp stayed there until he had been exchanged (on paper) for some paroled Confederate, whereupon he went back to duty with his regiment. In actual practice, however, paroled men tended to consider themselves more or less out of the war for keeps, and at times it was almost impossible even to keep them in camp, to say nothing of getting them back to their outfits. In mid-January 1863 the commander of the Annapolis camp estimated that fully three fourths of his men were arrant shirkers, and said that there were not five hundred men in his camp who either knew or cared what army corps they belonged to. He added: "If the men in my camp were a sample of our army we would have nothing but a mob of stragglers and cowards."[11]

Permitting oneself to be captured in order to get a parole, and thus a chance to slide out of the war sideways, had by this time become a widespread evil fully recognized by army authorities. Many men got to the parole camps without bothering to go through the formality of first being captured by the Rebels. There was a thriving trade in forged parole certificates. A man who got one would straggle off,

present himself at the parole camp, and either old-soldier it there or
take the first chance to set out for home. Or if he preferred he would
simply wander north at once, counting on his parole paper to serve
for a pass whenever the provost guard might halt him.[12]

Extensive as this practice was, however, most of the men who deserted used other means. There was an "underground railway" operating between Alexandria and Baltimore, its object being to get
soldiers past the guards and pickets around Washington. It appears
to have been operated by Confederate sympathizers, motivated either
by Southern patriotism or by a desire to earn an honest dollar. Its
agents would take a deserter at Alexandria, smuggle him across the
Potomac, and get him over to the Leonardtown road, where he
would be hidden until a little group of fugitives had been collected.
The men were then taken across country by way of Upper Marlboro
to Fair Haven on the Chesapeake shore, where a steamer would put
in to take them to Baltimore. On the boat the men would be given
civilian clothing, if they did not already possess it, and would be told
how to make their way north out of Baltimore.[13]

Alexandria, to be sure, was a good many miles upstream from
the army's camps. But Burnside's administration was never able to
keep the men in camp, not even though Burnside's provost marshal,
annoyed by "the alarming frequency of desertion from this army,"
had ordered corps and division commanders to redouble their vigilance, to patrol the immediate vicinity of their camps with infantry,
and to maintain cavalry on the roads farther out, arresting everybody
who lacked a pass. This was of slight effect. Deserters usually followed the roads that led via Aquia Creek through Dumfries and
Occoquan, riding in the wagons of sutlers, army traders, farmers,
or others, which were allowed to travel the muddy roads without
much examination. Sometimes the men passed themselves off as details sent out to repair the telegraph lines, which was fairly easy to
do since most patrols knew nothing whatever about the electric telegraph and could easily be made to believe that it took huge gangs
to keep the lines in order.[14]

But even this represented more trouble than was really necessary.
The principal thing was to get across the Potomac into Maryland,
for the contraband trade between North and South had such well-
established routes through places like Leonardtown and Port Tobacco and passed through an area so strongly Southern in its sym-

pathies that a deserter could usually count on getting north safely once he was over the river. Crossing was not too hard. Navy patrolled the river, but it was easy to hide rowboats along the shore and easy to slide across in them on dark nights. One naval officer frankly told the army people that the only way to stop the transriver traffic in deserters would be to break up all the rowboats between Aquia Creek and Washington, which clearly would be impractical.[15]

Now and then the army would load a regiment or so on a steamboat and, under navy convoy, cruise down to the "northern neck," the long peninsula between the Potomac and the Rappahannock southeast of Fredericksburg, in an attempt to break up the bases for the contraband trade. These attempts never amounted to very much, except, as one officer noted, that the pillage and freebooting indulged in by the troops probably confirmed the inhabitants in their disunionist leanings. The creeks and inlets which were the centers for this traffic were very shallow, and the steamers usually ran aground.

Both army and navy kept details on the Maryland side of the Potomac, and each service insisted that the other was muffing its opportunities. According to the navy, the army details there were rowdy, undisciplined, drunken, and insubordinate; army replied that the navy folk showed altogether too much friendship for local secessionists. Both services agreed that there was an immense traffic in contraband goods and spies back and forth between Virginia and Maryland. There was a regular mail and express route north from Richmond via Warsaw Courthouse and Leonardtown to Washington, with two scheduled deliveries a week and an established ferry service, and boss traders were growing rich by it. Cavalry went downstream and raided a ferry point on the Virginia shore, seizing coffee and sugar and tobacco and "nearly fifty barrels of villainous whisky" but causing the smugglers only momentary inconvenience. One Federal officer who had tried in vain to tighten the controls reported that "blockade running and dealing in contraband articles have become professions."[16]

So here was a veritable Yukon Trail running wide open not twenty-five miles away from the chief supply line of the nation's principal army, crossing deep rivers which were under steady navy patrol, and using highways which were fully controlled by Yankee cavalry and infantry. There are probably several explanations, including the fact that Americans of every generation seem to have a positive genius for smuggling, but the principal one appears to be that Burnside's army was just naturally the kind of army to which things like this were bound to happen. Operating deep in hostile territory, it was going to be run dizzy by enemy agents stealing its secrets and sending them south and stealing its soldiers and sending them north, and its high command simply was not going to know how to stop it.

By the end of January 1863, desertions from the Army of the Potomac totaled 85,123.[17]

A startling figure, which does not quite mean what it appears to mean.

It does not, for instance, mean that 85,000 men had willfully laid down their weapons and gone home. Heavy as desertions had been, they had not been that heavy. Most of the men who were on the army's rolls but not with the army had not so much run away as drifted away. They had been sloughed off by the army's own inefficiency. With many of them there probably had never been a conscious decision to desert, a moment when the soldier in his own mind ceased to be a soldier temporarily absent and became instead a civilian who was never going to go back unless somebody came and got him.

The hospital system, for instance, was practically guaranteed to leak men back into civil life, and to do it in such a way that the leaks could not easily be plugged. By a freak of chance this was so because the army had been making an honest and generally successful effort to give its men better medical care than any soldiers on earth had ever had before.

For uncounted generations—ever since military life was invented, as a matter of fact—all of the world's armies had apparently operated on the theory that the soldier was always going to be healthy. If he fell ill or got wounded he was a poor dog. Provided he did not die too quickly, he would eventually be put in a hospital and allowed to get well if he could, but getting well was pretty much his own responsibility and no concern of the army. From the military viewpoint, the ailing soldier was just a nuisance and the big idea was to get him out of the way.

But in this war it had to be different. Here the army was of the people and the people kept in close touch with their soldiers. If the soldiers had troubles the people quickly became concerned, and the people had devised a number of most effective ways to make their concern felt in high places. The war had not been going on very long before the War Department had to overhaul its hospital system from top to bottom so that the soldier could have better care.

In fact, before the War Department quite knew what was happening its hospital system was being overhauled for it, the instrument of overhaul being the United States Sanitary Commission. In its essentials, the Sanitary Commission was the women of America, brought together through thousands of spontaneously organized Ladies' Aid Societies and grimly determined that their menfolk in this war were going to be looked after properly. It also included doctors, bankers, merchants, and men vaguely but justly known as "civic leaders." It had almost unlimited financial backing, and it enjoyed enough sheer political influence to move mountains. By the middle of 1861 the commission had won quasi-governmental status, plus War Department permission to inquire into the sanitary condition of the troops, the provision of nurses and hospitals, and similar matters.

It appears that the War Department, which knows nothing about women, originally supposed that the commission would be quite happy with this permission to investigate and that the things investigated might go on as they had gone on before, but the War Department was quite mistaken. The commission was presently getting Congress to vote a thorough reorganization of the army's medical department, and in the peninsular campaign the commission was running hospital ships, providing nurses and medical supplies, getting sick and wounded men brought back to where their lives might be saved, and in general turning the army way of doing things upside down. By the end of 1862 the entire system of collecting, housing, and treating sick and wounded soldiers had been transformed.[18]

This, of course, was all to the good, and the soldiers had reason to bless every last member, officer, and paid employee of the Sanitary Commission. But in the process of providing medical care for soldiers in a manner to satisfy the women of America, the War Department also tried to make the state governors happy, and the result was a system by which a man who went to hospital could very easily slip out from under army control altogether.

What the department did for the governors was to establish general hospitals in the Northern states and to provide that sick or wounded men might be transferred to these from the front, either singly or in organized bodies, if it seemed likely that the change would help them to recover. This pleased the soldiers, who were glad enough to get back home, and it simply delighted the governors, who could gain much political advantage from getting them back. (For one thing, they could *vote,* and for whom would a soldier vote if not for an ardently patriotic war governor?) Before long most of the states had agents who visited army hospitals in the forward areas, looked up home-state patients, and pulled wires to get them sent to the home-state hospital. Thus there developed a steady flow of men moving from the areas of active operations to the Northern states. By the middle of the war it was estimated that between one and two hundred thousand men had been transferred to the various Northern hospitals.[19]

Which would have been all right, except that when a man was sent to a general hospital in his home state the odds were quite good that the army would never see him again.

The hospitals were practically independent. Each was run by a medical officer who was answerable to the surgeon general of the army, not to any line officer. The soldier who got into the hospital was completely out from under the control of his own outfit. Neither his company commander, his colonel, nor his army commander had any authority to order him back to duty. That could be done only by the medical officer who ran the hospital, who did not need to take anything from army brass. He had generally got his job through political patronage, and his patron would be the governor of the state, who, as a result, had effective control of the situation.

Thus all kinds of openings were offered to the soldier who was not eager to get back to the front. It was often possible to induce the hospital director to carry him on the rolls as sick long after he had recovered. If he had any useful little skills, if he could cut hair or mend cupboards or tend chickens or do any of the other little things that need to be done at behind-the-lines army posts, he was likely to be kept forever.

Medical directors were authorized to detail convalescents as nurses, orderlies, cooks, and so on, and an army officer familiar with such arrangements reported that in most cases the men so detailed "ceased to be soldiers in fact and spirit" and became "mere hangers-on of hospitals." Not long before his own dismissal McClellan was pleading for a strict investigation of each Northern army hospital "to ferret out the old soldiers hidden away therein." Such an inspection, he said, would produce more fruit in one week than the entire recruiting service would yield in three months. He added that not more than a tenth of the soldiers who went to the home-state hospitals ever rejoined the army, and cited the case of one regiment which had sent five hundred men to hospitals in the rear and had got back only fifteen or twenty of them.[20]

The general theory was that a man's own home was the best place for his convalescence. Normally, a soldier recovering at a Northern hospital had no trouble getting leave to go home, and if he could not get leave there was little or nothing to keep him from going home anyway. Once he got home, whether he was there legally or otherwise, no one in authority had any especial incentive to get him back. His own regiment could not touch him because he was absent from the hospital rather than from the regiment. The hospital was supposed to call him in and return him to his proper command as soon as he was strong enough, but it was more likely than not simply to forget about him. If the hospital authorities happened to be unduly conscientious about such things there were various dodges that could be tried. Away from his own regiment where people knew him, a man could pretend that he was a victim of some wasting disease brought on by overexposure. Naturally, a malingerer usually picked some malady whose symptoms were rather vague and nonspectacular; rheumatism was the favorite, and before the war was half over the army had been compelled to prohibit the granting of medical discharges for rheumatism under any circumstances whatever.

For one of the biggest loopholes of all was the fact that doctors in these Northern hospitals were authorized to issue medical discharges. In the forward areas a regimental surgeon naturally would try to make sure that such a release was given only to a man who genuinely deserved it, but a doctor at a Northern hospital was not likely to care very much, and the soldier who was unable to persuade the hospital authorities to give him a discharge was apt to be either tragically devoid of any kind of political pull or flagrantly and incurably healthy. Even if he tried to get a discharge, failed, and then went off home on his own hook, he still had a good chance to make everything legal. For when the War Department began trying to round up these hospital absentees, it ruled in its wisdom that any of them might get a lawful discharge if he could present a certificate of disability signed by any civilian "physician of good standing." The man who, safely perched in his own home town, was unable to come up with such a paper was a poor stick indeed.[21]

Yet most absentees seem not to have bothered to make the effort. It simply was not necessary.

When the war began there was a standard reward of thirty dollars payable to any peace officer or private citizen who caught and returned to custody a deserter from the army. For some incomprehensible reason, once the war began and desertion became a serious problem, this reward was cut to five dollars and expenses. A tangled web of red tape was then thrown over the business of collecting it. The applicant had to get a voucher from the local provost marshal stating that a genuine deserter, properly identified by name, company, and regiment, had in fact been turned in. The voucher also had to identify, by description or otherwise, the citizen who had brought the deserter in, and expenses incurred had to be specified in detail, with supporting documents to prove that they had actually been incurred and with other documents proving that it had really been necessary to incur them. Any government paymaster, naturally, could keep an applicant for five dollars and expenses at bay for a year with a setup like that. As an inevitable result, no city cop or county sheriff in his senses would bother to arrest deserters unless they became unmitigated disturbers of the peace.[22]

Before very long it was obvious to everybody that a man who deserted from the army ran very little risk of arrest or punishment. Everything about the situation encouraged the fainthearted and the chronic slackers to desert the first time they got the chance. If such a one, having returned to his home town, felt guilty or insecure, he could make things easier for himself by telling his fellow townspeople tall tales about the fearful treatment a man got in the army. A principal obstacle to enlistments, after the first year of the war, was the presence in every town and hamlet of these deserters "and the false stories they spread abroad of the cruelty and unnecessary hardships to which the men were subjected by their officers."[23]

Such stories of course were usually much exaggerated. Every generation knows the self-pitying ne'er-do-well who finds himself brutally mistreated when he is required to get up promptly in the morning, keep his clothing and his person clean, and turn in an honest day's work in return for his pay, food, and lodging, and such characters were quite as common and as vocal in the 1860s as at any other time. Although army discipline then lacked the impersonal tautness to which a later generation is accustomed, it apparently had a good deal more of the brutality which comes from sheer thoughtlessness and incompetence; and if the imperfect soldiers who drifted north told tales of hardships, those stories were not without a solid base in unpleasant fact.

At the end of 1862 a brigadier general controlling a camp for paroled prisoners in Illinois sent to the War Department an indignant protest about the treatment soldiers got when they had to travel long distances by railroad.

"If the railroad companies," he wrote, "will put a barrel of water in each car and will make coarse but decent arrangements, as they do in emigrant trains, for the men to get drink and answer the calls of nature in the cars, which is never done, officers could be responsible for their men. Now the instant the train stops the men rush out for these necessary purposes, as they claim, and any man wishing to desert 'gets left' and the conductor assists the deserter by refusing to stop the train, as he must 'make his schedule.' "[24]

Another officer was even more specific:

"Brave men, including many sick and wounded, have been crowded into common boxcars in the dead of winter without fires, or fuel, or lights, or any other conveniences that had been enjoyed by the cattle that occupied the cars before them, and in this condition the poor fellows were compelled to make journeys of hundreds of miles. In other instances the same class of cars were used in the hottest weather, and without having been cleansed of the filth left by the cattle, hogs, and other stock. Many deaths have occurred from diseases caused by the cold, suffocation, and stench endured in these trains, while a few were not able to hold out to the end of the route and were taken out dead."[25]

In other words, having shown the soldier that if he ran away he probably would not be bothered, the government was losing very few opportunities to make him feel that running away might be a fine idea. If the stupidity which could produce a Fredericksburg and a mud march failed to teach this lesson, the way in which hospitals in the combat area were directed might suffice. At about the time when Burnside was going through his final *Sturm und Drang* period, in January 1863, the surgeon general of the army had a doctor make a close inspection of the army's camps and hospitals at Falmouth. This

STORM AND STRESS.

officer reported that the regimental hospitals needed almost everything, from ordinary bed sacks on up. Hospital tents were cold. There were plenty of stoves, but they were of no use, some simpleton having ordered huge coal stoves which could not be used in tents. There were on the market plenty of little sheet-iron wood-burning jobs that would do nicely, but this kind the army had not bought. There was a lack of hospital clothing, and the nursing was of the worst: typhoid fever patients had been frostbitten because of lack of care.

"I do not believe," wrote the wrathy inspector, losing a bit of his professional poise, "that I have ever seen greater misery from sickness than exists now in the Army of the Potomac."[26]

Veteran regiments, he said, which numbered no more than two or three hundred men because all the weak had been weeded out by casualties and disease, and in which the line officers and surgeons had learned by experience how to care for sick men in the field— such regiments usually had hospitals which were "tolerably comfortable in their appointments." (The only catch was that such regiments had few or no sick men.) In the entire army there were perhaps three or four brigade or divisional hospitals which the inspector found fairly satisfactory. All of the rest, especially the hospitals of the new regiments, in which there was the most sickness, lacked almost everything.

The worst single problem was food, and men died because of it. Much of the army's sickness was the direct result of bad diet. The diarrhea, dysentery, constipation, and malnutrition which made men easy victims to other ailments were the natural end products of a steady diet of fried meat, hardtack, and black coffee. (Considering the matter after the war, Charles Francis Adams wrote: "My intestines were actually corroded with concentrated nourishment. I needed to live on bread, vegetables, and tea; I did live on pork, coffee, spirits, and tainted water.")[27] The army was even seriously troubled that winter with scurvy—scurvy, the deep-sea malady which even then was recognized as a deficiency disease, to be cured by a diet of fresh fruits and vegetables. The men in the hospitals at Falmouth that winter got exactly the same food that was issued to the healthy men in camp: salt pork, hardtack, and coffee.

This was not happening because the army could not get the right kind of food for sick men. It had bought lavish quantities of the very foods these invalids needed, and these foods filled whole warehouses at Aquia Creek. The whole trouble (as this medical inspector found and reported) was simply this: the army command was so abysmally incompetent that it was quite unable to move the good food from the warehouses to the hospitals.

For there was nobody who was empowered to make out the proper requisitions.

Unable to live by anything more inspiring, the army was living by its paper work, and when the paper work was done wrong, which naturally happened every day, military life being what it is, men died.

The warehouses full of good food lay only a few hours from the most remote of the regimental hospitals. Unfortunately, however, there did not exist any man or set of men whose job it was to see that the food got up to the hospitals where the men for whom it had been bought might actually eat some of it. Nobody made out the required papers, and without the papers the food could not move. In the quartermasters' offices there were the blank forms and in the warehouses there was the food, and in between there were open roads and empty wagons and teams of strong horses; but there was not a regular commissary of subsistence for the hospitals, and so the sick men ate salt meat and hard bread, and the vegetables and fruit and chicken and jellied broth stayed in the warehouses and spoiled, or vanished mysteriously down the channels of petty thievery and corruption. The sick men, often enough, went into new graves on the Rappahannock hillsides. And the men who were not sick faded out of the army as fast as the express trains could bring new boxes of civilian clothing, and it was necessary to picket all the roads around Baltimore and Washington, and President Lincoln had General Burnside's little paper setting forth the conditions upon which the present commander of the Army of the Potomac might consent to remain in office.

These conditions the President decided not to meet. Burnside went to the White House, and his last hour of command had visibly arrived. There issued presently an official document which, instead of cashiering anyone, simply announced that General Burnside was relieved of his command. Then Lincoln wrote a strange and canny letter to Joe Hooker, letting that soldier know that his remarks about the need for a dictator and his bitter criticisms of all of his superior officers had been heard and would be remembered in the White House, but nevertheless placing in his hands, as the prize of much hard striving, the command of this luckless army. General Franklin penned his own verdict on Burnside: "I can only account for his numerous mistakes upon the hypothesis that he is crazy."[28] Hooker remarked that he rather doubted if the army could be saved to the country.

It might be that that would largely be up to Hooker. The army would stick around, if he could give it reason to feel that there was any point in it. For the army was still there: the hard core of it, which had come up through great tribulation and which might be indestructible. A veteran in the 12th New Jersey commented that many men had been lost, but said that was only to be expected: "In a company of one hundred enlisted men, only about one third of the number prove themselves physically able and possessing sufficient courage to endure the hardships and face the dangers of active campaigning; the rest, soon after going into the field, drift back to the hospitals and finally out of the service."[29] The most drifted out, and a good many died, but about a third remained, and the men who made up that third would stand a great deal of beating. It might even be that the right man could win a war with them.

THREE

Revival

1. Men Who Are Greatly in Earnest

The war was the sum of all the things all the people in the country were doing. It was the weary private plodding through the mud or dying unattended in a cold hospital tent or defying his officers in order to trade coffee for tobacco with men whom he would try to kill as soon as the weather improved. It was also all of the people who were not in the army, whose lives touched this private's life at any point, and the truths about the war were various. At times the truth was what any of these people believed about the struggle that was going on, and at other times it was the contrast between what they believed and what was really so. By turns the truth was greed, and coarseness, and pain, and shining incredible heroism; and somehow, because the war was made up of people and of what people thought and felt and did, the whole of it was mysteriously greater than the sum of its parts. There was an ultimate truth lying half hidden behind what men were saying and doing, and it is rarely possible to single out any one happening and say, "This is what the war really meant." The war meant a great many things, and in the end it may have meant all of them together, with a saving intangible strangely added. But now and then the infinite complexity of this war seemed to be expressing itself briefly through one man or one event, where the currents that moved below the surface broke open with a foaming of great waters and showed how events were trending.

Specifically, in this winter of 1863 there was the barrel-chested governor of the Hoosier state, Oliver Perry Morton, a great bull of a man who fought for the sacred union of the states and also for the greater glory of O. P. Morton, and who did much which he had not set out to do.

Morton was the son of a country innkeeper, and he was born in rural Indiana one decade after Oliver Hazard Perry won his schoolbook victory over the detested British on Lake Erie. Morton's parents gave him the Commodore's name, which carried magic in the youthful Middle West, and by and by the "Hazard" was dropped. Morton, orphaned before he reached his teens, was reared through adolescence by two maiden aunts in Springfield, Ohio, worked for a time as apothecary's clerk, was bound out to a hatter, and wound up finally as an indifferent student in Miami University, where he managed to complete two years as "an irregular." He left college, married, read law in a country law office, moved to Centerville, Indiana, became county prosecutor and later county judge before he was out of his twenties, and then decided that he could do with more schooling. He went to Cincinnati and attended law school, and in the early 1850s returned to Centerville to become one of Indiana's most spectacular lawyers.

He was not its most profound lawyer, nor, from the professional viewpoint, one of its most distinguished. It was noted that in pleadings before the State Supreme Court, where cases were presented upon written briefs and oral arguments were almost unknown, Morton never amounted to much. The practice of law, for him, had to be personal combat, with a visible enemy present whom one could engage with all but physical violence. It is recorded that he did little office work, but that "before a jury he was irresistible." He was a bulldozer, a fighter; he was remembered as a great massive man having "a fine leg and a large soft hand," with strangely pale skin, a great deal of coarse black hair, and a voice like the crier in the tower of darkness. In court he was savage. An associate recalled that "he literally annihilated everyone connected with the Bar of Wayne County, and walked roughshod over all the other lawyers of his circuit."[1]

In that time and place the law courts had the limelight, and a gifted thunderer was known by the people and could hardly avoid a political career. Morton would not have tried to avoid it. He prospered financially, handling much railroad litigation, and he moved into Indiana politics—always, from the early nineteenth century, a rough-and-tumble affair—as inevitably as water flows downhill. Like most practical politicians, he knew the pitfalls that lurk in humor, and he carefully avoided them. Many a young man, he said, had wrecked himself by being witty. "A politician who goes into wit must expect to sacrifice everything else to it. He will gain no reputation as a sound man. His judgment will be suspected."[2] Morton sacrificed nothing to wit, and he early established repute as a sound man.

He was, in fact, a most orthodox Democrat to begin with, a sharp foe of the abolitionists, a man who voted in 1851 for the new Indiana constitution which ordered free Negroes not to come into the state and provided penalties for white folk who dared to hire them. In 1852 he voted for the Northern Bourbon, Franklin Pierce, and he was shaken out of soundness and orthodoxy only in 1854 by the Kansas-Nebraska Bill, which shook so many and so much. When the new Republican party came in he joined up as a moderate, riding along with but never espousing the anti-foreign Know-Nothing groups. In 1856 he ran unsuccessfully for governor and was accounted so much a moderate that his associate, the George W. Julian who presently became an implacable anti-slavery congressman, did not regret his defeat. At the party's state convention in 1860 Morton was anti-Seward, considering him too inflexible on the slavery issue, and pro-Lincoln. (It was at this convention that Morton was placed in nomination for lieutenant governor by "Mr. Meredith, of Wayne County";[3] the same Mr. Meredith who later, as colonel of volunteer infantry, was to carry Morton's blessing to Joe Hooker in successful quest for promotion.)

No one on the outside ever knows exactly what jars a man loose, and just what happened to Morton next is a bit obscure. But by the fall of 1860 the former moderate had become a fire-eater, and before November was out he was demanding that secession be beaten down by force: "If South Carolina gets out of the Union I trust it will be at the point of the bayonet after our best efforts have failed to compel her submission to the laws." In all the North he was one of the first public men to declare for the use of force against the new Confederacy. Early in 1861 he showed up, unscheduled, at a statehouse flag-raising in Indianapolis, injecting himself into a program of pleaders for compromise, state equality, and erring-sisters-go-in-peace, to declare sharply: "I am not here to argue questions of state equality but to denounce treason."[4]

He was presently put into a key position. Governor Lane resigned to enter the Senate, and Morton became governor by peaceful accession, moving up from the lieutenant governorship to which Solomon Meredith, to his own subsequent glory, had nominated him. A week earlier a convention of Indiana Democrats had voted opposition to "the coercion of sister states," and over in Ohio a leading Democrat warned Jacob Cox that if it came to fighting, 100,000 Ohio Democrats would take up arms to prevent any coercive force from getting even as far south as the Ohio River.[5] But Morton saw war coming and welcomed it, and by the end of April he was driving Indiana deeply into it, getting votes for men and supplies from the legislature, working hand in glove with a semi-secret "vigilance committee" of patriotic citizens which needled lukewarm legislators, worked to break up contraband trade with the South, and in general did its best to cultivate a warlike spirit along the Wabash.

Indeed, it seems that Morton had more energy and patriotic fervor than any one state could hold. He was war governor of Indiana, and working at it, but he quickly took Kentucky under his wing also and made it a Hoosier sphere of influence. Kentucky wobbled and swayed, trying to be neutral in a fight where a state could no more achieve neutrality than it could square the circle. Morton moved in, invited the Kentucky Unionist recruiter, Lovell H. Rousseau, to organize and train his troops in Indiana,[6] and all in all became known as the man who kept Kentucky in the Union. This was a slight exaggeration, for a good many men kept Kentucky in the Union, but Morton was active enough to deserve a good part of the credit.

A characteristic story was told of this period. Morton made one of his frequent visits to Louisville at the height of the neutrality argument, and as always he put up at the Galt House. A member of his party, sitting in the hotel lobby looking out of the window, saw a local secessionist leader walking along the street, laughing at some joke a friend had just told. The Morton man hurried outside, walked up to the Southerner, and promptly knocked him flat. When he was asked why he did this—for the Southerner had committed no offense— he replied stoutly that no damned secessionist was going to laugh while Oliver P. Morton was in town.[7]

A humorless man, this Morton, with humorless followers, operating in a time and a place which had little room for laughter. He was the embodiment of the Union cause, perhaps in a way its personal proprietor, in a state where almost more than any other in the North people were feeling the tearing, agonizing cross-strains set up by the war. The Ohio River flowed through a rich valley where the folkways and habits of thought ran back to planter-land tidewater quite as much as to town-meeting New England, and where the hateful stiffnecked particularism that had brought fire and sleet and candlelight to a young and happy people could be traced to Boston quite as easily as to Charleston. More people of Southern ancestry or Southern sympathies lived in Indiana than in any other free state. Not even in Kentucky, which yearned in vain for an unattainable virginal neutrality, had the war set people against themselves more poignantly.[8] If at times the war threatened to destroy more than it could possibly save, nowhere did that danger seem as real or as desperate as in Indiana. The man who proposed to take this tragically divided state and make it the keystone of the Union arch needed to be a man of uncommon force and daring.

Which, to be sure, was the least that could be said about Governor Morton. He was making himself one of the leading figures of a war which, among other things, clearly aimed to reduce the power of state governors, and he acted as if the governor of Indiana were an independent potentate with whom the government at Washington might negotiate but to whom it could issue no orders. Washington found out about this in what should have been a routine matter, the business of supplying overcoats to Indiana's soldiers.

Early in the war there were Indiana troops in the West Virginia mountains, where nights were cold, and these men lacked overcoats. Morton heard of it—he always heard of everything that happened to Indiana troops—and he made the life of the United States quartermaster at Indianapolis quite miserable, finding time also to spray letters and telegrams at Quartermaster General Meigs in Washington. Government sent him four thousand overcoats in response, but these went astray somewhere. Morton sent his private secretary out as a detective to trace the missing coats, took the matter up vigorously with General Rosecrans, the Union commander in West Virginia, and after six weeks of bickering announced that he personally would see about Indiana's overcoats thereafter. He accordingly bought some twenty-

nine thousand of them and had them distributed to Indiana troops.
Then, his natural force quite undimmed, he got the Federal government to assume his contracts.

The luckless quartermaster at Indianapolis found all of this most
irregular, especially since Morton in his haste had agreed to pay prices
far above the Federal maximum, but when the quartermaster (who
was only a major) protested, he was transferred away from there
and the business was settled Morton's way. Morton then established
the Indiana Sanitary Commission, with agents and depots in Washington, Louisville, Nashville, and elsewhere, to look after Indiana
soldiers, and was denounced for it by officials of the United States
Sanitary Commission, who saw in this "another development of that
obnoxious heresy of state sovereignty," but Morton stuck to it and was
proud of his accomplishment. He also, without any authority in law,
established an arsenal in Indianapolis for the manufacture of ammunition. Later he boasted that this was done "by me, on my own
responsibility."[9]

Between times Morton raised troops. When Braxton Bragg came
into Kentucky in the fall of 1862 Morton put on a big recruiting
drive. There was a bounty law, but the legislature had forgotten to
vote money to pay the bounties, and recruits hung back. Morton
personally borrowed $100,000 from a Cincinnati merchant, borrowed
$30,000 more from an Indianapolis bank, saw that the bounties
were paid, and eventually got the state to pick up his notes. When the
Confederate invasion reached its height he rushed green Hoosier
regiments across the river to meet the Rebels, went over himself to
witness Bragg's retreat, played his own strange role in the murder of
General Nelson, and pulled such wires as were handy to get Buell
removed from command. To Lincoln he wrote that the war would
never be won by "the cold professional leader, whose heart is not in
the cause." Victory would come, he said, only when leadership was
given to "the hands of men who are greatly in earnest, and who are
profoundly convinced of the justice of our cause."[10]

And Morton was greatly in earnest, which was the lump that
leavened the loaf. A passionate man, he stood among high-minded
Laodiceans who tried without success to command troops against
passionate, earnest men from the South, and he spent the strength
that was in him to get those who had no passion taken out of the
places of command. He tried for a time, vainly, to get himself com-

missioned a major general. Then, in the dead winter of the Union cause after Fredericksburg, the whole issue of success or failure in Indiana was placed in his hands, and the times quietly challenged him to show whether he was elemental force or windy bluff.

In the fall of 1862 the Democrats had won the elections in many Northern states—among them, most notably, Indiana. As 1863 began a solid majority of the legislators convening at Indianapolis were Democrats who seemed ready to unite in the belief that there must be a better way to settle this family quarrel than one which came home so painfully to the private pocketbook and the village cemetery. These men cocked their eyes at Governor Morton, who wired Stanton that his legislature was likely to adopt a joint resolution recognizing the Confederacy and urging states of the Northwest to sever all relations with a national government dominated by New England. Morton was perhaps a bit too nervous about this, as the legislators apparently did not plan to go quite that far. They did have certain definite ideas, however, chief of which was that peace-loving Democrats rather than fire-breathing Oliver P. Morton would hereafter control Indiana's part in the war.

Morton met this legislature head-on, sending it on January 8 a governor's message full of stirring patriotic sentiments. The legislature contemptuously refused to accept this. Instead, it voted thanks to Governor Horatio Seymour of New York for the message he had just sent to his legislature, a message which denounced emancipation (recently made national policy by Abraham Lincoln) and upheld the ancient theory of states' rights, for which the Confederates were shedding much blood in Virginia and elsewhere. Having done this, the legislature voted to investigate Morton's involved financial dealings, filed and endlessly debated a whole sheaf of resolutions denouncing practically everything the Republican administration had done, and then got down to the main course: a carefully drawn bill which would take all military power away from Morton and give it to a "military board" of hand-picked Democrats, most of them strongly anti-war and every man Jack of them vehemently anti-Morton.[11]

To good Union men this looked like taking Indiana out of the war and ultimately losing the whole of the Middle West, and to any eye it was clear that war-weariness had reached a climax. Many things were responsible for this, including the fact that this war was

most damnably complicated by plain old-fashioned politics, played
with venom and without much restraint even in the piping times of
peace, and played in wartime with all of its ordinary qualities at
double or triple strength. It could appear, in Indiana and elsewhere,
that the war was being fought for unadorned Republican supremacy
at all levels, from the county courthouse on up. It could also appear
that the Democratic party proposed to regain those courthouses even
at the price of stopping the war and conceding Southern independence. Beneath these appearances was the possibility that the whole
war was no more than a party fight, involving nothing much holier
than the proper division of the loaves and the fishes. These unhappy
appearances were at least partly true, although the whole truth lay
beyond them; and if the people were growing heartsick and confused
because of it all, they were getting the terrible casualty lists from
Fredericksburg and Stone's River for their daily reading matter, and
the incompetence in army command was cutting deeper and deeper
into their consciousness. So Indiana might possibly, this winter, fall
completely out of the war.

Morton himself had tried to warn the national administration. He
had forecast the Democratic victory in the fall election, giving Lincoln a précis of the opposition arguments—that selfish moneygrubbers
from New England were exploiting the Northwest and growing rich
by the war, that geographically and economically Indiana and her
sister states were forever tied to the Southland with the Mississippi as
the destined artery and outlet for their commerce, that the war had
been forced upon the South by the anti-slavery fanatics, and that the
Southerners had offered reasonable compromises which, if accepted,
could have led to a just peace. "In some of these arguments," Morton
had written, "there is much truth."[12]

Much truth, seen also by New York's Governor Seymour, who
feared that the war was concentrating economic power in New England, to the lasting harm of his own New York. Much truth, and also
much error and much failure to see what was going on in the world.
For the railroads had bitten clear through the fated Mississippi artery
and had tied the hinterland firmly to the markets and the banks of
the East, so that the Lost Cause with its bronze garlands and its
swords sheathed forever had perhaps been lost before the war even
began. Yet the strange, tantalizing fact that lies beneath that entire
war did remain as something for Lincoln, Morton, and all the others

to grapple with: doomed to defeat, with the very stars in the sky marching against it, the Lost Cause might nevertheless triumph simply because the men who had to fight about it could conceivably overthrow destiny itself.

History does not have to go logically, and its inevitables are never really inevitable until after they have happened. One of the things that are real about any situation is what the people involved in that situation think about it. What the people in 1863 thought was that the war in the end would go as they made it go, and if anybody had told them that circumstances were going to be controlling, they would have retorted that they would fix all of that by changing the circumstances. In this belief, as Governor Morton might have said, there was much truth.

Among the possible victims of circumstance in this winter of 1863 were the Democrats who made up a majority of the Indiana legislature. Without realizing it, these men were struggling against the fact that the American political system, wide enough for many things, had not by the founding fathers been made wide enough to contain a civil war. They were Democrats taking normal advantage of the fact that they had won an election, and what they were running into was the fact that there was no way, in this moment of all-out war, by which they could do that and nothing more. They wanted to oppose the party that was running the war, and in spite of themselves they could do no less than oppose the war itself. There could be no delicate shadings of action or belief. The administration was fighting for complete victory; to stand against the administration in the ordinary way, using the grips, feints, and arm locks of normal political struggling, meant in actual practice to stand for something less than victory—something a good deal less, perhaps, if the wrestling got really strenuous, so that the struggle might finally appear to be a struggle against the war itself rather than simply against the people who were conducting the war.[13]

So the air was full of rumors, and Indiana that winter was a place where reality blended with the outrageous shapes of Cloud-Cuckoo-Land itself. The victorious Democrats were luxuriating in their new legislative majority, whose precise use they had not yet determined, and were camped comfortably in the center of the stage. (Too comfortably, in fact, for they went sound asleep and were taken.) From the wings, to complicate their job and to precipitate crisis before they were ready for it, came strange far-off noises of wondrous gabbled conspiracies, with oath-bound armies swearing a fantastic fealty. Not for the last time, this prairie state was nurturing an invisible empire complete with weird ceremonials, and what mattered about it was not whether any of it was especially real, but simply that a great many people believed in it devoutly, some with springing hope and some with fear and hatred, but in any event believed.

The name of this invisible empire varied. It was known as the Order of American Knights, and as the Mutual Protection Society, as the Circle of Honor, the Knights of the Golden Circle, and the Order of the Sons of Liberty. It may have stemmed originally from some obscure pre-war fraternity in the South, and its members came together with the belief that the Lincoln government had somehow usurped authority and should be overthrown. The original declaration of principles simply restated a strong states' rights doctrine, upheld chattel slavery, and called piously for a restoration of the old Union.

It was perfectly legal for any Northern citizen to believe in these things, but it was very hard for him to do anything concrete about his belief without appearing to give aid and comfort to the enemy. So this Copperhead order went underground, proliferated its cells from city to city and from town to town, and took on a darker coloration. It came to favor a Northwest confederacy, then it undertook to encourage desertion from the Federal armies, and it prepared at last to give active help to the Southern cause. It bought arms, drilled members in military tactics, commissioned its own "major generals," prepared for active field operations, and called for the assassination of Abraham Lincoln.

Possibly a great deal of this was sheer unconscious make-believe. There was an uncommon amount of froth to the whole affair, and even now it is hard to say what was real and what just seemed to be real. This is not for any lack of facts. There are whole volumes of facts. This Copperhead order must have been one of the most thoroughly spied-upon organizations in human history. Reading the reports and the records, one at times feels that the secret-service men and the counterespionage agents must have been stumbling over one another's heels as they moved through its inner councils. All of these agents abundantly proved that the order had a huge membership—125,000 in Indiana alone, it was said—and they could cite chapter and verse to show that it was a malign revolutionary conspiracy which seriously tried to overthrow the government and lose the war.[14]

The only trouble is that one can never be sure how far the conspirators really meant it, and even the conspirators themselves do not seem to have been entirely certain. The great order never actually did much of anything. On the few occasions when Jefferson Davis tried to make use of it and sent operatives north to promote a little action, the soggy conspiracy came apart at the seams. The handful of hard-eyed Confederate veterans who came north to bring on some overt acts were a different breed from the well-intentioned, well-fed civilians who conspired in village lodge hall and in prairie grove. These Southern veterans were out for blood and they proposed to transform all of this mummery into irrevocable violence in which large numbers of the mummers would unquestionably get killed. It appears that they scared the conspirators almost out of their senses.

Yet in the winter and spring of 1863 this strange unreal plot was a genuine factor. It was believed in, North and South. In Richmond the war clerk-diarist, J. B. Jones, wrote confidently at the end of January that he had no doubt the year would bring "the spectacle of more Northern men fighting against the United States Government than slaves fighting against the South." On February 1 Jones noted:

"It is said and believed that several citizens from Illinois and Indiana, now in this city, have been sent hither by influential parties to consult our government on the best means of terminating the war; or, failing that, to propose some mode of adjustment between the Northern states and the Confederacy, and new combination against the Yankee states and the Federal administration." A fortnight later he was gravely remarking that when the Northwestern states did withdraw from the Union, Virginia probably would take them under her wing "if they earnestly desired to return to her parental protection." He added that if Indiana and Illinois joined the South, victory would be assured.[15]

If the business was taken as seriously as that in the capital of the Confederacy, one can hardly be surprised to find it treated as a matter of life or death in the capital of Indiana. Here men had it in their back yards, and to say that treason stalked the streets by daylight was to do more than indulge in a mere figure of speech. There was a war on, and Indiana regiments in the field were sending home resolutions denouncing all Copperheads—and here was where the Copperheads lived and moved and acted; here they uttered hair-raising threats in public; here their conspiracy was a matter of common street-corner knowledge.

In addition to all of which, the thing was a natural. It was dressed to command attention from skeptic and believer alike. It had an elaborate ritual of oaths and ceremonials which was intended to impress new converts but which probably had the ultimate effect of making a great many sober citizens feel that all Copperheads should be hanged. For this multifariously named order with its degrees and its grips and its ritualized impotent hatred created the atmosphere in which men who supported the Union could be ruthless. It made compromise impossible, and it drove both the war party and the peace party to extremes.

The new member of the order was taught a handclasp for recognition of other members: shake in such a way that the tip of the forefinger touches the pulse of the other man's wrist. He was given a sign of recognition to be used in public places when it was vital to know if other of the faithful were present: shade the eyes with the right hand, put the other hand on the left breast, and never mind if the pose looks odd to the uninitiate. There were verbal signals with which a beset Knight could call for help in a crowd: the word "Aokhoan!" uttered loudly (provided the beset Knight could just pronounce it), or at times the word "Nu-oh-lac," which was "Calhoun" spelled backward. The ritual set forth that a member who violated his obligations was to meet "a shameful death"; specifically, his body was to be divided into four parts, which were to be cast out at the four gates of the temple, the temple being the local Odd Fellows' hall, the room over the corner hardware store, or such other mundane spot as had been chosen for secret meeting place. Becoming slightly more practical, the order also warned its members that if one were brought into court or haled before a grand jury he should refuse to answer questions on the constitutional ground that he could not be made to incriminate himself.[16]

Clearly enough, all of this adds up to a great deal of mumbo-jumboism and nothing much more. But it was a cloak for men who felt deeply, even though they did not really feel deeply enough to risk their lives if they could help it. Until the moment of final risk came they might easily believe that they were going to risk everything, and if they felt that way they would talk—and, up to a point, act—accordingly. And this was going on in a gossipy, chatty, neighborly Middle West where there were really no secrets and mumbo-jumbo would become a matter of universal knowledge in no time. If the participants themselves could believe that this was real and no sham, those on the outside would believe the same.

So when the Democratic majority in the Indiana legislature prepared to whittle down Indiana's part in the war, Morton had his cue. The immediate issue was the bill which would take control of all military matters—troop recruitment, purchase of overcoats, all else—out of the hands of the governor and vest it in a board of hand-picked Democrats. There were in both houses of the legislature the votes to pass this bill, and Morton knew it. He could of course veto the bill, but the Indiana constitution contained an oddity, a provision that the legislature could re-enact a vetoed measure by a simple majority. The Democrats would infallibly pass this law over any veto which Morton might lay down.

If that happened, Morton said bluntly, there would be unshirted hell to pay; "it would involve the state in civil war in twenty-four hours," and "our people would be cutting each other's throats in every county." For Morton was not on any account going to give up his power, no matter what was voted and no matter what the law said. There was as he saw it but one way out, and "that was to break up the legislature."[17]

Indiana's constitution contained a second oddity: not less than two thirds of each house of the legislature constituted a quorum. Without a quorum, of course, no business could be done. So that winter the Republican members quietly bought tickets home and disappeared. The legislature could not act because it lacked a quorum, and so the Democrats went home, too, and Indiana's government consisted solely of Governor Morton and the rest of the executive branch.

The Democrats were unworried. Since it convened early in January the legislature had done nothing but orate, caucus, and investigate. No appropriation bills had been passed, there was no enabling legislation making appropriations legal, and the state treasury had no money and no way to get any. Morton might in effect prorogue the legislature, but sooner or later he would have to have money. To get money he would have to call in the legislature, because only the legislature could raise money. Once the legislature reconvened, the Democrats would have him over a barrel. It was an open-and-shut case, and all the Democrats had to do was wait a little while and be patient.

Except that there was a revolution in progress, and Morton was a perfectly genuine revolutionist. He was, in fact, one of the few men in all history who have understood how a dictatorship can be set up and operated in America. In the winter of 1863 he put that knowledge to work.

The muddle-headed conspirators who devised ancient-mariner recognition signals and who talked solemnly about casting the divided bodies of traitors out of the gates of mystical temples had been carrying on as if someday they would do a fearsome thing, but they were in fact legalists. They professed bloody revolution, and they were to go on doing so for another eighteen months, but in action they relied on a legislative majority. They knew that the majority would eventually make the decisions because the books said so. But when the showdown came the other side was ready to play by different rules, and all of the books went out of the window.

Morton proposed to rule Indiana so that it would stand in the front line of the war against secession. He could not do it legally without the money which he could get only from the legislature, and he had sent the legislature home. Therefore, unable to rule legally, he would rule illegally. He would get the money where he could and he would keep Indiana in the war, and Northern Democrats who did not like it might come around after the war was over and speak their minds fully. Until that time Indiana would have a one-man government named Morton, in whose presence no damned secessionist was going to laugh.

The money problem being at the heart of things, Morton organized a Bureau of Finance, which appealed to bankers, to heads of town and county governments, to the people themselves. Some of the towns and counties responded promptly, appropriating sums ranging from $2,000 to $20,000 and placing the money at the disposal of the governor. Additional money came from citizens and from business firms, and there was a loan of $15,000 from a railroad. There was also that state arsenal, which had acquired illegality ahead of time and which was now showing a fairly substantial profit.[18]

Most important of all, there was the Federal government, which was what really kept Morton in business.

The Secretary of War was Edwin M. Stanton, who had a knack for devious operations, and Stanton had at his disposal certain funds which could be used somewhat loosely. Morton went to Stanton asking for help, and Stanton dipped into these funds and got money for him. (Technically, it appears that the money was "advanced" to Morton as a disbursing officer dimly representing the War Department. The device was probably legal enough as long as the all-out-war crowd could make its own definitions of legality.) So Morton got a Treasury warrant for $250,000, and as he got it he reflected on the way they were stretching the law.

"If the cause fails," he said, "you and I will be covered with prosecutions, imprisoned, driven from the country."

"If the cause fails," said Stanton, who now and then could emit a very high-sounding sentence, "I do not wish to live."[19]

So Indiana got money and paid its bills, and Indiana troops remained in the field, and it continued a hard war for Hoosiers. Morton continued to be a dictator for two years, during which time he was considered a great man by ardent Union folk and an unspeakable tyrant by peace-minded Democrats. What few people noticed was that he and his opponents, between them, had helped to accomplish something which they had no faintest desire to accomplish. They had made a prairie revolution, and their handiwork lived after them.

Indiana had a dictator, and he was a man of force and power in his own right, but he really existed by grace of the Federal government, which was paying most of the bills and providing all of the law. Separatism was dying, and beneath the old concept of the sovereignty of the states there was opening a gulf filled with great darkness and echoing quiet. The Democratic legislators and the stage-struck conspirators had succeeded only in forcing the Republicans to go farther than they had consciously meant to go. If the Lincoln administration was demonstrating in South Carolina and in other Southern states that the real power was to be found henceforth in Washington, it was demonstrating exactly the same thing in Indiana.

2. The Imperatives of War

It was really the army's doing. The old tables were being broken up and far-reaching change was riding down the winds of war, and

even such a man as Morton himself, with his heavy hands and his
pale hairy flesh and his booming, be-damned-to-you-sir voice, was
more a symbol than a prime mover. In this winter of discontent
American institutions could be recast, not to fit the ideas of anyone
in particular, but simply to make it possible for the army to do the
things which it had been created to do. A process had been set in
motion which was beyond stopping, and the fact that these hundreds
of thousands of young men had been turned into soldiers had become dominant for the whole country.

The changes, of course, did not begin in the camps. In the camps
there was the old routine, with snow in the woods and mud on the
roads and unending drills on the hard-packed parade grounds, and
the immense restlessness of uprooted youth was reaching constantly
for an outlet.

When occasion offered there were mild sprees. March brought St.
Patrick's Day. There were many Irishmen in camp, and they saw
to it that the day was observed notably. The 9th Massachusetts held
open house for the 62nd Pennsylvania, broaching barrels of beer
and erecting a greased pole on the parade, with a fifteen-day furlough
pinned to the top. (The pole had been greased too well, and nobody
was able to get to the top.) A half-mile race track was laid out and
there were horse races, which wound up with an accident that killed
two horses and the regimental quartermaster, who had fancied himself as a gentleman rider.[1]

The Irish Brigade, naturally, put on the biggest party of all on
this day, and General Hooker and his staff and all of the officers of
the II Corps were guests. General Meagher turned out garbed as a
crimson-coated master of hounds, and at the close of the day he
had a huge banquet, with more guests than places at table. Ad-
dressing the throng, he begged the unseated guests to remember that
"Thomas Francis Meagher's hospitality is not so large as his heart."
Nobody really minded very much because there was an enormous
punch bowl filled with what one officer remembered as "the strongest punch I ever tasted," and the evening ended with a grand row
between Meagher and his brigade surgeon, who furiously challenged
each other to a duel that was never fought.[2]

Meagher was famous for his parties. The whole II Corps remembered a fabulous banquet the Irish Brigade had thrown in ruined
Fredericksburg on the fifteenth of December, while the dead men lay

still unburied on the frozen fields in front of the stone wall, and the echoing town itself presented bleak roofless walls to the wintry sky, with rival gunners on Marye's Heights and Stafford Heights blessing the place now and then with casual rounds of high explosive. Meagher's brigade had just received three new regimental flags, purest green silk made up by the ladies of New York, and nothing would do but a jollification. So they had taken over some half-wrecked hall and had invited in everybody who was anybody in the II Corps. Long tables had been set up amid the wreckage, loaded with chicken and cold turkey and ham, and good things to drink had been circulating liberally, and when the flags were presented to the Irish regiments there had been a great deal of oratory. In the end everybody had such a good time and cheered so loudly that even Burnside's moribund headquarters on the far side of the river had caught on and had sent staff officers over with frantic orders: stop the party and send everybody home, or the Rebels will take notice of all this noise and open a new bombardment.[3]

It was a hard-drinking army as far as its officer corps was concerned. Any officer could legally buy all the whisky he thought he could handle from the commissary stores, and the commissary whisky was originally famous as "a cheap and reliable article." Later on, as the original supply became exhausted, it was raw and harsh, although it continued to be cheap enough. Some officers would simmer it over a fire in order to reduce the harshness; others believed in setting fire to it and letting it burn awhile, arguing that this destroyed the fusel oil and other harmful substances. However they treated it, they used a good deal of it, and the soldiers' sleep was occasionally disturbed by singing and yelling from the officers' quarters. Colonel Cross of the 5th New Hampshire broke up one such party in his own regiment by stalking in with his drawn saber in one hand and a pair of handcuffs in the other.[4]

But the parties and the whisky were not for the enlisted man, except very rarely and by good luck. The VI Corps had a tale about one of its most distinguished brigadiers, who attended one of these festive occasions and came out full of a rich, sympathetic fellow feeling for his orderly, who presumably had been standing in the cold all evening, holding the brigadier's horse. The brigadier took his bridle reins and teetered gently on his heels and remarked to the orderly: "Do you know, I'd like to take a drink with you." Then

sadly he added that this just would not do because there was a great
gulf fixed between them. "You're an orderly, sir, and I'm a general,
sir; recollect that, sir." The orderly swayed in the dim light, exhaling
an aroma fully as fruity as that of the brigadier's and replied: "By
George, General, hadn't you better wait till you're asked?"[5]

For the most part, the private soldier found his life unexciting, not
to say dull. A Pennsylvanian that winter wrote in his diary that military glory consisted in "getting shot and having your name spelled
wrong in the newspapers," and a man in the 12th New Hampshire
recorded that he and his fellows had enlisted too early. Bounties
were running as high as fifteen hundred dollars per man up in the
White Mountain country, and the average citizen was cheerfully voting for higher taxes to pay for them because "every such enlistment
made his chances one less of having to go himself."[6]

It was a confusing sort of war, and if the enlisted man sometimes
wondered what it was all about it is not surprising. Up the Rappahannock, Federal pickets continued to make friends with the Rebels
across the water, to the horror of security-minded officers. A major
in the 2nd Rhode Island wrote that he had 340 of his men on riverside picket duty, under strictest orders to have no truck with the
men on the far side of the stream. Yet one day he heard the Confederates calling across to let the Rhode Island boys know that the
Yankee paymaster had just got to camp and that the Rhode Islanders,
accordingly, would get their pay very shortly. This, the major remarked glumly, happened barely fifteen minutes after the paymaster
had arrived. Next day the Rebels told the Rhode Island pickets that
the Yankee cavalry had moved on upstream, and one Rebel called
across to ask what had been done with a Rebel who had deserted into
the Federal lines the night before: would he be conscripted into the
Yankee army? The Rhode Islanders called back that that would not
happen, whereupon the inquiring Confederate asked them to look out
for him—he would be over himself as soon as it got dark.[7]

Scandalized by such laxity, the provost marshal of the army, Brigadier General Mason R. Patrick, a gruff old party with flowing white
hair and whiskers, who held little prayer meetings in his tent every
morning and then went forth (as the men supposed) to bite the heads
off tenpenny nails, reported that when the 62nd New York was on
duty by the river its officers took charge of rigging and sending out
the toy boats which carried on the illicit trade with the Rebel army.

One of Patrick's officers seized such a boat, laden with coffee and sugar, in an effort to break up the trade, and was immediately denounced angrily by a regimental officer as a spoilsport.

Worse yet, said Patrick, he had detected pickets of the 169th Pennsylvania in flagrant verbal communication with the Rebels. A Rebel had called across: "Any signs of a move?" and a Pennsylvanian had replied: "Yes, we've got eight days' rations and we expect to move in a few days." When the Rebel asked which direction the move would take, the Pennsylvanian obligingly told him that it would be upstream, to the right. Quite gratuitously the Yankee outpost added that they were going to use pack mules for transportation and hence obviously would not be following the line of the railroad.[8] What chance, asked General Patrick wrathfully, did an army have to deceive the enemy with that sort of talk going on?

From Ohio the governor was writing the War Department that for the past sixty days he had been trying to recruit men but that "success had been trifling," and the governor of Iowa was asking for five thousand stands of arms to use on dissidents who opposed recruitment and a vigorous prosecution of the war. Also from Iowa, a United States marshal was reporting that there had recently been a public meeting in Madison County at which armed men hurrahed for Jefferson Davis and declared that they would like to see Iowa join the Southern Confederacy. Simultaneously the governor of Illinois was wiring the War Department that "an extensive and dangerous traffic in arms" was going on between Illinois exporters and ultimate consumers in the Southland, and a draft-enrolling officer at Chambersburg, Pennsylvania, was quitting his job because indignant citizens had gone around and burned his sawmill.[9]

All of these things were happening, and it was hard for any man to say which incidents were really important and which were frothy bubbles on the surface. One significant occurrence could have been the publication of a formal document which was issued from the White House about the time General Burnside had his day and ceased to be as commander of the army.

This paper recited the findings of a recent court-martial and closed by asserting that "the foregoing proceedings, finding and sentence . . . are approved and confirmed"—as a result of which Major General Fitz-John Porter was cashiered and dismissed from tne service and was barred from ever again holding any office of trust or profit under the United States Government.[10]

Fitz-John Porter's was a name which had once carried weight. Brave, talented, and handsome, Porter had been McClellan's right-hand man all through the peninsular campaign; he had, in fact, done most of the actual fighting which kept McClellan's army from destruction when Robert E. Lee cast a net for it in the Chickahominy bottom lands. He had been trusted to fight Gaines's Mill and Malvern Hill by himself, and at Second Bull Run he had led a final forlorn-hope assault on Stonewall Jackson's invulnerable lines, and he had been respected and honored among men. Now he was being ruined, his career as a professional soldier closing in black disgrace. The signature at the end of the paper which condemned him was that of Abraham Lincoln.

This paper was rather surprising, for a conviction had not generally been looked for. Porter himself had been so confident of acquittal that he had recently gone to the White House to discuss with Lincoln himself his next assignment in the army. Since his day the verdict has come to seem cruel and unjust, the passage of time having indicated that the military court was hasty and biased, its principal function having in fact been to make somebody sweat for the loss of the second battle of Bull Run. John Pope, who commanded the army that lost that battle, had pointed the finger at Porter in a frantic effort at self-exculpation, and so Porter had come to trial.

Porter found himself accused, specifically, of violation of the ninth and fifty-second articles of war, the general idea being that he had refused to attack the Rebel flank as ordered by Pope and that the battle therefore had been lost. Porter had tried to show that his orders could not be executed, since the Rebel flank was nowhere near where Pope thought it was, but it had done him no good. He was a close friend of McClellan, and McClellan had been uprooted so that there could be an all-out war. The wind and the sun had bleached white the bones of Bull Run's unburied dead, Pope was in exile in Minnesota fighting the Sioux Indians, and not for another generation could there be a full understanding of the ins and outs of the tragic lost battle. Meanwhile, Porter had been broken, and there was in the action a meaning which did not appear on the surface.

While it was valuable to punish a scapegoat for Bull Run, a more important motive seems to have been operating in the background.

One interpretation can be found in the carefully worded memoirs of Alexander K. McClure, who as a Republican politician and editor had a fair understanding of what was happening in Washington then. McClure wrote that the military court, as set up by Secretary Stanton, was "studiously organized to convict." Lincoln, he added, approved the verdict even though he was by no means convinced that Porter was in fact a faithless officer. Said Editor McClure: "New conditions and grave military necessities confronted Lincoln; and while he did not approve of the judgment against Porter, he felt that Porter and others of his type merited admonition to assure some measure of harmony in military affairs, and he finally decided that to approve the judgment would be the least of the evils presented to him."[11]

The administration was groping through a red fog toward a shore dimly seen, and if McClure might not be qualified to say what was in Lincoln's mind, he could at least identify the angle from which the administration's action made good political sense. Porter was blameless, but he was being crushed because, in an excessively slippery situation, the civil authorities were finding it necessary above all things to get a solid grip on the army and on the war. Porter might not in fact be an obstacle in their way, but they thought that he was, which was what mattered. At the very least he had come to symbolize the obstacles which, being intangible, could not be dealt with directly.

Ordinarily the government would not need to ruin a general in order to establish its control, but these times were far from ordinary. Fear and hate and suspicion had been created in order that these incomprehensible soldiers who failed to hate their enemies might at least be inspired and directed by men who did hate. (Grim old Thad Stevens had recently offered in Congress a resolution denouncing, as guilty of "a high crime," anyone in the executive branch of the government who should so much as propose a negotiated peace with the South.)[12] Everybody in Washington was being victimized, and the bloodcurdling fol-de-rol of the Indiana conspirators was part of the emotional background. Porter was one victim. Another victim, looking with unutterable melancholy to a day beyond death and hatred, brooding darkly about what the people might buy with this sacrifice of their blood if they could be enabled to make their purchase with charity and without malice, was Abraham Lincoln. In between the two, the immediate victim and the tragic humorist who was appointed to sit in judgment upon him, there were many others. Among them was the coarse, savagely cruel, everlastingly vital little man with the straggly whiskers and the furious eyes, Secretary of War Edwin M. Stanton.

Stanton represented driving force. He was a terror to all traitors, to most Democrats, and to a good many officers of the United States Army. There were those who said that if one who came before him for a scolding barked back at him sharply the Secretary would change his tack and become ingratiating, and it appears that old-fashioned fortitude in personal combat may not have been one of his basic virtues.[13] McClellan had considered him a double-dealer who could talk falsely of friendship while he dug a pitfall before one's feet. Others spoke of his intolerable insolence, and it was a byword that his favorite cry to officers brought before him was a passionate "I'll dismiss you from the service!"

Stanton looked at the army and found its officer corps full of cliques—the friends of McClellan, the pals from West Point, the tent mates from the old Indian-fighting army from the Western plains. He saw, also, that this army somehow was not quite responsive to the will of the government. On the horizon lay the fleeting shape of a vision which was noble beyond utterance, but in the immediate foreground there were the blood and the mud and the inexpressible ignobility which doomed sick men to a diet of salt pork and hardtack, or squandered men's lives through sheer incompetence, or schemed and plotted for rank and promotion. The contrast was beyond endurance. So as a first step, and beginning with the destruction of the luckless Porter, Stanton would break up the cliques.

The technique was brutal, but the idea was sound enough. A rather obscure brigadier of cavalry, who served for a time in the provost guard in the capital and hence got a good look at the seamy side of things, applauded vigorously as he watched what the Secretary was doing.

"When Stanton was appointed," this officer wrote, "a military aristocracy of the regular army and of immense power had arisen in the bosom of the army of the volunteers. This aristocracy had at its head the commander-in-chief and stretched its roots into every corps, regiment, and bureau, defying the government at home with only a little less disdain than Davis manifested at Richmond. Our own army was first to be made subordinate to the President, and then the Southern army made subordinate to it. To relieve McClellan, court-martial

Porter, and eliminate all traces of West Point class traditions, uniting by nicknames, I consider victories as important as Appomattox, and these nothing but the wooden and numb audacity of Stanton dared to achieve."[14]

The crack about West Point nicknames, to be sure, indicates a general of volunteers whose feelings were hurt one day when he found that he did not belong to the club, and this doubtless colored what he had to say. Yet he did have a point. There was ever so much more to the Porter business than Porter himself. Porter was an innocent who stood in the line of fire, and he got hit. From this winter onward the army might have many defects, but one thing at least was certain: its higher officers would realize that a hard war was called for.

Others besides the offended cavalry general got the point. Major Dawes of the 6th Wisconsin, who never suffered from his own lack of a West Point nickname, wrote in March that army morale had been restored, and he set down the verdict of a front-line fighting man:

"By the prompt dismissal of disaffected and disloyal officers, the army is being purged of the damnable heresy that a man can be a friend to the government and yet throw every clog in the way of the administration and prosecution of the war."[15]

Fuzzier, yet speaking an honest emotion springing from the upswing that followed Stanton's purge, was the outburst written down by that eminent Bostonian, Major Henry Lee Higginson of the 1st Massachusetts Cavalry:

"We'll beat these men, fighting for slavery and for wickedness, out of house and home, beat them to death, this summer, too. . . . We are right, and are trying hard; we have at last real soldiers, not recruits, in the field, and we shall reap our harvest. . . . My whole religion (that is, my whole belief and hope in everything, in man, in woman, in music, in good, in the beautiful, in the real truth) rests on the questions now really before us."[16]

Neither Major Dawes nor Major Higginson quite said it. Yet there was something unexpressed, perhaps something finally inexpressible, lying beneath the change which they saw coming over the army and the war that winter and spring. America was changing, changing by violence, with much blood to be shed and many lives to be wrecked. Nobody was ready for it, and nobody could quite understand it now that it was happening. But somehow it was being determined that

democracy henceforth, perhaps for some centuries to come, would
operate through a new instrument. Sovereignty of the states was dying,
North as well as South, and going with it was the ancient belief that
the government which governs least is the government which governs
best.

Between that fact and the mangling of General Porter the connection might seem to be remote, but it was there. Neither Porter nor
the men who broke him could have told quite what was happening,
nor could they have said why it was happening. All men were victims and agents of the irresistible current of change. It was necessary
for some of them to die of dysentery, eating bad food in unheated
hospital tents beside the Rappahannock, and it was necessary for
others to hammer a desk and threaten army officers with ignominy,
and in the end something bigger than any man knew would come of
it all.

In this desperate war which America was waging—with itself and
with its own past, and with all of the habits of thought which had
grown up out of that past—the nation was unexpectedly finding that
it possessed enormous strength. The possession of that strength was
a fact of incalculable significance. None of the old means for wield-
ing and controlling it seemed to be any good. Yet the power existed,
and the one certainty was that someone would eventually control it
no matter what happened to the war, to the country, or to the country's traditional method of governing itself. So the necessity of taking
control of this immense power was going to dominate everything for
a time, and it was going to work through many instruments.

One of these instruments—least likely of the lot, perhaps, but extremely effective—was Joe Hooker, exercising the functions of the
profane hard-drinking soldier to bring the army back to fighting
pitch, and inspiring Boston's Major Higginson to a confused rhap-
sody about the higher values. Another was Secretary Stanton, smashing blindly at officer cliques to extend the power of the central
government. Still another was the great anonymous private soldier
himself.

He was the central fact in the whole situation. For the time being,
government existed for him. He fought without poetry, as the regular said of the New Englanders, and he died by platoons when the
time came for him to die, and all of the raw power which the coun-

try was beginning to assert had meaning only through him. Without in the least intending to, he was now driving the government on to a fuller assertion of its own powers.

He fought and he died without any particular complaint (except for remarks about bad food and incompetent leadership), but someone had to keep sending him up to the firing line. This job originally fell to the several states, and they had done nobly as long as individual Americans would respond to the call. But the unhappy fact was that volunteering had just about ceased. The states had tried coercion—that is, they had gingerly tried drafting their own people—but that was not working well either. The war had begun as an effort by one coalition of states to impose its will on another coalition of states, and it could not be fought that way any longer.

Hooker's army contained something like 120,000 men. Nearly 30,000 of these were men who had signed up for short terms—many of them were nine-month men, enlisted the summer before when Lee drove north into Maryland and made Northern pulses flutter—and their enlistments would expire in mid-May. There was no way to hold these men in service, since they had enlisted with the states and not with the Federal government. (Hooker was remarking that even the men who were willing to re-enlist would insist on being sent home and paid off first, so that they could join new regiments and collect fat bounties.)

The states were not what they had been. The corn belt had its troubles, with every governor sending plaintive cries to Washington asking for help. New York, which had refused to elect a fighting man, had a Copperhead for governor, a high-minded eloquent man who would stop now to reason and argue in a situation that was past reasoned argument. Horatio Seymour was an old-school Democrat, a man with a plausible smooth face fringed by under-the-chin whiskers, who dreaded the coercion of the states about as much as he dreaded disunion. He believed that hard-minded Republicans were shamefully making political capital out of a war which they had taken over for their own purposes—which, as a matter of fact, was perfectly true—and he was protesting that the only way to prevent the establishment of a despotic central government was to preserve the powers of the several states. The war, he declared, must not be turned into "a bloody, barbarous, revolutionary, and unconstitutional scheme" to destroy state sovereignty.[17]

Seymour stood at one of the extremes. He was an honorable extremist, driven by the cruel logic of events into speaking for forces which he would not ordinarily uphold, and behind him were men whom he himself would not endorse. Yet even loyal, all-out-war governors were complaining this winter that the government's policies were destructive. Andrew of Massachusetts, a fire-eating abolitionist who got into the war almost before Washington itself, had recently begged Lincoln to rely on nine-month militia regiments rather than on draftees, arguing that the draft would "disturb everything."[18]

The unhappy fact was that many governors had either lost control over their own states or had become men who did not believe in the kind of war that was now being fought. They were no longer supplying the army with adequate numbers of recruits, and since the war had become grim and unlimited, that seemed to be their principal reason for existence. The men who would come into the army willingly had just about been used up, and the men who would come in only if somebody made them come could not be brought forward in adequate numbers by mere governors. But to get on with the war now it was necessary above all else to keep the stream of recruits flowing into the army. The unsung private on the firing line might be voiceless, but unless he remained on the firing line the war was lost forever, and he was not going to remain there indefinitely unless he had company.

To keep him there and to provide him with the replacements he needed, the government had to use force. It was already using force on the states, and now it must use force on individual citizens as well. State sovereignty was dying in the smoke and dust of a dozen battles; dying with it was the old idea that the government of the United States could not reach out and tap the shoulder of the ordinary man. From now on the government must do exactly that or cease to be a government.

That was what government had come to, and that was what government now did. This same winter and spring of 1863 which saw the administration warning all army officers, via the ruined career of General Porter, that the civil government was in charge of things also saw the passage of a national conscription law.

The emphasis was on the word *national*. There was conscription already, with the states enrolling their citizens, appointing agents to harry them into camp, and making such deals as they could—at the price of fabulous bounty acts by cities, counties, and townships—to get a sufficiency of men under arms. But from now on Washington was not going to get its men from the states. It was going to reach out with its own lengthened arm and take them direct. The lists of men subject to conscription would be made up by representatives of the government at Washington and not by men named by the governors. The men who were called up would be called up by Washington. If penalties were inflicted for non-compliance, they would be inflicted by Washington, for a drafted man who evaded the call was no longer merely a citizen who had thumbed his nose at the state authorities: he was a deserter from the United States Army, and the Federal government might shoot him if it could catch him.

In the month of March, accordingly, the country went over to this new system of recruitment, which embodied, all in all, one of the most revolutionary changes ever made in the American form of government, since it permanently reduced the role of the states in the American political picture. State sovereignty, South, had fired cannon at Fort Sumter, leading to a great deal of this and that along the border. Now it was state sovereignty, North, which was coming under the guns.

Among those who immediately detected the sweeping nature of the change that was being made was New York's Governor Seymour. He protested heatedly that national conscription was unconstitutional, and he argued that the government should depend solely on the states even though the dome of heaven fell in. Ironically, there arose to his voice a splenetic echo from the heart of the deepest South, where Governor Joseph E. Brown of Georgia was making exactly the same kind of fight against Jefferson Davis. Brown was hotly telling Davis that "your doctrine carried out not only makes Congress supreme over the states at any time when it chooses to exercise the full measure of its power to raise armies, but it places the very existence of the state governments subject to the will of Congress."[19]

If the central government, cried Brown, can draft men, and if it is the central government which can specify who is to be exempt from the draft, then the central government could, if it chose, utterly destroy the state governments simply by drafting all state officials into the army. Congress, complained the governor of Georgia, was supposed to be the agent of the states. How now, if it could reach into the states and make its writ good within state territory? Were not the people thereby reduced to "a state of provincial dependence upon the central power?"

Indubitably. Yet it is recorded that while the angry plaints of Governor Brown caused Jefferson Davis to sigh wearily (and, the sighing over, to explode into icy polemics) they had no effect on Davis's program to raise the Confederate armies by conscription. Governor Seymour had no better luck in the North. The imperatives of war were at work, and there was a chill wind blowing in on theories and theorists. The New Yorkers and the Georgians who killed each other across the stone wall at Fredericksburg would have found cold comfort in the idea, but the fact was that they had left their respective governors high and dry.[20]

Thus while the administration moved to take the army away from the generals, it was also taking it away from the governors. The army would never again be an assemblage of troops contributed by the several states. (In 1861 Secretary Chase had protested that "he would rather have no regiments raised in Ohio than that they should not be known as Ohio regiments." He still felt that way, yet now he was one of the principal instruments of change.)[21] From now on it would be a national army.

One step led to another. Decreeing that the United States Government would be responsible for its own armies henceforth, the administration also gave thought to the question of making soldiers out of Negroes. The colored man seemed in some distracting way to be what this war was, at bottom, chiefly about. By presidential declaration the war now must go on until the colored man had been given his freedom. Might the colored man not fight as a soldier in the ranks, then?

So the decree went forth for the enlistment of regiments of colored troops, the tide of events having carried everyone some distance beyond Ben Butler's tent-side pronouncement that fugitive slaves were mere contraband of war. This was at first balm and a delight to the harassed Northern governors. If colored men could be enrolled, perhaps a state's quotas could be met that way, white men being loath to come forward. Andrew of Massachusetts thought this should be tried, and he hastened to enlist a solid colored regiment, the 54th

Massachusetts. Simultaneously he sent agents all across the North to enlist other colored folk for Massachusetts regiments.

This might have been a good trick for stay-at-home Yankees, busy with the prosperity of a wartime boom that went beyond anything in anybody's earlier imagination, if it had just worked. In the very nature of things, however, it could be carried only so far before it collapsed of its own weight. There were not any prodigious numbers of able-bodied colored men in all the Northern states together. When all was said and done, the North had been inhospitable to the Negro. Some of the states which stood strongest for the war had laws forbidding settlement by Negroes, and as fantastically underprivileged folk the free Negroes tended to live under bad health conditions and so produced many young men who could not pass army physical examinations. It became clear, at last, that even if the Northern colored population furnished recruits in the same proportion as Northern whites had furnished them the army would gain only eighteen thousand new soldiers.[22]

What this meant was that if any appreciable number of Negroes were to come into the army they would have to come from the South. Obviously, the national government was the only agency which could recruit them. (The irrepressible Governor Andrew did try to recruit some Massachusetts soldiers from among the colored contraband in the occupied areas, but the effort fizzled.) The colored recruit, therefore, rounded up by semi-literate, hard-handed agents who moved in the train of the armies, was, above all, a recruit to a national army.[23] His very presence in uniform testified to the existence of a new power in Washington.

All of these things happened, not at once and dramatically, but over a period of weeks. Their significance might or might not have been seen at the time. The atmosphere in Washington in the long winter that followed Fredericksburg seemed to be one of disintegration and despair, and it was none other than Governor Andrew who was writing that in Washington just then he found few men "of practical sagacity and victorious faith." Yet the sagacity and the faith were at work, and something was being done. The war was a long way from being won, but at last the things were being done which would make it possible for it to be won. Uncertainly and without a clear plan, Washington was removing obstacles from the army's path.

3. Soldiers' Bargain

Beyond any question, Joe Hooker was the handsomest commander the Army of the Potomac ever had. Crusty Publisher Alexander K. McClure grew fairly dreamy-eyed when he tried to describe him: "A man of unusually handsome face and elegant proportions, with a complexion as delicate and silken as a woman's." Major Dawes of the 6th Wisconsin spoke of Hooker's "Apollo-like presence," and a newspaper correspondent noted that the general had large gray-blue eyes, a rosy skin, and an abundance of blond hair, and said that he looked like an ideal soldier with his erect carriage and his square shoulders. To another correspondent Hooker looked "as rosy as the most healthy woman alive." Hooker had more than a little of the old McClellan touch, and the soldiers were always ready to cheer when they saw him, as if the tattered clouds of war's forgotten glory still trailed after him even for regiments which had gone through Antietam and Fredericksburg.[1]

He had won command at a bad time. The army was in disorder. A veteran in the 24th New Jersey said afterward that "at no period in its history were the troops more disheartened or less hopeful of achieving success," and a soldier in the 3rd Michigan wrote that winter that there had been many desertions and that "unless something is done to prevent it our ranks will grow pretty thin in a short while."[2] This man was an admirer of Hooker, but he was not sure whether the general could do much now that supreme command had been given him, and he wrote dubiously:

"We all feel that General Hooker will be like the poor man that won the elephant at the raffle. After he got the animal he did not know what to do with him. So with fighting Joseph. He is now in command of a mighty large elephant, and it will remain to be seen if he knows what to do with him."

Hooker himself was under no illusions. He was to show, in the end, a great capacity for deceiving himself, but at the start he knew exactly where he was. As he took over the command he examined the troubles of Burnside with brutal clarity, remarking that although the army was actually on the verge of dissolution Burnside had not even suspected it, the reason being that Burnside "has no other idea of the organization and government of an army than that of arranging it in such a way that the commanding general will have nothing to do. The nearer the army reaches that point, the greater the excellence in his estimation."[3]

That mistake Hooker himself would not make. The peculiar flaws in his make-up were not of the kind that would handicap him at the beginning. Editor McClure remembered being told by an officer who knew Hooker in the old California days that "Hooker could play the best game of poker I ever saw until it came to the point where he should go a thousand better, and then he would flunk."[4] The time for going a thousand better had not yet arrived. The game was still young, and at this point the general held it firmly in his own hands and played it with great skill.

If he shared with McClellan the ability to draw cheers from tired men who had seen much of war, he also shared with that departed officer an extreme distaste for letting army administration take care of itself. Quite unexpectedly Hooker turned out to be a first-rate organizer and military housekeeper. He looked upon himself, and caused others to look upon him, as the dashing leader of troops in battle; actually, in this winter of despair, his great service to his country lay in this prosaic matter of making certain that the men got enough to eat and stayed well.

Just now he needed to display none of his more flamboyant qualities, the qualities which seemed to be most characteristic of him, the dash and the rough soldiers'-campfire good-fellowship, and the "sublime courage at the battle front." (That last testimonial comes from an officer in the Iron Brigade, where they tended to be connoisseurs of courage.) The troops, indeed, might make up and gaily sing a little ditty[5] which stated:

> *Joe Hooker is our leader,*
> *He takes his whisky strong——*

But what they got from Joe Hooker first of all, what they got that made the rough places straight and convinced them that it was going to be a great day in the morning—what, in fine, was genuinely important to them and to the national cause—was the sober, unimaginative, routine work of eternally checking up on rations, clothing, hospitals, living quarters, and other little details which in the long run make all the difference.

The first trouble was food. The government had bought much very good food, including the fresh vegetables for want of which men sickened and died, in addition to the hardtack, salt pork, and coffee which were the iron rations of this army. The only problem lay in the fact that none of this good food got to the ultimate blue-uniformed consumer. With the canny eye of one who himself lacked innate virtue sufficiently to understand the inner motivations of sinful unwatched man, and who hence knew all of the angles, General Hooker looked into this with a very cold gaze. What he found was that the officers designated as commissaries of subsistence—the officers whose job it was to get this food from the warehouses to the mess kitchens—had discovered in Uncle Sam's bounty a good way to get rich.

The fresh vegetables, the onions and cabbages and potatoes and the patented desiccated vegetables—known to all ranks, inevitably, as "desecrated vegetables," since soldiers will always mispronounce a word if they can manage it—were being sold for cash money to outsiders, including a number of the unredeemed residents of rebellious Virginia. The money thus received went into the commissary officer's private purse, and the monthly returns were falsified in order to show that the soldiers themselves had been the recipients. Nobody had ever set up a system by which there would be a stream of monthly vouchers showing that all of this stuff had gone to the men for whom it had been bought. It was, as a soldier remarked later, "a system of single (not to say singular) entry that enriched many a captain and assistant commissary of subsistence for the rest of his life."[6]

On this singular system Joe Hooker landed with a heavy foot. There came from army headquarters presently an order announcing that flour or soft bread would be issued to the troops at least four times a week, with fresh potatoes and vegetables coming out twice a week and desiccated mixed vegetables at least once a week. Commanders of corps, divisions, brigades, and detached commands would require any commissary officer who failed to make such issues to file a written statement from the officer in charge of the depot warehouse proving that the warehouse did not have any of the foods in question.[7] That took care of the commissary officers.

Next came the matter of cooking. On the march each man cooked

for himself, and since the average soldier could do little more than
boil coffee and frizzle a strip of bacon or salt pork, the marching
ration consisted of fried pork, hardtack, and coffee. In camp things
were supposed to be better. And yet, administration having been lax,
and foods other than pork and hardtack and coffee having vanished
en route to the regiments, in most outfits here in the camps near Falmouth marching rations were the regular diet for troops which were
not marching at all. Regimental commanders now were required to
see to it that the regular company cooks went to work, and if there
were no company cooks they were instructed to create some, so that
the soldier could get decent meals in place of the intestine-destroying
stuff he cooked for himself.

It was true that most of these company cooks lacked skill. Some
noticeably lacked even the desire to be skillful, since most of them
were simply enlisted men detailed from the ranks to do a two-month
stretch in the mess kitchen. Nevertheless, bad as they might be, it was
at least possible for them to cook and serve fresh vegetables. They
could use the desiccated foods to make soups and stews, and when
fresh meat was issued they could do something besides fry it in pork
fat. The soldier cooking for himself, blessed with no kitchen utensils
except a little frying pan and a tin can in which coffee might be
boiled, could do none of those things no matter what raw materials
he might have.

One veteran, reminiscing years later, recalled the new order of
things:

"From the commissary came less whisky for the officers and better
rations, including vegetables, for the men. Hospitals were renovated,
new ones built, drunken surgeons discharged, sanitary supplies
furnished, and the sick no longer left to suffer and die without proper
care and attention. Officers and men who from incompetence or disability could be of no further use to the service were allowed to
resign or were discharged, and those who were playing sick in the
hospitals were sent to their regiments for duty."[8]

And so between the fresh foods and the better cooking, army surgeons presently noticed the disappearance of the cases of scurvy
which had been extending the regimental sick lists. At the same time
there was a sharp drop in the perennial scourge of diarrhea, together
with a general decline in "all the more serious diseases to which troops
in camp are liable, and especially those which depend upon neglect

of sanitary precautions." In addition, the surgeon general reported to Hooker that there had been "an improvement in the health, tone, and vigor of those who are not reported sick; an improvement which figures will not exhibit but which is apparent to officers whose attention is directed to the health of the men."[9]

Part of this was due to better food, and another part because somebody at last made it his business to see that elementary rules of sanitation were observed in the camps. The log-and-canvas hutments in which the men lived had become little better than pigsties, especially those in which the men had raised their shelters over shallow pits dug in the earth. It appears that young men living without women have no especial desire to be clean. Under Hooker's prodding the army's surgeons caught onto that fact and took corrective action. The canvas roofs of all huts were ripped off periodically so that the sun and the clean wind could strike the interior; wherever possible, the entire hut had to be moved to new ground at the end of each week. The worst of the camps were abandoned outright and the troops moved to new camp sites. It was required that blankets and other bedding be aired daily, that hut floors be carpeted with pine boughs or other material so that men would not bed down on the bare earth, and regimental commanders were ordered to require the digging of eighteen-inch drainage ditches around each habitation. Kitchen refuse had to be buried each day, proper sinks were dug for every camp, and "the men should be required to wear their hair cut short, to bathe twice a week, and put on clean underclothing at least once a week."[10]

Elementary as most of the rules seem to be, the mere fact that they were now embodied in official orders indicates the extent to which they had not been observed previously. The change that took place in this army, once decent food and decent living conditions became the rule, was remarkable. The soldiers themselves testified to the great improvement by setting up wild cheers whenever they saw their handsome general sitting proudly on his big white horse as they passed by. One wrote that "General Hooker proved a veritable Santa Claus to the army under his command." Another said that "the whole army was impressed with the feeling that strength, energy, and intelligence were all working together at headquarters," and a third remarked simply that "under Hooker, we began to *live*."[11] Writing long after the war, a Massachusetts soldier looked back ecstatically:

"Ah! the furloughs and vegetables he gave! How he did understand the road to the soldier's heart! How he made out of defeated, discouraged, and demoralized men a cheerful, plucky, and defiant army, ready to follow him everywhere!" Most of the accounts agree with another regimental scribe, who recorded that "cheerfulness, good order, and military discipline at once took the place of grumbling, depression, and want of confidence."[12]

There were furloughs. Thinking along non-military lines, Hooker concluded that if the men wanted more than anything else to see the folks back home the thing to do was to let them go, and there was presently a system by which one man in each company, in turn, could get a ten-day furlough. This could not take care of everybody, of course, but it took care of a good many, and the effect was good. At the same time, it was made harder to desert. The mails down from Washington were put under control of the army provost marshal, and stern orders were issued governing express packages. No package would be received for transmission to anyone in the army unless it bore an invoice stating that it did not contain civilian clothing, the invoice to be certified by the agent who had accepted the package for shipment. From President Lincoln there came an order granting amnesty to all absentees who returned to the ranks before April. At the same time, the kindhearted President was persuaded to relinquish his right to review all court-martial sentences, and it now became possible to shoot deserters. Picket lines around the army were tightened, parties representing themselves as telegraph-repair details had to exhibit written proof that they were telling the truth, and no wagons of any kind could go north without proper passes, while the pickets were ordered to shoot any wandering persons who failed to halt and account for themselves when challenged. Drinking in the camp was squelched (except among the officers, including especially the commanding general), and the guards on the bridges at Washington were presently confiscating five hundred dollars' worth of liquor a day. One result of this was that regimental sutlers, until the authorities caught on, did a land-office business in such canned goods as brandied peaches.[13]

There were also many drills—"constant and severe," as one soldier remembered them. If the men were down in the dumps, Hooker did not propose to give them leisure to sit around and brood about it, and from morning to night the drill fields rumbled with the tramp of many feet. Officers went to school evenings and next day went out to maneuver companies, regiments, brigades, and divisions in the tactics thus studied. There were reviews with the old McClellan touch, with everybody in dress uniform, brass bands blaring under the wintry sky, and Hooker looking on with visible pride. A man in the 16th Maine recalled "the evident satisfaction of Hooker and the conscious power shown on his handsome but rather too rosy face."[14]

It seemed that many men added that sort of qualification when they wrote an enthusiastic verdict on Hooker. He was too handsome, too roseate with good health and vigor, too confident that this army which was beginning to fit into his hand so nicely would prove an irresistible weapon. (He dismayed Abraham Lincoln once this spring by remarking jauntily that the question was not *if* he got to Richmond, but simply *when.*) The tide was visibly turning. Hooker himself had caused it to turn, perhaps he would ride the flood to fortune, yet it could hardly be quite that simple. There would always be a catch in it for this army—finest army on the planet, Hooker was calling it; he could march it clear to New Orleans if he had to, and the word would soon be "God help the Rebels."[15] It had labored under glamorous McClellan, braggart Pope, and plodding Burnside, coming uniformly to ill fortune under each. Now it had a general who seemed to blend the traits of all three of these predecessors, and it might be that it would do better under him. Yet even while he aroused confidence he created a small grain of doubt. The man whose beautiful skin was a bit too rosy might also, in the end, himself be a little too good to be true.

Yet the army did revive. The rank and file took Hooker at face value, and showed it by their actions. Hooker was proudly writing after a fortnight in command that desertion had practically ceased.[16] These soldiers, who were prepared to give everything, could drive no hard bargain for themselves. They wanted to be decently fed and clothed, and they wanted now and then to see some sign that the man at the top knew what he was doing. Beyond that they asked for nothing. They lived that winter in a strange vacant place in the middle of time. Behind them there were terrible names like Antietam and Fredericksburg, proudly written now on the regimental banners which sparkled like marsh-fire flames up and down the long blue columns. Ahead of them, as yet unknown, were other names equally great and terrible, and no one thought about them. The men were veterans and they would live in the immediate present, looking neither before nor after, coming once again to believe in themselves, proudly wearing the new corps badges which Hooker had cannily devised for them, parading when the President and the commanding general passed them in review—a great army with banners, marching through the mud and the dirt toward the battle smoke which veiled the stars.

There were changes at the upper level. Amid rumblings, General Franklin had departed, muttering sotto voce that he would not serve under Hooker. Gone, too, was Baldy Smith, to whom Burnside had confided the first hint of a great and amazing thing which was to happen. With Smith went Burnside's own troops, the faithful IX Corps, sent away to serve once more down the coast, or inland, or anywhere save with this luckless Army of the Potomac. Gone, too, finally, was the stout old Bull of the Woods, Major General Edwin V. Sumner, with his simple code and his unimaginative bravery and his rigid old-army loyalties. He had taken no part in all the back-biting which followed Fredericksburg, telling the congressional committee simply, "There is too much croaking in the army." In midwinter he was relieved, gone forever from the army which for better or for worse he had helped to stamp with his own imprint. He rested in the North awhile, then was ordered west to take command in Missouri and fell ill, an old man worn down by the war, his life coming to its close in a Syracuse sickroom. He lay in a stupor, and as he came out of it he seems to have thought of old battles—perhaps of Seven Pines and its reeking swamps, of the ambush by the Dunker church in the Maryland hills, or of the doomed advance toward the stone wall below Marye's Heights. He cried out suddenly: "The II Corps never lost a flag or a cannon!" His attendant came over to him, and Sumner repeated more feebly: "That is true—never lost one." He was raised in his bed, and the attendant gave him a glass of wine. He took one sip, intoned, "God save my country, the United States of America," dropped the glass, and died, an old soldier gone to join the great God of Battles.[17]

Hooker found new men for the vacant places, and in the process he did a strange and seemingly an uncharacteristic thing. For the all-important job of his chief of staff he asked the War Department to assign to him Brigadier General Charles P. Stone.[18]

Stone was a man out of the past, deeply buried in disgrace. A brigadier without a command, a soldier without a visible future, he was a ruined living symbol of the fact that the hatred which General

Burnside had failed to find among the fighting men had sprouted and flourished mightily among the stout civilians who controlled the destinies of the fighting men. This hatred, mixed with fear and grown old and gray and venomous, Abraham Lincoln greatly lacked, but it seemed that nearly everyone else in Washington had a share in it, most notably the very men to whom General Hooker had made his gestures and his overtures as he scrambled toward the top of the heap. General Stone had been its first sacrificial victim.

In the fall of 1861 General Stone had commanded troops along the upper Potomac. In a misguided moment he had thrust a brigade across the river to reconnoiter near Leesburg, and the brigade had blundered into trouble at Ball's Bluff and had been butchered. Butchered among many less notable had been its commander, Colonel Edward D. Baker, the Illinois-born Californian who had helped save Oregon for anti-slavery Republicanism and who was intimate with the leading men of the party which stood for all-out war. The war party wanted to punish someone for this disaster, and to do that job it had organized the Joint Committee on the Conduct of the War.

Looking into things, the committee had decided that General Stone was at fault and must be punished. It made no formal accusations and it took no direct action against him; it simply received and published accusations against his loyalty, turning him presently into an untouchable, a man who could not be defended, so that he was removed from his command and was even imprisoned for a time, although he had never been charged with any crime. The radical Republicans who had done this had nothing in particular against General Stone. They were simply using him to perfect the new technique which they had accidentally stumbled on. As an object lesson Stone had been extremely effective.

And it was this man whom Joe Hooker was now asking the War Department to send to him to become chief of staff of the Army of the Potomac.

Nothing came of it, to be sure. Stone had to remain on the shelf until Grant came along with a prestige that could overawe even the radical Republicans, and in the end Hooker took for his chief of staff Brigadier General Dan Butterfield, a stocky little ex-militia officer from New York. And yet Hooker's act in asking for General Stone is one of the most interesting things he ever did.

It was completely out of character, or perhaps it proved that

Hooker's character was not the open-and-shut case which on the surface it appears to have been. Hooker had schemed and calculated until it had seemed that there was no conceivable thing that he would not do to make political capital with the radicals. Yet now, untested in his perilous new job, he laid schemes and calculations aside and for one brief moment stood up as a straightforward soldier who would defy politics and politicians. He never bothered to explain what made him do it, and it seems that a passion for self-analysis may have been one of the few passions he lacked. He simply did it, leaving the fact that he had done it as a testimonial to something real in his strange, complex soul. It is a point to remember, because to speak up for General Stone took moral courage, a quality which Joe Hooker is rarely accused of possessing.

One like that was enough, and Hooker was not the man to go on sailing too close to the wind. Denied General Stone, he made do with General Butterfield, a strange but politically safe little man who had an unsuspected streak of poetry under his breezy bluster and who in an unexpected way left a permanent mark on the United States Army.

Butterfield was a New York businessman when the war began, and he raised New York troops and commanded a brigade on the peninsula under McClellan. He early noticed that when his brigade bugler sounded a call (which would be picked up and repeated at once by all regimental buglers in the brigade) there was apt to be confusion, since other brigades were usually within earshot. So he invented a little recognition call—three whole notes, followed by a couple of triplets—which would precede all brigade calls, and the boys quickly fitted a chant to it: "Dan—Dan—Butterfield!" It appears that one day in the camp at Harrison's Landing, shortly after Malvern Hill, Butterfield called his bugler into his tent, whistled a little tune for him, and asked him to sound it on his bugle. Somewhat struck, for generals did not ordinarily behave so, the bugler obeyed. The result did not quite suit Butterfield, and he did a little more experimental whistling, until finally he had it the way he wanted it. The bugler wrote the call down on the back of an old envelope, and Butterfield instructed him to use the tune thereafter in place of the call prescribed by regulations for "lights out." The regulation call, said Butterfield, was not musical; he wanted one which would somehow express the idea of a darkening campground with tired men snugging down to a peaceful sleep, and he hoped his new call would do it.

So the bugler used the new call after that, and other buglers heard it and liked it and came over to copy the tune, until before long it was used all through the Army of the Potomac. Later on, when some of the troops were transferred west, the bugle call was taken up in the Western armies, and at last it became regulation and has remained regulation to this day, the drawn-out haunting call that puts the lights out for soldiers and that hangs in the still air over their graves at military funerals—"Taps."[19]

In addition to having an ear for music, Butterfield appears to have had a personality that fitted Hooker's. Hooker could relax when the day's work was over, and Butterfield could help him. There were army officers who felt that the atmosphere at headquarters in those days was not wholesome. Greatly admired by his troops, Hooker was at no time a favorite among his generals. His military capacity they often admitted, but they were inclined to be dubious about the man underneath the soldier, and they did not like the tales about revelry at headquarters. Looking down a lengthy Adams nose through cold Bostonian eyes, Charles Francis Adams wrote (it may be with some exaggeration) that Hooker's tent was a place to which no gentleman cared to go and to which no lady could go.[20]

George Gordon Meade, irascible but fair-minded, wrote that he himself liked Hooker better than most and thought him a good soldier, but he added: "I do not like his entourage." In this entourage Meade specifically mentioned Butterfield and the new commander of the III Corps, Major General Dan Sickles. He wrote that they were cleverer than Hooker and that because they had political pull Hooker was likely to put himself under their influence. Meade would say nothing in particular against Butterfield and Sickles, but he primly told his wife that "they are not the persons I should select as my intimates."[21] Lumping Hooker, Butterfield, and Sickles together, Adams declared that "all three were men of blemished character."

Of the three, Sickles was the most obvious target. He wore notoriety like a cloak, so that if it never quite seemed becoming it at least looked natural on him. In an army so many of whose general officers have come to seem stuffed and posed, undistinguishable from one another in the shadowy portrait gallery of the half forgotten, Sickles remains a recognizable individual. Whether he was drinking, fighting, wenching or plotting, he was always operating with the throttle wide open. He might have had more faults than virtues, but everything about him was perfectly genuine.

Sickles came out of Tammany Hall. He was in his middle thirties when the war started, and even at that age he had already first conceived and then been obliged to discard a planned career of extraordinarily lofty proportions, for in the beginning he had told himself that he would become nothing less than President of the United States. He had lived too hard for that, had lived, loved, killed, and been cast into outer darkness by his fellow men, and the war offered him a chance to come back up the ladder a bit. He saw himself now as a military hero, and as a corps commander he could be on the way toward making his vision real. It would depend partly on the throw of the dice and partly on the valor of the men whom he was leading. Luck was with him on this second point, for his corps was made up chiefly of the divisions formerly led by Phil Kearny and Joe Hooker, and they were as good as the best.

Sickles had served in the New York State Assembly, had been corporation counsel in Manhattan, and when James Buchanan went to London as United States Minister, in the high and far-off times when the conflict between North and South looked like something that would wither and die of its own accord, Sickles went along as first secretary of legation. In London he had been somewhat gay, and he appears to have been one of the juniors who cooked up the once-famous Ostend Manifesto, which sought to commit the United States to the threat to seize Cuba by force if Spain, "actuated by stubborn pride and a false sense of honor," should refuse to get rid of the island by forced sale. Returning to America, Sickles had been a state senator and then member of Congress, a valiant states'-rights Democrat, a prosperous lawyer on the side, a militia officer and a student of the military arts, a fixer who knew all of the tricks of Tammany at its crookedest but who seems not to have taken graft himself. He had his sights fixed on the presidency, and he was making about as much progress in that direction as a Tammany man can.

And then he killed Philip Barton Key.

Son of the man who wrote "The Star-Spangled Banner," Key was a dabbler in politics, captain of a crack militia company, a drifter and a man about town, known for a time as "the handsomest man in all Washington society." He handled certain legal business for Sickles, and Sickles in turn helped to persuade President Buchanan to reappoint Key as United States attorney when his term expired. Key became friendly with Mrs. Sickles, had assignations with her in a shabby flat on Vermont Avenue in Washington, and one day was shot dead by Sickles on the sidewalk bordering Lafayette Square, across from the White House. Having killed him, Sickles walked down the street and surrendered his revolver and his person to Attorney General Black.

His trial was a circus. It belonged in the 1920s, in the era of sob sisters and flashlight bulbs. Edwin M. Stanton was one of defense counsel, and he and the other lawyers pulled out all of the stops. They raised—it appears to have been for the first time—the plea that Sickles was not guilty because of temporary insanity brought on by the shock of discovering that his wife had been untrue to him with his best friend. Like the plea, the verdict set an immutable precedent. Sickles was triumphantly acquitted.

So far, so good. The unwritten law ran strongly in predominantly Southern-chivalry Washington of the 1850s, and it was hard to think the worse of a man who killed by it. But Sickles then put himself beyond the pale by the simple act of forgiving his wife and restoring her to his bosom. It may be that after his own fashion he loved her.[22]

This was a shocker. Washington was scandalized to the eyebrows and remarked that Sickles's career was ruined. Mary Boykin Chesnut, the South Carolina diarist, sat in the House gallery one day and saw Sickles deliberately and totally ostracized. He was sitting all alone, like Catiline, every other member careful not to come near him—"left to himself as if he had the smallpox." His offense, Mrs. Chesnut conceded (demonstrating that the aristocracy of Charleston could be quite as censorious as that of Boston), was not that he had killed his friend but that he had condoned his wife's profligacy. Sickles wrote a defiant open letter to the press, remarking: "I am not aware of any statute or code of morals which makes it infamous to forgive a woman," but it did no good. Mrs. Sickles lived for eight years, an infinitely lonely little woman in a huge house that no one would enter. When she died after the war four major generals were among her pallbearers.[23]

When the war started Sickles resigned from Congress and went back to New York to raise troops. He got a commission from the governor to raise eight companies of volunteers and succeeded in getting this expanded into authorization to raise an entire brigade of five regiments. He raised it, saw it dubbed the Excelsior Brigade—New York regiments numbered 70 to 74, inclusive—and financed its camp for some time out of his own purse, while state and Federal authorities argued over the validity of his commission. At one time he rented a circus tent from P. T. Barnum to house several hundred of his recruits. At another, with a dozen companies or more quartered in a bare hall on lower Broadway, he contracted with a cheap bathhouse to give fourteen hundred men a shave and a shower bath at ten cents apiece. He got his brigade regularized at last, served with it under Hooker on the peninsula, and was promoted to divisional command just before Fredericksburg.

Now he was one of the intimates of the commanding general, and there were those who felt that no good would come of it. Yet if Hooker's tent that winter was not a place in which an Adams could feel at ease, a great deal of very hard work was done there and the army benefited by it.

Among other problems, Hooker tackled the cavalry. He began by consolidating all of the cavalry with the army into one corps, in place of leaving it split up by regiments among the different infantry divisions, and for its commander he selected a solid regular-army officer, Major General George Stoneman—not the ideal choice, perhaps, for what Hooker really wanted was a Sheridan, and Stoneman was neither fiery nor lucky. However, unification meant that the cavalry would at least have a chance to do cavalry's real job, and Stoneman was conscientious and did his best.

Cavalry's job that winter was practically impossible anyway. It was supposed to form a screen around the entire army, which meant that it had to patrol an outpost line one hundred miles long. This line for the most part ran through a broken country of dense second-growth timber which was crisscrossed by innumerable winding lanes and pathways, most of them so obscure that nobody but a regular inhabitant of the region could even find them, let alone tell where they led. The inhabitants of this country had the strongest of secessionist sympathies and formed an unofficial but highly effective Confederate intelligence network from which it was impossible to keep secrets. One Federal officer reported ruefully that even the women and children "vied with each other in schemes and ruses by which to discover and convey to the enemy facts which we strove to conceal."[24]

This meant bad times for Yankee cavalry. Little bodies of Rebel horsemen could always slip across the Rappahannock and concentrate on some remote forest-hidden farm. Knowing exactly where the Yankee vedettes and picket stations were, and guided through the timber by men or boys who could find their way blindfolded, they could descend on the isolated groups of Federals, smash things up, take prisoners, and get clean away before cavalry headquarters had a chance to know what was happening. Stoneman found that his cavalry was wearing itself out simply by doing outpost duty, which, under the circumstances, could not be done effectively anyway. He had twelve thousand men, of whom on any given day one third would be on duty, with another third either going or coming.[25] Nobody was happy, the army's secrets were open to inquiring Rebel eyes, and all of the horses were foundering. In addition, the outposts were getting so jittery that nobody could depend on the reports they sent back. Army headquarters had to warn cavalry that "those whose fears magnify trifling squads into large bodies of the enemy as richly deserve death as the base wretch who deserts his country's flag or his comrades in battle."[26]

That was all very well, but in the long run the only way to keep Jeb Stuart out of the Yankee lines was to go across the river in a body and attack him on his own home ground. This idea occurred to various people; among others, to youthful Brigadier General William W. Averell, who commanded one of Stoneman's cavalry divisions and who at West Point had been a classmate of Fitz Lee, now one of Stuart's brigadiers. This Fitz Lee had elevated the technique of annoying Yankee cavalry to a fine art, and he used to send taunting messages to his old pal Averell asking when the Yankee cavalry was going to begin to amount to something, and so on. His most recent message had been an invitation to Averell to come across the river and pay a little visit, bringing some coffee with him if possible. So Averell, who had won a reputation as a bold fighter against the Western Indians just before the war, at last came to Hooker and asked if he might not take his division across the river and look for a fight.

This was right in line with Hooker's ideas and he agreed, saying that there had not been many dead cavalrymen lying around lately but that if Averell went over and fought Fitz Lee there would be.[27] Averell hurried back to his division and made his men sharpen their sabers, promising them a chance to use them in action. In mid-March he led some three thousand troopers down to the Rappahannock at Kelly's Ford, pushed aside the Confederate river guards after a sharp little skirmish, and went barreling across country looking for Fitz Lee and trouble.

He found both quickly enough, but Lee came on the scene with only about half as many men as Averell had, and the Northern troopers were at last beginning to believe that they could face up to Stuart's men in an open fight. The Confederate columns were driven back half a mile or more, charging columns colliding head-on at full gallop in the dust and smoke, horse artillery banging away, everybody yelling and sabers clanging and the fields and roads and woods full of wild uproar. Lee's men counterattacked and were driven off, and opportunity quietly opened a door for young General Averell. He had the bulge on his old classmate now. He could move on and completely rout Lee's brigade and destroy its camp, and it was at a time like this that a good general had to have the instinct of a killer.

That instinct Averell did not have. He straightened his lines for a new attack, but then he began to get cautious. Prisoners told him that Stuart himself had come on the scene. This was true enough, although the prisoners forgot to add that Stuart had come all by himself, with no reinforcements. But the mere weight of Stuart's name was equal to a brigade or two in those days, and besides, Averell heard that Rebel infantry was near. So after a time he had his buglers blow the recall and the Yankee cavalry trotted back to its own side of the river.

The boys were proud of themselves—among other achievements, they had killed the fabulous Major John Pelham, commander of Stuart's artillery—and Averell was happy too. Before recrossing he had left a sack of coffee and a note for Fitz Lee: "Dear Fitz, here's your coffee. Here's your visit. How do you like it?"

But Hooker was angry. Cavalry morale might have been given a lift, but Hooker wanted more than that. In his own way he was a perfectionist—for a while, at least—and he wrote sharply that Averell had had a sweeping victory in his grasp and had lost it because of "imaginary apprehensions."[28] Many a victory this army had missed because commanding generals became nervous and saw things moving in the shadows. Under Joe Hooker this was not to happen. At

XII Corps headquarters, about this time, Hooker voiced his confidence.

"If the enemy does not run, God help them!" he cried.[29]

4. May Day in the Wilderness

The Confederacy's fortified lines ran for twenty-five unbroken miles, from Port Royal all the way to Banks Ford. Trenches zigzagged along the lower slopes of the hills, with gun emplacements above them sited so that the gunners could cover all possible approaches. Where the line came out in the open and ran across level plains it was anchored at proper intervals with built-up redoubts. Lee's army could take position anywhere along the immense shallow crescent which faced Fredericksburg and the nearby river crossings, and no imaginable frontal assault could dislodge it. Professional soldiers of that era were brought up on Napoleonic lore, and it was only natural for a young Confederate officer who was trying to explain how invulnerable these lines were to exclaim: "The famous lines at Torres Vedras could not compare with them."[1]

In December, when these field fortifications were not half so strong, Burnside had broken his army's back on them. Now Hooker had the army, and he was chock-full of bubbling confidence. Over and over he repeated that this was the finest army on the planet. He told one caller that he would take the army across the river before long and seize the Rebels where the hair was short, and in a moment of extreme expansiveness he said that he hoped God Almighty would have mercy on the Confederates because he, Joe Hooker, would have none. This led Senator Sumner, at the capital, to mark him down disgustedly as a blasphemous wretch,[2] but it also indicated that Hooker felt that he knew how to get at the Rebel army without going smack over the middle of those impregnable trenches.

Thanks to his own energy and good military sense, Hooker had one asset which his predecessors had lacked—a corps of excellent cavalry whose morale was beginning to be high. The boys had learned how to ride. It was no longer necessary for a cavalry colonel to look hawk-eyed at his ranks to make sure that his gawky troopers were not hanging onto the reins with both hands, letting their elbows flap like crows' wings, or seeking to control their horses by clucking or saying "Whoa," "Git-up," and "Go-along" instead of using bit and spur the way honest cavalrymen should. They had also learned how to fight, and they had lately been outfitted with new-model carbines, Sharps single-shot breechloaders, which lacked the range and penetrating power of the infantry rifle but which could be fired much faster and hence enabled cavalrymen fighting on foot to give a good account of themselves.

The army now had nearly twelve thousand of these troopers, and Stoneman was supposed to be a first-rate soldier. He was just over forty, a West Pointer who, as a young second lieutenant of dragoons, had served as quartermaster of the famous "Mormon Battalion" during General Stephen Kearny's march across the plains to California in the Mexican War. He was at Fort Brown in Texas when the Civil War broke out, and when the departmental commander, old General Twiggs, went over to the Confederacy and advised his subordinates to do likewise Stoneman defied him and succeeded in getting north with part of his command. At Fredericksburg he had commanded an infantry corps, and he was Hooker's own choice for cavalry commander.[3] The plan of attack which Hooker was shaping now would depend in large part on Stoneman's initiative and determination.

Hooker's basic idea was to pry Lee's army out of its fortified lines and make it fight in the open. By the first of April he had concluded that Stoneman's cavalry would be the instrument with which he would do the prying. Stoneman would take the cavalry far up the Rappahannock, cross over, and go swinging south until he hit the line of the Virginia Central Railroad, when he was to turn east and head for Hanover Junction, which was believed to be Lee's principal supply depot. If he could get there with ten thousand cavalry, Lee would have to retreat, Hooker would cross the river and pursue, and with Stoneman in front of him Lee would not be able to retreat with speed. There would be a big fight, and since Hooker's army had a solid two-to-one advantage just now—Lee's force was somewhat scattered, Longstreet having taken a good part of his corps down below Richmond to foil Yankee raiders in the Suffolk area—the Rebels would be shoved back into the Richmond lines. There would eventually be a siege which could have but one outcome.

So went the plan, and on paper it worked out very well. By April 1 Hooker was stripping his army for action, ordering all surplus baggage and equipment sent to the rear and warning the War Department to have siege equipment ready for delivery. Among other things, he wanted ten thousand shovels, five thousand picks, five thousand axes, and thirty thousand sandbags shipped to him in front of Richmond for the making of saps and parallels. He also asked Army Secret Service to prepare authentic maps of the Richmond defenses, and the commissary department was told to have one and one half million rations on boats, ready to be floated up the Pamunkey River to meet the army when it got that far.[4]

Hooker was a canny man, and Lee was not going to learn about this plan through any security leaks if Hooker could help it. Lincoln got a hint of it by letter around the first of the month, and a bit later when he came down to Falmouth to review the troops, Hooker told him some more. Things looked good, and Hooker took the large view, and in his chats with the President he kept beginning sentences with "After we have taken Richmond——" Lincoln listened soberly and found this excessive confidence depressing and warned Hooker and Couch, who was second-in-command: "In your next fight, gentlemen, put in all of your men." He may have been thinking of the fifty thousand soldiers whom Franklin had had on the field but had not used in the Fredericksburg fight. Whatever he was thinking about, Couch reflected, he was giving perfectly sound advice.[5]

A bit later Hooker sent Dan Butterfield up to Washington to give the President all of the details. Washington was full of leaks, then as now, and Butterfield was sternly ordered to tell the President everything but to say nothing at all to anyone else. This made it a bit embarrassing, for he was shown in to Lincoln's office just at the end of a cabinet meeting and found the President surrounded by expectant cabinet ministers, including the fearsome Secretary Stanton, who enjoyed being kept out of no secrets. Butterfield kept mum, stalled while the ministers got out, and stood mute while a New England senator, ears wide open, hung around making small talk with Mr. Lincoln. In the end the general saw the President alone, told him all, and returned to army headquarters with his mission accomplished.[6]

It was time to get going at last, and on April 13 the long columns of Federal horsemen went trotting along the dirt roads to the upstream crossings. Stoneman had picked a good man to go over first: Grimes Davis, the Mississippi-born brigadier who had snaked his regiments out of Harper's Ferry the previous September when Stonewall Jackson surrounded and captured the place in the Antietam campaign. Davis took his brigade over the stream several miles above the railroad bridge and came down fast on the southern side, while Stuart's pickets galloped desperately on ahead with the warning: Yankees over the river! Stoneman's main body was to cross at Rappahannock Bridge and at Beverly Ford, which was close to it. It got down to the banks and found the opposite shore strongly held, and Stoneman paused to consider whether he ought to be rash.

He had with him enough men to force a crossing—Sheridan or Bedford Forrest would have got over while Stoneman was counting noses—and in any case Davis was coming down from above to take the Rebels in flank, so that the resistance could not have been prolonged. But they were thirty miles or more from the rest of the army, and Stuart occasionally had unpleasant surprises for rash Yankee cavalrymen. Stoneman decided to wait so that he could have everything ready, and then it began to rain. It rained harder and harder, so that it was difficult for Stoneman to move his artillery, and while the cavalry waited the river began to rise prodigiously. Before long the water at the ford was deep and foaming and the rebuilt railroad bridge was wobbly, and Stoneman began to feel that the whole project was pretty risky. Messages were got to the other side, round about, and Davis angrily brought his brigade back and returned to the northern shore.[7]

Back in Falmouth, Hooker waited for news. On April 15 he wired Mr. Lincoln that the rain was a bad break, but added: "I am rejoiced that Stoneman had two good days to go up the river, and was enabled to cross it before it had become too much swollen. If he can reach his position the storm and mud will not damage our prospects." A few hours later Hooker messaged Lincoln that Stoneman's guns were stuck in the mud but that he had been ordered to go ahead without them. Lincoln, who was beginning to have his doubts, replied that as far as he could see "Stoneman is not moving rapidly enough to make the expedition come to anything." The President tallied up times and miles on his fingers. "He has now been out three days, two of which were unusually fair weather, and all three without hindrance from the enemy, and yet he is not twenty-five miles from where he started. To reach his point he still has sixty to go, another river [the Rapidan] to cross, and will be hindered by the enemy. By arithmetic, how many days will it take him to do it?" All of which, Lincoln concluded, was beginning to smell like another failure.

Lincoln was quite right. Hooker got the bad news from Stoneman next day—every creek and brook swimming-deep, roads impassable for guns and wagons and nearly so for horses, Rappahannock out of its banks and still rising. All the cavalry was north of the river, said Stoneman, and he thought this was a very good thing, for if it had crossed it would have an impassable river in its rear and the doubtless equally impassable Rapidan in front of it, with malevolent Rebels all about. All in all, the omens were bad. They were being cursed, he added, with "one of the most violent rainstorms I have ever been caught in."[8]

For the time being, that was that. Hooker fumed and entered a debit against Stoneman's name in his little black book, and the army huddled in its camps and waited for the rain to end, having missed a chance once again because a general lacked a driving spirit. And yet it may be that the army had not really lost much. Hooker's plan looked good on paper, but there may have been something too hopeful about the idea that Lee's whole army would meekly retreat just because some cavalry was threshing about in its rear. When Hooker set to work to make a new plan he adopted a different line.

This time he would not rely so much on cavalry. He would move by his right with infantry, flanking Lee out of his lines. Cavalry, as before, would cross far upstream and maneuver around to get on Lee's supply route, but the rest of the army would not wait for it. It would go upstream also, and if it moved fast and with proper secrecy it should be able to get across before Lee knew that it was doing anything, and when the infantry was south of the river it would move east. Instead of putting ten thousand cavalry in Lee's rear, Hooker would put seventy thousand infantry there, accompanied by artillery, and the cavalry would frolic about farther south and destroy railroads and supply depots.

Hooker had raised his sights. Originally he had been looking for a good way to make Lee pull back to the defenses of Richmond. Now he was thinking about annihilating the Rebel army outright. "I not only expected victory," he said later, "but I expected to get the whole army." Butterfield recalled that the real purpose of the campaign was "to destroy the army of General Lee where it then was."[9]

In general terms, Hooker's idea was that he would move so many men in behind Lee's left that Lee would have to retreat in a great hurry. The retreat would in effect be a flank march across Hooker's front, Hooker would attack, and that would be the end of the Army of Northern Virginia. Duly inspired, staff went to work to translate this plan into orders.

Staff had problems, because in making these plans one point was clear. If the infantry was going to outflank the enemy and take a position close in rear of the Rebel left it would have to go on a very long hike.

It could not move downstream for a flanking maneuver because the river below Fredericksburg was too wide and deep to ford and would have to be bridged. Also, moving in that direction would leave Washington uncovered, a point on which Mr. Lincoln was notoriously sensitive. Upstream there were two handy crossings—Banks Ford, not far from Falmouth, and United States Ford, half a dozen miles farther on. The Rebels held these in some strength and had dug trenches and gun pits, and anyway, these fords were so close to Fredericksburg that Lee could get his entire army to them on short notice. If it crossed the river at all, the Union Army would have to go some distance upstream.

There the problem began to get complicated. Just above United States Ford there was a fork in the river, with the Rappahannock coming down from the northwest and the Rapidan slanting in from the west to meet it in a looping, irregular angle. Operating in this angle was tricky business. John Pope had nearly come to total disaster there a fortnight before he fell into trouble at Bull Run, and from one end of the war to the other this area represented a puzzle which the Federals could never quite solve. To cross above United States Ford meant crossing two rivers instead of one. In addition, on the southern bank of the Rapidan lay the scrambled, brambly maze of the Wilderness, a long stretch of second-growth forest with narrow winding roads and infrequent clearings, where a soldier might walk into ambush at any moment and where the magnificent Federal artillery would have little room to operate.

Cutting across this Wilderness was one decent road, the Orange turnpike, which ran west from Fredericksburg to hit the Orange and Alexandria Railroad at Orange Courthouse. If Hooker proposed to cross the Rappahannock upstream, what he was up against was the job of getting over both rivers, striking the Orange turnpike, and moving east on it until he had emerged from the Wilderness—and all before the Confederates found out what he was up to and came out to waylay him.

His immediate strategic goal would be a tiny crossroads with the overgrown name of Chancellorsville, a dozen miles behind Lee's extreme left. If he could put his army there undetected, he might be able to make some of his boasts good. A simple march of four or five miles from Chancellorsville would get Hooker clear out of the Wilderness onto open ground southwest of Fredericksburg, and there, if he could just get there intact, he would have a fine chance to destroy the enemy.

This was a glittering vision for a general who had announced—perhaps just a shade ahead of time—that he would soon have the Rebels by the short hairs, and Hooker undertook at once to turn it into a reality. He was known as a slam-bang head-down fighter, but now he became the cool executive, concerned with matters of organization and logistics. Wagons would delay the march, so except for irreplaceable ammunition wagons and a few ambulances he would take no wagons. The soldiers could carry extra loads on their backs, and what they could not carry would be borne by some thousands of pack mules especially bought for the occasion. The foot soldier would have more than sixty pounds to carry, exclusive of his rifle, but he would just have to make the best of it.[10] It would not be for long, and victory would make up for everything. Pontoons would be sent up to the fords just in case the river began to rise again, and details would be appointed to strengthen that railroad bridge which had given Stoneman the jitters.

Stoneman still led the cavalry, and his function would be to cross where he had been supposed to cross before, to strike south, smashing up all Rebel cavalry outfits which crossed his path, and in general terms to create as much trouble as possible. His orders specified that he was to get in close to the enemy: "If you cannot cut off from his column large slices, the general desires that you will not fail to take small ones. Let your watchword be fight, fight, fight."

The rains stopped at last and the roads dried, the sun came out, and the Virginia spring was at its warmest and balmiest, and the Army of the Potomac pulled itself out of its camps and took to the highways.

The men were feeling good. As they started northwest on back roads, well out of sight of prying Rebels, the soldiers felt that this time they were headed for a victory, and their spirits went sky-high. As they left camp the bands played "The Girl I Left Behind Me," for leaving Falmouth seemed almost like leaving home, and along the roads the anemones and violets were growing, with dogwood in blossom in the groves and the peach trees glowing pink around deserted farmhouses. All along the river, cavalry patrols were rounding up local residents and making them stay inside their houses. There were going to be no secessionist civilians slipping across the river with news of this march if Joe Hooker could help it.[11]

The weather was hot and there was a long way to march, and the loads the men carried were heavy. The inevitable happened, and the roads soon began to be littered with discarded coats, shirts, blankets, and other things. The army found that it was being followed by people whom the soldiers dubbed "ready-finders"—civilians eager to collect the riches which the soldiers were dropping. A slightly scornful man in the 12th New Hampshire described them:

"An old horse or mule, sometimes, but oftener an old ox, a steer or a cow, strangely tackled by means of an old harness or yoke, spliced together and tied up by ropes, strings, and pieces of twisted bark to a primitive kind of a two-wheeled, nondescript kind of cart that no Yankee would care to make or imitate if he could, with an old man or woman or a young boy, and sometimes a girl, for a driver, and a cord or string of some kind tied to the bits or horns—as the animal motive power might belong to the equine or bovine order—for reins, and the pen picture is by no means complete, but only a scratch-sketch of some of the picking-up teams of the stay-at-home natives that used to follow our armies."[12]

By the evening of April 28 the first part of the job had been done, and there was a general feeling, as one man put it, that the Army of the Potomac at last "had got a leader who knew what to do and was going to do it."[13] In the woods and fields just back from Kelly's Ford—a few miles below Rappahannock Bridge, thirty-odd miles from Falmouth—were three army corps, V, XI, and XII, forty thousand men in all, with the skipper of the XII Corps, Major General Henry Slocum, in general command of the lot. These troops were there secretly, with Stoneman's cavalry screening all the crossings. Back at Banks and United States fords, close to Falmouth, was the II Corps, showing itself on the riverbank in order to make Lee think that the major effort was going to be there. In and below Fredericks-

burg, likewise keeping in plain sight and being busy with pontoons
and the like preparatory to making a crossing, were the I Corps and
the VI Corps under John Sedgwick, recovered now from the three
wounds he had received at Antietam. Behind these two corps was
Dan Sickles with the III Corps, awaiting orders. So far the troops
were exactly where the plan said they ought to be, and the Rebels
had caught onto nothing except that the Yankees seemed at last to
be on the move. Stuart's patrols were suggesting that Stoneman and
his cavalry might be preparing to move up into the Shenandoah
Valley.

Slocum got his three corps over the Rappahannock without much
trouble. Stuart's patrols were alert, and as the Yankee infantry
formed up on the southern side the Confederate squadrons stabbed
at them with galloping detachments, seeking to take prisoners for
purposes of identification. A few men on each side were killed in
these little forays—killed just as dead as if they had fallen dramatically
in some great battle, although none but the next of kin ever knew
anything about it—and Stuart found out what he was looking for
and sent word back to Lee: three army corps coming over the river,
looks like something big. Stoneman's cavalry went trotting down the
line of the railway, and Slocum led the infantry off southeasterly
toward the two fords over the Rapidan, Ely's and Germanna.

The boys crossed the Rapidan the next night, April 29. April had
brought too much rain, and the river was deep and swirling, black
under the moonlight with flecks of bubbling white foam. As the endless columns came down to the crossings huge fires were lit on each
bank to help the men see where they were going, and the flames put
a ruddy tinge on the dark water. Foot soldiers went slogging across,
waist-deep and more, and a few were swept away and drowned in
the strong current, and cavalry patrols took station in the crossings
to pick up the casualties. On the northern bank soldiers unloaded
the pack mules so that the animals could swim across, infantrymen
carrying the mules' packs and not liking it much. In some outfits the
officers forbade the men to take their pants off at the ford—Rebels
might attack as soon as they got across, and a line of battle couldn't
be formed without pants—but in others the commanders were more
sensible, so the men did not have to spend the rest of the night in wet
clothing. Men who were there remembered that the river was extremely cold, and not everybody had a chance to get around the big

bonfires and dry out. The men and animals came out of the river dripping, of course, so the climb to higher ground on the south side was soon very slippery and muddy for men carrying heavy loads.

All in all, however, it seems that there were more gay shouts and whoops of laughter than curses that night. Some pictorial quality in the scene, with the firelight dancing on the water and the white clouds drifting across the face of the moon and the limitless lines of men coming down over the northern hills, splashing through the water and shaking themselves out on the southern side, seems to have caught the soldiers' fancy. They remembered it long afterward, this crossing of the Rapidan in the April moonlight, and all of these precocious amateur strategists realized that Hooker was getting them safely around the dreaded entrenchments back of Fredericksburg, and everybody was ready to believe in his general, his army's chances, and his own lusty, irrepressible youth. The thickets and dim clearings and shallow ravines back of the Chancellorsville crossroads were still innocent that night. Men remembered that the whippoorwills sang.[14]

Next day was April 30. Slocum pushed his men forward. He was a good man, this Slocum, and from one end of the war to the other the Federals developed few better corps commanders. By noon George Meade had his V Corps at the Chancellorsville clearing, where a ponderous white manor house with tall pillars looked down on the country crossroads. The advance guard chased away a small Rebel outpost, and a bit later the head of Slocum's corps came up, Slocum himself riding in front. Meade rode to meet him, fairly bubbling over with enthusiasm—a rare state for Meade, a saturnine man who was sometimes lifted out of himself by hot fury at human error but rarely by any lighter emotion.

"Hurrah for old Joe!" cried Meade. "We're on Lee's flank and he doesn't know it."[15]

This was only a slight exaggeration. John Sedgwick had pushed his VI Corps across the river just below Fredericksburg, laying his pontoon bridges where Franklin had crossed in December, and he had his soldiers drawn up on the open plain south of the town, looking warlike and menacing, the idea being to make Lee think that a full-dress attack was about to develop. This was nothing but a bluff, and Lee was beginning to see through it. Stuart had warned him that a good many Yankees were crossing the Rapidan, and by nightfall Lee would conclude that Sedgwick was merely trying to annoy him and that the real attack was coming from his left rear.

Nevertheless, there was reason for Meade to feel exultant. This advance to Chancellorsville had already forced the Confederates to withdraw the troops which had been defending United States Ford, and two divisions of the Yankee II Corps were crossing there unopposed. By dusk Hooker would have fully fifty thousand men at Chancellorsville, together with the artillery reserve and a handful of cavalry. The open rear of Lee's field fortress on Marye's Heights lay barely a dozen miles to the east, with only one Rebel division—eighty-five hundred men or thereabouts—standing in the way. Almost equally close, and even less protected, were the main highway and the railway which led from Fredericksburg to Richmond, the life lines of Lee's army. Hooker had done precisely what he had planned to do, and he had done it with remarkable skill.

Meade's effervescence did not last long, however. What he wanted to do, he told Slocum, was to keep moving, take what troops were present and start down the road for Fredericksburg with them, "and we'll get out of this wilderness." But Slocum had a late message from army headquarters at Falmouth. Dan Sickles and his corps had been ordered to Chancellorsville, and Slocum was to make no move until they arrived, which would not be until next day. The army went into bivouac, with Meade slightly crestfallen.

Meade had touched on one cause for unease: they were still in the Wilderness. There was a little open plain about Chancellorsville itself and there were a few stunted farms scattered here and there, but in the main the army was surrounded by a forest which looked literally impenetrable—a mean sort of woodland, its second-growth timber clotted by vines and thorns and tangled underbrush, with boggy little streams leading from nowhere to nowhere, crossed by a few very narrow, inadequate roads. Advantages of numbers and guns could be canceled out if it should come to fighting here. If Hooker proposed to destroy the Rebel army, he had not quite reached the right place for it.

One other reason for doubt was cropping up that night, if anybody had bothered to notice it. Out on the byroads to the south and the west Yankee cavalry detachments were being driven in by hard-riding Confederates, Stuart himself riding at the head of one furious charge down a moonlit lane. These Yankee detachments were being driven in partly because they got confused in the patternless forest roads, but mostly because they were badly outnumbered. In view of the fact that Yankee cavalry was much stronger than Confederate cavalry that spring, this was odd.[16]

Stoneman had crossed the river and had gone riding south as ordered, heading for the remote, unguarded Rebel rear. Stuart had assigned one skimpy brigade to follow him—a detachment so weak it could hardly do more than keep him under observation—and with the bulk of his men had come pelting cross-country to join up with Lee. As a result he was now in shape to ride rings around Hooker's army. Having built up his cavalry so that it could dominate the field, Hooker had sent all of it away except for four regiments, and these were groping blindly against the cordon that Stuart was pulling in around the army.

However, all of that might not mean much. For once in history the Army of the Potomac tonight had the jump on its rival, and spirits were running high: Hooker's spirits, and the spirits of the men, who were laughing and shouting as they chopped firewood and pitched their pup tents in the little clearings and along the margins of the turnpike. Hooker reached the crossroads that evening and promptly issued General Order Number 47, which was read to all the troops at evening parade:

"It is with heart-felt satisfaction that the commanding general announces to the army that the operations of the past three days have determined that our enemy must either ingloriously fly, or come out from behind his defenses and give us battle on our own ground, where certain destruction awaits him."[17]

The soldiers were feeling good, and that was just what they wanted to hear. They believed in themselves again and Joe Hooker was responsible, and if now he said that the enemy was about to be whipped, everybody was ready to take him at his word. Parade lines broke up with men cheering and tossing their caps and knapsacks in the air, the brigade bands began to play, and the army sat around its campfires feeling jubilant, which it had not felt since the early days of the war.[18]

Next day was May Day. It came in with a slow misty rain, dank and chilly under the trees, a thin fog hanging in the narrow roads and the scattered fields. Dan Sickles rode in at the head of his troops, the day turned fair and the sun dried things up, and a little before noon

the army wheeled into thick columns and started out for Fredericksburg.

Three roads led there: river road meandering to the left to follow
the curves of the Rappahannock, turnpike in the center, old plank
road curving around to the right and joining the turnpike halfway to
Fredericksburg. Meade had his three divisions up in front and he
sent two of them along the river road and had George Sykes and his
regulars go along the turnpike. On the right, Slocum started down
the plank road with the XII Corps. The other outfits present were
ordered to stand by.

As the corps commanders understood it, they were to push ahead
until they were out of the Wilderness on open ground. There they
would join hands, with Meade's extreme left touching the river and
uncovering Banks Ford—a matter of some importance, this last, since
it would cut in half the distance from Chancellorsville to Sedgwick's
men. With all of this done, the army would be ready for the big fight.

The divisions on the river road had an uneventful time, but Sykes's
regulars ran into trouble. From Chancellorsville, going east along the
turnpike, the ground rose in a long slope heavily covered with jack
pines and scrub oaks and spiky bushes and cut up by little streams. It
was very bad walking, as the skirmishers who went on ahead soon
discovered. A couple of miles from Chancellorsville this gentle slope
reached a broad crest, where the Wilderness thinned out and the
country began to look more prosperous. Along this crest Sykes's advance guard ran into Rebel skirmishers.

There was a little intermittent firing, and then as the enemy skirmishers faded back they disclosed solid lines of Confederate infantry,
supported here and there by artillery. The guns began to plaster the
road and the wood with shells, and as the regulars struggled through
the underbrush to deploy, the opposition became heavier. Men were
hit, and the firing rolled out in long, echoing volleys, and Sykes realized that because the roads diverged he was in touch neither with the
rest of Meade's corps on his left nor with Slocum's men on his right.
From Slocum's front, as a matter of fact, more firing could be heard,
with a dirty-looking cloud of smoke going up toward the sky. The
Rebels began to assail the flanks of Sykes's line, and he sent word back
to Hooker that he needed help.

Back at Chancellorsville, Hooker had heard the firing and he sent
Couch down the road with Hancock's division to help. When Couch

came up he found Sykes pulling his men back into a better defensive position, the Rebel attack having become quite strong. Couch prepared to bring Hancock's men up, restore contact with Slocum and Meade, and resume the advance. Before he could do much about it, however, new orders came in from Hooker: call everything off and bring everybody back to Chancellorsville.[19]

Couch sent an aide back to protest that Sykes was in no real trouble and that they could soon butt their way through the Rebel line to the open ground where Hooker wanted to go, but it did no good. The aide returned with orders for retreat reiterated. Off to the right and left, Slocum and Meade were bringing back the rest of the troops, Meade storming and demanding, "If he thinks he can't hold the top of the hill, how does he expect to hold the bottom of it?"[20] Glumly Couch swung Hancock's men into line to act as rear guard, and the regulars marched back to Chancellorsville.

He was a cool customer, Couch. Slight, rather frail, a professional soldier who had won much reputation and lost nearly all of his health in the Mexican War, he was a man who had great personal courage. After Hancock's deployment the gunners in a distant Rebel battery saw massed troops on the turnpike and began to throw shells, trying to find the range. Couch turned to his staff and said, "Let us draw their fire," and led his officers up to an open knoll where the gunners could not fail to see them. The trick worked—gunners could seldom resist a chance to shoot at a cluster of mounted officers—and the infantry on the road escaped punishment. As it happened, nobody was hit, although it is written that the staff was not especially enthusiastic about any part of the deal.[21]

By evening the troops were back in the lines they had left that morning, the higher officers very dubious, enlisted men puzzled but not especially disturbed. Couch found Hooker full of reassurance: "It's all right, Couch, I've got Lee just where I want him." Couch said nothing, but made a mental note to the effect that the major general commanding was a beaten man.[22]

Couch may have been right. Hooker was talking too much, too loudly, too confidently—and, as Senator Sumner would have said, too blasphemously. To officers at headquarters he proudly announced: "The Rebel army is now the legitimate property of the Army of the Potomac." A little later he declared: "The enemy is in my power, and God Almighty cannot deprive me of them."[23] Then, descending to business, he dictated a circular order to corps commanders, instructing them to put their lines in a condition of defense, with wagon trains parked in the rear, and he closed with the statement:

"The major general commanding trusts that a suspension in the attack today will embolden the enemy to attack him."

Of all the hopes Joe Hooker ever had, that was the one destined to be the most completely realized.

FOUR

On the Other Side of the River

1. Some of Us Will Not See Another Sunrise

Perhaps Joe Hooker had lost his nerve. He could be debonair under fire, riding unconcerned into the middle of the fighting line, and the soldiers considered him very courageous. But here in the gloomy forest, with responsibility settling down over headquarters like the shades of blackest night, it was a little different. The showdown had come before he was quite ready. He had planned to be out in the open, and the Rebels had hit him ahead of time. There was a soft spot in the man, and the cruel test of war had found it. Now it was Robert E. Lee who was going to say what happened next.

Where do those soft spots come from? Somewhere between West Point and Chancellorsville—a few hundred miles in an air line, an incalculable distance as a man's life goes—there had developed in this man's character a little place that would collapse under pressure. No one had known it was there, Hooker least of all, but it was giving way right now as the moon came up over the forest and the campfires glowed under the trees, while the shooting died away on the picket lines and a misty light lay on the narrow roads.

Tragically enough, the army itself had its own soft spot, a place that might collapse if touched sternly, a soft spot that was part of the army's character just as Hooker's was part of his character. It was different in that its growth and development could be traced exactly. One can see where it began, and extensive casualty lists show what it led to, and the steps in between are quite visible. The army's soft spot was the XI Army Corps, Major General Oliver Otis Howard commanding.

The XI Corps was the Cinderella of the army, the unwanted orphaned child, and it was deeply aware of its own status. It seems to have felt, collectively, like a poor ignored wallflower at a high school dance. The corps contained many German soldiers, known to one and all as Dutchmen, a contemptuous title by which the soldiers expressed the national feeling—that men who talked with a foreign accent just did not need to be taken seriously. It is hardly going too far to say that what happened at Chancellorsville was the price the country paid for its indulgence in that feeling.

The nation had inherited something rich and strange when the German revolutionary movement of 1848 broke up in blood and proscription lists, with the best men of a dozen German states hastening to America. The nation had received these men, but it had never quite known what to make of them. These Germans were deadly serious about words which Americans took blithely for granted, words like liberty and freedom and democracy. They made up a substantial part of the ground which the free-soil men had cultivated in the 1850s, and when war came they had seen the Union cause as their own cause, with freedom for the black man as one of the sure ultimate goals. Their leaders were men who had lost their fortunes and risked their necks, taking up arms for liberty in a land of kings who resisted change, and these leaders called the Germans to the colors as soon as Fort Sumter was bombarded. Even more than the New England troops, these German regiments had welcomed and supported the Emancipation Proclamation. If the anti-slavery cause had an old guard, they perhaps were it.[1]

This old guard was the kernel of the XI Corps. About half of the men in the corps, as it happened, were native Americans; only fifteen of the twenty-six regiments were listed as German, and several of these contained a number of non-Germans.[2] But it was the German regiments which set the tone for the corps. They had brought to it officers with names like Von Steinwehr and Von Gilsa and Buschbeck and Schimmelfennig and Kryzanowski, they had come in with a number of incomparable bands and singing clubs, they had brought in both solid professional soldiers from Europe and a set of fortune hunters combed out of petty ducal courts, and in the end it appears that they had also brought their own tradition of incredible bad luck.

Louis Blenker originally had commanded most of these German regiments. He was out of the army now, dying of an accidental hurt received in a fall of his horse, but early in 1862 he had had a great name. He was a revolutionist in exile, a man who had led the men of Hesse-Darmstadt against Prussian troops and who had had to fly for his life when the revolution of 1848 was suppressed. A resident of New York when the Civil War came, he had raised the 8th New York, one of the first of the German regiments, and he and it had fought well at First Bull Run. Early in 1862 McClellan had given him a division composed of three brigades of Germans from the East and Midwest.[3] The Germans' woes had begun shortly afterward.

In the spring of 1862 this division was posted in Virginia, spraddled out from near Manassas to the edge of Alexandria. Just at that time the administration was giving John Charles Frémont an army command in western Virginia. Frémont was the unspotted hero of the abolitionists, and it seemed advisable to give him abolitionist troops whenever possible, so when he needed reinforcements McClellan was ordered to detach Blenker's Germans and send them to him.

It was a long hike up over the Bull Run Mountains and the Blue Ridge, across the Shenandoah Valley and on to Frémont's headquarters at Petersburg, deep in the Alleghenies, and American soldiers have rarely had a more miserable time than these troops of Blenker's had on what was supposed to be a perfectly routine cross-country move.

The first trouble was that through some lapse in paper work the division was sent out lacking the most elementary kind of equipment, from shelter tents (of which they had none at all) to overcoats, blankets, shoes, and rations. The next trouble was that the division got lost. The War Department forgot all about it. The division had moved out from under McClellan's control, but it had not yet come under Frémont's, and apparently no one gave Blenker a decent map. So the Germans went floundering cross-country through cold spring rains, losing sick men and stragglers wholesale, and leaving the country smoldering with angry complaints from the citizenry, who alleged that homes and barns and corncribs were being looted by ragged Germans who seemed not to have been fed for generations. On top of all other troubles, the division quartermasters had no money to use when they went out to buy provisions, so they simply requisitioned what they needed. They spoke poor English and they acted hastily, and anyway, the inhabitants were secessionists and objected to the whole process on principle. The Germans got the name of being the worst thieves and looters unhung. Crossing the Shenandoah, it seemed characteristic that some inexpert subaltern managed to swamp a ferryboat, and forty men were drowned.

Eventually the authorities realized that they had lost a division of troops, and Major General William S. Rosecrans was sent out to find the Germans and bring them in. He did so (after hunting around for several days), his eyes popping out of his knobby red face as he took a look at this lost command. Blenker's men, he reported to Stanton, "were short of provisions, forage, horseshoes and horseshoe nails, clothing, shoes, stockings, picket ropes and ammunition, without tents or shelters, and without ambulances or medicines for any important work." They were also practically out of horses, and the men had not been paid since December. All things considered, said Rosecrans, it was "not much wonder they stole and robbed."[4]

All in all, it took the division six weeks to get up from Alexandria and join Frémont's troops. The union was not happy. Frémont's native American regiments were discontented. Yankee soldiers were sniffing the air and reporting, "The air around here was found to be rather Dutchy," and Ohio soldiers objected to the presence of so many foreigners on Frémont's staff. It seems that these foreign officers rode their horses with the English rising seat, whereas the Middle Western boys believed that a man ought to get on his horse and go jogging along without any fancy tricks of equitation. Sentries coming to salute when these bedizened aides rode by were presently discovered to be saying something as they saluted. Upon investigation it was found that they were repeating: "Don't rise for me, sir," a gag which pleased everyone but the aides.[5]

Frémont's mountain campaign was less than a success. It almost duplicated, as a matter of fact, the experience Blenker's division had already had, with rations running out and soldiers collapsing from hunger, fatigue, and sickness. By the end of May fewer than six thousand of Blenker's original ten thousand were present for duty, Frémont's medical director was demanding "in the name of humanity" that something be done to restore the soldiers' health, and Carl Schurz was warning Lincoln that the whole outfit was half starved "and literally unable to fight."[6]

Things improved after Frémont left. His place was taken by Franz Sigel, another revolutionist in exile—little more of a soldier, unfortunately, than Frémont himself, but a good deal more of a man. When he took over the command the Germans were proud, and "I fights mit Sigel" became a catch phrase all across the North. When Sigel's command was finally denominated the XI Corps of the Army of the Potomac, the fact that Sigel led it helped to fix it, in the army's eyes, as a German command.

The rest of the army did not welcome this XI Corps. The corps had never licked anybody under Frémont and it had done little better under Sigel; it got to Falmouth too late to fight at Fredericksburg, and its camp there happened to be isolated from the camps of the other corps. Anyway, the soldiers were Dutchmen, or at least a good many of them were, and their broken-English dialect struck the other soldiers as comic.

When the spring of 1863 came, Sigel left. After Hooker he was the ranking general in the army. His corps was the smallest of the lot, and Sigel thought that in simple justice to himself it ought to be enlarged. Halleck had an anti-foreign bias and would do no favors for Sigel, who then asked to be relieved and saw that one request granted immediately. General Howard was also a man with a lot of seniority, and he had been complaining because Sickles, his junior, had been given a corps while he, Howard, still led a mere division. Sigel's departure offered a chance to pacify Howard, and he got the XI Corps,[7] which decided quite soon that it did not like him very much.

Howard was not the type to make soldiers warm up to him quickly. He addressed them as "my men," which did not go over any better in the 1860s than it would today, and he was a little too widely known as the Christian soldier, a major general who went to hospitals on Sundays to distribute baskets of fruit, which were welcomed, and religious tracts, which regrettably were not. This did not add to his popularity. His Germans were mostly freethinkers with a strong anti-clerical tradition, and his native Americans were inclined to be jocose about excessive piety. There were contradictions in the America of that generation, with deep religious feeling going hand in hand with rough skepticism, and these two warring traits had to be embodied in this one unhappy army corps. In addition, Howard brought in a pair of new generals, Charles Devens and Francis Barlow, who were ferocious disciplinarians and who displaced generals the soldiers liked. Howard wrote later that "I was not at first getting the earnest and loyal support of the entire command."[8]

So it was the soft spot, this army corps. It had a tradition of bad luck and defeat, it was unhappy with itself and with its leadership, and, worst and most dangerous of all, it was an outcast from the spirit and affection of the army.[9]

In this reaction the army simply reflected national sentiment. The Civil War had come to a nation which was suspicious of its immigrants. Its traditions and habits of thought still deified the simple, uncrowded, slow-moving society of an earlier day. In its adolescence the country was beginning to look back fondly to a lost golden age when there had been no problems that hard work and plain living would not solve. Fantastic growth and development were taking place, the old traditions were outdated, the new arrivals were part of this growth, and somehow the incomprehensible, unwelcome changes seemed to be their fault.

So men of foreign birth were, in plain fact, second-class citizens, and the men of the XI Corps wore the uniform of a country which did not like them. Hardly half a dozen years had passed since the Know-Nothings had been a powerful political party, and a country which hated foreigners almost as much as Negroes was now using the one to enforce freedom for the other and was suffering from emotional indigestion as a result. It might yet find that a fight to end slavery would also, in the end, be a fight to improve the lot of the immigrant, and that was something it had not counted on.

The way Hooker had his army lined up on the morning of May 2, it seemed unlikely that the XI Corps would have much to do, which was perhaps a measure of the general feeling that the men were something less than first-class troops.

The left end of Hooker's line ran along a wooded ridge from the Rappahannock to a clearing a few hundred yards north of Chancellorsville and was held by Meade and his V Corps. Next to Meade, covering the turnpike from Fredericksburg and the ground on either side of it, stood Hancock's division of the II Corps. On Hancock's right, bulging out in a big horseshoe curve to cover the plateau of Fairview Cemetery, a lonely country burying ground a few rods southwest of the Chancellorsville mansion, Slocum's XII Corps was dug in, with guns massed in the rear. Just west of this, holding a line that also bulged out to the south to take advantage of the elevated fields of Hazel Grove farm, were two divisions of Sickles's III Corps. On Sickles's right, running straight west along the turnpike for more than a mile, was the line of the XI Corps.

Hooker apparently was waiting for the Rebels to attack him. If they did they would be coming along the turnpike from Fredericksburg and they would hit either Hancock's men or Slocum's, shock troops, well entrenched, men who could be counted on. If they swung off to the north they would strike Meade's corps, equally reliable and occupying a practically impregnable position. Howard's men held the sector farthest removed from any possible point of attack, and to get at them Lee would have to march squarely across Hooker's front—a fatal maneuver, as any student of Austerlitz could testify. Anyway, the woods and underbrush around Howard's front were so thick and tangled that a regular line of battle could not get through. The Dutchmen might stack their arms and butcher their cattle and let their excellent bands play, while the real army of the Potomac took care of the fighting.

The day came in warm and sunny, and the army held its lines and waited. It was hard to know just what was going on. The Wilderness was bewilderingly dense, and Jeb Stuart's men were knocking Hooker's inadequate cavalry patrols back into camp every time they stuck their horses' noses out. In front of Hancock and Slocum there was a good deal of firing. Rebel patrols kept prowling forward, batteries sprang to life here and there, and there was a lot of skirmishing and sniping going on. Hancock's advanced skirmish line, commanded by the youthful Nelson Miles who had just recovered from the throat wound received at Fredericksburg, took a good deal of punishment. The skirmish line held and there was no attack, but from headquarters it seemed that the Rebels were tapping for soft spots, looking for a good place to strike.

Hooker toured his lines that morning, looking at trenches and rifle pits and murmuring: "How strong! How strong!" The soldiers sprang to their feet when they saw him, the handsome general with his handsome mounted staff riding at his heels, headquarters flag fluttering in the May sunlight, and a tremendous cheer rolled up from the lanes and clearings. Here was Hooker, and he had saved these men from the head-on assault on the evil Fredericksburg lines, he

had given them health and self-confidence again, he had promised
that Lee's army would be destroyed, and the very look of him was
the look of hope. So this morning, for the last time in its history, the
Army of the Potomac sent up a wild cheer of genuine affection and
enthusiasm for its commanding officer.[10]

Back to headquarters went Hooker, to wait for destiny on the pil-
lared veranda of the Chancellorsville house; and out in front Dan
Sickles saw what he believed to be a dazzling opportunity beckoning
from beyond the cedars.

Looking off to the south, Sickles's men had been getting glimpses of
Rebels in motion—a big column, with guns and wagons and infantry
trudging through the woods, apparently heading south.[11] The forest
was thick and open vistas were few, but by noon it was clear that
something big was under way and the high command took thought.
It was just possible that Lee did have some notion of circling
around and hitting the army's right, and Hooker sent a note to Howard suggesting that he consider the possibility of being flanked.

But this idea soon evaporated. There were many wagons in the
line of march—Stonewall Jackson's ammunition train and ambulances, infinitely ominous if anyone had known—and it looked as if
what Sickles's men saw might be Lee's army in full retreat. To be sure,
intermittent firing was still taking place in front of Slocum and Hancock, but that was probably just rear-guard stuff. Lee was flying lest
destruction overtake him, just as Hooker had predicted. Why should
not Hooker's good friend Dan Sickles take a couple of divisions, lunge
forward through the Wilderness, and smite this retreating column to
make victory complete?

Hooker struggled against this idea only briefly. It was what he
wanted to believe. Jubilantly he gave Sickles his orders. (Couch,
still glum, permitted himself to wonder: If the enemy really is in retreat, why do we pursue with only a small part of our force?)[12]

Sickles's soldiers had been having a quiet day of it so far. They
had lounged under the trees, smoked, joked, and speculated about
what was going to happen next. If a man put his ear to the ground
he could hear the rumble of wheels and the tramp of many feet, and
this seemed to jibe with the rumor that the Rebels were running away.
Rookies, it was noticed, swallowed the rumor whole and rejoiced.
Old-timers were more skeptical and said they could not quite see Lee
and Jackson retreating without a fight. But while they speculated or-

ders arrived, and Birney's and Whipple's divisions formed column and went south across the Hazel Grove plateau.[13]

Going in front as an advanced skirmish line was Colonel Hiram Berdan's brigade, the 1st and 2nd regiments of U. S. Sharpshooters, one of the most unusual outfits in the army. In the summer of 1861 Colonel Berdan had got permission to enlist these two regiments, with eligibility restricted to men who, at two hundred yards range, could put ten consecutive bullets inside a ten-inch circle. Solid companies had been enlisted from the different states—four from New York, four from Michigan, three from Vermont, and so on—and the men had been given special physical training not unlike that given commando or ranger battalions in more recent times. After a struggle Berdan got them equipped with breech-loading Sharps rifles. The army chief of ordnance had wanted to give them smoothbores, old Winfield Scott had warned Berdan that "breechloaders would spoil his command," and standard army equipment for a sharpshooter was a huge muzzle-loader with ponderous telescope attached, the whole business weighing around thirty pounds and fit to be fired only from a fixed rest. It seems that Lincoln himself finally decided matters in Berdan's favor, and with their breechloaders and their skill as marksmen the two regiments had won fame in both armies. Usually the different companies were detailed for temporary duty with different divisions, but today the brigade was fighting as a unit, a very snappy-looking unit, the men wearing dark green uniforms instead of the regular blue, with plumed hats and leather leggings and fancy calfskin knapsacks, a *corps d'élite* and fully aware of it.[14]

The sharpshooters went forward through dense thickets and over a soggy little creek, up the side of a ravine and through more thickets, until at last they reached open ground by an old iron foundry, where they got into a hot fight with Rebel infantry. Before long the Rebels wheeled up some guns and held the sharpshooters off, but Berdan took his men around a little hollow and captured two or three hundred of the Confederate infantrymen, neatly uniformed, husky-looking men from the 23rd Georgia, who remarked to their captors that they had come over to "help eat them eight-day rations."[15] The advance came to a halt. Sickles threw his divisions into line of battle and sent back word that he was among the enemy's trains and could do wonders if he were just reinforced.

This was what Hooker wanted to hear. Sickles was applauded and told to keep it up, Slocum was ordered to put some of his men in on Sickles's left, and from the right Howard was told to send Sickles a brigade. Such cavalry as Hooker had with him trotted forward to the Hazel Grove clearing so that it could ride out and slash fugitive Rebels as soon as the infantry broke through.

Cavalry got to the clearing, dismounted, and waited for orders. Past them came the Georgia prisoners, heading for the rear under escort, and the troopers jeered: "We'll have every mother's son of you before we go away." One stooped, elderly Confederate looked up sourly and replied: "You'll catch hell before night." Another was more specific: "You think you've done a big thing just now, but you wait until Jackson gets around on your right."[16]

Major generals do not often pay much attention to what angry prisoners say when they are kidded, and these warnings were ignored. It was more pleasant to listen to Sickles, who was among the enemy's trains. Headquarters was happy, the whole army was happy—except for the despised Dutchmen of the XI Corps, who held the right in lonely isolation and who as the day wore on began to be very nervous indeed.

The corps had had a quiet morning and stacked arms at noon to eat a leisurely dinner. Then a feeling of unease developed, sifting up from the lower ranks. Pickets went forward, south of the turnpike which formed the line of the corps, and they sent back disturbing reports: Rebel cavalry was active, parties of Rebel infantry were moving behind it, lots and lots of Rebels were moving over toward the right. West Pointers at corps headquarters wagged their heads and spoke of a rolling reconnaissance. Lower ranks knew nothing of such fancy terms but did know that something was developing and that it did not in the least look like a retreat.

The Dutchmen that afternoon discovered several things overlooked by higher authority. One was that a large part of the Rebel army was coming in closer and closer, giving every indication that it was looking for a fight rather than running away from one. Another was that the advance of Sickles had left the XI Corps completely isolated, with a gap of more than a mile separating it from the rest of the army. A third was that when Howard sent Barlow's brigade off to help Sickles pursue the fleeing Rebels he took away the corps' only reserve. These facts were very likely to add up to a full-fledged military disaster, and some of the soldiers were well aware of it.

Their situation invited a catastrophe. The corps was spread out in a thin line that was more than a mile long but for the most part was only two ranks deep. It faced south, and if the attack came from that direction everything would be fine, but if the attack should come from the west or from northwest there would be no way on earth to keep the corps from being completely wrecked. As the afternoon passed and evening approached it became more and more obvious that the Confederates were going to attack from west and northwest in overwhelming strength, but the soldiers who detected this could not make anybody hear them when they tried to tell about it. Of all the tragic experiences which blunders in high places inflicted on the Army of the Potomac, the one which took place on this evening of May 2 was the most nightmarish.

Eastern end of the corps line, the end that had meshed with Sickles's line before that ardent man went forward to pursue distinction in the bogs south of Hazel Grove, lay in fairly open ground, with Dowdall's Tavern and its yard south of the turnpike and the cleared space around the Wilderness Church and the Hawkins farm extending for half a mile or so on the north side. There was a low ridge crossing the road just here, and corps artillery had been stacked up north of the highway. The tavern had been designated a strong point and was set off by gun emplacements and rifle pits, most of which faced due south.

About the rest of the corps line there was nothing remarkable. It ran west along the road through dense woods, and after a while it simply came to an end. At the place where it ended two guns had been planted in the middle of the road. North of them, at right angles to the rest of the line, two regiments had been posted, facing west. They had been formed in one rank, the men three feet apart—a heavy skirmish line rather than a line of battle—and in front of them was a flimsy slashing of brush and saplings. Neither Hooker, Howard, nor anyone else could possibly have supposed that that skirmish line would be a real defense against a flank attack, but nobody supposed that there would be a flank attack—nobody, that is, except a considerable number of men of no especial rank or distinction, who as evening approached were quite certain that there was going to be hell to pay before the sun went down.

By ill chance many of these belonged to the brigade commanded by Brigadier General Nathaniel C. McLean, a good soldier recently demoted from divisional command to make room for Brigadier General Charles Devens. Devens came from Boston, and he seems to have felt that he had been brought into this second-rate Dutch corps to bring the men up to snuff. As a result he tended to be very stiff and military with his subordinates—the more so, perhaps, when those dealings took place via General McLean, between whom and Devens the situation was slightly delicate.

At any rate, Devens commanded the western end of the corps line, and it was McLean's men who first discovered that the Rebels were about to attack. Colonel Lee of the 55th Ohio had got so many reports of Confederate masses moving off to the right that he went to see McLean, who promptly took him to Devens. Devens pooh-poohed at him, but Lee stuck to his story, insisting that big trouble was coming down the wind, whereupon Devens loftily remarked that Western colonels were more scared than hurt. McLean and Lee went away, and presently Colonel Richardson of the 25th Ohio appeared, saying that his scouts had seen huge masses of Rebel infantry deploying not half a mile from the right and rear of the corps. McLean took him to Devens, who said icily: "I guess Colonel Richardson is somewhat scared; you had better order him to his regiment." McLean obeyed orders and Richardson returned to his regiment, called in his company officers, and told them to have the men eat supper early. While he was doing that, McLean took Lieutenant Colonel Friend of the 75th Ohio to Devens with a duplicate of Richardson's story. Devens unbent just a trifle and explained that corps headquarters, which would surely know if a flank attack were in the making, had sent him no alert. As a result, Friend hurried off to corps headquarters, where Howard's aides laughed at him and begged him not to bring on a panic.[17]

The brigade at the western knuckle of the line was commanded by Colonel Leopold von Gilsa, sometime major in the Prussian Army and a veteran of the Schleswig-Holstein war. Von Gilsa knew what was up, and when he received a note from his picket line saying that the enemy was massing, begging, "For God's sake, make dispositions to receive him!" he went to Howard with it. Howard explained that the forest west of Von Gilsa was so thick that no line of battle could ever get through it. Von Gilsa unhappily returned to his lines just as Leatherbreeches came riding over from Carl Schurz's division.

Leatherbreeches was a character. He was Captain Hubert Dilger, former officer in the Baden Mounted Artillery, who had taken leave and come to America when the Civil War broke out and who was now skipper of Battery I, 1st Ohio Artillery, in Schurz's division. He was a scientific gunner and a man of fantastic daring, and he was known as Leatherbreeches because of a pair of doeskin pants he liked to wear. At this moment he was out to do a bit of scouting. Schurz, the one non-professional soldier among all the higher brass in the XI Corps, had taken the alarm along with Von Gilsa and McLean and was quietly rearranging some of his men in the clearing around Wilderness Church so that they could fight facing west if they had to. He had told Dilger to be ready to meet an attack from the rear, and Dilger had got his horse and gone out to look things over for himself.

Von Gilsa warned him not to go west on the turnpike beyond the picket lines or he would be captured. But Dilger was not going to take anybody's word for anything, and he rode on out of sight—rode for nearly a mile, ran smack into a battle line of Rebel infantry, and very nearly met the fate Von Gilsa had predicted. He galloped madly north, being cut off from the XI Corps lines, and after a long detour that took him nearly over to the Rapidan he got up to the Chancellorsville crossroads, where he went at once to Hooker's headquarters to tell what he had seen. He was received there by a long-legged cavalry major, a very superior person who did not see why the commanding general's people should bother with mere artillery captains, especially those who spoke with a strong German accent. The major told Dilger to trot along and peddle his yarn in his own corps, where doubtless there would be someone who could find time to listen.

So Dilger went next to Howard's headquarters. There it was made clear to him that corps command did not approve of artillery captains going off on unauthorized scouting trips, and it was explained that since the Rebel army was in full retreat, with Howard leading Barlow's brigade off to join in the pursuit, Dilger must have things all mixed up. Dilger went back to his battery, where he told his men not to take the horses to water but to keep them handy—they might have to move the guns fast at any moment.[18]

On the picket line the men were more and more uneasy. They could see but a few yards in the bushes and vines and thick saplings, but the Confederate skirmishers were very close now and there was a good deal of shooting. Some oddity in the acoustics kept these shots from being heard by any generals, but the lower echelons were not fooled. Three of McLean's colonels rode out to compare notes with Von Gilsa, and when they came back Colonel Reily called his 75th Ohio together and said: "Some of us will not see another sunrise. If there is a man in the ranks who is not ready to die for his country, let him come to me and I will give him a pass to go to the rear, for I want no half-hearted, unwilling soldiers or cowards in the ranks tonight."[19]

The sun was getting low. Far away beyond the woods to the south there was a muffled sound of musketry as Sickles's and Slocum's men fought a Confederate rear guard. Most of the private soldiers in the XI Corps, knowing that all alarms had been passed on to headquarters, assumed that the generals must know what they were doing, and tried to relax. Some regiments stacked arms and began to eat supper, sitting on their knapsacks in rear of the rifle pits. Behind the lines a few details were butchering cattle. One of the German bands was playing "The Girl I Left Behind Me," and a tune called "Come Out of the Wilderness." A private in Reily's 75th Ohio sauntered off to a spring in the wood and dipped his tin cup in the water for a drink. An officer in the 25th Ohio lay on his side in a farmyard just back of the front line, holding the end of his reins while his horse cropped the grass.

There was a ripple of laughter and cheering from the soldiers in the shallow trench along the road, and the officer sat up to see what was going on. Into a little clearing in front of the trench innumerable deer had suddenly emerged from the wood to the west and were galloping madly toward the east, while the soldiers waved their hats and whooped. Then as the deer scampered off into the underbrush the quiet of the spring evening caved in with a tremendous crash.[20]

Out of the forest in the west there came a handful of rifleshots, then the wild weird falsetto of the Rebel yell, followed by great rolling volleys of musketry. A shell exploded against a tree beside the spring where the Ohio private was getting his drink, and he dropped his cup and ran for his regiment. Down the road two Confederate cannon suddenly wheeled into view and fired, and a solid shot crashed through the branches over the head of the officer who had sat up to look at the deer. Another shot slammed into a farmhouse beside which General Devens was lying on the grass taking his ease—he had bruised his leg the day before and it hurt him to stand—and the general belatedly realized that his subordinates had known what they were talking about. And Von Gilsa's skirmish line of two German regiments looked up to see all of the Rebels in the world shouldering their way through the tangle, firing their rifles and yelling like fiends, their line extending far beyond vision to right and left. The Germans got off a few hasty shots and then the flood rolled over them.

The men on the road were completely helpless. They spun about, trying to change position so they could at least face this onslaught, and were knocked out of the way before they could get started. The two guns at the knuckle were captured, and jubilant Confederates swung them around and began to fire down the packed roadway. Colonel Lee galloped to General Devens and begged him to order a change of front to the west. Devens, still trying to figure out what was happening, and perhaps also hoping that he would get some sort of word from corps headquarters, told him: "Not yet." Then the tide swept in, and the road was full of running men. Colonel Reily got his 75th Ohio swung around in the underbrush without waiting for orders and managed to hold out for ten minutes, fighting furiously. He was killed, the light of tomorrow's sunrise guttering out quickly, and 150 of his men were shot down, and then the 75th folded up and ran like all the others.[21]

In a matter of minutes Devens's entire division had collapsed. There was nothing else it could have done, for Stonewall Jackson had hit it with the full power of twenty-eight thousand men, attacking in a line more than a mile wide and four divisions deep, his men crashing through the woodland that was supposed to be impassable by any line of battle, getting their uniforms ripped completely off at times by thorns and broken branches, but coming on regardless. Devens's men had not a chance in the world. The fighting came in from their right and rear. McLean had to put his men on the opposite side of their breastworks, and Colonel Lee wrote dryly after the battle that "a rifle pit is useless when the enemy is on the same side and in rear of your line."[22] There was nothing the men could do but run.

So a confused, yelling, stumbling, running horde of men and horses was jammed in the turnpike, dense woods on either side, Rebel cannon slashing through the mass with shrapnel and canister. Here and there, in the forest, regiments and parts of regiments tried to make a stand, but it was hopeless. Jackson's men beat them down and swept over them, their battle line so wide that any strong point could be surrounded and taken in no time. Brigade and regimental organizations were utterly lost. Fragments of McLean's Ohio regiments were mixed together, trying in vain to put up a fight, but fugitives from the broken line to the west plowed through them, and then a great gust of Confederate rifle fire blew them back toward Chancellorsville. Some of the fugitives drew knives and cut their knapsack straps as they ran, not taking time to stop and unbuckle them. It was noticed, though, that most of the men hung onto their rifles, and many individuals paused in the rout now and then to fire at their pursuers.[23]

The disorganized mass rolled east and came presently to the open ground around the Hawkins farm and the Wilderness Church. Here Schurz had posted a few German regiments facing west, and for twenty minutes they put up a good fight, while Leatherbreeches wheeled his guns into line and swept the Rebels off the turnpike. But the odds were too great. The line was outflanked at both ends and attacked with overpowering numbers from in front, and Schurz's Dutchmen finally had to go back like everybody else. Dilger found himself fighting alone, his infantry supports gone, and the Rebels were creeping in on him through ravines and thickets. He stayed there, firing double-shotted canister, until the enemy were almost among his guns, then limbered up to leave. As the guns began to move, three of the six horses attached to one piece were shot. Dilger tried furiously to drive the gun away with three dead horses dragging in the harness, found that it was impossible, and at last withdrew without it.[24]

Last stand of the corps was made by the brigade of Adolph Buschbeck, another Prussian-trained soldier, who took over some inadequate rifle pits dug earlier in the day by the departed Barlow. Dilger paused here to help, elements of some of the retreating regiments tried to rally, and once more the Confederate tide was checked for a time. The sun went down, a vast cloud of smoke thickened the twilight, and there was an unceasing uproar. The Rebels paused to rearrange their lines slightly—they had got nearly as mixed up by all this Wilderness fighting as the Federals themselves—and at last they came on again, Buschbeck's line broke, and the rear guard withdrew toward Chancellorsville.

There was little disorder to this part of the retreat. Most of Buschbeck's men went back in regular columns, and Dilger stayed in the road as rear guard. The road was narrow and he could use but one gun, so he sent the others back, telling the men to report to the first artillery officer they found. Dilger himself stayed with his one gun, firing it like a pocket pistol—a couple of shots down the road, limber up and go back a hundred yards, unlimber again and fire some more: one man and one gun, standing off the advance of Stonewall Jackson. A nucleus of infantry gathered around him with some higher officers. Howard had come galloping madly back from the excursion south of Hazel Grove, the staff of a flag tucked under the stump of his amputated right arm. If there was anything that plain personal bravery could do to stem the rout, Howard was going to do it.[25]

Now they were going back across the big gap that had been created by the advance of Sickles's men, and there was no help in sight. For some odd reason the racket created by Jackson's assault had not penetrated far. Back at headquarters, Hooker had been standing on the veranda, surrounded by his staff, while his right wing was folding up, and nobody had known anything about it. Finally some echo of the firing reached the Chancellorsville house and an aide stepped out into the road to see what he could see. He got out there just in time to meet a tumult of horses without riders, men without officers, wildly bouncing wagons and guns, coming directly at him. He had time to yell, "My God—here they come!" and then the fugitives went streaming past headquarters, and Hooker vaulted into the saddle and went tearing forward to see what could be done.

Frantically Hooker ordered forward Hiram Berry's division—his own division in the old days, left in reserve when Sickles made his advance—and he rode forward with it, telling the men: "Receive 'em on your bayonets! Receive 'em on your bayonets!"[26] Someone was collecting cannon and posting them in a long line by Fairview Cemetery, facing west. Full night came down, and the moon came out, and the smoke and the noise rolled up over the thickets and the white narrow roadways.

The open clearing by Hazel Grove was another place which the first noise of battle failed to reach. Cavalry lounged at ease there, waiting for the order to go down and cut up Rebel wagon trains. With them were three or four batteries of artillery, likewise at ease, and a collection of ambulances, ordnance wagons, battery forges, and odds and ends of the rear echelon. Up to the 8th Pennsylvania Cavalry rode a courier, and to its skipper, Major Pennock Huey, he gave a message: General Howard was over by the Wilderness Church somewhere and he wanted some cavalry. There was no urgency to the message, no inkling that catastrophe had descended. Major Huey broke up his poker game, got his men on their horses, and took his regiment down a narrow woods lane in column of twos, sabers all in scabbards, the men talking casually of this and that.

A dozen yards from the turnpike the major suddenly realized that something had gone very wrong. He had barely time to order his men to draw their sabers and move at a gallop. Out into the turnpike came the cavalry, crashing squarely into the middle of Confederate General Robert Rodes's division of infantry. There was a wild confused melee, with nobody knowing what was happening, Rebels as surprised as Federals, troopers slashing with the sabers and taking bullets in return. A good many saddles were emptied, and Huey's survivors finally came drifting back to the Chancellorsville clearing, their mission unaccomplished.[27]

This was in some ways the least significant incident of a night filled with blunders and things gone wrong, and yet it may have been the most important thing done by Union troops that evening. For the Confederates, pausing to straighten out their lines before resuming the advance, got the impression that Yankee cavalry was on the alert and could be expected to make sporadic assaults, and the advance guard grew extremely wary whenever unidentified horsemen loomed up in the uncertain moonlight. And just a little bit later, when Stonewall Jackson and his staff came riding in from a scouting mission ahead of the lines, an overeager North Carolina infantry regiment fired a volley that knocked Jackson out of the saddle with a wound that was to take his life.

2. Hell Isn't Half a Mile Off

The explosion that wrecked the Dutchmen left Sickles's men isolated. They had heard little or nothing of all the firing in their rear, and when darkness came down in the dense thickets around the ironworks they had supposed that everything was going as it should. Sickles himself was skeptical when he first got the news about what had happened to Howard. Convinced at last, he pulled his men back to Hazel Grove, with Berdan's sharpshooters forming the rear guard, sniping at Rebel patrols which moved forward to maintain contact. The sharpshooters were interested mostly in the exploits of one of their chaplains, the Reverend Lorenzo Barber of the second regiment, who had taken one of the old-fashioned telescopic-sight rifles and had gone out on the skirmish line, where legend magnified his exploits prodigiously, leading to the assertion that he had shot Rebels out of trees a mile away. From that time on, it is recorded, Chaplain Barber always had a crowd when he held services. ."The chaplain practices what he preaches," said one soldier. "He tells us what we should do, and goes with us to the very front to help us in battle."[1]

Back in Hazel Grove, the fifteen thousand men Sickles had with him began to realize that their situation was potentially serious. Between them and the rest of the army there seemed to be a large number of Confederates. The moon was high, the sky was cloudless, and there was a ghostly light in the roads and clearings, with acrid layers of smoke drifting about like an evil fog, but under the trees the night was black as ink, and nobody's sense of direction seemed to mean anything in this tangled woods country. Most of the men had got wet wading creeks and swamps, and the night had turned chilly. Near Chancellorsville and the turnpike the night pulsed and glowed with intermittent gunfire. Hooker had put thirty-six guns in line by the little cemetery, and the gunners looked out over a land of hazy moonlight and deceptive shadows and fired whenever they believed that they saw movement.[2]

Sickles felt that he was in a desperate position, and he prepared to have his men fight their way back inside the Union lines. In the queer twilight about the Hazel Grove clearing he tried to form an assaulting column, with confused officers getting the men headed in the general direction of Chancellorsville, and he sent couriers flying down the dark woods roads to notify Hooker and Slocum. While he was getting his men lined up, an advancing Rebel patrol came into the clearing from the south, and the darkness all around twinkled and sparkled with rifle fire, stampeding all of the wagons and camp followers into wild flight back toward the Rappahannock and safety. The batteries which had been parked in the clearing swung into position and knocked the Confederates back into their own lines—a little exploit which the imaginative cavalryman, General Alfred Pleasonton, later magnified into a great save-the-Union repulse of Stonewall Jackson's entire corps.[3]

Back by Fairview Cemetery the gunners were alert. A few hundred yards west of them Berry's division and four or five thousand unpanicked survivors of the XI Corps had formed a line across the turnpike, and when the gunners fired at the Rebels their shell passed low over this line. That unnerved the infantry and now and then killed a few of them, since the shell fuses and propellants of that era were slightly erratic, but there was no help for it. The gunners fired at anything that looked like a target and opened a tremendous cannonade once when they saw a shadowy mass of Rebel infantry on the moonlit highway. The gunfire almost destroyed the party which was carrying the wounded Stonewall Jackson to the rear, did wound General A. P. Hill, and disrupted the formation of a division which he was preparing for a new assault.[4]

The Confederates had not yet lost sight of the fact that their big hope that night was to keep moving. Their lines were nearly as disorganized by victory as the Federal lines were by defeat, there were more Yankees than Rebels around Chancellorsville, and if the Yankees ever got properly reorganized the situation could easily be reversed. Jackson had the one great virtue of an aggressive soldier: he believed that no victory was complete as long as a single enemy was on his feet and breathing. When he was shot down he was trying to find a way to slide his troops to the northward, past the Chancellorsville clearing, and cut the Yankees off from their line of supply and retreat over the Rappahannock. On paper it is hard to see how he could have done it, since Hooker had an unused army corps in the vicinity, but in all that Wilderness nobody but Jackson really knew what the chances were that night, and if the man had not been shot he might just possibly have done what he wanted to do. In any case, the Rebels had not yet given up for the night.

Around the Chancellorsville house there was the utmost confusion. The clearing was a wild jamboree of stragglers, riderless horses, advancing troops, and galloping couriers, fragments of regiments trying to rally, wagons and pack mules going at the dead run down the roads and across the fields. Huge fires were burning in the woods, stretcher parties were coming and going, and here and there brass bands were industriously making music to restore the spirits of defeated men. Shells exploded overhead, the blast of the massed guns by the cemetery lit the sky like recurrent sheet lightning, and the fringes of the woods broke out with little pin points of flame as skirmishers and pickets fired into the darkness. There was an unending racket, and most of the time the low-hanging smoke blotted out the moonlight.[5]

In all of this seething confusion Sickles's couriers went astray, and his intention to fight his way back into the lines was known to no one. In addition, Sickles did not know that there was a solid Federal battle line drawn up across the turnpike and angling off through the woods to the south.[6] Men could see very little in that intermittent smoking moonlight, and what they could see was not reliable. Everybody was nervous, and nobody knew where anybody else was or what was apt to happen next.

In spite of everything, Sickles got his men moving at last and they went forward into the blind second-growth jungle, moving north to get to the turnpike. Sickles had three regiments in front—1st New York, 3rd Michigan, and 37th New York—and these advanced "by the right of companies," each company going in its own column of twos, a dozen yards or more separating each column from its neighbors. From the rear, divisional officers sent forward warnings to incline to the right—the columns were drifting to the left; they'd get into Howard's old lines if they weren't careful—and the attack became a blind, aimless drift, pressed forward by sheer weight of numbers.[7]

In the darkness the men heard voices, sentries challenged, the shadowy outline of earthworks came into view. There were a few shots from skirmishers, then a great sheet of flame lit up the jammed woodland and dropped a choking cloud of smoke, and the company columns ran and stumbled and collided with trees and with each other, trying to get up into line. A Michigan soldier recalled: "Some commence to fire, others follow suit, and all blaze away, not knowing what at, and all seems to be one vast square of fire. All begin to yell and cheer, some go forward, some to the right and others to the left." On the left the men ran into a Confederate entrenchment behind which alert Rebels were waiting, and there was blind hand-to-hand fighting in the darkness. A Pennsylvania private remembered the "awful grandeur" of this attack, and recalled "the demoniac yells of the Rebel forces—the flash of invisible guns marking the line of the enemy's defenses through the darkness—the gleaming of glittering bayonets in the pale moonlight."[8]

On the right the advancing Federals bumped into a line of Slocum's soldiers who thought the Rebels were charging them, and there was a desperate fight between opposing groups of Union troops. In the midst of all of this the Yankee gunners by the cemetery sprang to their pieces and began to hammer the contestants indiscriminately with canister and shell, and Rebel artillery off to the west began firing in reply. In the road and under the trees there was perhaps the most complete infernal mix-up of the army's entire experience, Rebel yell and Federal cheer mixed in together, officers swearing and beating ineffectively with their swords, men screaming, "Don't fire—we're friends!" and nobody able to straighten anything out.[9]

Looking back on it afterward, General Alpheus Williams of the XII Corps remembered "such an infernal and yet sublime combination of sound and flame and smoke, and dreadful yells of rage, of pain, of triumph, or of defiance." Less emotionally, General Slocum reported: "I have no information as to the damage suffered by our troops from our own fire, but fear that our losses must have been severe." A Massachusetts infantryman who watched from a vantage point near the cemetery wondered how anyone at all survived the assault and the cannonade, especially the latter. The Federal gunners were filling their pieces with all kinds of old iron, he said, including such things as trace chains.[10]

Far back to the rear, by Ely's Ford over the Rapidan, Yankee cavalrymen on a hilltop looked off through the night, and one of them described what they saw:

"A scene like a picture of hell lies below us. As far as the horizon is visible are innumerable fires from burning woods, volumes of black smoke covering the sky, cannon belching in continuous and monotonous roar; and the harsh, quick rattling of infantry firing is heard nearer at hand. It is the Army of the Potomac, on the south of the Rappahannock, engaged at night in a burning forest. At our feet"—for the flying debris of the army had got that far by now—"artillery and cavalry are mixed up, jammed, officers swearing, men straggling, horses expiring."[11]

Somehow, at last, the fighting lines were disentangled. Somehow, at last, part of Sickles's men got back inside the lines. The rest stayed in the Hazel Grove clearing and made the best bivouac they could. It was not a very good one. From a barn near the clearing, where wounded men had been taken, came a steady chorus of agonized cries, and off in the woods the men could hear the dreadful screaming of wounded horses. Sporadic outbursts of firing lit the sky, sometimes bringing nervous soldiers to their feet in expectation of attack. Men remembered oddly that when the racket of this fearful night subsided the whippoorwills were singing. Far to the rear, men of the

I Corps, hastily summoned as reinforcements, came marching up the hollow roads from United States Ford singing the John Brown song.[12]

It was probably the gunners by the cemetery who stabilized the situation, if anything about that chaotic mess could be called stable. After Jackson and Hill were wounded, the Confederates found that the gunfire had so broken up their attempted regrouping that nothing more could be done until morning, and some while after midnight the effort to continue the advance was officially suspended. The moon went down and the firing stopped, and both armies got what sleep they could.

Morning brought better visibility and a great deal more fighting. Hooker was worried about Sickles's men in Hazel Grove, and as soon as it began to get light he ordered them to come on back into the lines—a fatal decision, for it gave to the Confederates what turned out to be an invaluable artillery position, and the Confederates began moving guns into the clearing as soon as the Federals left.

Jackson had broken Hooker's right wing into fragments, but the Union Army still had a perfectly good position, and if Hooker had only realized it he was standing squarely between the two disconnected pieces of Lee's army, with a tremendous advantage of numbers on his side. But Hooker just was not realizing things at Chancellorsville.[13] Some paralysis of spirit was on him. The idea of a counterattack seems not to have entered his head. Instead he sent hasty word to Sedgwick, who was supposed to be keeping the Rebel rear guard amused in front of Fredericksburg, ordering him to march to the rescue at once. For the rest, he had the men dig in around the Chancellorsville clearing and prepare to hang on.

The digging was not easy, shovels and spades not being at hand. The men loosened the earth with bayonets or sharpened sticks and then scooped it out with tin plates, pieces of board, or their bare hands. Axmen went forward fifty yards in front of the line and felled trees to form an abatis, or entanglement—a highly effective obstacle when the trees were big enough and were felled so that their branches became intertwined. With some of the branches slashed off and others tied together, the fallen trees could be an almost impassable barrier for advancing infantry. The artillerists by the cemetery had been kept busy all night digging gun pits, and by morning the guns and gun crews were well protected.[14]

Confederate Jeb Stuart, meanwhile, had taken command of the infantry Stonewall Jackson had led. Old Stonewall himself was awaking from an amputation in a field hospital far behind the lines, beginning to drift slowly but surely toward the invisible riverbank which he was to speak of in his last moment on earth. Stuart had Jackson's own ideas about the virtues of an unceasing offensive. Dawn had hardly come before Stuart had his men swinging forward.

They swung first into the Hazel Grove plateau, getting there just as the last of Sickles's men were preparing to leave, and what had begun as an orderly withdrawal turned suddenly into a rout. (An XI Corps soldier who witnessed this noted with satisfaction that these III Corps cocks-o'-the-walk were "apparently as much panic-stricken, and as much stampeded, as any of Howard's men had been. The writer saw these demoralized and disorganized men with his own eyes.")[15] One of Slocum's brigadiers wrote bitterly that he saw an entire red-pants regiment of Zouaves legging it desperately for the Union lines, pursued by about half of its number of jeering Southerners. He tried to stop these Zouaves, he said, so that they could stand beside his men and fight, but the Zouaves kept on going and the 20th Connecticut came out and drove the pursuers back.[16]

This was the 20th's first fight, and there was in the regiment one man who had said openly, back in bivouac, that he was such a great coward that he believed he would certainly run away the first time he came under fire. His captain made a mental note to keep an eye on him, but when the fighting began he had other things on his mind and forgot the man. Suddenly he came upon him, down on one knee behind a log barricade, loading and firing as coolly as a veteran. The private looked up at him, bit a paper cartridge open, and grinned a leathery Yankee grin. "Hello, Cap'n," he said. "I believe the powder goes in fust, don't it?"[17]

The Rebels were beaten back and they rallied and came on again, along with thousands more. The attacking line may have extended two miles from end to end, but the ground was so broken and the wood so thick that nobody could see more than a fraction of it. Brigadier General John W. Geary, former mayor of San Francisco, commanded a division here, and his men disputed possession of a sketchy trench line with some possessive Southerners and got into a bitter fire fight at the closest range. Geary brought some guns forward, the Rebels hit him with their own artillery from in front and from the flank, and finally he had to retire after a fire "of the most terrific character I ever remember to have witnessed."[18]

Confederate General Archer came up with his brigade, striking at a part of the line held chiefly by the 27th Indiana. During the night that regiment's Colonel Colgrove, a red-cheeked, white-whiskered old chap who was a great deal sprier than he looked, had rounded up fragments of two broken regiments and added them to his command, and early that morning he had pounced on a couple of abandoned cannon and rolled them into his works, commandeering a stray artillery lieutenant and detailing a couple of dozen infantrymen to serve the guns. With this impromptu brigade the colonel was fighting briskly —in his shirt sleeves, as usual—and when the Rebel line came close he took personal charge of one of the guns, calling out to his major: "Here, boy, you run the regiment while I run this here gun."

Archer's men got up within seventy yards and then broke and went to the rear, and a new Confederate brigade charged forward. Colgrove led his men out in a counterattack, and the 2nd Massachusetts and 3rd Wisconsin went forward with them, and the Northern and Southern boys got into a blind, vicious fight in the midst of the abatis, where the low branches held the smoke close to the ground and men trying to fight were trapped and could not get free and so were shot or bayoneted. In the end the Rebels withdrew and Colgrove reported exultantly that these Indiana, Massachusetts, and Wisconsin outfits were "the three best regiments I have ever seen in action." At one stage the 2nd Massachusetts was fighting hand to hand with the 1st South Carolina, the two extremist fire-eating states fighting their fight out personally. Afterward a Massachusetts soldier wrote meditatively that although his regiment had been in a great deal of very hot fighting, this was one of the few times they had actually seen their enemies.[19]

Slocum's regiments had hard fighting that morning. Sickles's men and French's division of the II Corps, put in on their right, had it even harder. They were in line for the most part north of the turnpike, and the Confederates came surging in through the timber in three successive lines of battle, which in the confusion of the fighting eventually merged into one dense mass. General Hiram Berry, proudly leading Hooker's old division into action in the post he had coveted so long, scorned to send couriers with orders to his brigade commanders but rode back and forth delivering his orders in person.

He got too far up front at last and a Rebel sharpshooter in a tree shot him off his horse and killed him. A confused brigadier, noting his fall and thinking all was lost, led his brigade out of action (thereby leading himself entirely out of the war), but Sickles slammed in a New Jersey brigade to plug the gap. It made a hot counterattack, taking prisoners and capturing Rebel colors, but it got into position too far forward, hung on there for a time, and then had to retreat after heavy losses.

Another gap developed, and the 12th New Hampshire was thrown in—a rookie regiment, taking 550 men into their first fight. These took post on a little knoll and stayed there for more than an hour, most of the officers shot down and the men fighting Indian-style behind trees and logs. Nearly surrounded, the New Hampshire boys finally withdrew, fewer than 100 men around the colors, a lieutenant the ranking officer. They came out through a little ravine, and Sickles saw them and galloped up to check the fire of waiting Federal artillery with a frantic shout: "Hold on there—hold your fire—these are my men in front!" He rode up to the lieutenant who was leading the men in and demanded: "What regiment, and where's the rest of it?" Proudly the lieutenant answered: "Twelfth New Hampshire, and *here's* what's left of it."[20]

Stuart had abandoned Jackson's plan for a continual movement around to the north, to cut the Yankees off from United States Ford, and instead was shifting steadily to his right, to regain contact with the rest of Lee's army. What Jackson had tried to do the night before almost certainly could not have been done this morning, for Hooker had Meade and his V Corps planted right where they could foil such a move, although they were too far in the rear to take part in the immediate action. In any case, Stuart continued pressing toward the right, and the Federals considered that his left flank offered a chance for a counterblow, and French's brigades were moved forward. They made some progress, took prisoners, then came to a halt in the eternal woodland twilight while the Rebels rallied for a new push.

It was beginning to be clear that the Yankee line could not be broken by infantry alone. The Confederates tried over and over, but the Federals were well dug in, it was hard to keep an attacking line in order in the thick woods, and the artillery back by Fairview Cemetery was a mighty power. But the high clearing at Hazel Grove had passed under Confederate control and Stuart had a smart gunner working for him that morning, Colonel E. P. Alexander, and Alexander had been running battery after battery up onto this plateau ever since the Yankees left. By midmorning these guns were taking charge. They enfiladed a good part of the Union infantry line, they hit the Federal gunners at Fairview paralyzing blows, and they blew shot and shell all over the Chancellorsville clearing, disrupting supply lines and leaving the advanced units and some of the artillery with no way to replenish ammunition. They were aided in this by some thirty Rebel guns which had been drawn up near Dowdall's Tavern and by other guns over to the east of Fairview inside of Lee's lines, and presently all of these guns were taking Chancellorsville and everything near it under an overwhelming converging fire.[21]

The 8th Ohio, which had been left behind as artillery support when French's brigades went forward, was posted in a thick oak swamp toward the right of the line, and it reported that shell seemed to be coming in from all directions at once. The lines began to dissolve under this fire, the woods were full of fugitives looking desperately for the rear, and all of the narrow roads were choked with wagons, artillery, ambulances, stray detachments of cavalry, and frantic droves of beef cattle. The woods were on fire in a dozen places, underbrush blazing furiously, flames creeping up to the crown of the taller trees. The air grew unendurably hot, and the heavy wood smoke mixed with the battle smoke under the trees, almost suffocating the fighting men. From the south and east Lee's men kept edging in closer, rolling their guns forward and putting the crossroads under additional fire. The smoke went billowing upward, and the day was muggy and close and a monstrous clamor of exploding powder and clanging metal and shouting men went up the sky, while the starred Confederate battle flags came tossing closer and closer through the broken timber.[22]

Out in the open men fought in a blinding fog, and as they fought, in a clearing by the turnpike there appeared in the front lines a young woman, one of the characters of the III Corps, gentle, respected Annie Etheridge, who wore a black riding habit with a sergeant's chevrons and who had been part of the army since the early days of the war.

Annie had gone to war with the 3rd Michigan as a laundress. When the regiment first left Washington to go to the front, the other laundresses went home, but she stuck with the regiment, sharing its marches and its bivouacs. It is recorded that she was "a young and remarkably attractive girl," that she was "modest, quiet, and industrious," and that any soldier who dared to utter a disrespectful word to or about her had to fight the entire 3rd Michigan. Gallant Phil Kearny saw her, after a battle on the peninsula, caring for wounded men at a front-line dressing station, and he more or less adopted her into the division, providing her with a horse and saddle and a sergeant's pay and detailing her officially as cook for the officers' mess.

This morning, in the hottest of the fighting, Annie came riding forward with a sack of hardtack and a dozen canteens of hot coffee, and she trotted brightly up to a busy general and his staff and offered refreshments. The officers tried to shoo her back to safety, but she refused to budge until each one had had something to eat and drink. The Rebel bombardment was at its worst, and three horses in this mounted group were smashed by solid shot while she was about this business, but an admiring Pennsylvania soldier who watched it all wrote that "she never flinched or betrayed the slightest emotion of fear." A bit later she appeared from nowhere beside an all but disabled Union battery which had lost all of its horses, several caissons, and a good many men. The gunners were about to abandon their pieces, but Annie talked them out of it. She smiled at them and cried, "That's right, boys—now you've got good range, keep it up and you'll soon silence those guns." The men raised a little cheer, made her go to the rear, and returned to the service of their guns. One sweaty cannoneer remarked that all the officers in the army could not have had as much influence with them just then as "that brave little sergeant in petticoats."[23]

The Confederate fire grew heavier and heavier, scourging the length and breadth of the Chancellorsville clearing, breaking up battery after battery in the line by the cemetery. One shot split a wooden pillar on the veranda of the Chancellorsville mansion. Hooker was leaning against it at the time, and the shock threw him to the ground heavily, stunning him. His favorite specific, brandy, was brought to him as he lay on a blanket his staff had spread out for him, and he revived and got to his feet—just in time, because a cannon ball came along and ripped through the blanket where he had been lying. Other shells went through the mansion itself, where surgeons had taken doors off their hinges and set them up on top of chairs for operating tables. One shell killed a man while a doctor was operating on him.

others set the building on fire, and Hancock detailed the 2nd Delaware to get the wounded out. All around the building the ground was plowed up by the vicious missiles, and wounded men who had been carried from the burning building were killed as they lay helpless on the ground.[24]

Hooker was taken to a tent half a mile behind the crossroads, and he sent for General Couch. Other officers took heart when this happened. Couch was a desperate fighter, and if Hooker turned the command over to him he would unquestionably call some of the unemployed troops into action and turn the tables. But Hooker did not do that. He instructed Couch to take temporary command, but only for the purpose of withdrawing the men to a new defensive line back behind the crossroads, covering the road to United States Ford. Couch came out of the tent, disappointment visible on his face. Meade, who had been standing by hopeful that Couch would tell him to lead his corps forward, turned away dejected.[25]

The withdrawal began, and it fell to the lot of Hancock to cover the retreat.

Hancock had his division in line facing east, covering the turnpike from the direction of Fredericksburg. Lee's men had been pressing him all morning, but as the troops behind him caved in, Hancock's division began to get all of it, and the right wing had to be pulled far back. Before long the division was formed in two separate lines, back to back, only a few hundred yards apart. The last of the guns went away from Fairview, Stuart's and Lee's troops made contact with each other, and an enormous horseshoe of fire encircled Hancock's division, with shell coming in from every point of the compass except the sector between northeast and northwest.

Hancock was born for moments like this. He had a thundering voice and an unrivaled command of profane army idiom. The II Corps treasured for the rest of the war the way he had exploded the evening before when a panicked soldier from Howard's corps, still fresh after a two-mile run from the Rebels, dashed up to him in confusion and asked to be directed to the road leading to the river pontoon bridges and ultimate safety. (The corps historian noted primly of his answer that "it is best not to put it into cold and unsympathetic type.")[26]

To the east, Nelson Miles held an advanced skirmish line, and he boldly rode his horse up and down the line immediately behind the

men, holding them to their work. It was an effective stunt—the men
liked to know that a ranking officer was up front with them, taking
what they had to take—but it took an uncommon amount of nerve,
because the infantry on both sides usually fired just a little high and
the man on horseback was right where he could get the worst of it.
Miles seemed to glory in it, and once Hancock sent an aide spurring
forward to tell him that he was worth his weight in gold. A Rebel
marksman finally got him with a bullet through the abdomen and
Miles was carried off the field, supposedly dying—belly wounds were
almost invariably fatal in that war.

Colonel Cross of the 5th New Hampshire, bald-headed and red-
bearded, an old-time Indian fighter and soldier of fortune, had been
given command that morning of two other regiments besides his own
—he was a top-notch soldier, already marked for brigade command—
and he had with him a number of stragglers from the XI Corps whom
he had rounded up and pressed into service the night before. He was
up and down his line this morning, right in his element in this hot
fight. He came upon a soldier once cowering behind the useless protection of a flimsy cracker box. He kicked the box out of the way,
kicked the soldier and yanked him to his feet, crying that he would
disgrace the whole division. When a gun fell silent for lack of cannoneers, Cross ran to it and helped some of his infantry load and fire
it.[27]

Rebel guns now were firing from a distance of hardly more than
five hundred yards. This was canister range, and the Rebel gunners
were chocking their guns to the muzzle with anything they could
lay their hands on, including some twelve-inch pieces of old railway
iron which they happened to have with them. Amid the whirring
fragments that filled the air there was a file which struck in a tree
beside General Caldwell. The general looked at it coolly and was
quite unable to resist the temptation to remark to his staff that this
was real file firing.[28] The parallel lines of Hancock's eleven regiments
were being hit from in front, from the rear, and from the flank.

Into an orchard in the open space between the lines came Lieutenant Stevens with the 5th Maine battery, unlimbering and going
into action in desperate haste. Confederate guns from all around the
arc opened on the battery with fury, getting the exact range at once,
exploding shells overhead, firing canister and solid shot to hit just
short and go ricocheting in off the hard ground at waist height.

Horses were killed, caissons blew up, limber chests were smashed, men were slain, and Stevens made his gun crews fire slowly so that every shot would count, with half the guns detailed to fire at Rebel artillery and the other half under orders to shoot only at infantry. Ammunition ran low and the battery was a wreck. Stevens was down, all the officers were down, and Couch detailed an officer of regulars, Lieutenant Kirby of the 1st U. S. Artillery, to come in and take charge. Kirby went down with a mortal wound and was carried to the rear. (He survived in hospital for a fortnight and did not die before he received a lieutenant colonel's commission from Abraham Lincoln in recognition of his valor.)[29]

The dusty plain around the crossroads was covered with smoke from the guns and the exploding shell and the burning woods. The old mansion was all aflame, and a dense blanket of fumy, stifling smoke from the pine thickets was rolling across the open space, where the men and equipment for whom Hancock's men were buying time moved to the rear. In the thickets, wounded men were burned to death, and corpses were consumed, and all the debris left behind by retreating troops took fire. A fearsome stench came down with the smoke, and a Confederate brigadier leading troops up to the clearing wrote: "The dead and dying of the enemy could be seen on all sides enveloped in flames, and the ground on which we formed was so hot as at first to be disagreeable to our feet." A Federal officer noted soberly: "Fortunate were those that had to die, that they did so before the holocaust began," and cavalry far in the rear could see great plumes of soiled white smoke rising from the reeking woodland.[30]

It was getting on toward noon now, and Confederate troops were sweeping out into the open around Fairview Cemetery, setting up an enormous cheer, Lee himself visible in their midst. Hancock's guns were out of ammunition and almost out of men, and word came up from headquarters that he could leave now—the army was established in its new lines closer to the river. The advanced skirmish line where Miles had taken his wound came back first, withdrawing in good order except for a few companies which missed their direction and marched smack into the middle of the Confederate advance and were captured.

It was time to get the guns out, but most of the horses were gone and hardly any gunners were left. Hancock sent to the rear for a detail of infantry, and men from the Irish Brigade came up to the wrecked battery. The Irishmen found just one gun left in action, directed by a corporal who was firing his last shot. All of the battery's limber chests had either been exploded by enemy action or were now empty. If the guns got out they would have to be taken out by hand, and so prolonges were attached—long ropes fastened to the trails of the gun carriages, the men tailing onto the ropes three dozen at a time—and the lumbering, ungainly weapons were hauled slowly to the rear. Rebel skirmishers were barely 150 yards away when the guns began to move.

Now the infantry could leave—and high time, too, with the Rebel fire heavier than ever and enemy skirmishers coming in for pot shots at point-blank range. When the word to retire came through, the outfit nearest the enemy about-faced and started off at a trot. Hancock, who always saw everything, spotted them and came storming over at a gallop to demand: "Why are these men running?" Immediately the regiment slowed down to a walk, and at a walk the men left the field. One man who made this march admitted afterward that although they went out at a walk it was a good *brisk* walk.[31]

The new lines covered a wide angle of ground enclosing the Rappahannock bridgehead, and the flanks were firmly anchored, left flank running down to the Rappahannock and right flank running clear to the Rapidan. Hooker had more than enough troops, seventy thousand altogether, a good half of whom had not been in action, and his trench line was substantial. On the right and left the Confederates followed with inquisitive patrols, probing forward through the Wilderness to find out just where the new Yankee line might be.

In the center, coming from the Chancellorsville crossroads, a solid mass of Rebels was advancing as if Lee planned to break through the angle by sheer weight and drive the whole Union Army into the river. This part of the line was held by Meade, and he rode up to his divisional commander, General Charles Griffin, pointed to the approaching enemy column, and told him to drive it back.

Griffin was an old artillerist, one of the numerous excellent generals contributed to the Union Army by the regular artillery, and he still liked his guns. (One of his men once remarked that Griffin would have run his guns out on the skirmish line if he had been allowed to.) He now asked Meade if he might use artillery instead of infantry to check the Rebels. Meade told him that would be all right if he thought gunfire alone would do the job.

To an old gunner there could be just one answer to that.

"I'll make 'em think hell isn't half a mile off!" cried Griffin. He wheeled a dozen guns up into line. Dismounting, he told the gunners to load with double charges of canister, to wait until the assaulting column was within fifty yards, "and then roll 'em along the ground like this," stooping and swinging his arm forward like a bowler. The gunners did as directed. The head of the Confederate column was smashed in, and the rest drew back. For the time being, at least, the army was safe.[32]

Indeed, the high command that afternoon seems to have nourished some final shred of hope that perhaps a victory was being won. Half an hour after noon, with the army snugged down at last in this purely defensive position, Quartermaster General Rufus Ingalls wired an encouraging progress report to Dan Butterfield, who was back at the old headquarters at Falmouth:

"I think we have had the most terrible battle ever witnessed on earth. I think our victory will be certain, but the general told me he would say nothing just yet to Washington, except that he is doing well. In an hour or two the matter will be a fixed fact. I believe the enemy is in flight now, but we are not sure."[33]

3. Go Boil Your Shirt

Out in front the Wilderness smoldered, and a drizzling rain dampened the thickets and caused the smoke to drift in heavy spiritless clouds that hung low over the woodlands. Hooker's men held a line in the shape of a vast horseshoe, five miles or more from end to end, cleverly posted on high ground with ravines and bogs in front. Throughout the night the men were kept busy digging dirt and felling trees, and by the morning of May 4 the entire line was fortified. There were trenches four feet deep, with a solid breastwork of logs and earth facing the Rebels, heavy slashing of fallen timber out in front, a "head log" lying atop the breastworks with a four-inch slot under it for the riflemen. Brigadier General Thomas Kane, who as a patriotic amateur had helped organize the famed Bucktails in the first summer of the war and who now capably led a brigade in Slocum's corps, noted that "any force that the nature of the ground would allow the enemy to bring against us would meet with a certain and disastrous repulse," and said

that his men were confident of success and were looking forward to a
renewal of the fighting. In a letter to his wife Hancock wrote that "the
battle is not through yet by a long ways."

Yet the fighting was not renewed. The Confederates pushed skirmishers forward, and there was a bit of long-range artillery fire, but
for the most part the army sat in its trenches, peered out at a dull
inactive landscape of charred brush and smoking flatlands, and waited
to see what would happen next. Far away to the east there was a
sound of gunfire, but nothing much seemed to come of it. Rain came
down harder, and in places the trenches were flooded so badly that
details were put to work cutting gaps in the breastworks so that the
water might drain away.[1]

Hooker had left General John Sedgwick and his overstrength VI
Corps at Fredericksburg to beguile the foe, and when disaster took
place around the Chancellorsville crossroads Hooker sent word that
Sedgwick must advance, brushing aside any Rebels who opposed him,
and come over to join the rest of the army. Sedgwick had close to
twenty-five thousand men, and on paper his job looked easy: one
quick lunge up over the heights back of Fredericksburg and then a
straight hike of ten or twelve miles to Hooker's lines, and the job
would be done. In actual practice, as Sedgwick realized perhaps too
well, it was far from simple.

Lee had left Jubal Early, the army's reserve artillery, and some
ten thousand infantry to oppose Sedgwick's passage, and Early was a
stubborn character who never retreated unless he had to. He had
his men dug in along the line which had proved so impregnable when
Burnside assaulted it the previous December, and although this line
now was held by a skeleton force, the memory of the December
tragedy was strong and Sedgwick was very cautious. He got his men
up through town, sparred at long range during most of the morning,
and at last sent ten regiments out across the Fredericksburg plain,
over the ground where so many men had died in the last great battle.

Early's men were posted on Marye's Heights and in the sunken
road, and they proposed to stay there. The Federals charged twice
and were driven back with losses, and for a time it looked as if this
particular nut would be just as hard to crack as it had been when
all of Lee's army was on hand. The 5th Wisconsin was finally shaken
out as a skirmish line, and its Colonel Allen, who commanded the
advanced column of assault, addressed the men briefly: "When the

signal *forward* is given you will advance at double-quick. You will not fire a gun, and you will not stop until you get the order to halt. You will never get that order."[2] The men raised a cheer and went in on the run, the rest of the assaulting column at their heels. The charge wavered when it got close to the wall. Rebel defenders here were few, compared with last December, but they were firing fast and the position was all but invulnerable. Then the Federals at the right of the line swept in through a complex of kitchen gardens and board fences, vaulted over the wall, bayoneted the men who barred the way, and got a killing enfilade fire on the rest.[3] The surviving Confederates fled, guns were abandoned, and five months after Burnside had first imagined it the United States flag waved on top of the heights and this part of the battle had been won.

Sedgwick paused and took thought: plain, unassuming, weathered John Sedgwick, greatly liked by his troops, broad-shouldered and heavy-framed, an unmilitary-looking character with muddy boots, red shirt under his blue coat, old slouched black hat on his head, and a tangled brown beard, one of the best of the Yankee generals but not the man for daring decisions and rapid movement.[4] If he pursued Early's beaten detachment he might be able to wipe it out, but his orders said that he was to move straight on to Chancellorsville, and anyway, he had no cavalry to beat the bushes for fleeing enemies, so he reorganized his command and put it on the turnpike. He was methodical about it, and today he was being very cautious, and the afternoon was well along when he finally got the column moving.

If Hooker had been wide awake now Lee's army might have been crushed, but all of this was happening only a few hours after Hooker had been stunned by the cannon ball which fractured the pillar on the Chancellorsville mansion, and while Sedgwick's corps was tramping forward along the turnpike Hooker was meekly pulling his seventy thousand men back into the bridgehead entrenchments and was leaving Sedgwick to look out for himself. As a natural result, Lee posted a detachment to watch Hooker's trenches and took most of his army back to deal with this new threat to his rear.

Sedgwick's leading division ran into the Rebel battle line at Salem Church, half a dozen miles east of Hooker's inactive army. The division attacked gallantly and for a few moments had things all its own way. But Sedgwick had opened the fight without waiting for the rest of his corps to come up. The attacking division found itself out-numbered, and before long it was splintered and broken and forced to retreat, with the balance of Sedgwick's command reaching the field just in time to round up stragglers and form a new defensive line. When night came down the men found themselves drawn up in a ragged quadrangle near Banks Ford with Rebels on three sides of them and the river on the fourth, and the big question was not whether they could get to Chancellorsville to help Hooker but whether they themselves could get out of this fix without being captured in a body.

They put in a gloomy night. Losses had been heavy, the lanterns of the stretcher-bearers were bobbing through the woods and across the fields for hours, and Sedgwick stayed awake almost all night, trying to get word of his plight to Hooker and to get some sort of intelligent instructions in return. One soldier remembered that the "night was inexpressibly gloomy," and the 95th Pennsylvania re-called an episode of eerie horror. One of their number had been killed while climbing over a rail fence and by some appalling freak remained balanced upright astride the top rail all night, rocking slowly to and fro in the breeze, his comrades in bivouac a few hundred feet away able to see his white face distinctly in the light of the full moon. Rebel pickets held the line of the fence, and when they fired, the flash of their pieces put a lurid light on the ghostly figure.[5]

The next day was May 4, and Hooker's main body stayed in its lines while Lee tried to destroy Sedgwick's corps. Lee might have succeeded if he had been able to mount his attack in time, but one of his division commanders was sluggish and the ground was diffi-cult, and in the end Sedgwick was able to stand the Confederates off until after dark, when he finally managed to get his men back to the north side of the Rappahannock. From first to last his venture had cost forty-seven hundred casualties and had done no good whatever, except that for some thirty-six hours it had diverted Lee's attention from Joe Hooker.

May 5 came in rainy, with Hooker's men huddled in trenches or in dripping woods behind the lines. The Rappahannock was rising rapidly, and the pontoon bridges at United States Ford, only remain-ing avenue of communication between the Army of the Potomac and the North, were swaying insecurely on the flood. The eight days' rations had all been eaten or lost, supply trains were back around

Falmouth, and it seemed to Hooker that he and his army were in a desperately bad spot. Army intelligence said that Longstreet had brought his corps up from below Richmond to take a hand in the game, and after Sedgwick's defeat there was obviously nothing to keep Lee from assaulting Hooker's lines with everything he had.

Army intelligence was wrong about Longstreet, who was still far away. Its information came from Rebel deserters, who seem to have been planted for purposes of deception. However, Hooker was having a stiff case of McClellan caution, and that evening he called his corps commanders into council to see whether it might not be time to retreat.

The meeting was neither happy nor harmonious. Slocum was late and did not get to headquarters until after the meeting had adjourned. Meade was angry, full of fight and eager to resume the battle. Howard was somewhat subdued, feeling that his corps had been responsible for the army's troubles, but he too was all in favor of fighting it out. Reynolds was sullen and weary. He told Meade to vote his proxy for an offensive, and then lay down in a corner and went to sleep. Couch, slight and pale, looking more like a clergyman than a corps commander, was quietly bitter, making it clear that he would vote for an offensive if someone besides Hooker were to be in command but not otherwise. Sickles confessed himself an amateur soldier among professionals and was frankly ready to vote for a retreat. Hooker let his generals talk by themselves for a while and then came back in to say that his mind was made up and that the army would go back to Falmouth. As the meeting broke up Reynolds inquired savagely (quite loud enough for Hooker to hear him, one said): "What was the sense of calling us all together if he had decided to retreat anyway?"[6]

So here was the end to all the bright prospects and the fine talk, and Hooker's boasts would dance about in the newspaper columns to torment him for many a fine day. Meade's V Corps took station in the wet wood to act as rear guard, with a long picket line strung out in the darkness, and in the black night over atrocious roads the brigades and divisions of the rest of the army climbed out of their trenches and headed back for the river. There were the usual delays and mix-ups, and some regiments stood in line for hours, men falling asleep where they stood, so that orders had to be relaxed to permit the men to lie down in place and sleep in the mud and pelting rain if they could. Wind and rain grew worse, and somewhere after midnight the rising river broke the bridges. Hooker had already gone back to Falmouth, and here was the army on one side of the river and its commanding general on the other, all communication cut off and nobody able to say when or whether it would be restored. Somebody told General Couch about it, remarking that under these circumstances he, Couch, was now in effective command of the army. Couch replied that if that was so the army would turn around next morning and fight, but that meanwhile he was going to go to his tent and try to get a little sleep. Later the bridges were rebuilt and stern orders came from Hooker to resume the retreat, and by the middle of the morning the last of the rear guard was north of the river and the engineers were dismantling the bridges.[7]

The march from United States Ford back to Falmouth was slow and dreary. Tired and dejected, the soldiers fell out by platoons, some of them exhausted by fighting and marching, others fed up with the war and ready to quit. For the rest of the week all the countryside within a twenty-mile radius was swarming with stragglers, some of them in a lawless, ugly mood. They were pillaging houses for food, robbing citizens of their clothing and then putting it on in place of their own uniforms, and striking out for Alexandria and the road home. The provost marshal had squads of cavalry combing the woods and fields, but before long he was notifying the high command that he was outnumbered and asking for help.[8]

The rain did not let up—one diarist spoke of "a tremendous cold storm"—and the infantry came slopping in, soaking wet and covered with mud, in an atmosphere as glum as a funeral. Somewhat bewildered, a private in the 83rd Pennsylvania wrote that "no one seems to understand this move, but I have no doubt it is all right." He added that his outfit got back to camp completely exhausted, saying: "Most of the way the mud was over shoe, in some places knee deep, and the rain made our loads terrible to tired shoulders."[9] General headquarters was getting a count on the losses and was discovering that this Chancellorsville battle had cost more than seventeen thousand casualties, of which six thousand came under the heading "missing." A good many of these latter entries stood for men who had quietly died in the dark forest without being noticed by surviving comrades, but the list also represented many men captured by the Rebels, which indicated that things might not have been too good in some of the combat outfits. Desertions were heavy from the XI Corps, as might have been expected. Surprisingly enough, they seemed to be equally heavy from Slocum's XII Corps, which had fought magnificently on May 3, and from Reynolds's I Corps, which had not had to fight at all.[10]

Back in Falmouth, Hooker began to find out what his cavalry had been doing, and the story did not please him. Stoneman had started down from the river full of enthusiasm, apparently minded to carry out his orders to the letter. He was supposed to get as rapidly as possible to Hanover Junction, which was where the Virginia Central Railroad crossed the line of the Fredericksburg Railroad, for if that junction and its adjacent tracks and bridges were properly smashed, Lee's supply problem would have been impossible. Once he got under way, however, Stoneman had second thoughts. He sent half of his command off under Averell to keep Rebel cavalry at a distance, and Averell wandered over to Rapidan Station and went into bivouac there, confused and inert, as much out of the war as if he had been in Cuba. With the rest, Stoneman rode down to the line of the Virginia Central and then got entangled in his own eloquence.

Calling his regimental commanders together, he explained that "we had dropped in that region of country like a shell, and I intended to burst it in every direction, expecting each piece or fragment would do as much harm and create nearly as much terror as would result from sending the whole shell, and thus magnify our small force into overwhelming numbers."[11] This was putting it very nicely, and it showed that General Stoneman could thrash about in the rank second growth of the English language as valiantly as the next man, but it did not describe the part which Hooker had expected his cavalry to play. There had been nothing whatever to prevent Stoneman from marching his men into Lee's immediate rear. Practically all of Lee's transportation was collected at Guiney's Station, some eighteen miles south of Chancellorsville, and the guard there was of the sketchiest. Stoneman's division could have destroyed the lot, together with all of the supplies collected there, and Hooker's dream of the Rebel army in desperate retreat might have become a reality.

Instead of doing that, however, Stoneman broke his troops up into raiding parties (the "bursting shell" motif), which did spread a good deal of alarm in Richmond but which Lee simply ignored. A contributory factor may have been that Stoneman suffered extensively from piles at this time, so that riding was torture to him and the driving, twenty-hours-in-the-saddle kind of advance which Hooker had expected was just too much for him.[12] But whatever the cause, the result was that the cavalry had been wasted. One disgusted trooper wrote that "our only accomplishments were the burning of a few canal boats on the upper James River, some bridges, hen roosts, and tobacco houses." Hooker furiously relieved Averell of his command—a soldier remembered passing cavalry headquarters the day that order came out and seeing Averell seated in his tent, his head in his hands, the very picture of dejection—and a bit later he relieved Stoneman as well, putting Pleasonton in his place.[13] That would not undo what had been done, however, and the unhappy fact remained that the Hooker who had turned the Yankee cavalry into an effective instrument had not been able to get any service out of it when the big test came.

But if Hooker's cavalry had let him down, the worst letdown had come from Hooker himself. He had planned his campaign like a master and had carried out the first half of it with great skill, and then, when the pinch came, he had simply folded up. There had been no courage in him, no life, no spark; during most of the battle the army to all intents and purposes had had no commander at all. With a two-to-one advantage in numbers, Hooker had let his men fight at a numerical disadvantage at every important point on the battlefield. Howard's XI Corps had been mashed by an irresistible flank attack, but the real reason for that disaster was the fact that neither Hooker nor anyone else in authority would listen to the specific warnings which the unhappy Dutchmen had repeatedly sent in. Thereafter, while Lee and Stuart crushed his lines around Fairview and Chancellorsville, Hooker had held thirty thousand good troops out of action; he had cowered in his trenches while Lee broke up Sedgwick's corps; and then, to cap it all, he had hastily retreated across the river just as he was about to be given a chance to redeem the whole situation.

For on the morning the army recrossed the river Lee had actually been planning a full-scale assault on Hooker's lines. Those lines were strong; Hooker still had a two-to-one advantage in numbers, he had 106 guns in emplacements with 140 more in reserve, and by all military logic that assault should have resulted in a Confederate defeat as bad as the one at Malvern Hill.[14]

Yet it may be that military logic would have had nothing to do with it. Lee had not been contending with the Yankee army at Chancellorsville. He had been contending with Joe Hooker; he was more of a man than Hooker was, and Hooker knew it. Couch may have been right: if Hooker was to remain in command the thing to do was to get back across the river as fast as possible, because victory just was not in the man. Years later, when someone asked Hooker what went wrong at Chancellorsville, the general knew a rare moment of humility and remarked, "Well, to tell the truth, I just lost confidence in Joe Hooker."

In Washington there was deep dejection because of the battle—in Washington, which is always convinced that the soul-tearing doubts which come from looking at operations from the under side will immediately overwhelm every American citizen. Senator Sumner, tall and handsome, bearing on his face the indescribable shadow of the brain injuries left by Bully Brooks's cane, stalked into Secretary Welles's office, threw out his arms dramatically, and cried: "Lost —lost—all is lost!" Welles was hardly surprised. He had already noted that the War Department was shuffling papers, staring at the ceiling, and talking the vaguest of double talk, and by these infallible signs he knew the army had been beaten again. Horace Greeley cringed in print at the thought that the finest army on the planet had been defeated by "an army of ragamuffins." Lincoln had been hopeful as long as there was any room for hope, but he finally got the bad news in the form of a laconic telegram from Dan Butterfield. He read it, and his sallow face turned ashen-gray, and to a caller he said, as if dazed: "My God! What will the country say?"[15]

The President's anguished question went across the capital in muffled echoes, and government waited in deepest suspense for the answer. And at last, slowly, imperceptibly, it became evident that the country was not going to say anything at all.

There were sensitive weather vanes in Washington, and in the days following Chancellorsville they caught no breeze whatever. The profound depression which had settled down on the nation after Fredericksburg did not reappear. The editors and orators who could make political capital out of disaster flailed the air as usual and seemed to get no particular response. Most significant of all, perhaps —like the inactivity of the dog in the nighttime in the Sherlock

Holmes story—was the great quietude of Secretary Chase. Secretary Chase never wavered in the faith that it would be his deserved good fortune to displace Abraham Lincoln, once Lincoln's inability to fight a winning war became manifest. Here was Chancellorsville, the most inexcusable and costly of all the military defeats the Lincoln government had suffered, and yet in the reaction to it Chase saw no opening. He continued to believe that Joe Hooker should be in command of the army, and he made his attitude known, to the discomfort, said gossip, of Secretary Stanton and General Halleck, who were anxious to remove Hooker but who lacked the nerve to try it as long as the Secretary of the Treasury continued to back him.

There was a turning point in this war, and the country had passed it. It had done so undramatically and without realizing it, and the turning point itself can hardly be identified precisely even at this distance in time. It may have been the adoption of a national draft act, or the decision to recruit Negro troops, or even—so strange are the ways by which a people shows how its spirit is moving—the decision in the middle of a desperate war to build a railroad to the Pacific Coast and to create a million small farms in the Western wilderness by means of a national homestead act. Whatever it was, it had been there somewhere, invisible beneath the oratory and the headlines, the bloodshed and the suffering. Nobody had consciously made a decision about anything, yet here suddenly everybody was taking something for granted: that the war would be fought out no matter how many ups and downs it might have, that there would never be any turning back, that out of the horror of this lost battle in a forest fire there would come a renewed determination and an unutterable grimness. The high-water mark of the rebellion had been left behind, even though men would still have to die under a clump of trees on a heat-blistered ridge in Pennsylvania to make the fact manifest. From now on the road wound upward.

Nobody could see it at the time, least of all in the Southland. In the Army of Northern Virginia men's spirits had never been higher. Lee was reorganizing and was preparing to invade the North, mourning that Jackson was irreplaceable but sure that the superb fighting quality of his soldiers could overcome any handicap. Longstreet and his corps had returned, Longstreet confident that Lee's plan of invasion would succeed if he could just place his army on Northern soil in such a way that the Yankees would have to attack it: strange reminder of Hooker's lost faith that his position at the Chancellorsville crossroads would force the Rebels to march forth to certain destruction.

The Army of the Potomac settled back in its camps at Falmouth again. It was as if an evil fate condemned this army to be forever marching out of camp gaily and forever returning a bit later, its banners in the dust. (A solid year after this, when Grant took off for the Wilderness, veterans warned rookies not to burn the winter quarters—chances were they'd be back in them in a week or so.) The soldiers were utterly bewildered, knowing that they had lost a battle in which half of them had not fought at all, and the only thing clear was that topside had somehow got all of its arrangements most completely fouled up. As a symbol of this there was the experience of the Philadelphia Brigade, which had put in a dreary week guarding fords, hearing the sound of battle from a distance. Returning to camp with the dull realization that it had been beaten even though it had seen no enemies, the brigade found itself with a week's accumulation of orders, announcements, and what not, all of which were read off to the troops by regimental adjutants at evening parade. The first one —brigade staff had been too groggy to weed it out—was Hooker's jubilant May 1 announcement: ". . . the enemy must either ingloriously fly or come out from behind his defenses and give us battle on our own ground. . . ."[16]

There were recriminations, especially in the XI Corps, which discovered that the rest of the army and most of the country believed that the battle had been lost because of the cowardice of Dutchmen. Howard remarked in general orders to the corps that he could not "fail to notice a feeling of depression on the part of a portion of this corps." He added, perhaps unnecessarily: "Some obloquy has been cast upon us." Carl Schurz reported that the men had had about all they could take, and he appealed vainly to the War Department for justice: "We have been overwhelmed by the army and the press with abuse and insult beyond measure. We have borne as much as human nature can endure."[17]

The corps believed that a great deal of this was directly inspired from army headquarters, and General Schimmelfennig angrily complained that "the most infamous falsehoods" had been given to newspaper correspondents by members of Hooker's own staff. There was so much of this that German-Americans in New York City held a

mass meeting to try to clear the corps' name. Among the speakers
was General Meagher, who testified that his Irish Brigade had been
guarding roads to the rear during the battle and that of the many
stragglers he intercepted only a very few spoke with a German accent.[18]

The complaints made by Howard's corps, however, were as nothing compared with the backbiting that went on at the top levels of
army command. Most of the corps commanders had had their doubts
about Hooker from the beginning, and as they looked back on the
fumbled battle their doubts became nagging certainties. Couch tried
to get the others to join him in asking the President to remove Hooker
from his command. Slocum sided with him and went to see Meade
about it, and Meade, who was no part of a plotter, replied that he
would join in no round robin, although if the President asked him
for his opinion he would cheerfully give it. Members of the heavy-
handed Committee on the Conduct of the War came down to ask
questions and express opinions, and the administration did not help
matters much by taking clumsy soundings to see if there was a general present who would care to take Hooker's place. Nobody seemed
to want the spot, but word of the overtures got around.

Sedgwick and Hooker had an angry argument about the way Sedgwick had handled his part of the battle, and Hooker and Meade
quarreled over whether Meade had voted in favor of retreating. General Gibbon wrote that Hooker was looking for a scapegoat. Hooker's
own opinion may have been reflected in the comment of his chief
engineer, Brigadier General G. K. Warren, who wrote home that
"our great weakness, in my opinion, is the incompetency of many
of our corps commanders." Couch finally notified the President that
he would not serve under Hooker any longer and asked to be relieved of his command. His request was granted and he went north
to command home-guard levies in Pennsylvania, and command of
the II Corps went to Hancock. Hancock himself, famous throughout
the army for his vigorous cursing, had found himself shocked at
Hooker's boast that God Almighty could not keep him from beating
the Rebels, and he piously wrote to his wife that "success cannot
come to us through such profanity."[19]

One would suppose that the army was in a bad way. It had had a
humiliating defeat which seemed all the worse because of the high
hopes that had preceded it. The men had thought they were really

going to win this one, and one soldier asserted that "in no other battle of the East did the Union troops have so much confidence in their leader or so strong a hope of winning a complete and decisive victory."[20] The letdown had been sharp, casualties had been heavy, more than twenty thousand of the short-term troops had been paid off and had gone home, one full army corps was suffering from a slow burn because everybody considered it a set of cowards, and the principal generals were visibly and violently at odds with their commander. It seemed likely that all of the old cliques and officer-corps antagonisms would begin making mischief once again, and army morale might have been thought ruined beyond repair.

Yet actually the army was not in a bad way at all. It was not in the least demoralized, and if it was downhearted, the mood did not persist for long. A brigade historian wrote that the men were "puzzled to know how they had been defeated without fighting a decisive battle," but there was nothing remotely like the sullen discouragement that had followed Fredericksburg. Old-timers might have longed for a return of McClellan, in the mood of a middle-aged man yearning for the golden time of his early youth—a surgeon in the 20th Massachusetts noted that "the whole army cries for 'Little Mac'" —yet there was no particular loss of regard for Joe Hooker. It is possible that some of the blame for defeat which the men might have directed at Hooker was diverted in such a way that it came down on the ill-starred members of the XI Corps instead. General Schimmelfennig probably knew what he was talking about when he accused Hooker's staff of planting stories with the press. But the point is that the self-confidence which the army had reacquired during the winter was not diminished.[21]

Indeed, in a remarkably short time the army settled back into its old routine. There were drills and inspections and reviews—the weather was getting hot now, and by special dispensation drills and fatigues were held to a minimum around the middle of the day—and one morning Birney's division of the III Corps was paraded to witness a fancy ceremony. Birney had devised a new decoration called the Kearny Medal, a bronze Maltese cross to be given to enlisted men for valor, and this day the division stood at attention while the medal was pinned on the blouse of little Annie Etheridge, who had served hot coffee and cheered gunners under fire at Chancellorsville. On this same day the Iron Brigade also was paraded, and its 24th Michigan proudly came up to the line wearing for the first time the distinctive black hats which the brigade had made so famous, black hats turned up at one side, with a jaunty feather sticking out above the curled brim.[22]

Along the banks of the Rappahannock the Yankee pickets were carrying on trade and exchanging half-amiable insults with the Confederates across the water. The 46th New York, sending a little sailboat across, freighted it with a letter inviting the Rebels to come over for a visit in the evening. The letter closed with the words: "In the hope that Jeff Davis and Abe Lincoln will give us peace, we send our respects." One day a Confederate picket yelled across to a group of Federals: "Say, you Yanks, why didn't you shoot General Hill? He stood right here half an hour ago." The Federals replied that they were sorry to have missed a chance; they had seen him but supposed he was simply an officer of the guard and not worth shooting. One Confederate, asking loudly, "Where's Joe Hooker now?" was tartly informed: "He's gone to Stonewall Jackson's funeral."[23]

It was noticed that where New England troops had camped any stream or brook was sure to be improved by little dams and sluices, with water wheels made out of shingles and old fruit cans spinning merrily in the sunlight. A Maine regiment which was sent off on picket duty left little signs by its camp asking people not to disturb these grownups' toys because the owners would be back before long, and a colonel of regulars looked wonderingly at the display by a brook in a New Hampshire camp and meditated aloud that only mechanically minded Yankees would behave so.[24]

Four days after the battle the colonel of the 7th Wisconsin sent a note to his adjutant:

"There is a large crowd of soldiers in the grove below, engaged in the interesting game called chuck-a-luck. My chaplain is running his church on the other side of me, but chuck-a-luck has the largest crowd. I think this unfair, as the church runs only once a week but the game goes on daily. I suggest that one or the other of the parties be dispersed."[25]

Clearly enough, this was the climate of March and April all over again, and except for the new graves and the charred bodies in the Wilderness, and the thousands of maimed men in the hospitals, it was nearly as though Chancellorsville had not been fought. The battle had been almost totally devoid of results. The army had been defeated once more, but now, for the first time, the defeat did not seem to count.

A good deal has been said and written about the army's retreat to Falmouth in the rain after Hooker brought it back to the north side of the river. That retreat had in truth been a dreary affair, and the occasion is not referred to fondly in any memoirs or regimental histories. Yet there had been a different tone to it from that of the bleak marches that had followed earlier defeats. This time, as the tired men came back into camp, the early arrivals turned out to line the roads and watch the rest come in, and the watchers and the marchers called out derisive greetings to each other: "Here's another played-out set" . . . "Go lay down in the mud" . . . "Turn out the provost guard and pick up those stragglers" . . . "There comes the home guard" . . . "Go boil your shirt."[26] That kind of interchange can mask practically any emotional state imaginable except a state of dejection and despair. It was as a staff officer remarked: "The Army of the Potomac was no band of schoolgirls. . . . With the elation of victory or the depression of defeat, amidst the hardest toils of the campaign, under unwelcome leadership, at all times and under all circumstances, they were a reliable army still."[27]

The army had come of age. It was a professional army now in all but name. It was built around the volunteers of 1861, who had come in singing songs and dreaming dreams, and the songs had come down to camp doggerel and the dreams had been knocked out and the men were old soldiers now, proud with the pride of soldiers, able to do their jobs no matter who led them or how he did it. It was observed that now and then the waiting ranks would set up a cheer for some particular regiment or brigade. The cheers might simply be in welcome to old friends who had not been seen for some time, but more often they were the soldiers' spontaneous tribute to troops which they recognized as good fighting men. On this return from Chancellorsville Berdan's sharpshooters, who tended to be a rather hard-bitten lot, set up a mighty shout when the Iron Brigade came marching in. As it happened, the Iron Brigade had not been in action at Chancellorsville, while Berdan's men had been pretty thoroughly shot up, but something about the bearing of the Western soldiers made the sharpshooters toss their caps and yell—the Army of the Potomac, giving and receiving the only accolade it would ever know or care for. Long after the war one of Berdan's officers wistfully remembered the sight of "that famed body of troops marching up that long muddy hill, unmindful of the pouring rain but full of life and spirit, with steady step, filling the entire roadway, their big black hats and feathers conspicuous." To remember it, he said, filled him with "the pride of looking upon a model American volunteer."[28]

FIVE

Lincoln Comin' Wid His Chariot

1. The Grapes of Wrath

Out in front there were the eternal lines of weary men in dusty blue plodding through the sunlight into heavy mist and curling smoke, and it seemed that the only reality was the hard reality of combat and death. Yet in the background there was a great force adrift, and the future was beginning to take shape. No man could say what the future would be like, yet now and then strange hints of it seemed to come down the tainted winds. The gunfire and the shouts of men in battle and the unimaginable cruelties and agonies of war seemed to lift at times to permit a glimpse of something new and incalculable, bought with the lives of men who would never see it. A young soldier who was commissioned an officer in one of the new Negro regiments this spring heard his men singing one of the hackneyed war songs:

> *Yes, we'll rally round the flag, boys, we'll rally once again,*
> *Shouting the battle cry of freedom!*

and he wrote that he had never before heard such singing.[1] These colored men were not just repeating the empty words of a good marching tune. They were putting everything they had into a song that had suddenly taken on enormous meaning, and words like "the flag" and "freedom" had become revolutionary, the keys to a great future.

It might be, indeed, that this idea of freedom was something that had no limits whatever. It might begin as a limited thing, simple legal freedom from purchase and sale for the poor black man, and in the end it would become freedom for white men too, freedom also for all of the unguessed potentialities of an amazing country that had hardly begun to dream of its own destiny.

Thoughtful men occasionally talked as if they saw a gulf opening beneath their feet. Gideon Welles was as sober a conservative as party politics could bring to a president's cabinet, yet he saw something that spring as he meditated that privateering and support for blockade-runners might yet bring England into a war with America. Such a war, he wrote, could have unlooked-for consequences. Instead of being a conventional war it could bring about "an uprising of the nations." He talked with Lincoln about it, and in his diary he stated his belief: "If war is to come it looks to me as of a magnitude greater than the world has ever experienced—as it would eventuate in the upheaval of nations, the overthrow of governments and dynasties. The sympathies of the mass of mankind would be with us rather than with the decaying dynasties and the old effete governments."[2]

Wendell Phillips, the gadfly of abolition, was on the rostrum that spring crying out that the power which dwelt in this idea must be used as a telling weapon. He saw the war between North and South as something infinitely portentous, not confined to one continent:

"Wherever caste lives, wherever class power exists, whether it be on the Thames or on the Seine, whether on the Ganges or on the Danube, there the South has an ally. . . . Never until we welcome the Negro, the foreigner, all races as equals, and melted together in a common nationality, hurl them all at despotism, will the North deserve triumph or earn it at the hands of a just God."[3]

These were brave words, and they went farther than Phillips himself imagined. His catalogue of the rivers where caste existed was impressive but incomplete. He might have extended it: the Thames and the Seine, the Ganges and the Danube—and, very much closer home, the rolling Susquehanna as well.

Caste and despotism existed along the Susquehanna, and in 1863 some of the people most affected were rising to demand that something be done about them. They were not putting their demand in very intelligible words, for they were ignorant Irish immigrants and they had no better idea than anyone else of the ultimate meaning of a war for freedom. So confused were the times, and so mixed were the values which men believed they were serving, that these men actually seemed to be allies of the Confederacy, and patriotic Northerners tended to look upon them as traitors. But if their intent was not especially clear, either to themselves or to anyone else, they were at least speaking in a language that could not be ignored—the language of riot and gunfire and murder done in hot blood, so that the anthracite fields of eastern Pennsylvania seemed to be aflame in that spring of 1863.

On the surface, all that was happening was that the men who worked in the anthracite mines did not like either the war or the military draft and were going to extremes of violence to make their dislike known. Yet it is clear enough that the discontent went deeper than that. It went all the way down, as a matter of fact, to the injustices which the growing industrialization of a lusty, heedless country was inflicting on men who, if they did not look out, would soon be ground down into a submerged caste as unfortunate as any submerged caste along Mr. Phillips's rivers overseas. The Pennsylvania anthracite region, in short, was having a bad case of labor trouble, and since labor trouble was something relatively new in a nation which still believed itself to be a land of small farmers, it went more or less unrecognized and the authorities considered that they were dealing with a set of malignant Copperheads.

The anthracite area included principally Lackawanna, Luzerne, and Schuylkill counties. Population had mushroomed in the years just before the war, and production of anthracite had gone up from a scant million tons a year in 1840 to eight and one half million tons in 1860. Of protective legislation, mine safety regulations and the like there was not a vestige, and the clerk of the Schuylkill mining district was presently to write of "the danger to be encountered working in deep mines" in which "standing gas, decay of timber, the absence of ventilation, and standing water" made working conditions perilous. Within recent memories, mines had been small and each mine owner knew personally his handful of workers and was on friendly terms with them. The small holdings had coalesced into large ones, mutual acquaintance and understanding had vanished,

and the average miner knew the owner of his mine only through
the "ticket boss," who checked the cars of mined coal and so determined, impersonally, how much each man's earnings would be. Com-
petition for labor had disappeared, and large numbers of penniless
Irish were imported to work in the diggings. The era of company
housing had arrived—very bad housing, most of it, with one room
downstairs and two above, furnished with bedsteads made of square
timbers by company carpenters, a rough table, and a few benches,
with an open grate built into one wall for cooking and heating.
Along with company housing came the company store, run in such a
way that many miners received no pay whatever for their work. (A
full decade after the war a Pennsylvania legislator felt it necessary to
introduce a bill to require coal companies to pay their workers in
cash.)⁴

On top of all of this there were acute racial and religious difficulties. The miners were Irish and the mine bosses, to a man, were
English, Welsh, or Scotch. The grip of the Know-Nothing movement
was upon the land, and "No Irish Need Apply" signs were common
in city employment offices. Native Americans looked upon the Irish
miners as an uncouth lawless group given to fighting and drunken-
ness, the squalor of their existence somehow a national characteristic
rather than the end product of bad pay and worse housing. The
miners had never been received into the community. They were outsiders and they were made to feel that way, an oppressed class,
exploited in every conceivable way by a country which seemed determined to convince them that they did not belong. As a recent student of the case has remarked: "The situation in the Pennsylvania
anthracite coal fields in the middle of the nineteenth century was
such, in short, that industrial strife and disorder were to be antici-
pated. If one sought to improvise a combination of factors calculated
to produce trouble, he could hardly hope to improve on the example
offered by eastern Pennsylvania."⁵

So here, although he never dreamed of it, was what Wendell Phillips had been talking about. The war had brought all of these pres-
sures to a head and had laid on top of them the exciting idea that
freedom was a thing which men in this land would fight and die for.
As an inevitable result there was an uprising going on.

It was the draft which touched off the trouble. Plenty of recruits
had been obtained from the anthracite area. The 48th Pennsylvania,

which was a first-class outfit, was famous as a regiment of Schuylkill County coal miners, and in 1864 in front of Petersburg its miners were to dig the long tunnel which resulted in the famous battle of the crater.[6] It does not appear that the miners' objection to the draft reflected any especial reluctance to fight. Rather, it grew out of deep dissatisfaction with intolerable conditions of life, which made the draft look like one injustice too many. Men were compelled to enroll for the draft. Any man who had three hundred dollars (which no miner had) could buy exemption if his name was called. There was a suspicion that men considered "undesirable" in any mining community by the mine bosses were sure to be called up first, and tales were told of drafted miners being tied to cavalrymen's stirrups and marched off to war willy-nilly. All of the resentment which these Irish immigrants felt because of their second-class status boiled over, and there was bloodshed.[7]

It had begun the previous fall in a little mining town where a crowd of men beat a mine boss to death after an argument about the war. Not long after, in a neighboring town, two hundred miners raided a colliery, beat up the office staff, took possession of the company store, fired shots in the air, and announced that they would really make trouble if the hated store were ever reopened. Mobs visited homes of men supposed to be in sympathy with the draft, hauled them out of bed, and killed them. Organized bands appeared to have complete control over many parts of the anthracite region. A Pennsylvania newspaper asserted that the disturbances were the work of a mysterious secret organization known as the Molly Maguires.

It is very comforting in time of war or other national emergency to be able to see all colors as straight blacks or whites. Secretary Stanton saw things that way, and to him this whole affair was a Copperhead plot in which the emissaries of Jefferson Davis had doubtless been active. But the real difficulty would seem to have been that the miners were trying, somewhat ineptly perhaps, to put on some sort of labor-union organizing drive. There was a slightly vague Workingmen's Benevolent Association somewhere back of that Molly Maguire label; the miners for years had been making fitful efforts to get an effective labor organization started, and in the conditions then prevailing in the coal fields a union had to be both conspiratorial and militant if it hoped to survive. Under all of the talk about Copperheads and traitors, a bitter clash of economic interests is easily discernible. The retail price of coal in the cities had gone sky-high, and there was talk that this was all due to the greed and the violent behavior of the miners. A citizen of Mauch Chunk wrote in outrage that the rioters "dictate the price for their work, and if their employers don't accede they destroy and burn coal breakers, houses, and prevent those disposed from working." As remedies, he demanded that a large military force be sent to the coal fields, that martial law be declared, and that "summary justice be dealt out to these traitors." He also proposed that "protection be afforded to those willing to work."[8]

The civil authorities often appeared to be powerless, or at least in many cases very reluctant to use what powers they did have. General Couch, who was now commanding the military in Pennsylvania, wrote that "the ignorant miners have no fear of God, the state authorities or the Devil," and added that "the Democratic leaders have not the power of burnt flax over them for good." It seemed, indeed, that there was a good deal of sympathy for the miners. Governor Curtin flatly refused to use the state militia to enforce the draft in the coal fields, and in Schuylkill County, where the trouble was worst, it was alleged that the Molly Maguires dominated county politics and had judges and jurors under their thumbs. Couch reported that nothing but a vigorous use of Federal troops would answer.[9] Stanton agreed with him, and various detachments were sent into Pennsylvania. In at least one of these regiments, the 10th New Jersey, the soldiers themselves became sympathetic with the miners, and in the end the regiment's colonel begged the War Department to send his outfit back to the Army of the Potomac before it got entirely out of hand.[10]

The Pennsylvania politician in charge of conscription was A. K. McClure, the editor-politician who had a knack for getting oil onto troubled waters. His draft commissioner for Schuylkill County was another editor named Benjamin Bannan, and when Bannan drew a list of conscripts and notified the men that they must take a train for Harrisburg, where blue uniforms awaited them, the waters became troubled enough to demand McClure's attention. A few of the draftees were farmers, who seemed ready enough to go. Most of them were miners, who announced that they would go under no circumstances whatever. When departure day came a huge mob of miners surrounded the train, turned all of the draftees loose, and completely nullified the whole procedure.

Stanton took fire and sent word that the draft must be enforced "at the point of the bayonet" if necessary. McClure and Curtin begged him to go slow, but Stanton would not cool off, and the regiments showed up next day, ready for business. Then McClure did what hard-pressed public officials so often did in those days: he dumped the whole problem in Lincoln's lap via a carefully worded telegram in cipher.

To him, a day or so later, came a puzzled War Department officer bearing a verbal message from the President. Mr. Lincoln, this officer told McClure, was of course anxious to see the law executed, or —Mr. Lincoln had emphasized this point—at least appear to have been executed. What the President was talking about this officer did not know, but he said that Mr. Lincoln had added: "I think McClure will understand."

McClure did—the ways of Pennsylvania politics bring to a man a breadth of understanding at an early age, and McClure had been at it for a long time—and he went into a huddle with Governor Curtin and Bannan. McClure remembered that there had been enrollment districts which had been able to prove that their quotas were already filled by showing that numbers of their people had enlisted in other cities and hence had not been counted properly. Bannan, who was warning that the draft could not be executed in his region without a bloody fight, slipped away quietly. He returned next day with a big stack of affidavits showing that any number of Schuylkill residents had in fact joined the army in places like Philadelphia, Harrisburg, and where not. McClure solemnly inspected them, agreed that the draft quota had indeed been filled, and revoked the call for conscripts. There was a truce, and the law at least appeared to have been executed.[11]

A bit later the same dodge was worked in reverse. Philadelphia was the great Republican stronghold, and Washington's figures showed that Philadelphia that spring was shy of its quota by three thousand men. McClure got busy again. (He commented long afterward that "there were experienced lightning calculators in those days.") Many persons from other parts of the state had enlisted in Philadelphia and had been properly credited to their own districts. A magic hand passed over the figures, and it immediately became

evident that at least three thousand of these men were in fact Phila-
delphians. This brought no more troops to the Army of the Potomac,
but it at least kept the Republicans from losing Philadelphia, which
had seemed to be imminent, and all was well.[12]

Philadelphia was symptomatic. There was infinite bewilderment in
the land. The beloved Union for which men were dying was, after
all, an abstraction, and the Negro, for whom deaths were also being
recorded, was an utter social outcast, looked upon in the North with
very little more friendship than in the South. From New York to the
Mississippi River the average Northern worker had an uneasy fear
that emancipation would bring a great horde of low-wage Negroes
into the North, to take away the jobs and livelihood of honest white
men. Times were not easy. An inflationary boom was on, and prices
were going up faster than incomes. This came on top of older troubles which had been building up in America for years.

Here was a land of freedom and plenty, and somehow it had been
changing so that many people felt that the freedom was a trifle hollow and the plenty was a myth. Far down below the foundations
of society there had for years been a deep potential of unrest, of
which the senseless Know-Nothing agitation had been only a symbol.
Long before anyone fired a cannon at Fort Sumter, such dissimilar
men as Thaddeus Stevens and John C. Calhoun had warned of the
danger of "social convulsion." Stevens himself, a "radical" in the
jargon of that day, was in fact a typical Pennsylvania Republican
(in the modern sense of the term) on most issues aside from slavery.
He was as much a conservative, in his own way, as Calhoun himself,
a spokesman for solid established interests. It was precisely men of
that kind who had brought this war about, and the war had taken
the lid off things. In one sense, the great fight over slavery and the
Union had channeled off the resentments which might have produced the convulsion which Stevens and Calhoun had both feared.[13]
In another sense, it was giving those resentments an opening. In the
incredible last analysis, victory might yet mean that to destroy one
kind of slavery was to weaken all other kinds.

Meanwhile men were confused and bewildered, and there were
strange eddies and backwashes in the tide of history in 1863. If there
was trouble in Pennsylvania there were other troubles all across the
Middle West, following a familiar pattern: opposition to the draft,
sporadic riots, occasional murders, with the Copperhead leaders

tossed about on waves which they supposed they were controlling. What was coming up seems to have been less a will to end the war than a blind, angry determination to make it mean something, even though no one could say just what that something might be. As one perplexed Republican reported, "the people are desirous of some change, they scarcely know what."[14]

In southern Illinois most of the people were recent immigrants from the Southland, and although they were stoutly loyal to the Union they disliked the Negro and refused to fight to end slavery. The 128th Illinois, recruited from that territory, lost nearly all of its members by desertion, the men declaring that "they would lie in the woods until the moss grew on their backs rather than help free the slaves."

So that spring Federal troops went into Illinois, and the 16th Illinois Cavalry, not sharing the anti-Negro sentiments of the 128th, found itself clumping and clanking across Williamson County to quell disturbances and lay the fear upon all Copperheads. They hit the countryfolk with a hard heavy hand. The Union League, newly organized by loyalists as a counterweight to the Knights of the Golden Circle, had been busy sniffing out treason, and it provided the cavalry with long lists of places where deserters were hidden. The regiment split up into platoons which went about the countryside, each with its little list, and the alarm was spread and people took to the woods. A young officer in charge of one of these squads found himself deeply puzzled by the whole business. He had enlisted to fight the Southern Confederacy and here he was, harrying the people of his own state in their own homes, and he wrote, bewildered:

"What were we there for? It is true that they had been harboring and secreting deserters from the Union Army, but for this was their property to be consumed by fire and were they to be marched off to some fort, there to be guarded as prisoners of war?"

It was a poor day, he recorded, when they brought fewer than twenty-five prisoners into camp, but he acknowledged that "such jumping fences, such riding through fields and woods, such searching smokehouses, garrets, barns, and cellars, such hanging men to trees for the purpose of extorting secrets, such breaking up and dispersing courts and grand juries, such foraging"—in plain violation of all law, as he felt—"I never before heard of at any time, in Illinois or any other state."[15]

Thus in Illinois, with barns and hayricks ablaze, and farm folk hiding out in the timber while troopers rode through the cornfields with drawn sabers glinting in the sun. There was also Ohio, and in Ohio there was a man named Clement Laird Vallandigham, until recently a Democratic congressman, who was minded now to become governor of Ohio and to make some use of the discontent and weariness and perplexity born of the war. Vallandigham was a tall handsome man with a politician's too-easy smile, a talent for using words, and a long record of unwavering opposition to the coercion of the South. Barely a month after Lincoln's election Vallandigham had warned a caucus of Ohio's congressional delegation that he would under no circumstances agree to the use of force against the South. Some of those present understood him to threaten war in the North if force should be tried. He was cold, calculating, profoundly ambitious, with a way of expressing himself that sounded self-righteous at times, a man not above appealing to prejudice when it would serve his turn. Early that winter of 1863, as a lame-duck congressman (his district had been gerrymandered to prevent his re-election) he had taunted the Republicans in the House:

"The war for the Union is, in your hands, a most bloody and costly failure. . . . War for the Union was abandoned; war for the Negro openly begun, and with stronger battalions than before. With what success? Let the dead at Fredericksburg and Vicksburg answer." He wanted peace, and peace at once, and he cried: "Ought this war to continue? I answer no—not a day, not an hour. What then? Shall we separate? Again I answer no, no, no!" His program was simple, based upon faith: "Stop fighting. Make an armistice. Accept at once friendly foreign mediation."

Under the surface Vallandigham saw, or at least professed to see, the same specter that had haunted Calhoun and Stevens, and the belief that desperate forces might be let loose by continued war ran under his impassioned sentences like a somber leitmotif: "I see nothing before us but universal political and social revolution, anarchy and bloodshed, compared with which the Reign of Terror in France was a merciful visitation."[16]

So here was Vallandigham, stumping Ohio for the governorship, seeking to capitalize on the people's deep belief that a word should be spoken that would explain this war and give it meaning. Also in Ohio, by the oddest chance, was Major General Ambrose E. Burnside, and his path was about to cross Vallandigham's.

After his ineffectual effort to purge the high command of the Army of the Potomac, Burnside had been quietly shelved. His offer to resign his commission had not been accepted, and he had been assigned to command the Department of the Ohio, which included the states of Ohio, Kentucky, Indiana, and Illinois. There was no great number of troops in his department and not much fighting was going on there, and the assumption seems to have been that even this well-meaning author of misfortune could hardly bumble his way into any very serious trouble now.

But Burnside was an intensely loyal man, and the wave of unrest that was going across the land troubled him. Like Stanton, he saw things in unshaded blacks and whites, and it seemed to him that a great many things which were being said and done in his department smacked strongly of outright treason. He began to issue restrictive orders, prohibiting the citizens from keeping or bearing arms, and placing limits on the right to criticize the military policy of the administration. He climaxed these at last by promulgating General Order Number 38, which stated flatly, if somewhat clumsily, that "the habit of declaring sympathy for the enemy will not be allowed in this department. Persons committing such offenses will be at once arrested, with a view to being tried . . . or sent beyond our lines into the lines of their friends." To make it perfectly clear, the order added that "it must be distinctly understood that treason, expressed or implied, will not be tolerated in this department."

Having said this, Burnside appointed a military commission to try any persons who might offend against General Order Number 38 and waited to see what would happen next.[17]

What would happen next would be a speech by Vallandigham, who was opening his political campaign with a big meeting in the town of Mount Vernon on May 1, the same day the Army of the Potomac was gathering around the Chancellorsville crossroads, with Hooker feeling the first chill wind of doubt and with Meade wondering how the bottom of a hill could be held if the top was untenable. It appears that Vallandigham accepted Burnside's order as a challenge, and a huge crowd was on hand to hear him respond to it. American flags floated from the tops of hickory poles (emblems of the Democracy ever since Andrew Jackson's day), and there was a great horse-drawn float carrying thirty-four pretty girls, who represented the thirty-four states of the whole Union. It was noticed that many men in the crowd wore in their lapels the emblems which had given the anti-war Democrats their name of Copperhead—copper heads cut from pennies and mounted on pins or clasps. In the crowd, lounging close to the platform with pencils and notebooks, were two officers of Burnside's command prepared to take down Vallandigham's words.

These officers did not give Burnside a very coherent account of the speech, contenting themselves with taking down stray phrases and sentences, but with the huge crowd cheering him on, Vallandigham spread himself. He talked sarcastically of "King Lincoln," specifically denounced General Order Number 38, and repeated all of his familiar arguments, seeing the war as a step toward despotism and demanding an immediate peace. It was a wild, fire-eating speech, coming tolerably close to an outright declaration of sympathy for the Confederacy, and when Burnside's officers got back to Cincinnati they gave the general notes which ruffled his whiskers. Reading them, Burnside concluded that he had an open-and-shut case. Without bothering to discuss the ins and outs of the matter with anybody, Burnside issued an order for Vallandigham's arrest.[18]

A night later an officer on Burnside's staff collected a company of infantry and took a special train from Cincinnati to Dayton, which was where Vallandigham lived. A little after two in the morning—graveyard watch, town silent as the tomb soldiers' footsteps echoing off the cobbles of quiet streets—heavy hands beat loudly on the door of Vallandigham's house. From an upstairs window the orator asked what was wanted and was told to open up, men had come to arrest him. A revolver was fired into the air, and Vallandigham lifted his voice to yell, "Asa! Asa! Asa!" into the night, this call being the alarm signal for anti-war Democrats. Musket butts smashed in the door, and the officer and a squad of soldiers went to Vallandigham's bedroom and told him he had just time to get dressed and catch a train. Protesting bitterly, and dressing the while, Vallandigham went with them, and that morning he was lodged in a military prison in Cincinnati. In Dayton an angry mob sacked the office of a Republican newspaper, starting a fire that burned out several non-partisan business establishments, and from his prison cell Vallandigham issued statements denouncing the author and the manner of his arrest and asserting: "I am here in a military bastille for no other offense than my political opinions."

This was true enough as far as it went, but the military were in control, and on May 6 Vallandigham went on trial before Burnside's military commission, accused of violating General Order Number 38. The two officers who had taken notes testified for the prosecution: Vallandigham had denounced the war as "wicked, cruel, and unnecessary" and had said in so many words that it was not being waged to preserve the Union but "for the purpose of crushing out liberty and erecting a despotism." He had unquestionably violated Burnside's order, if that order had any validity.

Vallandigham did not think it had any, and he refused to recognize the commission or to plead his own cause, contenting himself with summoning one witness, another Democratic congressman, the widely known anti-war man S. S. Cox, who had been among the speakers at Mount Vernon but whose remarks had been somewhat less inflammatory. Vallandigham was returned to his prison cell, and a lawyer went to the United States Circuit Court to demand a writ of habeas corpus.[19]

Rightly or wrongly, writs of habeas corpus did not run in this case, and the court refused to intervene. So on May 16 the military commission announced that it had found Vallandigham guilty of violating General Order Number 38 by publicly expressing "sympathy for those in arms against the government of the United States, and declaring disloyal sentiments and opinions with the object and purpose of weakening the power of the government in its efforts to suppress an unlawful rebellion." It sentenced him to be imprisoned for the duration of the war. Burnside promptly confirmed the sentence, ordering the man confined in Fort Warren at Boston.

Up to now Vallandigham had been just another candidate for the Democratic nomination for governor of Ohio. By act of Burnside he immediately became a martyr, nationally famous, and the land erupted with mass meetings of furious Democrats denouncing military despotism. Vallandigham's nomination for the Ohio governorship was a foregone conclusion. Worse yet, it was equally certain that the Democratic party in Ohio—and possibly everywhere else in the North—would now pass firmly into the hands of the faction that wanted to make immediate peace with the Confederacy. And this mess was dropped on Lincoln's desk while Lincoln was still trying to digest the bad news from Chancellorsville.

Unfortunately Burnside was not yet out of ammunition. Having struck a blow at treason in Ohio, he looked over into Illinois, where in addition to Southern-born residents who hid deserters and supported the Knights of the Golden Circle there was a pestiferous newspaper, the Chicago *Times,* which had long been saying in print exactly the sort of thing Vallandigham had said on the Mount Vernon platform. Burnside never had been able to tell a good strategic move from a bad one, and he was always fated to make a defect rather than a virtue out of the fact that he never knew when he had bitten off more than he could chew. Early on the morning of June 3, by his express order, cavalrymen rode up a Chicago street and mounted guard at the door of the *Times* office, and an hour or so later two companies of infantry from Camp Douglas came marching into the place. They took the building over, stopped the presses, and prevented further publication of the paper.

Thus after suppressing freedom of speech Burnside had suppressed freedom of the press, and it was up to Lincoln to say whether it was going to be that kind of war from now on.

Lincoln moved warily. Both actions had been taken without his knowledge, and the Vallandigham case was by far the hotter potato of the two. It may be that as he cast about for an expedient the President remembered Burnside's earlier statement that offenders against General Order Number 38 might be sent "beyond our lines into the lines of their friends." In any case, that finally seemed to strike him as a solid idea, and he canceled that part of the military commission's verdict which ordered Vallandigham imprisoned. Instead he had him sent down under guard to General Rosecrans, who was holding the line in front of Murfreesboro, Tennessee, and one morning not long after that a squad of soldiers escorted the orator out into the desolate no man's land between Union and Confederate lines and turned him over to the Confederacy, to do with as the Confederacy might choose. Suppression of the Chicago *Times* was revoked outright, the troops were removed, and Burnside was warned to arrest no more civilians and shut down no more newspapers without prior authorization from Washington.

The Confederacy hardly knew what to do with its new guest. He flitted cross-country to Charleston, South Carolina, his position sufficiently embarrassing both to himself and to his hosts, and eventually he took a ship for Canada. Before he sailed he found time to hold a quiet conversation with a representative of Jefferson Davis's government, in which he is alleged to have betrayed an inner fear—that the Confederacy might yet fold up, leaving Vallandigham without a cause. The Northern peace party, he insisted, was on the climb, and if the South could just hold out for another year everything would be fine, as the Democrats would then "sweep the Lincoln dynasty out of political existence." He offered one curious piece of advice which was totally ignored but which might profitably have been listened to: Whatever happens, do not again invade the North, because if you do all parties there will unite to throw you out and Lincoln's hand will be so strengthened that he will be able to go on with the war with new vigor.[20] (Lee was perfecting his plans for a march into Pennsylvania, and farther west John Hunt Morgan was marshaling his troopers for a dash across the Ohio, and it was as if this leader of the Copperheads was crying, Don't take our Copperhead uprisings so seriously. We won't stick if it comes to real fighting; we are men of politics and fine words and that is all we can ever be.)

In Canada, a martyr-in-absentia, Vallandigham issued statements and exhortations to the faithful in Ohio, and when the Ohio Democrats held their state convention in Columbus in June they drew an enthusiastic crowd of forty thousand people. For the balance of the summer Lincoln was painstakingly explaining his course in regard to Vallandigham's arrest, sounding at times, perhaps, rather more like a clever lawyer than a statesman but at least explaining, and leaving one difficult question for the opposition to answer as best it could: "Must I shoot a simple-minded soldier boy who deserts and not touch a hair of the wily agitator who induces him to desert?"[21]

For Lincoln was shooting soldier boys that spring, and desertion was no longer being treated as a minor fault. The V Army Corps was drawn up in an open field one day, solid masses of bronzed veterans grouped around three sides of an open square, tattered flags motionless above them. One of the soldiers remembered afterward:

"The impressive silence was not broken by a single sound. Each line of soldiers looked more like the section of a vast machine than a line composed of living men. The silence was suddenly and sadly broken by the sounds of approaching music—not the quick, inspiring strains with which we were so familiar, but a measured, slow and solemn dirge, whose weird, sorrowful notes were poured forth like the moanings of lost spirits. Not a soldier spoke, but every eye was turned in the direction from which came the sad and mournful cadences, and we saw the procession."

First came a band playing the "Funeral March." Then came sixty men from the provost guard, spick-and-span in dress uniforms, rifles at the shoulder. After them were four soldiers carrying a black coffin, followed by a condemned deserter in blue pants and white shirt, a guard on either side of him; then four more men with another coffin, followed by another prisoner, and another detachment with another coffin, and so on—five condemned deserters in all, each preceded by his coffin, with a final detachment from the provost guard bringing up the rear. The procession came to the open side of the square, where five graves had been dug. A coffin was put on the ground before each grave, and each prisoner sat on the end of his coffin. Black blindfolds were put on the prisoners, thousands of men looking on in utter silence, and then the chaplains came up beside the condemned men for a final word and a prayer. The chaplains retired, and a firing squad of twelve men took post facing each prisoner, one blank charge in every twelve rifles, so that any member of a firing squad might later, if it comforted him, think that perhaps he himself had not actually killed anyone. An officer stepped out, brisk and businesslike, sword hooked up at his side, and the great silence was broken by his thin cry: "Ready—aim—*fire!*" And the thing was done, five bleeding bodies lay across the coffins, and the band piped up a quickstep while the soldiers marched off the field.[22]

That was the spring when words were no good in America. The war had given the country problems for which the past offered no guide—problems, indeed, which grew out of the total explosion of the shell which the past had built around human institutions—and men were not going to talk their way out of them. It was what they did that was going to count. A musket butt could smash in a man's door in the dead of night, troopers with drawn sabers might drag farmers off to prison camp under a prairie moon, veterans of great battles might have to stand in formal ranks to see deserters executed, and what it all added up to could be told only after men had acted.

Yet there was an immense vitality at work. In their reaction to war-weariness and defeat both the people and the government were showing signs of a new temper. Here was no inert resignation to despair. Trouble was being met head-on now—stupidly, in some cases, brutally in others, but at least squarely. The country was no longer numb. Slowly and with infinite pain, strength was being gathered, and the danger soon would be that the ultimate answer might be sought in strength alone. The Republican stalwart, War Governor Buckingham of Connecticut, was exultantly telling his legislature to get on with the war: "Let the retribution be so terrible that future generations shall not dare to repeat the crime." The final tragedy would occur if retribution alone should become the answer.

The word could not be spoken yet. The grapes of wrath were being trampled out, and there was a great clamor of many voices. There would have to be, finally, an hour of decision, with the uproar coming to its own terrible climax. After that, if anyone could understand and speak for the myriad people who were crying their complaints, a voice might be heard.

2. Glory! Glory! Hallelujah!

Things were looking up, and it seemed that the crisis had been passed, and the newspaper editor took up his pen and wrote his jubilation for all the world to read.

"Aladdin with his wonderful lamp could scarcely have worked a more magical change," he announced. "All honor, we say, to the men who have battled long and bravely to secure this consummation— who have stood up in the dark days of the enterprise and pressed onward, through the most discouraging difficulties, until their efforts have been finally crowned with glorious success!"

The editor was a loyal Pennsylvanian, editor of the Crawford County *Democrat,* writing in the very middle of the Civil War, but he was not talking about the progress of the national arms, the suppression of Copperheads, or the state of the war for union and freedom. Instead he was being inspired by the fact that a new railroad line had pushed its way into the heart of the Pennsylvania oil fields, and what he was growing most lyrical about was the sight of half a dozen locomotives all puffing at once, long trains of cars laden with oil barrels waiting in the yards, a brand-new brick refinery, a handsome hotel, many new dwelling houses, the ensemble now visible "where, but a few months since, stood the primeval forest." This was in the town of Corry, which in a short time had mushroomed from nothing at all to 10,000 inhabitants and a $12,000,000 annual business. At Meadville the editor saw further marvels, including a new depot with a 327-foot train shed, and a fine hotel "which has brought to this little city of the west the luxury and magnificence of New York living." He paid his respects to "the old fogies who have imagined that our town was finished and should be fenced in," and he announced unhesitatingly that "a new era of prosperity is about to dawn upon us."[1]

The editor was quite right. Prosperity was at hand, for Meadville and for Corry and for all the rest of the North, and it might seem that the great news of the day was not so much the progress of the armies as the miracle that was taking place behind the lines. Pennsylvania was having an oil boom, with a new product and a new technology coming up to provide wealth and employment that had not previously existed. (In 1859 oil production was a scant 84,000 gallons; three years later it had gone up to 128,000,000, the cheap kerosene lamp was beginning to displace candles and whale oil, and a pious young businessman named John D. Rockefeller was watching attentively.) Yet this new industry was only one of many, and possibly the year of jubilee was at hand. All across the North a tremendous transformation was taking place, and if an editor babbled about magic and Aladdin's lamp, it was hardly surprising. The country was on its way with a rush and a roar, gaining new strength almost by geometrical progression, and perhaps the war was a spare-time venture, with most of the country's attention fixed on more important matters.

(General Robert E. Lee was beginning skillfully to move toward the upper Rappahannock, concealing the shift behind a show of strength along the hills back of Fredericksburg, and Jeb Stuart was assembling the largest cavalry corps the Confederacy ever saw on the open hills and fields near Brandy Station, preparing for a hard thrust into the North. His equilibrium regained, Hooker watched closely and prepared countermoves, and men began to see the prospect of a great climactic battle on Northern soil.)

In the West the wagon trains rolled across the frontier without a halt. The same Eastern newspapers that printed news from the fighting fronts announced that interested parties could obtain maps of the Western regions at the front office, and much was printed about the best routes to the new mining fields of Nevada and Colorado, of Idaho and Montana—great names now, as important in their way as names like Fredericksburg and Chancellorsville. Every day from twenty-five to one hundred wagons were ferried across the Missouri at Council Bluffs, and on the Iowa side the road was usually packed for half a mile or more with wagons waiting their turn. One man noted a solid string of twelve hundred wagons on the road leading west from Omaha, and a traveler in Kansas reported that he met five hundred wagons every day bound for Colorado and California. Some of the men who made this westward migration were frankly anxious to get beyond the reach of the army draft, yet the army lost little. The country had men and riches to spare; it could fight a great war and at the same time open a wilderness to settlement, and the government was actually encouraging the move by giving away, free, 160-acre farms to anyone who would take the trouble to occupy and improve the land. (It gave away two and one half million acres to homesteaders during the war years.)[2]

The farm belt had been drained of men of military age. In one Wisconsin village which contained 250 men of voting age, 111 had gone into the army, and in an Illinois rural township 117 of 147 men liable to the draft had volunteered. Yet the farm states were far more populous than when the war began, and farm production had increased beyond imagination. In the cities there were new factories building reapers, mowers, revolving horse rakes, two-horse cultivators, rotary spaders, grain drillers, and other appliances, and between the immigrants and the new machinery the lost labor of the volunteers simply did not matter. Like the Pennsylvania editor, men who took time to look about them were impressed with the sense that a prodigious change was taking place. The president of the Illinois Agricultural Society wrote ecstatically:

"Look over these prairies and observe everywhere the life and activity prevailing. See the railroads pressed beyond their capacity with the freights of our people; the metropolis of the state rearing its stately blocks with a rapidity almost fabulous, and whitening the northern lakes with the sails of its commerce; every smaller city, town, village, and hamlet within our borders all astir with improvement; every factory, mill, and machine shop running with its full complement of hands; the hum of industry in every household; more acres of fertile land under culture, fuller granaries and more prolific crops than ever before; in short, observe that this state and this people of Illinois are making more rapid progress in population, development, wealth, education, and in all the arts of peace than in any former period, and then realize, if you can, that all this has occurred and is occurring in the midst of a war the most stupendous ever prosecuted among men."[3]

Traffic on the Great Lakes was booming. Passenger travel had declined, and many of the passenger boats had been dismantled so that their engines could be installed in freighters, but these freighters were carrying a huge trade. The same Civil War which saw naval warfare revolutionized by the introduction of ironclads saw also a revolution in Great Lakes traffic. Iron steamers were coming in, the canal at the Soo had been opened, and the iron mines of upper Michigan were sending more and more ore down to the lower lakes. The first year's shipment of ore, shortly before the war, had amounted to a mere 132 tons; by the middle of the war ore was coming down to Cleveland at 235,000 tons a year, to be smelted there or to be sent on by rail to Pittsburgh, which was creating its characteristic pillar of smoke against the sky.[4]

For the transportation industry, 1863 was the most prosperous year in history. Hundreds of locomotives and thousands of freight cars had been built since the war began. The Pittsburgh foundries that turned out guns and armor and mortars for the military were also busy with castings for the locomotive manufacturers, with machinery for iron mines and gold mines, with equipment for the oil refineries, with the production of railroad rails, with countless other items needed by an industrialized nation.

At Washington the Patent Office was active. Americans were inventing things in these war years at a greater rate than ever before, and while some of these had to do with war goods, most of them had nothing to do with the war but were aimed strictly at civilian wants. There were new patents for passenger elevators, steam fans for restaurants, milk-condensing machinery, steam printing presses, flypaper, fountain pens, roller skates, dredges, washing machines, and heaven knew what else.[5] With so many men gone in the army, there was naturally an emphasis on labor-saving equipment, but a heavy flood of immigration from Europe was coming in without ceasing, so that the population increased steadily month by month despite the losses in camps and on battlefields. No fewer than 800,000 immigrants arrived during the war years, bringing with them something like $400,000,000 in cash, and if the war was costing the unheard-of sum of two millions a day, there would be no trouble about paying for it.

The export trade was thriving. New York merchants had been panicky when the war began, remembering that two thirds of the export trade normally was in cotton and wondering how this deficit would ever be met. With the war in full stride they forgot their worries. Manufactured goods went overseas. One New York exporter, in the first three years of the war, sent $800,000 worth of sewing machines to Liverpool, and a New York merchant exulted that Yankee clocks "are ticking all over England." Most important of all, there was wheat. England and Europe had had drought, and crops were down. Civil War America was raising wheat, corn, and hogs as never before, and England's purchases of American wheat and flour increased prodigiously over the pre-war level. English factory hands were idle because Southern cotton could not be imported, and in Richmond men still believed that eventually this pressure would bring England in on the side of the Confederacy. What they overlooked was that while England could get along somehow without American cotton, it could not under any circumstances get along now without American wheat. Back of the export figures lay that solid fact which in the end was to make British intervention impossible—a fact which the South could not even see but which was a force as mighty for the Union as an army with banners.[6]

(In Richmond, Vice-President Stephens was starting off under a flag of truce, hoping to get to Washington to present proposals for peace. It was believed that he would reach Washington while Lee reached Pennsylvania, and that the irresistible pressure of the Army of Northern Virginia on a North undermined by Copperheads would compel the Lincoln government to talk to him and to offer acceptable terms. One-legged Dick Ewell, perkily riding his horse with a peg leg sticking out at an angle, was leading Confederate troops on the road of invasion, and the only man in his outfit who had ever heard of a rocky Pennsylvania knoll named Culp's Hill was a young fellow who used to live there.)[7]

Railroads and shipping, iron ore and wheat, patents and immigrants—the North was exploding with new strength and energy. A sober man of business in New York reviewed the war boom a few months later and found it unlike anything that had ever happened before.

"There is a mania abroad," he wrote. "There are thousands of new schemes, and new companies, forming almost every day; and although many of them prove failures, yet there is one remarkable fact connected with them, differing entirely from those speculations in years gone by. . . . Men are not now going to banks and getting notes discounted that have been endorsed by neighbors. The fact is the people have got the money and they are looking about to see what to do with it. These companies are organizing for the very purpose, and most of them are honestly intending to develop the material interests of the country, and to this end hundreds of millions of dollars in the last four years have been devoted."[8]

There was money to be made, and a young officer in the Army of the Potomac was writing in wonder about "my country, hardly feeling this draft upon its resources, and growing richer every day."[9] It was noteworthy that the richest fields for money-making were no longer, as in the past, merchandising, shipping, and real estate speculation. The big money now was in manufacturing, in mining, and—as an inescapable by-product—in the manipulation of stocks. The factory system had arrived full blast. The sewing machine, coming in just in time to make it possible to meet enormous army orders for uniforms, had created a vast new ready-made-clothing business, and 100,000 people were employed by this trade in New York alone. Textile factories were consuming, among other things, 200,000,000 pounds of wool annually and were making fabulous profits. One manufacturer reported that he was making $2,000 a day. A new stitching machine for joining soles to uppers had revolutionized the boot-and-shoe industry, and big factories were going up in New York and Philadelphia, in Lynn and Danvers and Haverhill. The distilling trade enjoyed a delirious boom, and profits for one fat war year were estimated at $50,000,000. St. Louis (which as a distilling center got a generous slice of that profit) boasted of its new Lindell Hotel, built at a cost of a million and a half, with twenty-seven acres of plastering and thirty-two miles of bell wire. Chicago built eight large packing houses and sixteen smaller ones in a single year. In 1863 alone, Philadelphia put up fifty-seven new factories. A party of 230 Western businessmen was taken on a promotional junket to Portland, Maine, by aggressive city boosters. War-torn America displayed a great new fondness for horse racing, the new tracks in Boston, Chicago, and Washington drawing enormous crowds. Twenty-seven cities built street railways, there was an unprecedented rise in the sale of school textbooks, and fifteen colleges and universities were founded, including such institutions as Vassar, Swarthmore, and Cornell.[10]

In Richmond the Confederacy's chief of ordnance was dolefully noting that the North had thirty-eight arms factories able to turn out nearly 5,000 infantry rifles every day. This, he said, "exhibits a most marked contrast to our own condition," as the South was making only 100 a day. Theoretically, he added, Southern capacity was nearly 300, but skilled workmen were lacking.[11] What nobody was able to see at the moment was that this volume production of weapons with interchangeable parts was teaching Northern industrialists one of the great secrets of mass production.

The New York merchant who had exulted in the prosperity born of the war declared that "the mind staggers as we begin to contemplate the future," and concluded that there was coming to the nation a greatness "which no other country in the world has ever seen." He had reason to talk that way. There had never been anything like this before. Whole generations of growth and development seemed to be crammed into a few years. Here was eternal Yankeeism triumphant, grinning because it was possible to grow rich out of a ruinous war, but here also was ever so much more than that—a dazzling expansion of strength, a welling up of vitality and energy that could create faster than any possible destruction, a tapping of powers so profound that the whole get-rich-quick tribe could not quite reduce them to a mere matter of dollars and cents.

Perhaps it is time to ask what was really going on here, anyway. Had the war already been won, with a doom from beyond the stars pronounced in advance on a rash Confederacy which never really had a chance?

William Tecumseh Sherman saw it so. That grim soldier with the ultra-modern viewpoint had called the turn before the war even began when he warned a Southern friend: "In all history no nation of mere agriculturists ever made successful war against a nation of mechanics. . . . You are bound to fail." Apparently his prophecy was being borne out. This war which was bleeding the Confederacy to absolute exhaustion was making the North stronger than ever before, stronger than men had dreamed possible, stimulating a growth which in a few generations would create the mightiest power in history. A Northern victory, it might seem, was inevitable.

But the war was not over and the war had not yet been won. The war, on the contrary, could very easily be lost, and Robert E. Lee had with him seventy thousand lean and hungry men who would quickly arrange it that way if something were not done about them. If destiny had arrived at a verdict, it was a verdict which could still be reversed. All of the weight of power might lie on one side, yet in actual contemporary fact Northern victory was not in the least certain. The spreading factories and the burdened busy trains and the limitless fields of wheat were not going to appear on the firing line, and it was on the firing line that this affair must finally be settled. Up there, under the muzzles of the guns, there would be living men, as self-centered and as shortsighted and as careless of historical imperatives as any men that ever lived, and in the end it was all going to be up to them. If a general lost his nerve or a brigade lost its head, or if the thousands of obscure young men in dirty, sweat-stained uniforms failed by whatever justifiable margin to come up to the mark, then the riches and the power and the might were phantoms to drift away with the battle smoke as the flags came tumbling down.

It was not going to be easy, either. Lee's men were at their peak. Chancellorsville may have been a delusive victory, yet it had seemed to confirm their jubilant feeling (and Lee's feeling, too, that strong gray man who never once let emotion run away with him) that there was no enemy anywhere whom they could not lick. Jackson was gone, but Longstreet was back, and a division commanded by one George Pickett was beginning the long hike northward to keep a certain engagement that was written, perhaps, in the Doomsday Book. Lee's army was beginning to move northward, and its men stepped off the miles as if they had heard the bell of destiny ringing for them.

In the Army of the Potomac there was no such jubilation. The army had little room for either elation or despondency any more. It had mostly a grim antic humor and a deep hard-bought toughness, and although it would unfurl the colors, strike up the band, and march in step when it passed through a town, it slouched along most of the time without parade or display, hiding whatever it most relied upon under an irreverent and derisive spirit. While it still kept to its camps around Falmouth there was an exchange of prisoners, and there were returned to the army men who had spent months in Southern prison camps, skinny, tattered men who were dirty beyond anything anyone had ever heard of. One of these rejoined his outfit, drew a neat new pile of clothing, and invited his squad to go down to the river with him and scrub the dirt off him—there was so much of it, and it had been there so long, that he was sure he could never do much with it himself. So his friends went down to the river, and everybody stripped and got into the water. The men went to work on him with soap and scrubbing brushes, while his miserable discarded rags went floating off downstream. At last one of the scrubbers wiped away a mound of lather with a sweep of his brush, peered closely at the ex-prisoner's torso, and announced flatly that something was wrong with his skin. The other men looked more closely, agreed, scrubbed some more, and discovered suddenly that the man still wore his undershirt.

The ex-prisoner expressed great pleasure and surprise at this discovery. He had thought, he said, that that undershirt had been lost six months ago, and it was a comfort to him to know that he still had it. As they peeled it off and cast it adrift he asked to be allowed to keep it for a souvenir, but the men hooted loudly and refused to hear of it. . . .[12]

Rumors of the Confederate movement reached camp, and Hooker sent his cavalry up the Rappahannock under orders to cross over and, if possible, see what the Rebels thought they were up to.

Pleasonton had the cavalry now—a stylish little soldier with a pert straw hat and kid gloves and a shifty eye—and he was more of a cavalryman than Stoneman had been, though he was a long way from being Phil Sheridan. His reports were better than his battles, and he gained fame that way. There were those who noticed that he was a good deal of a headquarters operator, but he had close to ten thousand mounted men at his command, and they had learned how to ride and shoot, and in spite of Chancellorsville their morale was high. Pleasonton had some good subordinates, too, most notably a brigadier named John Buford, a solid man who was hard to frighten and who was greatly admired by the men of his division. There were others: harum-scarum Judson Kilpatrick, for instance, a lanky little man with stringy side whiskers; a fantastic mustachioed soldier of fortune, Sir Percy Wyndham from England and the Continent; and a flamboyant hell-for-leather horseman named George Armstrong Custer, who possessed the great basic virtue of liking to fight. All in all, the cavalry corps now was a different outfit from the clumsy, lumbering conglomeration which had been wearing out good horses on Virginia roads earlier in the war.[13]

Pleasonton got his men down to the upper fords of the Rappahannock all unnoticed, and in the mist of an early dawn on June 9 he sent them down to the river to cross with a whoop and a wild splashing gallop. They promptly crumpled up the Confederate outpost line and went careening up from the riverside toward the open fields and knolls around Brandy Station, where Stuart had just been reviewing his own cavalry.

What followed was the biggest cavalry fight of the war—a wild, confused action in which cavalry charged cavalry with sabers swinging, dust clouds rising so thickly that it was hard to tell friend from enemy, and the rule was to cut hard at the nearest face and ride on fast. For once in his life Stuart was taken by surprise. A vicious fire fight developed in the meadows near a little country church, where dismounted troopers of the 8th Illinois Cavalry fired their carbines so fast that some of the weapons burst, and a flanking column went thundering up a side road and came within an inch of capturing Fleetwood Hill, where Stuart had his headquarters tents. In the final nick of time Stuart got his squadrons back, and there were charge and countercharge all up and down the Fleetwood slopes, Confederate troopers riding through a battery of Yankee horse artillery and cutting down the gunners, and the air was full of dust and the thunder of pounding hoofs and the clang of steel and the sickening sound of head-long columns crashing bodily into one another.

By the narrowest margin Stuart's men held the hill. One of Pleasonton's columns went astray somehow and did not get into action, and scouts notified Pleasonton that gray infantry was showing itself around Brandy Station, which made him feel that there might be such a thing as going too far. In the end, the Yankee cavalry rode back to the river and went back where it came from, the corps as a whole having left approximately ten per cent of its members behind as casualties. Among these, shot dead from his saddle in the first yelling charge up from the riverbank, was Mississippi-born Grimes Davis, who had shown a great knack for making rowdy volunteers take regular-army discipline and like it, and who had begun to look like one of the army's most promising cavalry officers.

This fight was not without effect. The Federal cavalry had finally been beaten and had had to withdraw, but it had at last stood up to the Rebel cavalry in open combat, and the men were immensely pleased with themselves. A Confederate critic remarked ruefully of this battle that "it *made* the Federal cavalry," and a New York private said gleefully that "the Rebels were going to have a review of their cavalry on that day, but our boys reviewed them." This soldier could not understand why the Yankee troopers had been withdrawn after what he considered a winning fight, but he concluded hopefully that "the head officers knew all about it." A Massachusetts major, after admitting that "there was more fighting than generalship," added that the Rebels here "lost their prestige and never recovered it."[14]

That may have been overstating the case a bit, but the cavalry had reason to feel proud. By and large, the Yankee troopers were men who had come up the hard way. They had learned a good deal on the way up, much of it at the hands of their enemies. Gone were the fancy uniforms and the cumbersome equipment provided for by old-army regulations—light blue trousers, dark blue waist-length jacket with brass scales on the shoulder, the whole topped with what one man recalled as "a predacious-looking hat with yellow cord." This struck the men as overfancy, and anyhow, after an hour on the road in dry weather everybody got so dusty that nobody could tell what they were wearing, and by now most of the men had provided themselves with plain infantry pants and tunic and forage cap. They generally managed to buy or steal great piratical boots, into which they stuffed their pants legs, with a revolver tucked into the right-leg boot along with the pants.[15]

They were beginning to discover that the revolver was a better weapon than the traditional saber. The handgun furnished cavalry at the start of the war was just about useless—a cumbersome museum piece known as a dragoon pistol, a muzzle-loader a foot long with a ramrod swiveled on the under side of the barrel. It kicked so hard that the man using it was in nearly as much danger as the man he was shooting at, and it had such a hard trigger pull that one cavalryman insisted that if a man shot at an enemy in battle, "by the time his pistol was discharged he was liable to be shooting at the men in his own regiment." This man added that "it was never wise to choose for a mark anything smaller than a good-sized barn."[16]

In the course of time the army replaced these miserable weapons with up-to-date revolvers, with which the men felt much more at home than they felt with sabers. These latter were supposed to be carried at all times in scabbards which dangled from a man's waist belt, but the metal scabbard and its rings jingled and made a lot of noise, and the weapon was just a nuisance to a man on foot. So the average trooper simply lashed his scabbard firmly to the near side of the saddle, nearly parallel to the horse's body, so that his left leg was over it when he was on his horse. That way he did not have to bother with it when on foot, it stayed put and did no flopping or jangling when he was riding, and if he needed it he could draw it quickly enough. Left to himself, though, he usually preferred to use his revolver.

Most cavalrymen were notorious foragers, not to say thieves, if only because the possession of a horse enabled them to carry more booty and make a quicker getaway than were possible for a foot soldier. As a general thing they found an easy rationalization for their marauding. A slightly prejudiced Illinois trooper wrote of the luckless Virginia farmers: "These simple people seemed to think that they could send their sons into the Rebel army to destroy our country and murder our soldiers, and that we would not only protect them but spend our time in guarding their chicken roosts, pigpens, and beehives. But they soon learned that Western soldiers came for other purposes." The cavalry tradition stipulated that a good trooper was a good provider, having forage for his horse even when government issue failed and, for the matter of that, having occasionally a new horse as well. When a cavalry regiment camped in a hitherto untrodden part of the country, it invariably happened that certain of the men would show up with new horses, and if an officer made inquiries it is recorded that he generally got "an irrelevant answer." A farmer would come in, as likely as not, to make complaint and would be invited to look over the picket rope and claim his horse if he could see it. That rarely did much good. As one veteran put it: "It was odd how a little art would change a horse's appearance so that his own dam would not know him, let alone owner or breeder. . . . With a pair of scissors, a very nice imitation of a brand would be made to appear on shoulder or hip. A little hair dye would remove all white marks, and the same scissors would so change mane and tail as to make the animal unrecognizable. . . . Almost any change in appearance or gait could be produced at short notice by the cunning trooper."[17]

Once in a blue moon a lucky cavalry outfit could loot by official order rather than in defiance of the rules. After the Brandy Station fight the army prepared to move, and as a security measure headquarters ordered all sutlers to leave the army. Here and there a sutler would evade the order, trusting to luck that he could move along by unused side roads and keep within shopping distance of the bivouacs without drawing the attention of the provost marshal. On the move up from the river one sutler miscalculated disastrously and met a whole column of cavalry while he was plodding along a narrow lane which he had thought the army would not use. Cavalry jangled to a halt because the sutler's wagon blocked the entire lane, and in a few moments an officer of the provost guard came trotting up to see what the trouble was. He took the situation in at a glance and wasted no words on the sutler. Instead he raised his voice and called to the head of the column: "What regiment is that?" First Massachusetts Cavalry, he was told. "Well, 1st Massachusetts Cavalry," he cried, pointing to the wagon, "go through that sutler!" The troopers came on with a whoop, and one of them asserted that in less than fifteen minutes "the contents of that wagon were distributed through the whole length of the regiment."[18]

Aside from lifting cavalry morale, the fight at Brandy Station had one other effect. The glimpse which had been obtained of Confederate infantry so far upstream persuaded Hooker that Lee was beginning to move around the Federal right flank, presumably by way of the Shenandoah Valley but possibly on a narrower arc, and he alerted his army for a countermove. It struck him that if Lee was moving north and west the thing for the Army of the Potomac to do was either to pitch into the Confederate rear or to march straight for Richmond, but Washington overruled him: Lee's army was his objective and the protection of Washington was his responsibility, and he had better go where Lee went and stay between him and the capital.

This made Hooker grumpy. Herman Haupt went to him a few days after Brandy Station to ask what the next move was to be, and he found Hooker in a very bad humor. Hooker said that he had no plans: he had made various suggestions and they had been turned down; from now on he would do nothing except what he was ordered to do, and if trouble came of it, it would not be his fault. Haupt did not care a great deal for this attitude and eventually he told Halleck

about it. Meanwhile Hooker unbent a bit and by mid-June orders
went out to evacuate the great supply bases at Aquia Creek and
Belle Plain and start the army north.[19] (Haupt noted that the order
to evacuate a base, with the consequent destruction of many supplies,
was always welcomed by quartermaster and commissary officers, because such a move automatically settled the deficiencies in everybody's accounts.)

By June 15 the army was on the roads again. The Virginia coastal
plain can get hot in June, and the Army of the Potomac remembered
the first few days of this march up from Falmouth as the worst march
of the entire war. The sun came out blistering hot, roadside springs
and brooks were scarce, and unfriendly Rebels had filled many of the
wells with stones. The roads were ankle-deep in dust, and each regiment moved in a choking opaque cloud. When a column did reach a
small spring the rush of men to fill canteens quickly turned it into a
mud puddle, and in any case the water in canteens reached blood
heat in no time. Any number of men were prostrated by the heat—a
Sanitary Commission nurse wrote that there were 120 cases of sun-
stroke in one division—and a good many deaths occurred.[20]

To add to the discomfort, GHQ was in a hurry, and long marches
were ordered. The XII Corps did thirty-three miles to Fairfax Courthouse in one day, and Humphreys's division of the III Corps was
kept marching all night, following the railroad to Manassas Junction.
When morning came with no break for breakfast the men began to
chant "Coffee! Coffee!" until they were finally turned into a field and
allowed to take a nap until noon. The Philadelphia Brigade remembered doing twenty-eight miles on the dustiest of roads, and as the
army moved on at this killing pace it littered the whole countryside
with stragglers. John Gibbon, commanding a division in the II Corps,
sternly announced in general orders that "in the vast majority of
cases the straggler is a skulking cowardly wretch who strives to shift
his duties upon the shoulders of more honest men and better soldiers." He told his men that the 15th, 19th, and 20th Massachusetts
regiments customarily reached camp at night with few or no absentees, and said that showed that "straggling, even in the worst weather,
is inexcusable." The historian of the 15th proudly recorded this tribute
to his regiment's steadfastness but admitted that on the very evening
the order was issued the 15th came into camp with only fifty-three
men to stack arms. The remaining three hundred men in the outfit
came stumbling in at all hours.[21]

Cavalry horses, like foot soldiers, often gave out on this march. Many of these were simply abandoned by the troopers, and it often happened that after a rest they would revive and go sauntering along, following the army. This was a boon to many footsore infantry stragglers, who would capture the beasts, rig makeshift reins and bridles out of strips of tent cloth or other material, and go riding along bareback—until, no doubt, the provost guard got them. It was noticed that stragglers who were congenital shirks would hide out in barns or sheds when sundown came in order to escape the guard, but that good men who had honestly been trying to keep up would tramp along until late at night to overtake their regiments.

A few days of this intensive marching pulled the army far away from the Rappahannock, and its bivouacs presently ran from the Bull Run Mountains all the way up to the Potomac. It was generally believed by the men in the ranks that if Lee had not already gone north of the river he would do so shortly, and some of the old-timers were wagging their heads and telling each other that they were going to have Antietam all over again. Nobody in his right mind wanted to repeat that fight, but the men who had marched through Maryland remembered it as a green and pleasant land where the citizens were glad to see Union soldiers, and there was a general feeling that this army could not fail to win once it got north of the Potomac.[22] After a few days of forced marches the high command let the men take it a little more easily as they got nearer the river, and the army caught its breath and found its spirits reviving.

Late one afternoon the I Corps was hiking along the road toward Leesburg. The column went past an old plantation, and on a rail fence by the roadside there was an unexpected audience—some dozens of the plantation's colored folk, perching on the fence and rolling their eyes hugely as the Lincoln soldiers went by. The mounted officers at the head of the column passed along, and the color guard with the cased dusty flags, and then came the infantry, rank upon endless rank, tramping the miles off with the stolid silence of veterans. The colored folk were simple people who knew very little about many things, but they were familiar with the apocalyptic visions and the wild sharp poetry of Scripture, and as they looked at these tired soldiers they saw what the reviewing officers would never see—Freedom stepping lightly along the hills, the King of the Earth striding by with a ram's horn in his hand, the walls of Jericho itself collapsing to the sound of far-off trumpets—and before long they began to rock and sway on their perch, and they shouted "Hallelujah!" and "Bless de Lord!" and some of them cried out that Lincoln was a mighty warrior.

In front of the fence, close to the road, stood a gray-haired bent old patriarch, and he finally spoke up to ask where Lincoln was personally. Soldier-like, the men answered that he wouldn't be along for a while yet—he was back behind the mule train, and maybe it would be tomorrow before he showed up. The slaves on the fence took this in, and they continued to shout, and before long the old man by the roadside began to sway and chant, and the first thing anyone knew he was leading the colored people in a song, all of the bodies rocking back and forth with the music, while the tanned soldiers with their gleaming rifles marched by:

> *"Don't you see 'em, comin', comin', comin',*
>   *Millions from de odder shore?*
> *Glory! Glory! Hallelujah!*
>   *Bless de Lord forever more!*
>
> *"Don't you see 'em, goin', goin', goin',*
>   *Past ol' massa's mansion door?*
> *Glory! Glory! Hallelujah!*
>   *Bless de Lord forever more!*
>
> *"Jordan's stream is runnin', runnin', runnin'—*
>   *Million soldiers passin' o'er:*
> *Lincoln comin' wid his chariot—*
>   *Bless de Lord forever more!"*

One of the soldiers who marched past them wrote that it seemed to him as if he could see the rocking figures and hear the singing far into the night, while the army kept on its way to the river.[23]

Yet this army rarely heard the echoes of a glory-hallelujah chorus as it tramped the long roads of war, and it was much more likely to punctuate its endless rambling narrative with a ribald jeer than with a chant about Jordan's flowing stream.

Part of the army came up to the North by a road that took it straight across the old Bull Run battlefield. It was ten months since the great battle there, but many dead had never been buried. The day was as sultry here as everywhere else in Virginia, and the men tramped along the historic turnpike, with bleached skulls and ribs and shinbones lying in the meadows amid heaps of rotted clothing. The men glanced casually aside from time to time, but they kept walking along and they said nothing, except to curse wearily when galloping staff officers or couriers crowded them. Finally they passed a too-shallow grave by the roadside. From it there extended a dead hand, withered to parchment, reaching bleakly toward the sky as if in some despairing, unanswered supplication. A New Jersey soldier saw it, reflected upon it, and was moved to mirth.

"Look, boys!" he called, pointing to the lifeless hand. "See the soldier putting out his hand for back pay!"[24]

The men guffawed briefly and tramped on without another glance.

3. White Road in the Moonlight

Off beyond the Blue Ridge Lee's army was moving, and Federal outposts in the Shenandoah Valley collapsed before a tidal wave of Rebel soldiers who struck as suddenly and as hard as if Stonewall Jackson himself still led them. Stragglers from the routed Union detachments scrambled back through Harper's Ferry, and a long rabble of civilian refugees went rocketing clear up into Pennsylvania, blocking the roads, picking up strength as they went, taking horses and cattle and household goods with them, as if the destroying angel and the original flood were hard upon their heels. Among these refugees, bewildered and lost, were hundreds of free colored folk, headed for no discernible goal short of the north star. Word had gone forth that the Confederates were rounding up all colored people and sending them south into slavery, and no Negro cared to wait to see if the rumor were true or false.[1]

Clearly enough, this was invasion again and not a mere cavalry foray, and the North took the alarm. At Washington's request, Northern governors called out the militia, and as far away as New York the natty home-guard regiments fell in at their armories, counted themselves and their equipment, and took the trains for Pennsylvania. At Harrisburg, where national guardsmen felled trees and dug up wheat fields to build fortifications, there was infinite excitement. The toll bridge over the Susquehanna did the biggest business in its history as people cleared out from before Lee's advance guard. There was the greatest demand for railroad tickets the city had ever known;

the state capitol was stripped of its valuables—including the expressionless oil paintings of bygone governors—which were crated for shipment to some safer place, and around the railroad depot the pavement was blocked with trunks and boxes piled up six deep.[2]

To President Lincoln, from disturbed opposition party governors, town councils, and frightened pro bono publicos, there came an old familiar plea: Put McClellan back in command of the army, put him at least in command of our brave but untrained militia; if this is done the people will rise en masse and we may yet get out of our scrape. Lincoln filed most of these pleas with his miscellaneous papers. To one of the complainants, Governor Joel Parker of New Jersey, he coolly replied that Lee's march north represented opportunity, not disaster, for the Union cause, and he reminded the governor that no one outside of the White House could quite understand "the difficulties and involvements of replacing General McClellan in command."[3]

Between Joe Hooker and General Halleck there passed many telegrams, a running debate by wire, Hooker trying to get some sort of firm instructions, Halleck vetoing Hooker's suggestions but offering few of his own. The Army of the Potomac moved closer to the Potomac, and Pleasonton and the cavalry galloped west to go knifing at Stuart's protective cordon in front of the Blue Ridge gaps in an effort to get authentic news of Lee's movements. Stuart was on the job and his squadrons struck back, and for four days in mid-June there was a series of desperate little fights around Middleburg and Aldie.

Yankee cavalry lived up to its new reputation in these fights. On one occasion the 1st Rhode Island, led by dapper French Colonel Duffié, went swirling through Middleburg and made Stuart himself take to his heels, paying for it a few hours later when Stuart came storming back with reinforcements in a countercharge that tore the little regiment to pieces. The fields in this part of the country were cut up with stone fences, and the Federals displayed a talent for fighting dismounted, the troopers lining up behind the walls and using their carbines like infantry, and the Confederates were pressed back to the mountain wall so that in the end Longstreet had to send infantry forward to help bar the way.

After one of these running fights a Federal cavalry officer rode across the stony upland field and studied the dead Confederates, lean men in homespun, their saddles and harness and other equipment mostly homemade and makeshift, many of their carbines made by cutting down the barrels of infantry rifles. He compared this with the abundant equipment that was available to the Yankee cavalry, and he mused: "How desperately in earnest must such a people be, who, after foreign supplies are exhausted, depend on their own fabrics rather than submit."[4]

Desperately in earnest they were, and in the end they finally held the gaps, so that no Yankee saw what was happening beyond the Blue Ridge. But what went almost unnoticed at the time was that this succession of fights screened the Army of the Potomac as well. With June two-thirds gone and Lee beginning to slip his infantry over the Potomac and up across Maryland toward Hagerstown and the Pennsylvania line, Stuart was somewhat in the dark as to the location and intent of the Federal infantry. This fact was to have important consequences.

As Lee got the bulk of his infantry north of the Potomac, the need for Stuart's screening operation ended, and it became important to get the cavalryman up into Pennsylvania with the advance echelons of the army. The obvious way would be to have Stuart pull his troops back through the Blue Ridge gaps, follow the rear of the army across the Potomac, and then go spurring northward on Lee's right flank. The route was roundabout, however, considering that Stuart was expected to pick the advance guard up around York, and going up the valley to the fords behind infantry and wagon trains would mean delay. Stuart accordingly proposed that he repeat his famous old stunt of riding clear around the sluggish Yankee army, crossing the Potomac somewhere east of the Blue Ridge, and striking north cross-country to meet Ewell. The way would be shorter, and there probably would be a chance to annoy the Yankees by molesting supply lines. For this plan Stuart got Lee's approval.

It appears that Stuart believed that Hooker's army was lying behind the Bull Run Mountains, facing west, in a formation that had no very great depth. Also, he considered that the Federals were being pretty static just then. That conception had been given him by John S. Mosby, the famous Rebel ranger, who had just been riding through Hooker's camps and found them all quiet. It seemed to Stuart, therefore, that by making only a short march to his right he could get around Hooker's flank and that he could then march north, west of Centreville, and hit the Potomac at Dranesville or thereabouts.

The Federal "rear" which he felt ought to be disturbed was, under this conception, the territory between Bull Run and Washington.

In accordance with his orders, then, Stuart began his march at 1 A.M. on June 25. He immediately ran into trouble. The Federal army was sprawled out over more territory than had been supposed. The VI Corps was at Centreville, well to the east of the spot that was thought to mark the army's rear, and the III Corps was at Gum Springs, which was on Stuart's projected route to the Potomac. And although Mosby had been correct when he reported that the army was quiet, his information had gone out of date and the whole army was on the move, filling all the roads and making Stuart's move impossible. Stuart had to make a disastrous long detour south and east, and the upshot was that he rode his cavalry right out of the campaign.[5]

Meanwhile, Hooker had not been entirely in the dark. As early as June 18 he got his pontoons into the Potomac opposite the mouth of the Monocacy, ready to lay bridges if a crossing became necessary. By June 23 he had definitely located the advance Confederate corps north of Hagerstown, Maryland. On that date one division of Rebels led by Jubal Early was up in the Pennsylvania mountains, laying irreverent hands on the Caledonia Ironworks owned by Thaddeus Stevens. Stevens's resident manager gave Early a moving argument about this property, saying that to destroy it would simply put several hundred people out of work; it would not hurt Stevens, because the place had been operating at a loss for a decade. Early was as skeptical as the next man, and he remarked dryly: "That's not the way Yankees do business," after which he ordered the whole place destroyed, with provisions and livestock confiscated for the benefit of the Confederacy. Visiting the place later, Stevens figured that he was out $75,000, and said the destruction was total—"They could not have done the job much cleaner."[6]

Hooker waited no longer but ordered three army corps to move over the river at once, and by June 27—while Stuart was still floundering north toward the Potomac, and his brigadier, Fitz Lee, was sending him a hot bulletin to the effect that the Federal army was converging on Leesburg, doubtless planning to cross the Potomac—the entire Army of the Potomac was in Maryland, and one wing of the army was moving west to the passes in South Mountain.

This was tolerably fast action, all things considered. Hooker's army had completed its crossing only twenty-four hours after the last of Lee's infantry had crossed, and the whole of it was in Maryland before either Stuart or Lee knew that the crossing had even begun.

But if Hooker was handling the army skillfully, the fact was not impressing his immediate superiors, Secretary Stanton and General Halleck. They were still refusing him the reinforcements he was demanding.

The Army of the Potomac was lean just now. The Chancellorsville losses had not yet been made good, twenty thousand short-term troops had taken their discharges and gone home, and the forced marches in the sweltering heat had greatly extended the sick list, so that Hooker had fewer than seventy-five thousand effectives with him, not counting cavalry.[7] To be sure, there were plenty of other Federal troops within reach—the eternal Washington garrison, the brigades and regiments that were scattered about in Maryland, whole divisions down on the Virginia peninsula—but these were not for Joe Hooker. Halleck and Stanton would not let him have them, and when he asked for them he got pin-prickings and naggings in return.

Halleck and Stanton obviously did not want to see Hooker in command of the army in another battle. Yet with the greatest battle of all drawing nearer every day they could not quite nerve themselves to remove him. They had in mind, possibly, what Meade was calling "the ridiculous appearance we present of changing our generals after each battle." They also had in mind Hooker's chief cabinet sponsor, Secretary Chase, who was still a power in the land and still firmly committed to Hooker, which meant that to fire Hooker was to invite a shattering political upheaval. So these two set out to make things unpleasant for Hooker in the hope that he would take the hint and resign, and the Hooker who had criticized McClellan so bitterly in the old days began to find out what McClellan had been up against.

It is never safe to come to any firm conclusions about what Stanton really had in mind, but the probability is that he simply mistrusted Hooker's nerve. The blue funk that had suddenly materialized at Chancellorsville might appear again, and Stanton was taking no chances. For the time being, however, Hooker was a first-rate general. Considering the fact that the War Department had not given him a free hand but had limited him to the role of following Lee and trying to parry his blows, Hooker handled the army very well that June. But he felt himself a man on the end of a tether, with Washington restraining his every move, and he was a hot-tempered man, never famous for his patience. There was bound to be a blowup sooner or later, and if one thing did not touch it off some other thing would.

It came to a head at last over the same sore spot that had bothered McClellan during the Antietam campaign—control of the garrison at Harper's Ferry. Hooker could see no point in trying to hold this indefensible spot and he demanded permission to withdraw the troops and use them elsewhere. Halleck refused, and Hooker gave way to petulance and, just conceivably, to an inner reluctance to face once more the searching test of battle in supreme command. Whatever may have been his real reason, he hotly sent off a telegram of resignation, and the War Department accepted it with bland promptness. That night a War Department official took a special train west, and in the early morning hours of June 28 he entered Meade's tent, aroused that sleeping soldier, and informed him that he was now the commander of the Army of the Potomac.

Meade was genuinely surprised, so much so that when he first woke up and saw the War Department man standing by his cot he believed foggily that he was being placed under arrest, and he hastily searched his conscience to consider what he could have done to deserve it: He tried to decline the promotion and was told that that was impossible, he had been put in command whether he liked it or not. Dressing hastily, Meade made his way to Hooker's headquarters to give that officer the news.[8]

Meade was a good, decent man, and nothing in all his story is much more creditable than the attitude he had taken toward his own promotion. Ever since Chancellorsville he and other ranking officers had expected that the army would get a new commander, and Meade had heard some gossip that he himself would be named. Considering the matter dispassionately, he concluded that the appointment just was not coming to him, and on June 25 he wrote a long letter to his wife explaining why he felt that way. For one thing, he told her, there would be great opposition from the innumerable cliques and factions of the officer corps itself, and Meade soberly analyzed these:

"They could not say that I was an unprincipled intriguer who had risen by criticizing and defaming my predecessors and superiors. They could not say I was incompetent, because I have not been tried, and so far as I have been tried I have been singularly successful. They could not say I had never been under fire because it is notorious no general officer, not even Fighting Joe himself, has been in more battles, or more exposed, than my record evidences. The only thing they can say, and I am willing to admit the justice of the argument, is that it remains to be seen whether I have the capacity to handle successfully a large army. I do not, however, stand any chance, because I have no friends, political or others, who press or advance my claims or pretensions, and there are so many others who are pressed by influential politicians that it is folly to think I stand any chance upon mere merit alone. Besides, I have not the vanity to think my capacity so pre-eminent, and I know there are plenty of others equally competent with myself, though their names may not have been so much mentioned."

Having explained all of this, Meade went on to twit his wife gently: "Do you know, I think *your* ambition is being roused and that you are beginning to be bitten with the dazzling prospect of having for a husband a commanding general of the army. How is this?"[9]

He was genuinely but uneffusively fond of his wife, and in the early days of army life he wrote to her about the "terrible agony" of parting from her when the army sent him off to a distant post. On their twenty-first wedding anniversary he wrote her that he doubted if any other couple alive "have had more happiness with each other than you and I." If he was irritable and touchy in camp, possessed of a famous temper and imperfect means for controlling it, it never cropped out in his letters home. He was deeply and quietly religious, content to do his duty in the sphere where God had placed him, expressing his gratitude to God whenever his health (about which he worried a good deal) improved enough to let him feel robust. A professional soldier, he was inclined to distrust volunteers, and he had no use whatever for abolitionists.[10]

This latter trait, as a matter of fact, had got him into the bad books of one of the most influential of all abolitionists, Senator Zach Chandler of Michigan, which was doubtless one reason why Meade felt that he would never be given Hooker's place. Meade had been stationed in Detroit when Fort Sumter was fired on, and while he was a staunch Unionist he was dismayed by the arrogance of the fire-eaters, to whom Southern secession looked like a simple riot which would be suppressed by the mere appearance of Federal troops. Detroit civic leaders called a huge mass meeting to whip up patriotic fervor and pass resolutions, and they invited all army officers stationed in Detroit to appear on the platform and publicly take the oath of allegiance to the Union. Meade and his fellow officers flatly refused to do this, notifying the War Department that they would freely take all the oaths the department asked them to take but that they would not take any in the circus surroundings of a mass meeting. For this stand Meade was publicly denounced at the meeting, and Senator Chandler had distrusted him ever since.[11]

With the War Department man, Meade went to Hooker's tent. Hooker took the news as gracefully as a man could under the circumstances, and he called in Dan Butterfield, his chief of staff, and sat down with Meade to explain where the army was and what current plans were. (Meade had long since expressed his dislike for Butterfield, and he had tried this morning to bring in G. K. Warren, the army's chief engineer, as his chief of staff. He was talked out of it by Warren himself, who explained that it would simply be impossible to break in a new chief of staff when a collision with the enemy might take place at any moment.) Butterfield and Hooker flared up once when Meade, after looking at their map, remarked unguardedly that it seemed to him the army was rather scattered, but that was smoothed over and the men got down to business.[12]

Hooker told Meade that Lee had no pontoons with him and therefore could not be planning to cross the Susquehanna River, to whose bank Ewell's corps had progressed. If the rest of Lee's army followed Ewell, Hooker continued, Lee must be planning to move down the western bank of that river in order to cut off Baltimore and Washington, which meant that the line of march of Lee's invasion would follow a huge semicircle, curving northeast, east, and southeast. The Army of the Potomac, Hooker explained, had been placed so that it could move by a shorter arc inside of this semicircle, covering Baltimore and Washington and falling on Lee's flank if there was an opening. The explanations completed, Hooker withdrew and the army was Meade's.[13]

He got it at a bad time—bad for him, and bad for the army. In the whole career of this body of troops, no greater test was ever put upon it than this business of getting a new commander on the very eve of the war's most crucial battle. It had had bad commanders and it had had fairly good ones, and all of them had been heckled and second-guessed by Washington, by the press, and by their own subordinates, but never before had there been anything like this.

Meade's appointment on the eve of battle was an act of sheer desperation, done solely to get rid of a man whose heart and nerve were distrusted. What happened now would be largely up to the men themselves. In effect they had no leader. They were almost within rifleshot of a supremely aggressive enemy, and there was no time for a shakedown, no time for high strategy and careful planning, no time for reorganization and regrouping. Whatever happened during the next week, the one certainty now was that the soldiers themselves would run this next battle. The most that could be expected of Meade was that he would make no ruinous mistakes. For the rest . . .

For the rest there were the men in the ranks, the hard brown survivors of the old 1861 regiments, the new levies that had come in to pick up the tone and the casual, unemotional spirit of the old-timers, the men who occasionally cheered one another in tribute to bravery and stoutness of heart which they themselves had seen, but who looked for no cheers or tributes from any other source. These men now were coming up from the river, and the weather was hot again, and the order was out for forced marches—Meade disagreed with Hooker's strategy, feeling that his cue was to follow Lee north and force him to turn and fight—and for a day or so the fate of the Union was going to rest on the sinewy legs of the men who had to do the marching.

The army came up from the Potomac, and some of the men were taken up a narrow strip of land between the river and the Chesapeake and Ohio Canal, the march continuing long after dark, rain coming down and mud underfoot and Cimmerian darkness all around. Humphreys was in command—Humphreys, grandson of the naval constructor who had designed the U.S.S. *Constitution,* a slim dapper driver who had taken over Berry's old division in the III Corps. Humphreys was a grim courtly man who just before he took his troops up to the stone wall at Fredericksburg had bowed to his staff and had said pleasantly: "Gentlemen, I shall lead this charge; I presume, of course, you will wish to ride with me?" Since it was put like that, staff had so wished, and five of the seven officers got knocked off their horses. He was a stickler for the regulations, and the United States Army has possessed few better soldiers, and he was driving his men north now without regard for human frailty.

The march went on and on, and men fell out and lay down in the mud and went to sleep. When the rain stopped, men who kept going lighted candles and stuck them in the muzzles of their rifles, and the straggling column lurched on, will-o'-the-wisp fires flickering in the night, and the riverbank was lined for ten or fifteen miles with officers and men who could not keep up. One survivor wrote that "it was impossible to say whether colonels and brigadier generals had lost their commands, or regiments and brigades had lost their commanders." When day came, after a sketchy bivouac, the column pulled itself together—Humphreys was the man to see to that—and by noon all hands were accounted for and the march was going on compactly again.[14]

Up past Frederick they went, pulling for the Pennsylvania line, and the men's spirits rose with the green fields and blue mountains about them, citizens cheering them on when they passed through towns, girls standing by farmhouse doors to wave flags and offer drinks of cold water. The army had its own method of greeting these girls. The wolf-call whistle was unknown to soldiers of that era, but they had an equivalent—an abrupt, significant clearing of the throat, or cough, which burst out spontaneously whenever a line of march went by a nice-looking young woman, so that at such a time, as one veteran said, "the men seemed terribly and suddenly afflicted with some bronchial affection."[15] Coughing and grunting, and vastly pleased with themselves, the men followed the dusty roads, and while they had no idea where they were going, it seemed to them that at last they were marching to victory. As one man put it: "We felt some doubt whether it was ever going to be our fortune to win a victory in Virginia, but no one admitted the possibility of a defeat north of the Potomac."[16]

The advance crossed the line into Pennsylvania, and the veteran 2nd Massachusetts went into a little town at the head of one column and found that word of their coming had gone on ahead. The citizens were out in force, and on each side of the main street there were long tables spread with all sorts of good things to eat, pretty girls standing behind the tables, wanting nothing so much as to serve good Union soldiers. There was much coughing and grinning and waving of hands, and the men fixed their mouths for apple butter and pie and soft bread, when bang-bang-bang! from the northern edge of town there came the sound of rifleshots, and couriers came galloping back, and the regiment swung its rifles to the right shoulder and went double-quicking on through the village to help the cavalry drive off Rebel skirmishers. But when they got to the open country there were no Rebels, and nobody seemed to know what the scare had been about, and the 2nd Massachusetts awoke at last to the knowledge that the regiment had been had. They could not retrace their steps back into town, regiments farther back in the line got all of the lunch, and to the end of their days the Massachusetts boys were convinced that the whole thing had been a put-up job devised by scheming characters envious of the regiment which marched at the head of the column.[17]

On every road the long columns went north. To the 3rd Michigan, the march seemed pleasant, what with pretty girls and cheering villagers, and one veteran wrote that "the roads around here are beautiful and macadamized and we enjoy marching over them very much. Every man in the ranks feels jubilant." To an Irishman in the 9th Massachusetts there was poetry in the very landscape: "The picturesque farmhouses and granaries appeared under the bright sunlight as white as driven snow. The undulating farming lands were covered with their rich nodding plumes of yellow grain which rose and fell in the breeze, before the approaching eye, on plateaus, valleys, and hills with pleasing effect. The scenery of it all, in its greatness, when viewed from a vantage ground, was a magnificent spectacle." Not all of the notes were quite so enthusiastic. Some soldiers found that when they tried to buy fruit or food they were badly overcharged, and when this happened the men sometimes helped themselves to contents of store or roadside stall and, departing, airily told the proprietor to "charge it to Uncle Sam." On such occasions the inhabitants would try to shame the men by saying that Lee's soldiers had been much more gentlemanly, but this rarely seemed to have any effect.[18]

Then came the news that Meade had replaced Hooker. It was unwelcome news, for the enlisted man still liked Hooker, and outside the V Corps Meade was hardly more than a name. In the ranks men asked angrily: "What has Meade ever done?" and bleakly answered: "Nothing!" But if most of the soldiers felt that the government had made a mistake in this change of commanders, they kicked up no fuss over it. The ardent hero worship of the old volunteer days was gone now, and it would never come back again, partly because the heroes were departed but mostly because the men themselves had lost their old need to make and worship heroes. The soldiers were sorry to see Hooker go, but they did not bother to carry on about it.[19] The man at the top might be anybody. It no longer seemed to matter very much. In the ranks there seems to have come slowly and painfully the realization that the man who would finally get the army through its trials was a profane, weary man with no stars on his shoulders and scant hope of any in his crown, the everlasting high private who was being challenged now, once and for all, to show what kind of man he really was.

Meade announced his accession by a circular to corps commanders, calling on officers to explain to their men the immense issues involved in Lee's invasion of Pennsylvania. Meade said that "the army has fought well heretofore," and he believed that it would fight "more desperately and bravely than ever if it is addressed in fitting terms." He added, somewhat maladroitly—the capacity to sound an inspirational note simply was not in this gnarled gray-bearded man—that corps and other commanders "are authorized to order the instant death of any soldier who fails to do his duty at this hour."[20]

The army moved on, some of its segments doing thirty miles and more in a day, and in rear of the moving troops there was pandemonium. A newspaper correspondent who got to Frederick just after the army marched out noted that the place was full of stragglers, with all the liquor shops running full tilt and drunken soldiers wandering all over town, trying to steal horses or sneak into private dwellings, "inflamed with whisky and drunk as well with their freedom from accustomed restraint." On the road north from Frederick he found more of the same, and he wrote bitterly:

"Take a worthless vagabond who has enlisted for thirteen dollars a month instead of patriotism, who falls out of ranks because he is a coward and wants to avoid the battle, or because he is lazy and wants to steal a horse to ride on instead of marching, or because he is rapacious and wants to sneak about farmhouses and frighten or wheedle timid country women into giving him better food and lodging than camp life affords—make this armed coward or sneak thief drunk on bad whisky, give him scores and hundreds of armed companions as desperate and drunken as himself—turn loose this motley crew, muskets and revolvers in hand, into a rich country, with quiet, peaceful inhabitants, all unfamiliar with armies and army ways—let them swagger and bully as cowards and vagabonds always do, steal or openly plunder as such thieves always will—and then, if you can imagine the state of things this would produce, you have the condition of the country in the rear of our own army, on our own soil, today."[21]

The debris that was set afloat by this backwash of the moving army littered towns and hamlets all along the Maryland-Pennsylvania border, underlining the regrettable fact that not all soldiers are shining sons of light; emphasizing, too, the queer gaps in this army's discipline, which meant that a hard march usually cost the army about as many men as a hard battle. How could it have been otherwise? Here was an army in which the whole problem of command had gone unsolved. In the past ten months the army had fought four great battles—Bull Run, Antietam, Fredericksburg, and Chancellorsville. It had had a different commander for each one, and now with a fifth battle approaching it had its fifth commander. Of the seven army corps, not one was being led now by the man who had led it at the time of Antietam. All but three of the nineteen infantry divisions had changed command since then. Fewer than half of its fifty-one infantry brigades were led by men who had the proper rank for the job, the rank of brigadier general, and only ten of the fifty-one had led their brigades for as long as ten months.

In the regiments the condition was apt to be even worse. Army regulations rewarded regimental officers who kept their men out of the hottest action and penalized those who took them into the thick of the fighting. When regimental strength declined, as it invariably did, since there was no adequate system for providing replacements, a regiment sooner or later was apt to fall below the minimum strength at which it was permissible to muster in a full colonel or to maintain a regular regimental staff—quartermaster, surgeon, commissary officer, adjutant, and so on. Most of the veteran regiments were commanded by majors or captains, and promotion for these men was impossible no matter how much they might deserve it, simply because their regiments were too small to carry higher ranks. (The three New York regiments in the famous Irish Brigade had been consolidated to two companies apiece now, and these battalions were led by company officers.) If a brigade made up of such regiments was reinforced with a brand-new rookie regiment and the brigadier then got shot or fell ill or resigned, command of the whole brigade would go by seniority to the untested rookie colonel even though the junior officers who led the veteran battalions knew ten times as much as he knew about leading troops.[22]

The leadership which men got under this system was apt to be haphazard and unpredictable, and when the army moved it was bound to dribble men to the rear, unraveling a loose fringe of ne'er-do-wells and fainthearts and out-and-out skulkers to ravage the countryside and to scandalize right-thinking war correspondents. Yet it was noticed that in those outfits which did have good leadership there was very little straggling, and indeed it was more or less an axiom in the Army of the Potomac that a regiment, brigade, or division which fought well also marched well. A commander who "looked after his men," as the expression went, and who insisted on soldierly behavior, would always get a response.

The II Corps had gone under Hancock after Couch departed, and Hancock was driving it along the highways unmercifully in the end-of-June heat and dust, but very few of his men were leaving the ranks. They remembered afterward being driven so hard that when they had to ford any creek or river they were not allowed to fall out to remove their shoes and socks, which meant that they had to march with wet feet and so got very footsore by the end of the day. It was on this march that the skipper of one of Hancock's best regiments, Colonel Colville of the 1st Minnesota, was sternly placed under arrest because he had let his outfit make a little detour in order to cross a certain stream by a footbridge instead of sending the men splashing straight ahead through the shallows.[23]

As it reached Pennsylvania the army began to encounter militia regiments—regiments dressed in fancy uniforms, carrying the full complement of equipment, with muskets polished until the barrels shone like mirrors. The veterans looked at these militiamen with dour curiosity and uttered wisecracks designed to put the holiday soldiers in their places. North of Frederick the XII Corps encountered the New York 7th, a dandy regiment wearing, among other things, nice white gloves. There was a rain coming down and the roadside was muddy, and the militiamen were not looking their best as Slocum's veterans cast critical eyes on them. The XII Corps advised the militiamen to come in out of the rain before the dress-parade uniforms got spoiled, asked them where their umbrellas were, and suggested that the boys join the army someday and see what soldiering was like. On another road the VI Corps met a Brooklyn home-guard regiment dressed in uniforms of natty gray, and the veterans coldly advised the militia to dye those uniforms blue: if they ever got into a fight the Army of the Potomac was apt to shoot anybody it saw who came to the field in a gray uniform. Now and then a veteran would ask the home guards where they buried their dead.[24]

As it moved the army covered a very wide front, thirty-five or forty miles from tip to tip. Orders were vague because plans were vague. Lee's army was somewhere between York, on the east, and Chambersburg, on the west, and as June ended it became apparent that the Confederates were beginning to pull their far-flung detachments together, heading toward some sort of concentration east of the long barrier of South Mountain. Meade considered that when it came to a fight the line of Pipe Creek, a meandering little stream along the Pennsylvania border, would be a good place for the Army of the Potomac to make its stand. He was uneasy about it—Halleck was warning him that he was pretty far west and that Lee might be able to make a dash around his right and strike at Baltimore or Washington—and he kept his men pushing on, tentacles of cavalry reaching forward, looking for a contact. In York an agent of the Sanitary Commission got inside the Rebel lines and took a look at one of Ewell's camps, finding the Rebels "well stripped for action and capable of fast movement."

"Physically, the men looked about equal to the generality of our own troops, and there were fewer boys among them," this man wrote. "Their dress was a wretched mixture of all cuts and colors. There was not the slightest attempt at uniformity in this respect. Every man seemed to have put on whatever he could get hold of, without regard to shape or color. . . . Their shoes, as a general thing, were poor; some of the men were entirely barefooted. Their equipments were light as compared with those of our men. They consisted of a thin woolen blanket, coiled up and slung from the shoulder in the form of a sash, a haversack swung from the opposite shoulder, and a cartridge box. The whole cannot weigh more than twelve or fourteen pounds." He asked one of these lanky Rebels if they had no shelter tents, and the soldier was scornful of such comforts, saying, "I just wouldn't tote one."[25]

John Buford was leading his cavalry division north from Frederick and Emmitsburg, prowling close to the slope of South Mountain, trying to find the enemy. On the last day of June, after narrowly missing a collision at the little town of Fairfield, he drew a bit farther to the east and late in the afternoon brought his men into the town of Gettysburg, a pleasant place in the open hilly country where many roads converged, with the long blue mass of the mountain chain lying on the horizon off to the west. Confederate patrols had been in the town, and they went west on the Cashtown pike as Buford's troopers

came in. Somewhere not far beyond them, clearly, there must be a
solid body of Rebel infantry. Buford strung a heavy picket line along
a north-and-south ridge west of town, threw more pickets out to cover
the roads to the north (army intelligence warned that Ewell's corps
was apt to be coming down those roads from Carlisle before long),
and snugged down for the night with headquarters in a theological
seminary.

The brigade which was responsible for picketing the roads north of
town was commanded by Colonel Tom Devin, and as Buford and
Devin talked that night Devin doubted that there was any substantial number of Rebels anywhere near him. He would keep a good
watch, he said, but he could handle anything that could come up
during the next twenty-four hours. But Buford was convinced that
most of Lee's army was within striking distance, and he warned Devin
sharply.

"No, you won't," he said bluntly. "They will attack you in the
morning and they will come booming—skirmishers three-deep. You
will have to fight like the devil until supports arrive."[26]

Buford was more anxious that night than his staff had ever seen
him, and he kept his scouts moving all night, west and north of town.
He impressed on his subordinates that they must be alert—"Look out
for campfires during the night and for dust in the morning"—and he
messaged Meade that there might be trouble next day. He was told to
hang on, Reynolds and the I Corps would be up sometime in the
morning, and Howard with the XI Corps would not be far behind.

There was a bright moon that night, and most of the army kept to
the road long after the sun had gone down. Nothing had actually
happened yet, but there was a stir in the air, and the first faint tug
had been felt from the line that had been thrown into Gettysburg, a
quiet hint that something was apt to pull the whole army together
on those long ridges and wooded hills. The soldiers kept on marching,
and a strange thing happened, significant because it showed how little
the men who led this army understood the spirit of the men they were
leading. Somewhere in the officer corps a little plot was hatched: the
men would be told that McClellan was back in command, and they
would be so inspired and heartened that they would fight and win this
battle before they found out that the rumor was false.[27]

In various moving columns that evening staff officers galloped up
in mock frenzy and shouted out the news: "McClellan is in com-

mand again!" The boys cheered and tossed their hats, and for half an hour the business was a sensation, yet it appears that something about the news failed to ring true, and most of the soldiers were not greatly deceived. Here and there veterans wagged their heads and agreed that maybe if they lost this next battle and were forced back into the lines around Washington, McClellan would indeed be called in to save the day—otherwise, not a chance.

Inspired or otherwise, the men kept moving. Colonel Strong Vincent, leading a brigade in the V Corps, took his men through a little town, where the moonlight lay bright on the street, and in every doorway there were girls waving flags and cheering. The battle flags were broken out of their casings and the men went through the town in step with music playing, and Gettysburg lay a few miles ahead. Vincent reined in his horse and let the head of the column pass him, and as the colors went by he took off his hat, and he sat there quietly, watching the flags moving on in the silver light, the white dresses of the girls bright in the doorways, shimmering faintly in the cloudy luminous dusk under the shade trees on the lawns. To an aide who sat beside him the colonel mused aloud: There could be worse fates than to die fighting here in Pennsylvania, with that flag waving overhead. . . .[28]

There was the long white road in the moonlight, with the small-town girls laughing and crying in the shadows, and the swaying ranks of young men waving to them and moving on past them. To these girls who had been nowhere and who had all of their lives before them this was the first of all the roads of the earth, and to many of the young men who marched off under the moon it was the last of all the roads. For all of them, boys and girls alike, it led to unutterable mystery. The column passed on through the town and the music stopped and the flags were put back in their casings, and the men went marching on and on.

In the Gettysburg cemetery, quiet on a hilltop just south of the town, there was a wooden sign by the gatepost—just legible, no doubt, in the last of the June moonlight, if anyone had bothered to go up there and read it—announcing that the town would impose a five-dollar fine on anyone who discharged a firearm within the cemetery limits.

SIX

End and Beginning

1. The Economics of Eighty Per Cent

West of Gettysburg the land rolls to the mountains in a long easy ground swell, without whitecaps or breakers. The ridges run north and south and they are broad and rounded, with wide shallow valleys between. It is good farming country, and by July most of the land is bright with growing crops. Here and there are open groves, with farmhouses and big stone-and-timber barns close by.

On the morning of July 1, 1863, Yankee cavalry held one of these ridges a mile west of town. The troopers were a mixed group, New York and Illinois men mostly, with a couple of squadrons of Hoosiers, and their pickets looked down a gentle slope toward a little brook, Willoughby Run, which came lazily south and crossed the graveled pike that ran toward Cashtown, a little village half a dozen miles to the west, close to the mountain wall. The pickets looked west, and the dawn came up behind them, throwing long gray shadows across the hollows and lighting the blue crest of South Mountain. Men who glanced back noted an ominous red sky in the east, with a promise of heat.

The light grew, and a dun-colored column of troops came snaking eastward. John Buford had had it pegged: the column was preceded by a triple line of skirmishers who overflowed the wheat fields and pastures beside the Cashtown road and came along jauntily, their muskets ready. These Confederates belonged to the division of Harry

Heth in A. P. Hill's corps. Hill was sick that morning, and it seems he did not believe there would be many Yankees around Gettysburg. Heth thought the Gettysburg stores might contain shoes, and he wanted to get them, or so it is stated, at any rate, although Jubal Early's men had gone through the place a week earlier, and it was most unlikely that they would have overlooked anything useful. It may be that these Confederates simply were looking for a fight. They had seen nothing in Pennsylvania so far but militia, and as far as they knew there was nothing but militia in front of them. And so as Buford had predicted, they came booming over the western ridge, skirmishers three-deep, striding forward into the rising sun.

The first Federals to get a good look at them were a corporal and three men of the 9th New York Cavalry near Willoughby Run. The corporal sent his men back to spread the alarm while he trotted across the stream and up the hill for a closer look. Rebel skirmishers loosed a few long-range shots at him, and he rode back to the little bridge, and as the skirmishers came over the ridge he fired a few times with his carbine and then turned and galloped back to the main line. With that harmless exchange of shots the battle of Gettysburg had begun.[1]

If the Confederates were looking for a fight, Buford was just the man for them. Unsupported cavalry was not expected to stand off infantry, and for a couple of hours or more Buford's two brigades would be entirely unsupported, but Buford liked to fight and he did not propose to leave until somebody made him leave. He dismounted his regiments and spread them out along the ridge, one man in every four standing fifty yards in the rear holding horses, the rest squatting behind fences, bushes, trees, or what not and peering at the Rebel skirmishers over their stubby carbines.

Buford had to keep part of his men patrolling the roads that came down from the north, because the word was that Ewell's troops would be approaching from that direction before long, so his fighting line was a bit skinny. He had six guns with him—Battery A, 2nd U. S. Artillery, under Lieutenant John Calef—and he sent them out the Cashtown road to take position in the center of the line of dismounted cavalrymen. Calef swung his guns into battery, trained a piece on a knot of mounted Confederate officers three quarters of a mile off, and nodded to the gunner, who jerked the lanyard. The flash and the echoing report and the bursting shell notified the Confederates that they were expected, and the ridge to the west blossomed out with rolling spurts of dust as the Rebel guns went in at a gallop to unlimber and return the fire. Rebel skirmishers began working their way up from Willoughby Run, and there was an intermittent clatter of rifle and carbine fire.

Two or three hundred yards east of the ridge where the cavalry and the guns were posted there was another rise of ground, slightly higher and much longer, and a little way south of the Cashtown pike on this high ground there was a Lutheran theological seminary, its white bell tower rising above walls of ivied brick. Buford went back to this building and climbed up in the tower to survey the situation. It did not take him long to see that if Yankee infantry did not come up soon the cavalry would be in a bad spot. Rebel infantry was present in strength and more was coming up all the time, and Heth was putting additional guns into battery on the far side of Willoughby Run. Buford sent gallopers hurrying away to give the news to General John Reynolds, who was to bring the I Corps up toward Gettysburg from the south. The Confederate skirmish line pushed in more closely, the racket of the firing was getting louder, and men were being hit. Confederate artillery was blasting the crest of the ridge, and Calef was firing fast in reply, and the weight of metal was all in the Confederates' favor.

South of Gettysburg, Reynolds's infantry could hear the firing, and they quickened their pace. Reynolds galloped on ahead of them and rode into town, got a quick size-up of the situation from a scout, and turned west and rode fast to the seminary. Buford saw him from the belfry, called out, "There's the devil to pay!" and came clattering down in a rush. He told Reynolds what he knew, and Reynolds got off a hasty note to Meade: the enemy was coming on, but "I will fight him inch by inch, and if driven into the town I will barricade the streets and hold him back as long as possible."[2] A courier went pounding back with the note, and the head of the infantry column swung west as it neared the town, crossing the fields to get over to Seminary Ridge.

The column was led by Major General James Wadsworth, a vigorous white-haired old man who had been a well-to-do gentleman farmer in New York State before the war and who was turning into a good general. His men liked him immensely. He was a stickler about things like adequate rations and decent housing, and in winter quarters the men found it not at all unusual to wake up before dawn on cold mornings and see the old chap poking his nose inside to find out for himself whether the huts were warm and decently ventilated. He had run unsuccessfully for governor of New York against Copperhead Seymour the previous fall, scorning to go home and campaign on the ground that it did not befit a soldier.[3] Now he was leading his division into action, an old Revolutionary War saber in his hand, Reynolds galloping back to meet him to tell him where to put his troops.

Wadsworth's division contained just two brigades, but they were good ones. One of them was composed of four New York regiments and one regiment from Pennsylvania, led by Brigadier Generaı Lysander Cutler, and the other was the Iron Brigade, Influential Citizen Meredith riding at the head of it. As this brigade approached Gettysburg, Meredith or someone else ordered the flags uncased and set the fife-and-drum corps playing at the head of the column, and the Westerners fell into step and came swinging up the road, their black hats tilted down over their eyes, rifle barrels sparkling in the morning sun. There were eighteen hundred fighting men in this brigade, and the men were cocky. Officially they were the 1st Brigade of the 1st Division of the I Army Corps, and they figured that if the army were ever drawn up in one long line for inspection they would stand at the extreme right of it, which somehow was cause for pride. On the ridge to the west there was a crackle of small-arms fire and a steady crashing of cannon, with a long soiled cloud of smoke drifting up in the still morning air, and at the head of the column the drums and the fifes were loud—playing "The Girl I Left Behind Me," probably, that perennial theme song of the Army of the Potomac, playing the Iron Brigade into its last great fight.[4]

On Seminary Ridge, Reynolds divided the column, telling Cutler to form line north of the Cashtown pike and calling the Iron Brigade into action on the south side. The veteran regiments wheeled into line and the dismounted cavalrymen came sifting back through the intervals to take their horses again. They had done well enough, holding A. P. Hill's men off for two hours, and now they could go to the rear while the infantry took over. Back with them went Calef and his battery, one gun limping along with but two horses left to pull it. Into the place Calef had vacated came the 2nd Maine battery, Captain James Hall, the same who had so impressed the rookies on the line at Fredericksburg by his extreme coolness under fire, sitting his horse and making chit-chat with a brigadier while the Southern gunners used him for a target.

There was no time now for Captain Hall to put on a show for nervous infantry. The Rebels had a good deal of artillery in action, and twelve guns promptly opened on this Maine battery, getting it in a deadly cross fire. Confederate infantry was getting in close, too, and skirmishers were shooting down the gunners. Cutler's boys relieved this situation slightly when they opened fire, but the Confederates were coming on with a rush, their line extending farther to the north than Cutler's line, and before long the Federals found themselves flanked, with a couple of Southern regiments advancing on their right and crumpling them up. The infantry was ordered to retire, the 147th New York did not get the order and was left isolated, in danger of being captured en masse, and Hall suddenly found that he was all alone on the ridge, with a Rebel column on his right barely sixty yards off. Coolly he ordered his right and center sections to swing over and blast the charging column with canister, while the two guns of his left section continued to duel with the twelve guns on the ridge to the west. The enemy charge was broken, but it realigned itself and came on again, skirmishers creeping forward to pick off the gunners. Hall's men did their best, but as a Federal infantry officer who saw the fight remarked, "Artillery against skirmishers is like shooting mosquitoes with a rifle."[5]

Clearly it was time for the guns to go. Hall wrote later that he ordered the battery to retire by sections, "feeling that if the position was too advanced for infantry it was equally so for artillery." His right section went back seventy-five yards, unlimbered again, and opened fire to protect the retirement of the other pieces. The Rebels got in close and killed all of the horses of one of the guns in this right section, so that the men finally had to remove the piece by hand. As Hall's last gun was being removed all of its horses went down, and Hall was about to ride back and bring it off personally when Wadsworth came up and told him not to waste time worrying over one gun—the thing to do was to get the rest of the guns into position back nearer the town to cover the retreat. Hall obeyed, but he did detail a sergeant and five men to go out and see if they could not yet save the gun. They tried but none of them came back, and the gun stayed there, a bleak silhouette on the smoldering sky line.[6]

As Hall's guns retired, Calef's regulars came up again to take their place, accompanied by Battery L, 1st New York Light Artillery. These guns went into line and the Rebel guns stormed at them, killing horses and men and smashing gun limbers. Cutler reassembled his infantry, and the brigade formed line at right angles to its original position, drawn up in the roadway facing north. A hundred yards in front there was the cutting of an unfinished railway line running parallel to the road, and somewhere beyond it the isolated 147th New York was still hanging on, invisible in the smoke. Two regiments of Southerners took shelter in the cut and swept the road with a steady fire.

South of the highway things had gone better. General Abner Doubleday, stiff and formal and just a shade pompous, still wearing his laurels as an "old Sumter hero," had come up ahead of his division, and Reynolds told him to take charge south of the road while Wadsworth looked after affairs to the north. Doubleday led the Iron Brigade forward to the crest of the rise overlooking Willoughby Run, where there were a plot of trees and a little farm, and Archer's Confederate brigade was coming up the slope in a long line, skirmishers out in front.

Like so many other generals of that era, Doubleday felt that troops going into action needed a word of encouragement, and he called out to the men that this spot was the key to the whole battlefield and must be held "to the last extremity." The men yelled back: "If we can't hold it, where will you find men who can?" or so Doubleday reported later: he had a weakness for touching up the things soldiers said in action. He got the 2nd and 7th Wisconsin into line, and they ran into Archer's men head-on, while the 24th Michigan and the 19th Indiana worked around toward the south and took the Confederate brigade in the flank. Rifles blazed all along the slope and in the grove, and the Confederates suddenly realized that they were up against the first team. The Iron Brigade could hear the Southerners telling each other: "Here are those damned black-hat fellers again. . . . 'Tain't no militia—that's the Army of the Potomac!"[7]

Reynolds rode forward with the battle line. He was a handsome man and a first-rate soldier, who had come up originally with the Pennsylvania Reserves and who had once declined command of the army because he did not think he would be given a free hand. The morning Meade replaced Hooker, Reynolds had carefully put on his dress uniform and sash and had gone formally to call on him; and when Meade, who looked like a wagon master that morning, with an old uniform and muddy boots and a general air of unmilitary slouchiness, had tried to express his embarrassment at being promoted over the man who until recently had been his superior, Reynolds had decently stopped him, assuring him that the post had gone to the man who most deserved it. Now Reynolds was studying the battle, trying to make out just how much weight lay back of the Rebel attack, and a Southern sharpshooter in an old stone barn got him in the sights of his rifle and shot him dead.

Reynolds went down, and his aides took his body to the rear and put it in an ambulance, and the Iron Brigade closed in savagely on Archer's men, getting them off balance, pushing them down into the valley, and driving them back in wild rout. A muscular Irish private in the 2nd Wisconsin ran forward and seized General Archer bodily and made a prisoner of him, hundreds of lesser Confederates surrendered, and the rest of the brigade went staggering back to the high ground to the west.

North of the road, too, there was a success. The 6th Wisconsin had been sent over to help Cutler's men, and it suddenly charged forward to the railway cut, the 84th and 95th New York following it. The Wisconsin men were running in an uneven V-shaped line, the colors at the peak of the V, Colonel Dawes riding along, yelling: "Align on the colors! Close up on that color!" The men swept into the railway cut at the end of the Rebel line, getting a deadly enfilade fire down the length of the Rebel regiments packed between the steep banks, the southern rim of the cut flamed with musket fire, and there was a vicious flurry of hand-to-hand fighting. A Wisconsin private grabbed for a Confederate flag, a Confederate shot him down, a comrade leaped forward swinging his musket like a ball bat and brained the man who had shot him, a corporal ran in and got the flag—and then, all along the line, the Federals were shouting: "Throw down your muskets! Throw down your muskets!"

Hundreds of Southerners obeyed. Dawes shouted for the colonel of the nearest Southern regiment, and the dazed colonel came forward and handed over his sword. Six of his subordinate officers came up and did the same, and Dawes had an awkward moment, standing there with his arms full of swords, until his adjutant relieved him of them. Some of the Rebels escaped by running out at the western end of the cut, but hundreds surrendered, and the beleaguered New York regiment north of the cut was rescued. It had lost two thirds of its men in half an hour's fight.[8]

So for the moment the Federals had won a decided victory, with two Southern brigades beaten back and a good bag of prisoners going to the rear. (General Archer, understandably, was not in good spirits. En route to the rear he met Doubleday, whom he had known before the war, and Doubleday somewhat tactlessly came forward, crying: "Archer! I'm glad to see you!" Archer refused to shake hands, muttering, "Well, I'm not glad to see you by a damn sight." The Irish private who captured him had manhandled him, and his feelings were all out of joint.)[9] Doubleday reflected that Howard and the XI Corps would be up shortly, and it seemed to him that the day was off to a fine start.

It was a start, but no more. A new infantry line appeared on the western ridge, and more and more Confederate guns came up to blast at the Union line. It was not yet noon, and although there was a brief lull there was trouble in the air. The Confederate battle line kept reaching farther and farther to the north—A. P. Hill's corps was twice the size of Reynolds's—and as Doubleday's own division came up it was hurried into position north of the turnpike to match the extension of Confederate strength. All available Federal guns were in action. Hall's half-wrecked battery was called back from its position on the edge of Gettysburg, and it came galloping up the grade of the unfinished railway. A couple of Rebel guns had an exact line on that cutting and they slammed in solid shot and shell, and because the banks were high Hall's men could neither turn around nor go back but had to keep on for half a mile, taking cruel punishment all the way. They got out of the horrible little ravine at last, turned to the left, and went into battery over near the seminary, where Doubleday had men building a half-moon embankment of fence rails and earth as a strong point.[10]

From the north Buford's pickets were frantically reporting that a heavy new Rebel column was coming in, and these enemies appeared presently on Oak Hill, a rounded tree-clad knoll at the northern end of Seminary Ridge, taking the Yankee line in flank. Doubleday sent the last of his reserves up to meet this threat—a division led by General John C. Robinson, a salty old regular of whom a soldier said that "in a much-bearded army, he was the hairiest general I ever saw."[11] Robinson got his men in behind some stone walls and beat off the first Rebel attack, but there were dust clouds all along the northern horizon marking the impending arrival of still more Confederate troops.

Up from the south came the head of the XI Corps, the Dutchmen who still carried Chancellorsville on their shoulders. The men were tired, and on the long hike up from Falmouth their shoes had given out and some of them were barefooted, and they did the final half mile or so into town on the double under the hot July sun.[12] Howard galloped west to the seminary, taking command by virtue of his seniority, and he told Doubleday to stand firm—the Dutchmen would protect his right flank. Two of Howard's divisions he sent straight north through town, planning to seize Oak Hill, but before the men got there a new Confederate battle line was tramping south through the open country east of the hill, and there was nothing for it but to form a hasty line and try to beat them off.

Just south of Gettysburg there was a high hill with a cemetery on top, and Howard put his headquarters there, holding with him General von Steinwehr with some artillery and two thin brigades of infantry. Steinwehr had been a Prussian professional, and he immediately put his men to work digging pits for the guns and banking earth up against the stone walls about the cemetery. A soldier remembered how strange it was to see batteries galloping helter-skelter into the burying ground, knocking over tombstones and setting up their guns, as often as not, on top of graves.[13]

The right end of the Yankee line north of Gettysburg was in charge of Brigadier General Francis Barlow, the slim, clean-shaven young New York lawyer who had gone into the war as a militia private and now commanded a division, and he tried to anchor it on a little knoll near a stream known as Rock Creek. He planted guns there, a stout regular battery under Lieutenant Bayard Wilkeson, whose father, a correspondent for the New York *Times,* was at that moment coming up toward Gettysburg to see what the news might be. Barlow put the 17th Connecticut in to protect Wilkeson's guns and made note that still another Southern column was materializing on the far side of Rock Creek, away to his right and rear.

The XI Corps line measured perhaps a mile, from Barlow's knoll to its western end. It lay in flat open country, and between its left flank and General Robinson's position below Oak Hill there was a

quarter-of-a-mile gap. Up into this gap came Leatherbreeches Dilger
and his six brass smoothbores of Battery I, 1st Ohio, and these guns
immediately got into a spirited duel with the Rebel guns on Oak Hill.
Dilger believed that the place for smoothbores was as close to the
enemy as they could get—they were splendid for close-range work
but were not of much account for the longer distances—and when
a battery of rifled guns came up beside him he asked its commander,
Lieutenant William Wheeler, to lay down a covering fire while he
went forward. Wheeler did so, and Dilger's battery trotted straight
ahead for several hundred yards, halting once under fire while Dilger
had the men collect fence rails and other debris to fill a ditch that
blocked the way. Dilger at last got into position at the range he liked,
and while he fired Wheeler brought his own guns up to join him,
and in a short time the two batteries had dismounted five Rebel
cannon.[14]

It was early afternoon by now, and the Rebel line formed a long
semicircle from southwest clear around to northeast. From end to
end this semicircle flamed and crashed, and Howard sent couriers
off, breakneck, to the nearest Federal troops, Slocum's and Sickles's
corps, begging them to come on to Gettysburg as fast as they could.
West of Willoughby Run (although the Federals did not know it)
was Lee himself. He had not at first planned to bring on a general
battle, but he was finding that the setup was practically ideal, with
the Yankees badly outnumbered and outflanked, and he ordered an
advance all along the line. The wild uproar of battle rose to a
crescendo and the great blazing semicircle began to roll forward.

Something had to give, and the break came first on the knoll where
Barlow had his guns. Rebel infantry charged in close and laid down
a killing fire, and two Confederate batteries hit the knoll with everything they had, and Barlow went down critically wounded. Young
Lieutenant Wilkeson was coolly picturesque on his white horse amid
his guns, but a sharpshooter killed him, the supporting infantry gave
way, and then the guns limbered up hastily and went to the rear.
At the other end of the line Confederate infantry drove for the gap
between the two corps formations. The left-flank element of the XI
Corps, 75th Pennsylvania, changed front to the left to meet this
threat, lost 111 men in fifteen minutes' fighting across a snake-rail
fence and then had to run for it. All along the line regiments caved
in, and the position was lost.[15]

For the rest of the life of the Army of the Potomac there would be arguments about this, and other troops were to complain that the miserable Dutchmen had let them down again, but the line simply could not be held, and when the men rallied a few hundred yards in the rear the Confederates who had been advancing beyond Rock Creek got in behind the right flank and shook them loose once more. Before long the whole corps was in retreat again, and from the cemetery Steinwehr saw the rout and sent one of his two brigades out through town to form a rear guard.

Dilger's and Wheeler's batteries had to limber up quickly, with four Southern batteries lashing at them and yelling Southern infantry only a hundred yards away. As the guns moved off a solid shot smashed the axle of one of Wheeler's pieces. He halted and put his sweating gunners to work arranging a rope lashing to sling the dismounted gun beneath one of the limbers—hot enough work it was, too, under the blistering sun, with Rebel bullets whipping in all around and the plain draining itself of men in blue. They got the gun fixed at last and went off again, but a gun is one of the most perverse of all inanimate objects, and before the battery had gone far this one broke loose from its lashing and thumped down on the ground. Wheeler left it there and went off without it. (After the battle he came back and found it, remounted it, and put it back in service.)[16] From time to time Dilger halted a section and fired a few rounds of canister at the pursuers.

From Oak Hill all the way to the south of the seminary there were boiling smoke clouds and a tremendous racket of guns and rifles and yelling men. On the extreme right of this line General Robinson had planted the 16th Maine, with instructions to stay there no matter what, and these men were fighting against enemies who had come in so close that the Federals could hear the Rebel officers shouting orders to their men. The 16th's colonel protested that he had only two hundred men and could not stay where he was, but Robinson repeated that orders were to hold on at any cost. The regiment edged back a trifle and found itself isolated on a narrow, wedge-shaped ridge, Southern infantry firing fast from behind a rail fence on one side, a new battle line charging in on the other. This could end in just one way, and everyone present knew what that way was going to be. The color-bearer went dodging along the line at last, and each man tore off a piece of the regimental flag and tucked it in his pocket, and then it was every man for himself, and those who were still on their feet struck out for Cemetery Hill south of town. That evening thirty-five of them reassembled there.[17]

Farther south the line was in no better shape. The whole of Robinson's division was cut to pieces, more than sixteen hundred of its twenty-five hundred men being shot, among them Brigadier General Gabriel R. Paul, a white-haired regular who got a bullet through both eyes. A Pennsylvania infantry brigade led by Colonel Roy Stone got into a tremendous series of fights around the unfinished railroad cut, captured it, lost it, recaptured it and lost it again, seized it for a third time, and then was blasted out for good by two Rebel batteries posted to shoot lengthwise down the cut. The brigade retired with a loss of two thirds of its numbers, and Colonel Stone wrote proudly that his men fought "as if each man felt that upon his own arm hung the fate of the day and the nation."[18]

They all fought that way, but there were just too many Confederates present, and after the XI Corps line collapsed the line west of town was bound to go. Cutler's brigade retreated at last, leaving a thousand men dead and wounded on the ground, and when he came to write his report Cutler remarked sadly: "I can only hope that the country may not again require that these brave men shall go through so severe an ordeal."[19]

Off to the left, near the rail-and-dirt barricade which Doubleday had had the men build near the seminary, the Iron Brigade grimly hung on in the grove which the general had told them to hold to the last extremity. The last extremity had visibly arrived. The Rebels were attacking from three sides, and the brigade was dissolving in fire and smoke and ear-shattering noise. General Meredith was knocked out when his horse was killed and fell on him, the 19th Indiana lost eight color-bearers, Colonel Fairchild of the 2nd Wisconsin went down with a wound that was to cost him an arm, and Private Patrick Maloney, who had captured General Archer, was killed.

And here in the middle of it all was the 24th Michigan, with a county judge for a colonel and a county sheriff for lieutenant colonel and all the line officers carrying presentation swords; the regiment that had once been ostracized because its valor was unproven. Since Fredericksburg the regiment had been accepted, but in the unfathomable economics of army life the men seem to have felt that they still owed the rest of the brigade something, and here on Seminary Ridge the bill had come up for payment. Three times Colonel Morrow sent back word that the position was untenable, and each time General Wadsworth grimly ordered him to hold on anyway. Some of the survivors remembered forming line of battle six times that hot afternoon, with the rank battle fog lying low under the trees and unappeasable enemies coming in from all directions at once. Four color-bearers were killed, and the regiment sagged toward the rear, and Colonel Morrow ordered the fifth color-bearer to jab the flagstaff in the ground and stand beside it for a rally. The man was killed before he could obey, Morrow himself took up the flag and waved it, a private ran up and took it away from him, muttering that it wasn't up to the colonel to carry the colors, and then this private was killed and another man took the staff. Then he too was shot, and Morrow got the flag after all, after which a bullet creased his skull and he himself went down.[20]

Back went the Iron Brigade to the barricade by the seminary, held by a tough handful of the troops who had been fighting north of the turnpike. The Rebels paused for breath and realignment, then sent a strong column straight in on the low breastworks, and the colonel of the 7th Wisconsin complained that he had trouble making his men hold their fire until the Rebels got to close quarters. The range suited him finally, and the Westerners put in a smashing volley. The whole front rank of the Rebel line seemed to go down in smoke and dust, but there were other ranks behind that kept on coming, and the artillery flailed those ranks without mercy.[21]

Howard had sent word that the guns were to make a last-ditch stand on Cemetery Hill, but Doubleday's chief of artillery had understood him to say Seminary Hill and so he had plugged in a dozen guns, hub to hub, beside the half-moon barricade and they were firing canister as fast as the men could load. Over in the turnpike was one of the veteran artillery outfits, Battery B of the 4th Regulars, the battery General Gibbon used to command when he was a captain fighting Indians out West. It was led now by Lieutenant James Stewart, and he was on his horse amid his guns, facing always toward the enemy—partly because he was a brave man and partly because his horse was a veteran with certain fixed ideas about battle. In some previous action a shell fragment had cut off most of the horse's tail, and ever since then this beast steadfastly refused to expose his rear to the foe when the shooting started. Stewart swung his guns around now and hit the charging Confederates in flank, and for the moment the assault was beaten back.[22]

It was only for the moment. A. P. Hill was piling his men in remorselessly and they were great fighters. Their line outflanked the Union line both north and south, and there was no possibility of stopping them. The line by the seminary crumbled and finally collapsed, and when the retreating Federals left the ridge they had to run the gantlet with Rebel battle lines closing in on them from north and south while still other Rebels fired at them from the west. The 7th Wisconsin lost more men on this retreat from the seminary than in all the rest of the day's fighting, and Buford's cavalry came back in to fight dismounted in valiant protection of the left flank. Some of the horse holders turned their animals over to retreating infantrymen so that they themselves could get into the scrap.

From Cemetery Hill the men in reserve looked down on a wild panorama of retreat. Thick battle fog lay on the ridge and the late afternoon's sun shone down through it, and out of it came the swaying lines of beaten men, turning now and then to fire a defiant volley, batteries lunging down roads and lanes with men clinging to gun limbers and caissons, shreds and patches of smoke lying in the hollows and on the plain, with flags making bright spots of color here and there as the breeze caught them. One man recalled seeing a color-bearer plant his flag and turn to face his pursuers, part of his regiment clustering about him. The smoke from their rifles floated up, the charging Confederates fired heavily in reply, and the knot of soldiers around the colors broke up in flight. The man with the flag remained by the staff, shaking his fist at his foes as they came nearer, then someone drew a bead on him and he went down and the flag went down and the retreat was unbroken again.[23]

Going through the town was worst of all. All of the lines of retreat converged here, and a considerable number of Confederates had got into town, and there was a maddening chaos in the streets and between the houses—thoroughfares all clogged with guns, wagons, and ambulances, retreating regiments colliding with each other and getting hopelessly intermingled, Rebel gunners hitting the place at long range so steadily that a number of soldiers were wounded by bricks and other debris knocked down from buildings, Rebel infantry regiments firing unexpectedly down the streets, dense smoke clouds settling down so that nobody could see which way he was going. One of the High Dutch regiments, the 45th New York, went double-quicking down a side street to avoid a traffic jam and ran into Confederate infantry fire. It turned and ducked down an alley and found itself in a cul-de-sac. There was no way out but the way by which it had come in, which was blanketed by rifle fire. Barely a third of the men got out of it and went back to Cemetery Hill. Steinwehr's rear-guard brigade helped, and Dilger ran a gun section out in a street near the public square and held the pursuit back for a time, but before the day ended several thousand Federals were taken prisoner in Gettysburg.[24]

The rest of the army pulled itself together on Cemetery Hill in the smoke-stained evening. Losses had been appalling. The I Corps had taken between 9,500 and 10,000 men into action and had approximately 2,400 left. Its divisions and brigades were mere remnants. The Iron Brigade, which had had the worst of it, had lost almost exactly two thirds of its 1,800 effectives, and for the rest of the war it existed as a shadow, always a great name but never again a mighty force in battle. The 2nd Wisconsin had brought only 69 men back to the hill. As the 7th Wisconsin came up the slope a shell wounded Sergeant Daniel McDermott, who had carried the regimental flag in every battle of the war, and splintered the flagstaff. They laid McDermott on a caisson which lumbered along just ahead of the regiment, and he rode up onto the hill, still feebly waving the tattered flag on the broken staff. The 24th Michigan, largest regiment in the brigade, had had the most fearful loss: 399 of its 496 men had been shot, for a loss of 80 per cent, and whatever it was which the men had felt they owed the rest of the brigade, it would seem to have been paid by now. In a house in Gettysburg the Confederates had laid a number of the 24th's wounded, and later that evening Colonel Morrow was carried in to share the quarters with them. As he was brought in the wounded men raised their heads and asked him if he was finally satisfied with his regiment.[25]

Howard's corps had suffered heavily too. There had been fewer outright casualties, but nearly 4,000 men had been captured in the wild mix-up attending the retreat through town, and 1,500 more had fled to the rear, to be rounded up later that evening by the provost guard of the oncoming XII Corps.[26] All in all, as evening came down there were no more than 5,000 fighting men left of the two corps which had fought that day. These were grouped in a semicircle on and around Cemetery Hill, and between the height of the ground and the trenches and gun pits Steinwehr had dug they put up a bold front, but if the Confederates had followed up their victory they probably could have taken the hill and everybody on it. The expected attack did not come, however. Lee's orders were vague and seem not to have been well understood, and the Confederates themselves had been badly mauled in the day's fighting and were ready for a rest.

As the exhausted Federals took position on the hill they met Howard, still defiant, riding back and forth with a battle flag tucked under the stump of his right arm. Better yet, they met Hancock, who had been sent up by Meade to look things over and see whether the whole army should go to Gettysburg and make a finish fight of it. Hancock got there just as the retreat was ending, and he had a brief passage at arms with Howard. Howard outranked him and did not see how Meade could send a junior to take charge, and he was slightly stuffy about it for a time. But in the end the two men straightened things out without too much of an argument and saw to it that an orderly line of battle was formed. Hancock decided that Gettysburg was a good place for a fight, sent Meade a note saying so, and continued to look about him.

Straight east from Cemetery Hill there was a saddle of high ground running for half a mile to another high point, Culp's Hill, all rocky and overgrown with trees. A ravine cut into this saddle from the north, halfway between the hills, and Rebel patrols were edging forward into it, and it occurred to Hancock that if the Rebels got up on Culp's Hill the whole Union position would be ruined. He spurred over to the west side of Cemetery Hill, where Doubleday was collecting the remnants of the I Corps, and told him to send a division over to occupy Culp's Hill.

Doubleday demurred: his men were disorganized, they were almost out of ammunition, many of their officers were dead, they had had a hard day, someone else would have to go to Culp's Hill. Hancock was not the man to take excuses, and in his pocket he had Meade's letter giving him control for that evening over everybody around Gettysburg. He stood up in his stirrups and he raised one hand and he thundered largely, and a soldier who watched noted that despite the heat and dirt of the day Hancock then, as always, wore spotless white linen, gleaming cuffs visible at the ends of his sleeves.

"Sir!" concluded Hancock. "*I* am in command on this field. Send every man you have got!"[27]

So Wadsworth and his division went over to Culp's Hill, and the day's fighting was over. The sun went down, and the air was all tainted with smoke and death. Slocum's men came up, and some of Sickles's, and Hancock galloped back to Taneytown to see Meade. Sometime after midnight he and Meade reached the battlefield, and Meade went around to see what he could see, in the warm July moonlight, of the field where his army had begun its greatest fight. From southwest all the way around to northeast, Confederate camp-fires glowed in the night.

2. All the Trumpets Sounded

Philippe Regis de Trobriand, French-born colonel commanding the 3rd Brigade of the 1st Division of the III Corps, climbed to the bell tower of St. Joseph's Convent in Emmitsburg, eight miles south of Gettysburg, to see what he could see. On the lawn in front of the convent his five regiments had stacked arms, and wisps of smoke from the fires of innumerable coffee boilers were floating up through the trees in the still evening air. Some guns were in park across the road, and there was a great coming and going of couriers, staff officers, and other mounted persons. Off to the north there was an uneven jerky rumble coming down the wind, faint but unmistakable. Colonel de Trobriand looked around, found that he could learn nothing in this belfry that he did not already know, and came down, his jack boots clumping incongruously in the quiet halls. At a window he came upon a group of nuns peering shyly out at this invasion of soldiers. Being a Frenchman, he stopped for a word with them, and he chided them lightly for giving way to the venial sin of curiosity.

"Permit me," he said, "to make one request of you. Ask St. Joseph to keep the Rebel army away from here; for if they come before I get away I do not know what will become of your beautiful convent."

The nuns vanished and the colonel went on down and came out on the lawn, and the brigade quieted down for the night. Early next morning—July 2, clear and warm after a rainy night—orders arrived, and the brigade fell into line and took the dusty road north toward Gettysburg, and a Michigan man in the ranks knew a moment of homesickness, reflecting that the bells chiming for morning mass sounded just like the church bells in his home town. As they went on up the road the colonel thought about the way war had broken the peaceful isolation of the convent, and years later he wrote: "I have never returned to Emmitsburg, but it would astonish me very little to hear that the two armies had gone to Gettysburg to fight on account of the miracle performed by St. Joseph, interceding in favor of these pious damsels." Meditating thus, the colonel got his brigades up to the hills south of Gettysburg and joined the rest of the army.[1]

The morning was hot and the army was tired. Most of the men who had not fought the day before had been on the roads far into the night. An air of foreboding lay upon the battlefield, heavy as the muggy weight of the July heat. There was an occasional spat-spat of picket firing, and now and then a battery loosed a few rounds at some temporary target, but these outbursts only emphasized the ex- pectant quiet. The Army of the Potomac waited grimly, and in rear of Cemetery Ridge the 120 ambulances of the II Corps were ranked on a slope, the chief of ambulances making the rounds to see that each wagon was properly equipped—keg of water under the end of each of the two leather-covered benches, supply of beef stock and bandages under the front seat, a stretcher properly hung on each side. Tough Colonel Cross of the 5th New Hampshire, promoted re- cently to brigade command, rode past and grinned, and called out: "We shan't want any of your dead carts today."[2] Farther up the slope, Meade had set up headquarters in a two-room cottage.

Meade had put his men where the ground was high. His line curled around Culp's Hill on the east, ran west across the saddle to Cemetery Hill, made a ninety-degree turn to the left in a little wood called Ziegler's Grove on the western slope of this hill, and then went straight south for a mile or more along Cemetery Ridge. This ridge lost altitude, trailing off at last to lower ground covered with small trees and broken by tiny watercourses, and rising finally to two dominant hills—Little Round Top, very craggy and full of boulders, and a quarter of a mile south of it a higher hill, Big Round Top, sometimes known locally as Sugar Loaf.

From Culp's Hill through Cemetery Hill the line was held by Howard's men and Slocum's men and the remnants of the I Corps. Hancock's II Corps held Ziegler's Grove and the open ridge immediately south of it, and Dan Sickles had been told to put his III Corps in beside Hancock. It was Meade's idea that Sickles could hold whatever part of the ridge Hancock's men could not cover, and that in addition he would be able to occupy the Round Tops. George Sykes had brought his V Corps up during the night and was held in reserve behind Cemetery Hill.

The position was strong, and some of the officers remarked that if the Rebs attacked here it would be Fredericksburg in reverse, and they frankly liked the idea. But Sickles was not happy. He held the low part of the ridge—it was so low where he was that it practically ceased to be a ridge at all—and he believed that the ground would be very hard to defend. The Round Tops would be a good anchor, but Sickles did not think he could stretch his two divisions to reach them. Meade's orders did not seem clear, and Sickles had some of his men posted farther west than Meade had intended, down in flat land bordering a little brook known as Plum Run. As the morning wore on Sickles grew very uneasy, and he kept looking out at the Emmitsburg road in front of his position.

This road ran southwest from Gettysburg, skirting Ziegler's Grove and going down over rolling country, getting farther and farther away from Cemetery Ridge. Half a mile due west of the low ground which Sickles was occupying the road passed over a broad flat hill on top of which there was a peach orchard, and this hill was somewhat higher than the ground where Sickles's men were. Sickles believed that if the enemy put men and guns in the peach orchard they could drive him out. He noticed, too, that an uneven fold of high land ran off southeast from the peach orchard in the direction of the Round Tops. This ground was rugged, with little hills and ravines and woods and rocky ledges, and if the Rebels got in there they would be squarely on the Federal left flank and it might be extremely hard to dislodge them.

Sickles finally grew so worried that he rode over to headquarters and asked Meade to come down and have a look. Meade refused. Ordinarily he was a front-line operator, but now that he was army commander he was a little immersed in details at headquarters. He believed that morning that the real fighting was apt to break out near Culp's Hill, and anyway, he did not care much for Sickles, and at last he bluntly told Sickles to put his men where the original orders told him to put them, and be done with it. When Sickles still protested, Meade unbent enough to send Artillerist Henry Hunt over to survey the ground and make a recommendation. Sickles and Hunt went away, and Meade went back to his other concerns.

To make Sickles feel still worse, when he got back to his troops he found that the cavalry was gone. Buford's troopers had been covering the left flank, but through some misunderstanding Pleasonton had taken them away from there without sending anyone in to replace them. Sickles felt naked. He put a skirmish line out on the Emmitsburg road, and the skirmishers kept having little brushes with Rebel patrols, and around noon Hunt suggested that Sickles make a reconnaissance to find out just what the enemy was doing off to the west. So Sickles called in Colonel Berdan and told him to take four companies of his sharpshooters, with the 3rd Maine Infantry for support, and go out to investigate.[3]

Noon came, and everything was quiet except for a vicious little fight on the skirmish line in front of Ziegler's Grove, where General Alexander Hays was posted with the third division of Hancock's corps. In the empty land halfway between his line and the enemy's there was a big barn, and Federal and Confederate skirmishers were bickering over it, each side wanting to possess it as an advanced post for sharpshooters. The firing grew rather heavy, and General Hays decided he would ride out and look into it. He would go alone, he said, except for one mounted orderly.

A little Irish private on a big white horse was detailed for this job, and Hays looked him over and asked him brusquely if he were a brave man. The private grinned and said nothing, but Hays was a brigadier general, and when he spoke to an enlisted man he liked to get an answer, so he barked angrily: "Will you follow me, sir?" The Irishman saluted and said: "Gineral, if ye's are killed and go to hell it will not be long before I am tapping on the window." So the general and the private made the trip, Hays carrying his divisional flag and the orderly riding close at his elbow. Neither of them was hit, and Hays got the skirmishers straightened out.[4]

Meanwhile, Berdan was leading his men west. They crossed the highway and passed through a belt of woods, coming out on the southern part of Seminary Ridge, and before long they passed a farmhouse. A small boy, who must have been having a big day for himself, came out from behind the barn, big-eyed and excited, and pointed to another wood ahead of them, crying: "There are lots of Rebels in there—in rows!" The men laughed at him and doubtless told him to go down in the cellar and be safe, and they kept on going. They found out shortly that the small boy knew exactly what he was talking about.

They found a line of Rebel skirmishers, got into a fight with them, and when the skirmishers withdrew and Berdan's men pursued they ran into any number of Rebels all in rows, just as the boy had said. For twenty minutes the opposing lines blazed away at each other under the trees, the 3rd Maine coming up beside the sharpshooters. Berdan realized at last that he had found what he was looking for, and he took his men back to Sickles's line east of the road and told Sickles that a solid body of Rebel infantry was moving around to the left.[5]

That was enough for Sickles. Here was Chancellorsville all over again, with the Confederates marching through the wood past Sickles's front, and hot-blooded impetuous Sickles was unable to contain himself. This time he did not jump to the conclusion that the Rebels were in retreat. On the contrary, he knew perfectly well what they were up to—a smash at the Federal left flank—and the only trouble was that Sickles decided to answer the threat himself without waiting to consult headquarters, and in his haste he came up with the wrong answer. He did ask Hunt if he could move forward to the Emmitsburg road, but Hunt warned him that this was a question for Meade to answer, and then Hunt rode away. So Sickles issued his orders anyway. He took his whole corps forward, a mile-long line of battle with waving flags and rumbling batteries rolling west in the afternoon sunlight. John Gibbon, commanding Hancock's 2nd Division on Cemetery Ridge, looked out in amazement and wondered if a general order to advance upon the enemy had somehow missed him.

What Sickles got out of his advance was a longer line than he had had before. He wanted to hold the road and the peach-orchard hill and to bend the rest of his line back to the Round Tops, and he did not have enough men for it. Humphreys's division took position in the road, and Birney's division crammed the little orchard with men and guns and extended its line back toward the southeast, down a little slope from the orchard, across a rolling wheat field, and up through a maze of thickets and boulders and rocky crevices to a little hill which went by the descriptive name of Devil's Den. At Devil's Den, Birney ran out of troops. He got some guns up there beside his infantry—uncommonly rough work it was, too, manhandling the clumsy weapons up the little hill through rocks and trees and gullies—and he managed to plant one regiment and two guns down in a valley that separated Devil's Den from the Round Tops, but he could do no more than that. His line was thin, and he had no reserves.

Just as the men were getting into their places Meade decided to call a conference of his corps commanders. Sedgwick was coming up with his VI Corps, his men winded after an all-night hike of thirty-five miles, and the army was complete at last. Meade issued the conference call, but before the generals assembled Meade heard about what Sickles had done and he rode over, at last, to see about it personally.

When he joined Sickles and looked out at the new line he became wrathy. Sickles's corps was half a mile out in front of the rest of the army. Its left had no support, on the right all connection with Hancock had been broken, and the peach orchard looked to Meade like a vulnerable spot which the enemy could assail from three sides at once. He spoke of these matters with some heat, and Sickles asked him if he should take his men back to the original line. Meade said that he should, and then what the army had been waiting for all day began to happen, starting with an earsplitting crash of artillery. Confederate James Longstreet had put forty-six guns in line where they would bear on the orchard and the rest of Birney's line and they all began firing at once. A long cloud of smoke went rolling up above the distant trees, and Birney's line was laced with exploding shell.[6]

Meade immediately reversed himself. He barked at Sickles that it was too late to withdraw now—Sickles would have to stay where he was and the rest of the army would try to support him. Then Meade went galloping back to headquarters, where he told Sykes to get his corps down to the left end of the line as fast as he could. He had no sooner given this order than another cannonade opened on the right of the Federal line, and the hills to the northeast and northwest became alive with a long semicircle of flashing guns. Enormous echoes went rocking back and forth from the ridges, Gettysburg was ringed in fire and smoke and shaking sound, and the Federal gun positions on Cemetery Hill were caught in a cross fire that smashed tombstones, splintered gun carriages, tore men's bodies apart, and sent the horrible mixed fragments flying through the blinding smoke. So confusing was this fire that a Massachusetts regiment which had been crouching behind a stone wall facing north finally crawled over on the enemy's side of the wall, figuring that it was on the whole somewhat safer.

One shell exploded directly beneath a Federal gun, putting the entire gun crew out of action, and an artillery officer remarked with approval that men ran in and put the gun back in action before the wounded were removed. Another shellburst put twenty-seven men out of action—a fantastic toll for one shell, in those days—and an Ohio private noted later that the ground around one battery was hit by 115 separate projectiles. The Federal gunners fired furiously in reply. Northeast of Culp's Hill they pulverized a Rebel artillery battalion, smashing guns and killing men and, in the end, knocking the props out from under the murderous bombardment of Cemetery Hill.[7]

On Sickles's front General Hunt kept piling battery after battery in from the artillery reserve, and the guns took position just behind the peach orchard along a little country lane and got into a tremendous fight with Longstreet's gunners. For a time they followed the old tactics that had been worked out at Antietam, twenty or thirty guns concentrating at a time on one Rebel battery, shifting to another when they had put the first out of action. One gunner reported that they silenced five batteries in succession. But they were not having things all their own way, and the Confederate fire was heavy, especially in the peach orchard, where shell and solid shot took a frightful toll. A New York battery there found itself fighting two enemy batteries at once, one section dueling with one while the other two fought the other. The Rebels had the exact range. Supporting Yankee infantry hugged the ground behind fences and mounds of earth, trees were stripped and broken, men and horses were mangled, and the battery commander wrote that he was in "as sharp an artillery fight as I ever witnessed."[8]

Then the high quaver of the Rebel yell went up from field and wood and the infantry came out—John B. Hood's famous division, charging in from the southwest, driving straight for the Devil's Den, forcing its way through ravines and thickets and sweeping over the rocky little hill and around into the valley between Devil's Den and the Round Tops.

The two guns and one regiment which Birney had put in this valley put up a prodigious fight, but they had to give ground, and the defenders of Devil's Den itself were swamped. This was miserable ground for a fight, the rocks and gullies breaking up formations so that there seemed to be no connected lines of any kind. Men fought by regiments and by companies and squads, a choking haze of smoke lying close to the ground. The Rebels got in among the guns and captured three of them, and Birney sent off desperate appeals for help. Colonel de Trobriand, who was in the wheat field and the wood beside it, had to send two of his regiments over to help, and he was left holding part of his line with the 5th Michigan deployed as skirmishers, volleying away against a host of Rebels who found shelter in a muddy little ravine that ran across his front. He said later that if the Confederates had jumped up and charged then his whole brigade would have been demolished. Even as it was, his line was visibly melting away, and it seemed to him that each of his men was fighting as if "the destiny of the Republic was attached to the desperate vigor of his efforts." He wedged the 17th Maine in behind a little stone wall, and to the left the terrible uproar of firing and shouting men came closer and closer and he knew that Devil's Den was being lost.[9]

Sickles took a brigade away from Humphreys and sent it pounding over double-quick, but the line had been stretched too thin. The brigade came in just as fragments of the battle line were breaking to the rear. De Trobriand's Maine regiment was flanked out from behind its wall, his Michigan skirmish line collapsed, and at last the whole left of Birney's line gave way in wild confusion. The men who had been defending the valley below the Round Tops were driven back, yelling Confederates came charging through, and a solid Rebel brigade swung off and went plunging straight ahead for Little Round Top, upon which at that moment there was no one in Union blue except a few men in a signal detachment.

Here was unrelieved and final disaster, coming on fast and yelling like fiends, for if the Rebels ever got Little Round Top the whole of Cemetery Ridge would have to be abandoned and the battle would be lost once and for all. Up on the hill with the signal men was General Warren, and he spotted the danger just in time and hurried off for help. Just north of the hill he met George Sykes bringing his corps down to reinforce the left as Meade had ordered—George Sykes, stiff and crusty and very much old-army, looking always a little tired and out of sorts, uninspired and uninspiring, but all soldier for all of that. Sykes was sending two brigades down into the flat land along Plum Run to reinforce Birney, and at Warren's request he shot another brigade straight south to defend Little Round Top.

This was the brigade of Colonel Strong Vincent, who had sat in the moonlight a couple of nights earlier to reflect that a man could do worse than die on Pennsylvania soil under the old flag. Vincent got to the southern slope of the hill and swung his four regiments into line just as the Confederates came lunging up the valley. The Confederates clambered up over the boulders to finish things, the Federals squatted behind the boulders and met them with fire, the valley was filled with smoke and flame and a great deafening clamor, and the Rebels shifted their strength to break in the flanks of this new Yankee line.[10]

At the extreme left of Vincent's line was the 20th Maine led by Colonel Joshua Chamberlain, who had been college professor and minister of the gospel before the war and who was becoming a good deal of a soldier. Vincent went to the southern end of the hill with him, pointed down the slope, and told him to take his 350 men down there and hold the ground at all hazards, and the 20th ran down the hill and collided with a powerful flanking column that bent the left half of the regiment back at a ninety-degree angle and threatened to overwhelm the whole outfit by sheer weight. Chamberlain had to space his men several paces apart to keep the Rebels from getting around his left, and when the first wild rush was beaten back the Rebels settled down among the logs and trees and rocks for the sharpest fire fight this Maine regiment was ever in. The reeking smoke filled the air, the Yankee line swayed and staggered as if the weight of the attack were a tangible force that shoved men off balance, and the valley rang with rifle fire, with the clang of metal ramrods in hot musket barrels, with the yells and cries of Northerners and Southerners caught up in a great fury of combat.

Far behind him Chamberlain heard a new burst of shooting and yelling, which for all he knew might mean that the other end of Vincent's line had caved in. Nearly half of the 20th was down, ammunition was almost gone, here and there the colonel could see men preparing to swing their muskets as clubs when the next Rebel assault was driven home. In sheer desperation—for that next assault would inevitably crush the entire line—Chamberlain ordered his men to fix bayonets and charge.

No one could hear a shouted order in that terrible racket, but somehow the word was passed along the line, by gesture and by example, and the men glanced right and left, nerving themselves for the shock. A young lieutenant suddenly waved his sword, yelled: "Come on! Come on, boys!" and ran toward the Confederate line, which was barely thirty yards away. The color guard followed him, streamers of smoke eddying about the shaken flags. There was a moment of hesitation, and then with a wild cry the whole regiment charged in a long, ragged line.

Perhaps it worked because it was so unexpected. The Confederates fell into confusion as the charge hit them—Chamberlain remembered one Rebel officer firing a pistol with one hand while he held out his sword in token of surrender with the other—and the whole first line broke and ran. The second line collapsed a moment later, the Maine regiment swung up over the slope of Big Round Top, and Chamberlain at last had trouble getting his men to halt and adjust their line, the men crying that they were "on the road to Richmond." They sent upward of four hundred prisoners to the rear.[11]

Yet if that wildly improbable counterattack had saved the army's flank, it had saved it only for the moment. This was a day on which crisis followed crisis. While they were hitting the 20th Maine the Confederates were also working around the right of Vincent's line. They made better progress here, and the right-flank regiment, 16th Michigan, was broken and driven back. Vincent ran down into the melee to rally his men and the Rebels shot him dead, and once more the way was open for Confederate conquest of Little Round Top.

General Warren was still on hand, watching, and he saw this new disaster and once again rode madly off for help. The first regiment he met was the 140th New York, part of General Stephen Weed's brigade in Sykes's corps, and while he was still fifty yards away Warren began shouting to Colonel Patrick O'Rorke to bring his men up the hill as fast as they could run. O'Rorke protested that he was under orders to follow the rest of the brigade somewhere else, but Warren replied: "Never mind that, Paddy! Bring them up on the double-quick—don't stop for aligning! I'll take the responsibility!" And because Warren was known to be intimate with Meade, O'Rorke assumed that he could square things, so he took the 140th up on Little Round Top at a dead run.

He had no time whatever to spare. The Rebels who had broken the Michigan regiment were coming up the hill. O'Rorke jumped off his horse, tossed the reins to his orderly, called out: "This way, boys!" and ran down the slope toward the enemy, his men at his heels. It was as strange a counterattack as the army ever saw. The men went in with unloaded weapons. They did not stop to fix bayonets, they did not even club their empty muskets: they simply ran straight at their foes, and the only weight their charge had was the weight of their running bodies. Perhaps the mere appearance of fresh troops was enough for the moment. The Confederates wavered and drew back, and the 140th went into line beside Vincent's brigade, and in a few minutes the rest of Weed's brigade was on the hill with them.[12]

So was a battery of six three-inch rifles, whose sweating gunners had practically carried their guns to the hilltop piece by piece since there was nothing resembling a road up this rocky height. This battery began to fire on Rebel reinforcements in the valley—the gun muzzles could not be depressed enough to hit the men on the sides of Little Round Top itself—and from the Rebel line in front and from a host of sharpshooters in Devil's Den a new fury of rifle fire hit the Federals. General Weed was killed as he gave some order to the battery commander, and when that officer bent over him to examine his wound a sharpshooter got him too, and he fell dead on top of the general, and all of the hill with its steep slopes and its rocks and its tangled underbrush was smoking and crackling like a volcano.

In front of the Round Tops everything was coming loose. The Devil's Den line had long since dissolved, the wheat field was gone, and all of the uneven half mile between Round Top Valley and the peach orchard was smoke and flying bullets and wild shouting. Two of Sykes's brigades came in to hold the ground between the peach orchard and the wheat field, and their division commander, General Barnes, lined them up and made a few patriotic and inspirational remarks, while the men cheered bravely. (So says the record, at any rate. One of the private soldiers involved wrote that the general told them: "Boys, I want you to put in a few licks for Pennsylvania. The Bucktails will go in on your left. Forward!")[13]

For a time these brigades made progress, and Hancock sent a whole division in to retake the wheat field and drive the Rebel line back on its supports—the ghost of the old Irish Brigade storming along beside red-bearded Colonel Cross and his soldiers, the men who had broken the Rebel line at Antietam and swarmed nearly to the stone wall at Fredericksburg and held on in the great last-ditch fight at Chancellorsville. These men got into woods and hollows south of the wheat field, and Sykes's division of regulars came in on their left, and it seemed briefly that the whole position had been stabilized.

Then Longstreet sent in a fresh division, and the Rebels caught the peach-orchard angle from three sides at once, just as Meade had foreseen. In from the west came General Barksdale and his Mississippians—the same general and the same troops who had held the Fredericksburg water front against the bridgebuilders—and they charged straight through a picket fence, knocking it down by sheer impact, and they shot and stabbed at a Pennsylvania regiment that was dug in behind it, and after a flurry of hand-to-hand fighting under the shattered peach trees the Union defenders turned and ran and the peach orchard was gone.

With this position lost, there was no way on earth to save Birney's line. (It was "Birney's" line only by courtesy now, the reinforcements far outnumbering the original defenders, all the units so mixed up that nobody quite knew where anybody else was.) The Rebels who had broken in the angle drove straight on toward Little Round Top, and they took the entire line in flank, destroying one segment after another. The artillery which General Hunt had lined up behind the peach orchard enfiladed the charging Rebels and killed them by platoons, but these Southerners were tough and they kept on going, and one after another the brigades which had restored Birney's line found that the Rebels were coming in on their right rear.

The volunteer brigades Sykes had sent in discovered it first. They faced south, and a color-bearer rode up to his brigade commander and said: "Colonel, I'll be damned if I don't think we are faced the wrong way. The Rebs are up there in the woods behind us, on the right." The colonel investigated and found that the man was right, and sent an aide back to tell the division commander. The aide ran into a host of armed Rebels right where division headquarters was supposed to be, and the whole Union line seemed to have vanished in smoke and confusion. Rebel units were intermingled with Federals, some regiments were surrounded without knowing it, the 4th Michigan saw its colonel killed with a bayonet while he was still in the saddle, and the only order or pattern in any of it was the fact that defeat and collapse progressed steadily from right to left, from the peach orchard toward Devil's Den.[14]

The division Hancock had sent over was forced to retreat, more than a third of its men killed or wounded, three of its four brigade commanders shot down. (Among them was Colonel Cross, carried to the rear in one of the ambulances which he had gaily said would not be needed this day, wounded mortally.) When this division fled the regulars were flanked, and as they went back toward Plum Run they crossed open marshy ground and came under a storm of musket fire, losing nine hundred of their two thousand men. The skipper of the 11th U. S. Infantry reported grimly that he had lost half of his men "without inflicting the slightest damage upon the enemy."[15] Of Birney's entire line, reinforcements and all, nothing whatever was left except a dense carpet of dead and wounded men lying on the ground, and broken waves of fugitives going back toward Cemetery Ridge, some in good order and under control, some altogether out of control and in no order whatever. And there was a huge gap in the line of the Army of the Potomac.

This gap immediately got bigger. After the peach orchard fell, Humphreys's line along the Emmitsburg road was doomed, particularly so since a division of A. P. Hill's men assaulted it in front while Longstreet's men were flanking it from the south. As the left end of this line began to crumble the artillery had to leave. Humphreys tried desperately to swing his line back so that he could maintain contact with the troops that had been driven out of Birney's line, but he found that there was nothing left to maintain contact with and the Rebels were getting his own line under what he later described as one of the hottest rifle and artillery fires he ever saw.

Near the orchard some Massachusetts gunners were removing their guns by hand, all horses having been killed, and a man who watched them wrote that "it is a mystery to me that they were not all hit by the enemy's fire, as they were surrounded and fired upon from almost every direction." Humphreys was riding amid the thickest of the fighting. A captain on his staff threw up his hands and cried, "I'm shot!" Humphreys rode up beside him to hold him in his saddle, when a cannon ball went through the wounded officer's horse and tore the head off an orderly who was starting to lead it to the rear, and Humphreys's own horse, already six times wounded, got another bullet and sprang into the air, throwing the general to the earth. Humphreys got up, took an aide's horse, and went on trying to patch up his collapsing line.[16]

Things had gone past the point where a general could help much. The 7th New Jersey was coming forward on the run up a narrow lane, and it collided with a Federal battery going to the rear, frantic drivers lashing frantic horses, battery and infantry hopelessly tangled in the cramped dirt road, guns overlapping guns and locking wheels. The 2nd New Hampshire, running back from the peach orchard, got involved in the mess, and Rebel skirmishers trotted forward and took the whole mad turmoil of yelling men and plunging horses under fire, and a few companies of the New Jersey regiment tried a bayonet charge just in time to be routed by a new Rebel line. Barksdale was pushing his Mississippians on relentlessly, riding back and forth behind the infantry lines, driving his men on. One of Humphreys's brigadiers detailed an entire company to concentrate its fire on the man, and at last Barksdale went down mortally wounded, with five bullets in his body.

On the Emmitsburg road, regiments were going to pieces in smoke and fire, trying to cope with a flank attack and at the same time beat back a heavy assault from in front. The colonel of the 11th New Jersey was shot as he began to put his regiment through a confused left wheel. The major took over and spun round like a top when a bullet caught him in the knee. Someone notified the senior captain that he was in command, but he was killed just as he got the news, and the captain who took over from him was immediately wounded. Four men picked him up to take him to the rear, all four were shot down, and the captain was hit again and killed. One more captain tried to take charge and was killed, and a corporal finally rallied what was left of the regiment behind a little hedge.[17]

At the right of Humphreys's line, Gibbon had sent forward two regiments from his division to try to fill the gap between the two army corps. A whole Rebel brigade hit them and tore them apart, and their commander, Colonel George Ward of the 15th Massachusetts, who had lost a leg at Ball's Bluff and was now going around on an ill-fitting peg, went stumping along the line with a cane in one hand and a sword in the other, until a Confederate rifleman killed him, and what was left of the two regiments went to the rear. The 12th New Hampshire hung on for a while by a log house beside the Emmitsburg road, and a Rebel battle line suddenly appeared over a rise in ground just in front, yelling and firing like mad, and the two battle lines volleyed at point-blank range in blinding smoke.

For a few minutes the Union line there held as the sun went low and the smoke brought the dusk in ahead of time, and back on Cemetery Ridge an officer saw unreal drama in the parallel battle lines: "The smoke of their rifles encircled them, the flashes lighted up the field upon which the shadows of evening were advancing, and the scene resembled one of those battles which are seen in pictures, where the lines of battle are formed with mathematical exactness." Then Confederate guns around the peach orchard came into action and the Yankee line broke, and the Rebel columns advanced with wild cheers.[18]

Between the Round Tops and Hancock's position there was nothing now except a vast, disordered retreat. The III Corps was altogether out of the fight, and its survivors were going east for the reverse slope of the ridge, to reorganize there if possible, but in any case to get there, out of the danger zone. The brigades that had gone in as reinforcements had suffered heavy losses and, like Sickles's men, were at least temporarily out of action. Most of Slocum's corps had been ordered down from the right of the line, but it had not arrived yet, and great masses of Rebel soldiers were coming up the slope almost unopposed.

Sickles had been carried to the rear, one leg gone—he went back jauntily, smoking a cigar, game enough for a regiment—and Meade told Hancock to take charge and stop the rout. It was a good choice, for Hancock was probably the best combat general on the Federal side that day. Yet neither Meade, Hancock, nor anyone else could do anything unless somewhere, on that long slanting plain, some of the fighting men dug their heels in and bought a little time. There was not much any general could do about this. If out of what it originally was and what it had learned the army had developed the swift instinctive reflexes which are all that will serve in the moment of disaster, then the situation might be saved—by Meade, by Hancock, or by sheer good luck. If not, then the war was about over.

For ten minutes or so it would be entirely up to the gunners. Lieutenant Colonel Freeman McGilvery of the artillery reserve had been pulling batteries and parts of batteries out of the retreat, and he was building up a line of two dozen guns just behind Plum Run. It was an army axiom that guns unsupported by infantry could not hope to beat off a charge, but the gunners averaged pretty tough in this army and McGilvery proposed to see what they could do on their own. While he was organizing the line he sent word out to Captain John Bigelow, who had the 9th Massachusetts battery posted in the barnyard of a farmer named Trostle, a few rods west of Plum Run, informing Bigelow that no matter what happened the Rebels must be held off until this new rank of guns could be installed.

The Massachusetts boys had never been in action before this day but they were making up for it very fast. Several Confederate batteries had their range and were firing fast and accurately, but Rebel infantry was coming in so close that Bigelow told his men to forget about counter-battery fire and knock off the foot soldiers. For a time the gunners loaded their guns with canister all the way to the muzzles, firing at pistol range, and then they switched to shell with the fuses cut entirely off so that the projectiles would explode the instant they left the muzzles of the guns. Fighting thus, they gained just the time McGilvery needed, and when he finally called them in the battery had lost half of its men, sixty of its horses, four of its six guns, and all of its officers.[19]

McGilvery's guns no sooner opened fire than the Rebel infantry charged home. A Mississippi regiment which had overrun Bigelow's guns followed the survivors in, broke in among McGilvery's guns, and got into a desperate hand-to-hand fight with the cannoneers, who hit them with rammers and handspikes and even grappled with them like rowdies rioting back of the grandstand at the county fair, everybody yelling and cursing, officers firing pistols, dense smoke settling down over everything. One entire regular battery was put out of action, and for a moment it seemed that this Mississippi regiment might break all the way through and get into the Union rear. But the fire of the other pieces never stopped, and the rest of the Confederate line was compelled to halt, and the Mississippians at last sullenly withdrew.[20]

It was getting dark and the air was streaky and blurred with smoke, and the advancing Confederate masses were almost indistinguishable in the twilight. Reinforcements were coming up from the Union right and rear at last, and officers were casting forward looking for the spots where these new troops were needed the most.

Among these officers was Hancock, and he saw a Confederate brigade advancing toward him, its uneven line coming up out of a little hollow a hundred yards off. He trotted back, saw a Union regiment coming up in column of fours, and galloped over to it. It was the 1st Minnesota out of his own corps. Hancock pointed to the Rebel line, whose flags were just visible in the murk.

"Do you see those colors?" he demanded. The regiment's Colonel Colville had just been released from arrest, which he had incurred by refusing to make his men wade a creek on the march north. He looked forward and nodded laconically.

"Well, capture them!" barked Hancock.

Down the ridge came the 1st Minnesota, still in column of fours, and it hit the slightly disordered Rebel column and knocked it back. The Rebels quickly rallied from the shock—they greatly outnumbered this lone Minnesota regiment—and they formed a firing line in the underbrush and woods on the edge of the ravine, and the Minnesota men swung into a line of their own, and the fire lit the dusk like great flashes of irregular sheet lightning. The Confederates worked their way around on each flank and got the 1st Minnesota into a pocket, sending their fire in from three sides, and the whole war had suddenly come to a focus in this smoky hollow, with a few score Westerners trading their lives for the time the army needed. Off to the left McGilvery saw what was up, and while the Confederate batteries by the Emmitsburg road concentrated their fire on him he swung his guns around and pounded the underbrush with canister, and on the other side Hancock found some more troops and sent them in. After a time the Confederates began to draw back, and when they came out into the open the guns hit them hard, and finally they went into full retreat.

What was left of the Minnesota regiment came back to reorganize. It had taken 262 men into action and it had 47 men left, and the survivors boasted that while the casualties amounted to 82 per cent (which seems to have been a record for the Union Army for the entire war) there was not a straggler or a prisoner of war on the entire list.[21] They had not captured the flag that Hancock had asked them to capture, but they still had their own flag and a great name, plus those 47 exhausted survivors, and as they came back it might have been as John Bunyan wrote: "So he passed over, and all the trumpets sounded for him on the other side."

North of there Meade himself was on the firing line, and he and his staff saw another advancing Confederate line which had got clear up on top of the ridge and was possessing itself of some Union cannon. For a moment it seemed that no one but the commanding general was there to meet this assault, but an officer cried, "There they come, General!" and looking back, Meade saw a Federal battle line coming in on the run. He spurred back, waved his hat toward the Rebels, and started riding forward again in the middle of the firing line, hat still in his hand, calling to his staff: "Come on, gentlemen!" His aides finally got him out of the front line, the line charged, the Confederates ran back out of the guns and down the slope, and Cemetery Ridge was clear.[22]

Behind the ridge there was a great tangle of men and animals and equipment, jammed together like the debris of a hopelessly defeated army. On the hillsides, beaten regiments and brigades tried to reassemble. Walking wounded were limping toward the rear, ambulances were clattering down the bumpy roads, broken batteries were jolting back for a refit, and dazed stragglers and non-combatants were wandering about in a daze, drifting back and forth like the shreds of smoke that came seeping in through the trees from the west. Over all there rolled a great pall of sound: many guns firing, an unending crackle and sputter of small arms, and above all the yelling and screaming of many men. Slocum's corps was being moved up, and one column was coming along a country lane in the twilight, marching toward a firing line which it could not yet see; and it seemed to these men that the high screech of the Rebel yell coming out of the darkness ahead "was more devilish than anything which *could* come from human throats." These men were veterans, but there was something about this twilight march, with those unearthly cries just ahead, which put them on the edge of panic.

They passed a little cabin, and by the roadside in front of it there was a bent old woman—an "old crone," as one soldier ungallantly called her—and she caught the feel of their unease, and as the ranks passed her she kept repeating soothingly: "Never mind, boys— they're nothing but *men*." A soldier who heard her wrote that these commonplace words "seemed almost sublime as she uttered them, standing unmoved by all the uproar of battle," and he said that they calmed the men so that they shook off their panic and were brave soldiers once more.[23]

Cemetery Ridge was secure at last, and yet still the day would not die. Far to the right a great crescent of fire and smoke was climbing the sides of Culp's Hill, encircling the lone Union brigade which held that point, and it seemed to observers in the rear that all of the wooded hill was ablaze with jagged bolts of chain lightning. Among Slocum's men who had been holding this hill were many New England lumbermen, and these men had spent the day with their axes making stout breastworks of solid logs. When Slocum took his men away to reinforce the line on Cemetery Ridge he had left General George Greene's brigade behind, and these men in their good breastworks were putting up a desperate fight. Four times the Rebels surged up the slope through the trees, a solid division of first-rate troops, and each time the fire over the logs drove them back. Yet part of the Union line, which ran through low ground southeast of the hill, was overrun, and as the darkness came down the Union position here was still insecure. It was as certain as anything could be that the Confederate attack would be renewed at dawn.

On the saddle between Culp's Hill and Cemetery Hill there was one final brush with disaster. While the fight raged on Culp's Hill the Union troops along this saddle saw a long Rebel line forming in the plain to the north, just east of Gettysburg, and the ranked batteries came to life and fired at it long-range in the fading light. The line moved closer, dipping down into lower ground, wheeling a little toward the west, and then striking straight up the ravine where Hancock had spotted danger the evening before. On a little knoll at the head of this ravine stood the 5th Maine Battery, six brass smoothbores, and it fired so fast at the advancing line that gunners dropped exhausted in the hot dusk and had to be relieved by volunteers hastily called from the nearest infantry regiment. On up the ravine came the Rebels, and the rising ground shielded them from the waiting batteries on the east side of Cemetery Hill. It was dark now, and the Union line on the rim of the ravine was traced in fire as the infantry went into action.

Along part of the rim the sparkling lights suddenly went out. The Rebels were in the Yankee line, fighting hand to hand with Von Gilsa's brigade, and they shattered it and sent it flying. The Maine battery kept on firing until it had shot away the last of its ammunition, and beside it the 33rd Massachusetts and what was left of the Iron Brigade got the Rebels in flank at close range, and most of the charging line went to pieces and slid back downhill in the dark. But some of the Confederates—very tough men, these, from Louisiana —kept coming on, and they ran in among the guns on the eastern slope of Cemetery Hill, and once again there was savage fighting between gunners and infantry, cannoneers clubbing Rebels with anything they could lay their hands on, including fence rails. The Louisiana boys spiked a gun in Ricketts's battery, overran a New York battery beside it, and tried to drag some gunners off bodily as prisoners, and here once more the Federal grip on a key position was being broken.

Then over the top of Cemetery Hill a shadowy mass came rolling forward—Carroll's brigade from Hancock's corps, sent over on the run when Howard called for help. The daylight was entirely gone now, and in the darkness Carroll's men could see nothing except the points and splashes of flame in the overrun batteries, and they came running blindly down the slope, shouting breathlessly as they ran. There was a confused sound of pounding feet and colliding human bodies, grunts and yells and curses and a crackle of rifle fire—and the last of the Confederates were driven out, Carroll's brigade drew up along the lip of the ravine, and the line was secure once again.[24]

The day's fighting was over at last. The noise died down, and the smoke drifted away, and a huge brilliant moon came up, flooding all of the ghastly battlefield with a rich mellow light.

3. And It May Be Forever

Around the foot of Culp's Hill the men had an uneasy night. There was a hollow meadow where the ground was low and spongy, dark as a pit under the trees and streaky with thin smoky moonlight in the open, and where there should have been alert skirmish lines there were listless exhausted men who had lost their sense of direction and had no idea where their enemies might be. Near the foot of the hill there was a spring, and shadowy figures from both armies came up in the dark to fill canteens, lounging nearby for low-voiced casual conversation. Some of Slocum's men who had just returned from Cemetery Ridge came wandering in to get some of the water. One of them remarked that "the Rebs had caught Hail Columbia" over on the left that evening.

A Confederate heard and sprang up, yelling: "Hell—those are Yankees!" and it was as if his shout reminded the men that they were in the midst of a battle. Someone fired his musket, other shots were fired, and men struck blindly at each other in the dark, swinging clubbed muskets and firing with their fists. The uproar aroused the authorities, and after casualties had been given and taken, including on each side a moderate haul of disgusted prisoners, officers came in and pulled the rival forces apart and established orderly military lines across the swale with sentries in front.

Behind the sentries men tried to sleep, but they did not do very well at it. The sentries kept peering forward into the gloom, and when one of them heard footsteps or thought he saw movement he fired. Men on the other side would fire at the flash of the rifle, still other men would fire at them, and a fusillade would break out all along the line, with no one able to see what he was shooting at. The sleeping men would stumble to their feet, grab their weapons, and get ready to beat off an attack. Then quiet would slowly return, the men would go back to sleep, and fifteen minutes later it would happen all over again.[1]

Nobody in the army got much sleep that night. It was hot, and the fighting had gone on until after the last of the long summer twilight faded, and there was so much rearranging of battle lines that one soldier wrote: "The entire army seemed to be in motion the greater part of the night." There was a great scarcity of drinking water. (One man remembered kneeling by a hoofprint in a muddy cowpath and laboriously spooning into his tin cup enough dirty water to make some coffee.)[2] Ambulances and stretcher parties were busy all along the western slope of Cemetery Ridge, where there was more than enough work for them. Searching the hillside with them were many private soldiers who had been assigned to no stretcher details but who were simply looking for missing comrades. One of the things that held those thin regiments together was the strong sense of personal attachment the men had for each other. Most of the men in any given company came from the same town or county and knew each other from before the war, and a man who was left wounded on the field knew that his friends would come out to help him if they could. So men went across the torn thickets and meadows in the late moonlight without orders, hunting for comrades who had not come back.

Behind the lines there were the field hospitals, and every house and barn within reach had been filled with wounded men. Brigadier General Zook of the II Corps, shot through the belly with one of those wounds which medical knowledge of that day could not cure, was carried back to a small house on the Baltimore Pike. The house was full of wounded men, most of them screaming—the overworked doctors had not got to the place yet—and the floors were hideous and slippery with blood. An aide asked Zook if he should bring the chaplain to him, but Zook shook his head and said quietly that it was too late, and after a while he died.[3] Colonel Cross had died before midnight, gasping: "I did hope I would live to see peace and our country restored. . . . I think the boys will miss me." The boys would, those who were left—his old 5th New Hampshire had lost 100 out of 150 men that day, and its surviving fragment was detached from the army and sent home to recruit as soon as the battle was over. One of the soldiers paid his tribute to the redheaded colonel in words which any troop commander in that war might have been proud of: "He taught us to aim in battle, and above all things he ignored and made us ignore the idea of retreating. [Cross used to boast that his regiment simply did not dare to retreat without orders.] Besides this he clothed us and fed us well, taught us to build good quarters, and camped us on good ground."[4] Cross was camping on far ground tonight, and many good men had gone to keep him company there.

Late at night Meade called a meeting of his corps commanders. They met in a stuffy little box of a room at headquarters, the principal generals of this army, and they quietly talked over the fighting they had had that day. The army's losses had been fearful—probably twenty thousand men in two days—and the immediate, temporary loss made it a good deal worse than that, since, as always, a good many thousand additional men had got blown loose from their regiments, had wandered off heaven knew where, and would not be back in line for days to come. Nobody seemed to think that the army ought to retreat, but nobody thought that it ought to attack, either. The moral dominance of Robert E. Lee over the Federal commanders was all but complete. In a crisis like this they were

bound to come up with the one idea: hold on if we can, wait and
see what Lee is going to do, and then try to stop him.

For some reason—perhaps because he was new in command and
did not know many of his generals very well—Meade turned the
meeting into a formal council of war, with specific propositions put
up for a vote and with Dan Butterfield writing down the answers.
The verdict was unanimous: the army should stay where it was and
await attack. Meade nodded and said, "Such, then, is the decision,"
and the meeting broke up. As the generals left, Meade stopped John
Gibbon, who commanded Hancock's 2nd Division along the crest
of Cemetery Ridge near Ziegler's Grove.

"If Lee attacks tomorrow, it will be in your front," said Meade.
Gibbon asked him why he thought so, adding something to the effect
that if Lee did attack there he would be repulsed. Meade replied that
Lee had attacked both flanks the day before and had failed, and if
he attacked once more he would hit the center. Gibbon went off to
an improvised bed in an ambulance, reflecting that this was an odd
application of the law of probabilities.[5]

When the first streaks of daylight came it was apparent that Lee
was not yet through with the Federal right flank. His men had seized
nearly half of the Culp's Hill line the evening before, and they held
a half-open door leading directly to the army's unprotected rear.
Slocum had all of his corps reassembled, and during the night he and
General Hunt had been planting guns on some high ground by the
Baltimore Pike. At dawn these guns opened a rapid bombardment
at no more than eight hundred yards' range—Ewell's men were that
close to the Federal rear—and after fifteen minutes the gunfire was
stopped and Slocum's men prepared to charge. But the Rebels were
ready first and they made their own attack before the Federals could
take off, and there was bitter fighting all up and down the wooded
hillside and across the hollow ground where the men had blundered
into each other in the darkness. Try as they might—and they tried
with uncommon desperation—the Confederates could not get to the
top of the hill. The Federals here had the unusual experience of
standing in good trenches where they could inflict much more loss
than they received, and they laid a blistering fire on the slopes while
the guns in the rear fired as fast as the men could load. Some of the
fire fell short, and a few of the advanced Federal regiments were hit.
Doughty Colonel Wooster of the 20th Connecticut saw one of his

men lose both arms from the explosion of a Federal shell, and he angrily sent back word to the battery commander that if it happened again he would pull his men out of line, face them about, and charge his own guns. (Long afterward, at a veterans' reunion, a member of this regiment told his comrades: "He was just the man to keep his word, and you were just the boys to execute his threat.")[6]

The lines on top of the hill were unshaken, but there was still a good deal of Rebel strength down in the lower ground to the southeast, and the high command wanted a counterattack. No one was sure how many Rebels were in there, and a division commander ordered skirmishers thrown forward to feel the line and get a little information. Somehow this order reached the front as a straight order for attack by the two leading regiments, 2nd Massachusetts and 27th Indiana. Colonel Charles R. Mudge, commanding the 2nd Massachusetts, blinked when the aide gave him the order, for he knew there were many more Rebels just ahead than any two regiments could handle.

"Are you sure that is the order?" he demanded.

The aide assured him that it was.

"Well," said Mudge, "it is murder, but that's the order." He raised his voice to a great parade-ground shout. "Up, men—over the works! Forward, double-quick!"

The two regiments put up a cheer and charged out into the little meadow. There were three Rebel brigades within range, concealed among trees and rocks, and they cut loose with what wintry-faced old Colonel Colgrove of the Indiana regiment later described as "one of the most destructive fires I have ever witnessed." The charge collapsed before it reached the trees and the survivors came back to a little stone wall, where they beat off a countercharge. Colonel Mudge was killed, his regiment lost four color-bearers, nearly 250 men were shot, and the only advantage was that the division commander now knew that the enemy held the far side of the swale in great strength.[7]

One more valiant Confederate attack was made. Slocum had plenty of men now—two brigades from the fresh VI Corps had come in to help—and the charging Confederates never had a chance. Their left-flank elements came under a killing fire from Federals down in the flat, and the hilltop trenches were still invulnerable. In front of the 7th Ohio some seventy Confederates raised the white flag of surrender, and when the Federals ceased fire a doughty Rebel staff officer rode up, indignant, and tried to stop the surrender. The Federals killed him and took their beaten enemies into their lines. By ten-thirty the attack had been beaten off for good, and the Confederates had sullenly withdrawn to the lines they had occupied the day before, leaving thousands of dead and wounded behind them.[8]

As the fighting around Culp's Hill ended, an uneasy quiet came down on the great battlefield. It ceased briefly when the old row over that barn in front of Hays's division broke out again, with Hancock's and A. P. Hill's gunners suddenly running to their pieces and exchanging salvos in an immense meaningless cannonade. The barn took fire at last, its flames burning thin and insubstantial in the hot midday sunlight. The quarreling skirmishers fell back, and the cannonade died down as quickly as it had begun. It had happened almost by reflex action, as if the armies were so edgy that anything could touch off a fight, and the silence that followed was uneasy and insecure. Somehow, invisible but sensed by everyone, a slow fuse was burning toward one final, supreme explosion. The battle was following its own course now, and perhaps nobody controlled it. These two armies had come together, a gigantic thunderhead was stacked up higher than anything the war had known before, and it was full of a terrible, shattering tension that sooner or later would have to discharge itself. The soldiers held their places and waited for it in silence.

Whatever was coming, it was going to hit Cemetery Ridge when it came. From private to commanding general, everyone took that for granted. The soldiers cowered behind low stone walls and insubstantial earth-and-rail breastworks, the heat of the sun heavy on their shoulders. In front of Ziegler's Grove one regiment which still carried the old-style smoothbore muskets emptied its cartridge boxes on the stone wall in front, for easier access in reloading, and most of the men tore apart their buck-and-ball cartridges and made up new ones containing a dozen or more buckshot apiece.[9] General Hunt went along the ridge, making sure that the guns were ready and that caisson and limber chests were full. Off to the left, where the ridge sagged, McGilvery had thirty-nine guns in line, and he had his men building a little earthen embankment in front of the guns for protection.

Not far away, up in the front line, was a brigade of nine-month men from Vermont. They had enlisted in the preceding fall and had gone down to Washington green as grass. A diarist in one regiment wrote of their train ride across New Jersey that "such a night of suffering and misery is far beyond the power of any pen to portray," because they had to ride in unheated cars. In Washington they had manned the fortifications all winter and spring, and they had not been any too happy about it. Such veterans as they met showed lack of respect for their status as soldiers, and their historian noted moodily that "we have been called, by some, nine-monthlings, hatched on two-hundred-dollar bounty eggs." Being Vermonters, they did not care very much what other people said about them, but they did want to fight, and they were pleased when, near the end of June, they had been pulled out of the forts and sent up to join the Army of the Potomac.[10] Now for the first time they were in the presence of the enemy, even though the enemy's infantry was invisible under the trees on Seminary Ridge, and they showed a certain nervousness as they waited.

The enemy's artillery was far from invisible. It was very much in evidence, as a matter of fact. All morning there had been a ceaseless, ominous activity, with more and more Confederate batteries coming up into one prodigious line that began at the peach orchard and ran north along the Emmitsburg road and just west of it—scores and scores of guns, more of them than the Federals had ever seen in one row, bleak and silent in the bright light, their muzzles staring blankly toward the center of Cemetery Ridge. Farther north the Confederates had still more guns glinting out of the shade on Seminary Ridge, and off to the northwest on Oak Hill a few long-range pieces were placed in order to bear on Ziegler's Grove and the cemetery.

Meade was busy in his little headquarters house on the far slope of Cemetery Ridge. There were many things to see to, and there was much coming and going of the staff. There were occasional interruptions too. Somehow a civilian got in to see Meade that morning, a man who lived on the outskirts of town, coming in angrily to protest that the Federal troops were using his house for a hospital, were burying dead soldiers in his garden, and were strewing amputated arms and legs all over his lawn. He wanted damages, and he demanded that Meade give him a paper which he could use as a claim on the government. Short-tempered Meade blew up at him, told him that if this battle were lost he would have no government to apply to and no property that was worth anything, and hustled him out of there with the warning that if he heard any more from him he would give him a musket and put him in the ranks to fight.[11]

Twelve o'clock and after, and John Gibbon thought about Meade and went to see him. He found the general looking haggard and asked him to come over to division headquarters and have some lunch—Gibbon's mess staff had picked up an old rooster somewhere and the bird had just been cooked. Meade demurred, saying that he was needed where he was, but Gibbon told him that he must keep up his strength and that the paper work could wait, and Meade finally gave in. With Hancock and some staff officers the generals sat down by an ambulance near the crest of the ridge and ate the chicken. (Rather a tough old bird, as Gibbon remembered it.) Meade finished early and went back to headquarters, and the rest of the group sat there and idled. Hancock called an aide and began dictating an order regarding the supply of beef for his corps.

One o'clock, and the day was hotter than ever, and there was still that great fragile quiet upon the broad shallow valley between the opposing ridges, with the endless row of Confederate cannon ranked there in the open, not a sound or a sign of movement. Then at last there was a quick bright flash of light, and a white puffball of smoke floated up from a gun down near the peach orchard and hung, slowly turning and expanding, in the windless air, and the dull clang of the discharge echoed over the hollow. Silence for a few seconds, then another flash and smoke puff and echoing report from the same battery. There was a quick ripple of movement all along the line of Confederate guns as hundreds of gunners sprang to their feet and ran to their places. Then every gun in the line was fired in one titanic, rolling crash—the loudest noise, probably, that had ever been heard on the American continent up to that moment—and a hurricane of exploding shell came sweeping over Cemetery Ridge and the air was all smoke and stabbing flame and unendurable noise and deadly flying iron.

For just a moment Hancock tried to finish his dictation. The gesture was impossible, and it was not solely because nobody could hear what he was saying. The surrounding circle of couriers, orderlies, horse holders, and aides swirled away in what Hancock's chief of staff described as "a scene of confusion such as is seldom seen even on a field of battle." Men and horses were blown to bits where they stood. Some of the horses broke away and galloped off riderless in a frenzy of terror. The ambulance which held the luncheon equipment bounded wildly over the rocks when the team took to its heels after the driver fell from his seat, killed by a shell fragment. Officers were running for their horses, shouting at the top of their voices, and Gibbon, who could see neither his horse nor his orderly, ran up the ridge toward the battle line.[12] From end to end of the ridge Federal gunners were scrambling to their feet to open fire in reply.

One hundred and thirty Rebel guns were smiting the Yankee line, and it was like nothing the oldest soldier had ever imagined before. Men who thought that at Antietam and Fredericksburg they had seen and heard the worst that a massed cannonade could do confessed that this went beyond the bounds of their experience. Dazed Federal gunners, firing the eighty-odd guns on the ridge in feverish haste, found that exploding Rebel shell overhead and all around them made such a stupendous racket that the sound of their own guns was muffled, as if the guns were being fired a great way off.

One of General Hays's soldiers, whose brigade had to shift its position slightly just then, wrote afterward: "How that short march was made I don't know. The air was all murderous iron; it seemed as if there couldn't be room for any soldier upright and in motion." Farther to the left, a veteran in the 1st Minnesota got the same impression, declaring that "it seemed that nothing four feet from the ground could live." Infantry lying flat behind walls and barricades was nearly suffocated by the choking clouds of smoke. One man recalled that the men were very quiet. Usually, in a cannonade, the infantry would make wisecracks, and when shell flew overhead the men would offer derisive advice to the Rebel gunners: "Shorten your fuses" . . . "Depress your guns." But this was like no previous bombardment, and the men were silent, hugging the ground and saying nothing.[13]

The artillery was taking a frightful pounding. Caissons and limber chests were exploding, sending huge fountains of black smoke high in the air. Gun wheels were broken, men and horses were killed, and the dead and wounded were torn apart afresh by shell that skimmed low over the earth. Vicious fragments of broken rock, as dangerous as actual shell fragments, whirred through the air when the projectiles hit the ground. Ziegler's Grove seemed to be filled with flying fence rails, limbs of trees, and splinters from broken gun carriages and limbers. Through it all Colonel Richard Coulter, commanding blinded General Paul's brigade, was walking along holding his limp left arm in his right hand and asking, bewildered: "Who in hell would suppose a sharpshooter could hit a crazy bone at that distance?"

General Hunt somehow made his way along the line, ordering the gunners to save their ammunition even if they had to cease firing altogether. An infantry attack, he was sure, would follow this bombardment, and he wanted to have shell enough to break it up before it reached the line. Off to the left, in McGilvery's line of guns, his order was obeyed, but on the II Corps front Hancock countermanded it, feeling that his infantry would stand the punishment better if its own artillery kept on firing. So the cannoneers kept to their work, firing smoothly and without fuss, battery commanders standing amid the turmoil calling: "Number One, fire! . . . Number Two, fire!" as methodically as if they were firing parade-ground salutes.

All along the line there was what General Gibbon called "the most infernal pandemonium it has ever been my fortune to look upon." In the entire valley there was nothing to be seen but a dense coiling smoke bank, glowing and sparkling wickedly with the unceasing flashing of the Rebel guns. On Cemetery Ridge the smoke hung a couple of feet off the ground, so that only the legs of the busy gunners were visible. The cannonade was taking a horrible toll of the horses, and as he watched the poor beasts Gibbon was struck by the stolid, almost apathetic way in which they endured their ordeal, standing motionless in their places even while those beside them were kicking in their death agonies. Going over to a certain little clump of trees near the center of his line, Gibbon met the officer who commanded there, Brigadier General Alexander Webb, who was sitting on the ground smoking his pipe, as if the whole battle were no concern of his, and it occurred to Gibbon suddenly that men behaved under fire very much as horses did.[14]

Oddly enough, the extreme front line was the safest place on Cemetery Ridge. The Confederates were making just one mistake in this shattering bombardment: uniformly, they were firing just a little too high. Along the II Corps front the infantry suffered comparatively little from the shelling. Gibbon went far out in front of his firing line, trying in vain to see what the Confederates might be doing behind their flaming line of guns, and he found that he could walk erect there in almost complete safety. The farther back one went, the greater was the danger, and beyond the crest, over on the eastern slope of the ridge, it was worst of all. Most of the shell just cleared the crest and curved down to strike or explode in the rear, out of sight of the gunners who had done the firing.

As a result the whole rear-guard population—orderlies, clerks, cooks, servants, musicians, ambulance drivers, and just plain stragglers—went streaming back along the Baltimore Pike as fast as they could run, scourged out of what had seemed like a safely protected hillside by the worst shelling they ever saw. A soldier who saw them go wrote with satisfaction that "it seemed as if half of the army was running away, but it was only the noncombatants," and a regiment acting as train guard a mile or so down the road speedily rounded up five hundred fugitives to turn over to the provost guard.[15] It was impossible to take wounded men back from the ridge through this zone of fire, and caisson drivers who had to take fresh ammunition forward needed to be fantastically brave or reckless.

Most dangerous spot on the whole slope may have been the field immediately around Meade's headquarters. A newspaper correspondent there wrote that from two to six shells were exploding around the little cottage every second, and he counted sixteen dead horses lying mangled by the fence, grotesque in death with their halters still tied to the top rail. An ambulance went careening by, one horse galloping madly on three legs, a solid shot having removed the fourth. One shell knocked away the front steps of the cottage, another broke one of the two pillars by the door, another went through the low garret, still another smashed the second pillar. Meade came to the doorway to look things over, and a shot smashed through the doorjamb, missing him by inches. He got his staff out in the yard, figuring that flying splinters made the inside of the little house more dangerous than the outside.

Unconsciously the men huddled in the lee of the building, which was far too flimsy to stop any shell. Noticing this, Meade chuckled grimly—extreme coolness under fire was always his long suit—and he leisurely recounted an anecdote of the Mexican War. At Palo Alto, he recalled, old Zachary Taylor had come upon a wagon driver crouched behind his two-wheeled cart in the midst of a cannonade and had called out: "You damned fool, don't you know you are no safer there than anywhere else?" The driver had replied: "I don't suppose I am, General, but it kinda feels so." Staff no doubt laughed dutifully and rather hollowly, and Meade then decided that there was no sense trying to carry on headquarters business here and moved everybody over to Slocum's headquarters, out of range.[16]

How long all of this went on no one ever quite seemed sure, and the estimates ranged all the way from thirty minutes to two hours; but eventually, almost imperceptibly, the weight of the bombardment grew less. Hunt had pulled some wrecked batteries out of the II Corps line and was persuading others to cease firing, and along the right of the line many guns had exhausted all of their shell and solid shot. As the Federal firing died down, firing from the Confederate guns slackened also. The smoke still lay heavy between the armies, and Gibbon was trying in vain to peer through it from his post out in front, when the signal station on Little Round Top wig-wagged a message to army headquarters: Here come the Rebels!

The smoke lifted like a rising curtain, and all of the great amphitheater lay open at last, and the Yankee soldiers could look west all the way to the belt of trees on Seminary Ridge. They were old soldiers and had been in many battles, but what they saw then took their breath away, and whether they had ten minutes or seventy-five years yet to live, they remembered it until they died. There it was, for the last time in this war, perhaps for the last time anywhere, the grand pageantry and color of war in the old style, beautiful and majestic and terrible: fighting men lined up for a mile and a half from flank to flank, slashed red flags overhead, soldiers marching forward elbow to elbow, officers with drawn swords, sunlight gleaming from thousands of musket barrels, lines dressed as if for parade. Up and down the Federal firing line ran a low murmur: "There they are. . . . There comes the infantry!"

Lee was putting fifteen thousand men into this column—George Pickett riding into storybook immortality with his division of Virginians, Heth's division led today by General Pettigrew, two brigades of Pender's division under General Trimble, coming out of the woods to march across a mile-wide valley to the heights where the Yankees were waiting with shotted guns. Rank after rank came out of the shadows, and the Rebel cannon were all silent now, gunners standing aside to let the infantry come through, and for the moment the Federal guns were silent too, as if both armies were briefly dazzled by the war's most dramatic moment. In the Confederate line there were officers on horseback, and if the Federals looked closely they might have seen one who held his sword high over his head, his black felt

hat on the point of it as a guide for his brigade—General Lewis
Armistead, who was coming over the valley to meet death and an old
friend.

Back in the spring of 1861, when the country was just breaking
apart and officers of the regular army were choosing their sides, there
was a farewell party one evening in the officers' quarters of the army
post at the little California town of Los Angeles. The host was Captain Winfield Scott Hancock, and he was giving the party to say
good-by to certain Southern officers who were going east to Richmond, where they would take commissions with the new Confederacy. The departing guests were sad—it was not easy for those
regulars to cut loose from the army they had given their lives to—
and a tragic shadow lay across the little gathering, and just before
the party broke up Mrs. Albert Sidney Johnston sat at the piano and
sang "Kathleen Mavourneen." Good-by and good-by, the gray dawn
will be breaking soon and our old comradeship in this intimate little
army world is fading, it may be for years and it may be forever. When
the song was ended Major Armistead came over and put his hands on
Hancock's shoulders, tears streaming down his cheeks, and said:
"Hancock, good-by—you can never know what this has cost me."[17]
Then the guests left, and next morning Armistead and the others
started east, and a little later Hancock himself came east to fight on
the Northern side, and he and Armistead had not seen each other
since. Now Hancock was on his horse on Cemetery Ridge, waiting
with the guns all around him, and Armistead was coming up the
slope with his black felt hat on the end of his sword, and the strange
roads of war the two old friends had followed were coming together
at last. . . .

Long and bright and perfectly aligned, the lines came down the
far slope and began crossing the valley, and the open space in front
was dotted by little bursts of smoke as the rival skirmishers began
to shoot at each other. This was the moment General Hunt had been
waiting for, and all along the left of the Union line the guns opened
fire and began to hit those neat ranks, tearing ragged holes in them.
On Little Round Top the rifled guns that had been lugged up over
the rocks the afternoon before were finding the range, and McGilvery's long line was flaming and crashing, and the Rebels were closing
the gaps as they moved forward—no Rebel yell now, the men were

coming on silently, they were still out of musket range. The yelling
and the firing and the stabbing would come later.

Pickett's division was at the southern end of the advancing line,
and Pickett's objective was the clump of trees under which General
Webb had been smoking his pipe. Pickett wanted to mass his troops
for greater impact, and he had his brigades do a half left wheel to
bring them closer to the center. The maneuver was done smartly, and
the waiting Yankee infantry praised it, but as the brigades swung
around they offered their flanks to McGilvery, and his gunners took
cruel advantage. Pickett's men were in the open and the range now
was hardly half a mile, and shell ripped down the ranks from end to
end, one shell sometimes striking down ten men before it burst.
Along Hancock's line the guns were silent, for they had nothing left
but canister and they would have to wait for point-blank range.
Gibbon was riding along the line—an aide had found a horse for
him at last—cautioning his men to take it easy and not to fire until the
enemy got in close, and the gray lines came swinging up the rise,
nearer and nearer.

Webb's brigade would get it first, and the Confederates continued
to crowd in toward the center, building up the strength that would
overwhelm the little rectangle of torn, littered ground which the brigade was holding. Webb had two Pennsylvania regiments in line
behind a low stone wall that ran just in front of the little clump of
trees and extended a few rods toward the north, and the rest of his
brigade was on the crest of the ridge, perhaps a hundred yards in
the rear. Hancock had put three batteries in here, and they had been
almost completely destroyed. Beside the trees and down close to the
wall were the two guns that remained of Battery A, 4th U. S., commanded by a girlish-looking young lieutenant named Alonzo Cushing. The ground around these guns was hell's half acre. Four guns
had been dismounted, caissons and limbers had been exploded,
nearly all of the horses had been killed, and there were just enough
men left to work the two guns that remained. It had been impossible
to remove the wounded, and they lay there amid smashed wheels,
fragments of wood and indescribable mutilated remains of men and
animals. One gunner, dreadfully cut by a shell fragment, had been
seen to draw a revolver and put himself out of his pain by shooting
himself through the head.

Cushing had been wounded three times, and he was there by his two guns, a sergeant standing beside him to hold him erect and to pass his orders on to the gunners. (He was calling for triple charges of canister.) The Rebel artillery had renewed its fire, and this part of the line was being hit again, and the advancing Rebel infantry was up to the post-and-rail fences by the Emmitsburg road now, barely two hundred yards away. One of Cushing's two guns was knocked out, and he was almost entirely out of ammunition. The Federal infantry opened fire and the smoke cloud settled down again, thick and stifling. Dimly the men behind the wall could see the Confederates coming in over the fences, brigade lines disordered, the spearhead of the charge a great mass of men sweeping over the fences and up the last of the slope like an irresistible stream flowing uphill.[18]

Farther south the nine-month Vermonters got their chance at last. Hancock was down there with them, pointing to the exposed flank of Pickett's line, and the Vermont regiments swung out, wheeled toward the right, and opened up a blistering flanking fire at close range. Some Pennsylvanians and a New York regiment went in with them, and the Confederate lines here gave way and began to fall back, and as the men wavered McGilvery's cannoneers pounded them afresh, three dozen guns hitting them all at once.

Just south of the clump of trees the stone wall ended and the men had raised a little breastwork of earth. Behind this barrier were the regiments commanded by Colonel Norman J. Hall—the same officer and men who had floated across the Rappahannock in pontoon boats to drive Rebel sharpshooters out of Fredericksburg so many months ago. The advancing Confederates here went down into a little hollow, seeming to vanish from sight. Then they came up out of it, appearing suddenly, as if they had popped up out of the earth, so close that Hall's men could see the expressions on their faces. The breastwork blazed from end to end as the men from Massachusetts and New York and Michigan opened fire. The Rebel line staggered visibly, came to a halt, and opened its own fire in reply, and then it began to drift slowly to its left, toward the dense crowd by the clump of trees.[19]

In front of Ziegler's Grove, to the north, Pettigrew's division was coming up to the Emmitsburg road. It had lagged slightly behind the rest of the Confederate attack, but it still kept its formation, and Hays's men looked in admiration at the trimness of its lines and, as they admired those lines, made ready to destroy them. The 8th Ohio had been posted west of the road in skirmish formation, and this regiment drew back and got into a little country lane on the Rebel flank and opened fire. Along the ridge and in the grove the Federals waited, and the foremost Federal brigade stood up to level its muskets, and the Rebel line came very near. Then at last every musket and every cannon in this part of the Yankee line opened at once, and the whole Confederate division disappeared in an immense cloud of smoke and dust. Above this boiling cloud the Union men could see a ghastly debris of guns, knapsacks, blanket rolls, severed human heads, and arms and legs and parts of bodies, tossed into the air by the impact of the shot. One observer wrote: "A moan went up from the field, distinctly to be heard amid the roar of battle, but on they went, too much enveloped in smoke and dust now to permit us to distinguish their lines of movement, for the mass appeared more like a cloud of moving smoke and dust than a column of troops."[20]

The mass rolled in closer, the Federals firing into the center of the storm cloud. The men with the improvised buckshot cartridges in smoothbore guns had a target they could not miss, and the XI Corps artillery on Cemetery Hill was sending shell in through the gaps in the Yankee line. Suddenly Pettigrew's men passed the limit of human endurance and the lines broke apart and the hillside was covered with men running for cover, and the Federal gunners burned the ground with shell and canister. On the littered field, amid all the dead and wounded, prostrate men could be seen holding up handkerchiefs in sign of surrender.

But if the right and left of the charging Confederate line had been smashed, the center was still coming on. Cushing fired his last remaining charge, and a bullet hit him in the mouth and killed him. Most of the Pennsylvanians behind the wall sprang up and ran back to the crest, and the few who remained were overwhelmed as the Rebel line rolled in and beat the life out of them. Most of the Rebels stayed behind the wall or crowded in amid the clump of trees and opened fire on the Yankees on the crest, their red battle flags clustering thick, men in front lying prone or kneeling, men in the rear standing and firing over their heads. A handful leaped over the wall, Armistead in the lead, and ran in among the wreckage of Cushing's battery. Armistead's horse had been killed and his hat was down on the hilt of his sword now, but the sword was still held high, and through the curling smoke the Union soldiers got a final glimpse of him, one triumphant hand resting on a silent cannon.[21]

This was the climax and the bloody indisputable pay-off; the next few minutes would tell the story, and what that story would be would all depend on whether these blue-coated soldiers really meant it. There were more Federals than Confederates on the field, but right here where the fighting was going on there were more Confederates than Federals, and every man was firing in a wild, feverish haste, with the smoke settling down thicker and thicker. From the peach orchard Confederate guns were shooting straight into the Union line, disregarding the danger that some of their own men would be hit, and the winging missiles tore ugly lanes through the disorganized mass of Yankees.

A fresh Union regiment was moving up through Ziegler's Grove, and as the men came out into the open they heard the uproar of battle different from any they had ever heard before—"strange and terrible, a sound that came from thousands of human throats, yet was not a commingling of shouts and yells but rather like a vast mournful roar." There was no cheering, but thousands of men were growling and cursing without realizing it as they fought to the utmost limit of primal savagery. The 19th Massachusetts was squarely before the clump of trees, and the Confederate mass kept crowding forward, and for a time the file closers in the rear of the Massachusetts regiment joined hands and held the thin line in place by sheer strength.[22]

Gibbon was down with a bullet through his shoulder, Webb had been wounded, and Hancock was knocked off his horse by a bullet that went through his saddle and drove a tenpenny nail and bits of wood deep into his thigh. Except for one valiant staff officer, there was not a mounted man to be seen. Hunt was in the middle of the infantry, firing his revolver. On the open crest of the ridge men were volleying at the Confederates behind the wall and among the trees. From the left, regiments were running over to help, coming in through the smoke like a mob gone out of control.

These were Hall's men, and men from Harrow's brigade on the left—famous old regiments, 20th Massachusetts and 7th Michigan and "that shattered thunderbolt" (as an officer on Gibbon's staff called it), the remnant of the 1st Minnesota. They were not "moving by the right flank" or "changing front forward" or executing any other recognized tactical maneuver, and they were not obeying the commands of any officers, although their officers were in their midst, yelling hoarsely and gesturing madly with their swords. No formal tactical move was possible in that jammed smoky confusion, and no shouted command could be heard in the everlasting din. One soldier wrote afterward that the only order he remembered hearing, from first to last, was "Up, boys—they're coming!" right at the start.[23] This was not a controlled movement at all. It was simply a crowd of armed men running over spontaneously to get into the middle of an enormous fight, Yankee soldiers swarming in to get at their enemies, all regimental formations lost, every man going in on his own.

Some of the men stopped and fired over the low earthen barricade toward the front where there were still Rebels in the open. Others jammed in toward the clump of trees, firing through gaps in the crowd ahead, sometimes hitting their own comrades. Off to the left the Vermonters were still out in front, facing north, tearing the Confederate flank to tatters, and from the right Hays's men and the guns in the grove were firing in obliquely. The heavy smoke went up toward the sky, so heavy that Lee over on Seminary Ridge could get nothing but an occasional glimpse of red battle flags adrift in the murk.

Back on the crest, facing the clump of trees, the line swayed as men worked up their nerve. The mounted staff officer was shouting, men were yelling to each other, and a color-bearer jumped up and ran forward, waving his flag. The staff was broken by a shot, and he grabbed the stump and held the ragged colors above his head, and by ones and twos and then all along the crest men sprang to their feet and followed him, firing as they ran. Armistead was stretched out on the ground now with a bullet in him, and the other gray-coats who had got in among the guns were down too, and the Federals came in on the Rebel mass among the little trees, and the smoke hid the hot afternoon sun.

Pickett's men were in a box now. On their left Pettigrew's division had evaporated, on the right they were dissolving under an unceasing flank fire, in front they were getting a head-on assault that was too heavy to take, and there was no support in sight. Longstreet had sent a brigade up to cover their right, but in the blinding fog the brigade had lost its direction and was heading straight for McGilvery's ranked cannon, which blasted it with deadly aim, and the Vermont regiments wheeled completely around and got the brigade in flank. It fell apart and its bits and pieces went tumbling back to

Seminary Ridge. And suddenly the tension was gone and the firing was dying down, and the Confederates by the clump of trees were going back to their own lines or dropping their muskets and raising their hands in surrender. Meade came riding up to the crest just now, and an officer met him and told him that Lee's charge had been crushed, and Meade raised his hand and cried "Thank God!" The last of the fugitives went back toward their starting point, Federal gunners following them with shell, and Gibbon's weary soldiers were sending a great mass of Rebel prisoners back to the rear. The fighting was over.

Hancock was on a stretcher, dictating a note to Meade. He believed that a quick counterattack now would take the Rebel army off balance and finish it, and he urged that the men be sent forward without delay. He added proudly: "I did not leave the field so long as a Rebel was to be seen upright." An aide came up to him and handed him a watch, a pair of spurs, and other trinkets. They came from Lewis Armistead, whom the aide had found dying there beside Cushing's last gun. Armistead had asked that these mementos of an old friendship be sent to Hancock, and he had gasped out some sort of farewell message.[24] "Tell Hancock I have done him and my country a great injustice which I shall never cease to regret" was the way the aide had it; he may have dressed it up a good deal or, for that matter, he may have dreamed it all, and it does not matter much either way. Armistead had died, going beyond regrets forever, and as if he had been waiting for this last message, Hancock had the stretcher-bearers carry him off to the field hospital.

The smoke drifted away and the noise died down, and a soldier who looked out over the ground where the men had fought said that he looked upon "a square mile of Tophet."[25]

4. Valley of Dry Bones

One day they would make a park there, with neat lawns and smooth black roadways, and there would be marble statues and bronze plaques to tell the story in bloodless prose. Silent cannon would rest behind grassy embankments, their wheels bolted down to concrete foundations, their malevolence wholly gone, and here and there birds would nest in the muzzles. In the museums and tourist-bait trinket

shops old bullets and broken buckles and twisted bayonets would re-
pose under glass, with a rusty musket or so on the wall and little
illustrated booklets lying on top of the counter. There would be neat
brick and timber cabins on the hillsides, and people would sleep
soundly in houses built where the armies had stormed and cried at
each other, as if to prove that men killed in battle send forth no
restless ghosts to plague comfortable civilians at night. The town and
the woods and the ridges and hills would become a national shrine,
filled with romantic memories which are in themselves a kind of forgetting, and visitors would stand by the clump of trees and look off to
the west and see nothing but the rolling fields and the quiet groves and
the great blue bank of the mountains.

But first there would have to be a great deal of tidying up.

The day after the battle began muggy and cloudy, and there was
a tremendous rainstorm. (There always seemed to be a great rain
after a hard battle in that war, and men believed that something in
the firing of many guns brought rain clouds and jarred the moisture
out of them.) The long line of Rebel cannon along the Emmitsburg
road had been pulled back, and when Slocum and Howard sent scouting parties out to the north and east of town they found no Rebels
except wounded men and a few stragglers. On Seminary Ridge the
Confederates were still in evidence, and for a time Meade appears
to have been uncertain whether the battle was really over.

But the Confederate Army had had enough. It had lost 25,000 men,
artillery ammunition was nearly exhausted, supplies were low, and Lee
was holding his line on Seminary Ridge merely to let his trains and
his advance guard get a decent start on the long roads back to Virginia. A wagon train seventeen miles long, loaded with wounded
men, crawled over the mountain road toward Chambersburg. It was a
nightmarish procession of pain. A great many of the wounded men
had received no medical attention whatever, the almost springless
wagons rolled and jolted over the uneven road, and no halts were
permitted for any reason. The cavalry officer in charge of the train
said that he learned more on that trip about the horrors of war than
he had learned in all of his battles.[1]

As the signs of a Confederate retreat multiplied, Meade worked
the VI Corps forward to take up the pursuit, but he was in no hurry
about it. If the Rebels wanted to go back to Virginia, it seemed like a
good idea to wish them Godspeed and let them go.

Meade was able to see some things very clearly. He knew that the victory had been brutally hard on his army, and above all things he was determined not to do anything that might create any risks. A quick checkup after the battle showed him that he had no more than 51,000 men armed and equipped and present for duty. This total was approximately 38,000 below the number he had had just before the battle. Casualties had been about 23,000, so it was evident that the impact of battle had jarred fully 15,000 uninjured men loose from the ranks. They would be back later, but for the moment they were lost, and the army was not half as large as it had been when Hooker took it down to the Rappahannock fords two months earlier.[2] The I Corps was hardly as big as an ordinary division, and the III Corps was not a great deal better off. (Both of these famous corps were mortally hurt, as it turned out; in the army reorganization of the following winter they were broken up and their survivors were transferred to other units.) The II Corps had lost more than a third of its men, and its best generals, Hancock and Gibbon, would be out for months. The XI Corps had suffered nearly as much and in addition had had another blow to its reputation and morale, with the rest of the army making caustic remarks about its wild flight through town, the astounding number of prisoners it had lost, and its inability to keep the Rebels out of the guns on Cemetery Hill on the evening of July 2. Some of the army's finest combat units had been all but destroyed —the Iron Brigade, the 5th New Hampshire, the 1st Minnesota, the 2nd Massachusetts, and the 16th Maine, among others—and artillery losses had been so severe that Hunt had to consolidate some of his best batteries. Three of the seven army corps were under temporary commanders.

Of all these things Meade was acutely aware. The old habit of caution was strong at army headquarters, and another heritage from the McClellan era was cropping out just now: Meade somehow had been persuaded that the Rebel army in this campaign was larger than his own. So he waited where he was, ignoring the clear signs that he was in the presence of a badly beaten enemy, and he moved his patrols forward very carefully.

The soldiers themselves had no doubt about how the battle had come out. On the afternoon of July 3 they had seen something they had never seen before—the principal attacking column of the Army of Northern Virginia running in desperate disordered fragments back to its lines after a smashing repulse—and some of the men on Cemetery Ridge had stood up exultantly and cried "Fredericksburg!" as they watched. As they went forward through the town and down to the Emmitsburg road they were dazed by the human wreckage they saw. Toward the left, where for a time nothing but artillery had beaten back the Rebel attack, they found bodies dreadfully broken and dismembered. An officer who went over that part of the ground wrote that on no other field had he seen such appalling numbers of dead. In places where the infantry fire had been especially intense the dead men lay in great rows, and in the twilight it seemed as if whole brigades had made their bivouac there and had gone to sleep. On the ground covered by Pickett's charge one officer wrote that "I saw men, horses, and material in some places piled up together, which is something seldom seen unless in pictures of battles, and the appearance of the field with these mounds of dead men and horses, and very many bodies lying in every position singly, was terrible, especially as the night lent a somber hue to everything the eye rested on."[3]

A fearful odor of decay lay over the field. A cavalry patrol went through Gettysburg to scout the Cashtown road to the west, and as it came out by the fields where dead bodies had been lying in the heat for four days the cavalrymen sickened and vomited as they rode. The country here was the ultimate abomination of desolation: "As far as the eye could reach on both sides of the Cashtown road you see blue-coated boys, swollen up to look as giants, quite black in the face, but nearly all on their backs, looking into the clear blue with open eyes, with their clothes torn open. It is strange that dying men tear their clothes in this manner. You see them lying in platoons of infantry with officers and arms exactly as they stood or ran—artillery men with caisson blown up and four horses, each in position, dead. You meet also limbs and fragments of men. The road is strewn with dead, whom the Rebels have half buried and whom the heavy rain has uncovered."[4]

Here and there by the road the cavalrymen met oddly embattled farmers, armed with pitchforks and flails, who had rounded up small batches of Rebel stragglers and wanted to turn them over to the authorities. These farmers, it appeared, were moved not so much by patriotic fervor as by old-fashioned rage. In their retreat the Confederates had left the roads and had marched across the fields, trampling down the ripening wheat and rye in great swaths, and if the farmers could not have justice, they at least wanted to see the destroyers locked up.

The town of Gettysburg looked as if some universal moving day had been interrupted by catastrophe. Streets were barricaded up to window levels with everything that would serve—wagons, rocking chairs, bureaus, stoves, fence rails, old lumber, and piles of rocks— and there were scars from cannon balls and bullets. In row houses facing Cemetery Hill the Rebel sharpshooters had found vantage points in second-floor rooms, and they had knocked out walls between houses to provide communication along their line. One civilian had been killed—a girl named Jennie Wade, shot down by a stray bullet while she baked bread in her kitchen. When she died she had in her pocket a picture of her fiancé, Corporal Johnson Skelley of the 87th Pennsylvania, and she never knew that two weeks earlier Corporal Skelley had been mortally wounded in the fighting around Winchester, Virginia.[5]

Details were at work all over the field, collecting the last of the helpless wounded and burying the dead. This last was an almost impossible job, since more than five thousand men had been killed in action. Federals who were buried by men of their own regiments were given little wooden markers, with the name and regimental identification carved with a jackknife or scrawled with pencil, but in hundreds and hundreds of cases no identification was possible and the men went into the ground as "unknown." Long wide trenches were dug and the men were laid in them side by side, and sometimes there was nothing more in the way of a gravestone than a little headboard at one end of the trench stating the number of bodies that were buried in it. In places the burial details just gave up and did not try to make graves, but simply shoveled earth over the bodies as they lay on the ground.[6]

There was an immense harvest of discarded weapons to be picked up. As a first step the men attached bayonets to the rifles which lay on the field and stuck them in the ground for collection later, and along Cemetery Ridge there were whole acres of these, "standing as thick as trees in the nursery." Ordnance officers who took charge of these weapons noted an oddity. Out of more than thirty-seven thousand muskets which had been left on the field, nearly a third were loaded with more than one cartridge. In the excitement of battle men forgot to fix percussion caps, sometimes even forgot to pull the trigger, and reloaded automatically without realizing that they had not fired. One man remarked briefly that "not all the forces attacking or attacked are fully conscious of what they are doing," and veterans were free to admit that in this as in all other battles there had been a great deal of wild, ineffective shooting. Whole regiments at times fired volleys with the line of muskets pointing vaguely toward the sky at an angle from the vertical of no more than forty-five degrees, and men were often seen to fire with both eyes tightly shut. An Ohio soldier in the XII Corps reflected that in the Culp's Hill fighting on the morning of July 3 every man in the corps had fired 250 rounds, and he mused that "the mystery exists how any Rebels escaped."[7]

It was a rough war for wounded men. Immense field hospitals had been established in the low ground east of the Baltimore Pike, by Rock Creek, and the heavy rains of July 4 flooded this ground, and some of the helpless wounded men were drowned. An attempt was made to get some of the less seriously wounded over to the railroad, where they could be sent back to established hospitals in Baltimore, York, and Harrisburg, but Stuart's cavalry had broken the railroad and for a few days no trains were running. The wounded lay where they had been dropped, unsheltered on the bare ground, and the best that the army's medical inspector was able to report was that within a few days they were "made as comfortable as circumstances would permit," although it was admitted that things would have been better if the Medical Corps had been able to get straw for the men to lie on.[8]

The wounded men were not much given to complaining. A man in the Corn Exchange Regiment saw an amputee sitting outside a hospital tent, perky enough, considering that he had but one leg, playing cards with a wounded comrade. An orderly passed by hauling a hideous load of amputated arms and legs from the operating tent, and the one-legged man looked up with interest, laid down his cards, and asked the orderly to stop and let him inspect the haul. He wanted to take one more look at his lost leg, he said, and he would be able to recognize it because of a certain bunion. The orderly had no intention whatever of shuffling through his ghastly cargo, and he rebuked the soldier and told him that if he believed in the resurrection of the body as a good Christian should, he could wait for the Last Day and take a good look at his missing limb then. The cardplayer agreed that that made sense and went on with his game.[9]

Slowly, and with immense effort, this shot-to-pieces army pulled itself together and took to the road. The VI Corps was out in front, and it had suffered little in the battle and had rested from its prodigious twenty-four-hour hike, but Meade was still cautious and John Sedgwick was equally so, and the pursuit was not pressed. Pulling the army out of Gettysburg was like pulling a shod foot out of deep mud—something to be done slowly and carefully, with infinite pains— and the air of urgency was gone. Colonel Chamberlain of the battle-bruised 20th Maine looked back at his regiment's final bivouac and reported:[10] "We returned to Little Round Top, where we buried our dead in the place where we had laid them during the fight, marking each grave by a headboard made of ammunition boxes, with each soldier's name cut upon it. We also buried fifty of the enemy's dead in front of our position of July 2. We then looked after our wounded, whom I had taken the responsibility of putting into the houses of citizens in the vicinity of Little Round Top, and on the morning of the fifth took up our march on the Emmitsburg road."

The Emmitsburg road had been the last long mile for many men— for handsome John Reynolds riding to meet an unknown Southern sharpshooter in a farmer's barn, for the black-hatted Western regiments with their fife-and-drum corps playing them into battle, for many unheard-of men who stepped off it into unmarked graves on slanting rocky fields—and for a few days it had been a famous military highway, pumping a stream of troops off to the unfathomable chances of war. Now it would be a quiet country road again, with a farmer's load of hay or drove of cattle as its most exciting wayfarers, the mountain wall to the west dropping long shadows across it in the blue summer evenings, the dust and the clamor and the rumbling guns gone forever. It was over at last, this enormous battle with its smoke and its grimness and its unheard-of violence, and here again was a simple road leading from one country town to another, with a commonplace little name that would ring and shine in the books forever.

Meade was on the road with his troops, an infinitely weary man with dust on his uniform and his gray beard, feeling responsibility as a paralyzing weight. He had been one of the few men who could have lost the war irretrievably in one day, and he had managed to avoid the mistakes that would have lost it. He would continue to avoid mistakes, even if he had to miss opportunity. Lee's army was at bay on the northern bank of the Potomac, the river too high for fording and all bridges gone, and there might still be a chance to sweep down on him, to force him to battle again and to destroy him and his army and the star-crossed, legendary cause which they represented in one last, blazing, triumphant assault. But it was a chance and no more than that. Meade could see all of the things that might go wrong with it: could see the Potomac, moreover, as a border between two countries, so that the important thing just now might be to get the Southern army across that border back into the land where it belonged. Meade brought his army up to the river very slowly. Nevertheless, when he found that the Rebels were still there, well dug in on a great crescent of rising ground not many miles from the old Antietam battlefield, he put his own men into line of battle and took them carefully forward.

It was more than a week after Gettysburg by now, and some of the army's temporary losses had been made good. The army rolled forward on a front six miles wide, battle flags snapping in the wind, sunlight glittering from thousands of bright muskets, guns clanking along ready to go into battery on command. A soldier who marched with it was struck with the picture: "Throughout the miles of deep lines it presented a beautiful sight as with the swinging cadenced step of veterans they moved over cultivated fields of grain, over roads, orchards, and vineyards, on plain, valley, and hill. Obstructions were leveled by the pioneers in advance, and regardless of damage the army of blue swept over the ground with heavy tread, leaving in their rear destruction and desolation."[11]

The long blue lines halted and skirmishers were sent out in front to guard against Rebel surprises, and that night there was a heavy rain and the army entrenched, while Meade summoned his corps commanders to determine whether the army should attack or not. The corps commanders were decidedly against it, and the army waited for a day. On July 14 Meade put it in motion again, having quietly concluded that he would try to do what his lieutenants had advised him not to do. But now it was too late. The Army of Northern Virginia had gone south of the river at last, leaving a small rear guard for a delaying action. Meade's cavalry and infantry picked up some Rebel wounded and stragglers, killed the General Pettigrew who had commanded the left wing of Pickett's great assault, and captured a gun or two. That was all. If the war was ever to be won, it would have to be won later—and somewhere else.

All of which was to the infinite displeasure of Abraham Lincoln. The President had learned a great deal about the military art since those early amateurish days when he had decreed that all Union armies should advance willy-nilly on Washington's birthday and had juggled troops frantically back and forth from McClellan's army to the Shenandoah Valley in a vain effort to catch Stonewall Jackson by telegraphic order. It could even be argued now that he was as canny a strategist as the North possessed, and he had followed the army's slow progress down from Gettysburg in an agony of impatience. He still saw things as he had seen them three weeks earlier, when the governor of New Jersey had asked him to reinstate McClellan: Lee's advance into Pennsylvania had been an opportunity for the Federals, not for the Confederates; if the affair were handled right neither Lee nor his army should ever get back to Virginia; and all of this talk about "driving the enemy from our soil" struck him as deplorable blindness. Vicksburg had fallen and the back door to the Confederacy lay open; one more blow and it would all be over. This war could be won, once and forever, between Pennsylvania and the Potomac River, in this month of July 1863, if someone really set out to win it.

The flaming driving spirit of war, which could find no congenial home anywhere among the top commanders of the Army of the Potomac, had actually found its place at last in the mysterious heart of that melancholy, quizzical civilian, the President of the United States, the man who had confessed that he could not so much as kill a chicken for Sunday dinner without wincing at the sight of bloodshed. Lincoln wrote a harsh letter to Meade, crying in effect: *Why* couldn't you, just this once, go in and smash things and let me worry about picking up the pieces? He wrote it, and then characteristically he did not send it, letting it gather dust in a White House pigeonhole.

Halleck warned Meade that the President was dissatisfied, and Meade, worn almost to a frazzle, with a temper that was never stable, flared back that in that case, since he had done his level best, he would like to be relieved of his command. Halleck soothed him with a friendly, appreciative letter, and Lincoln in turn swallowed his vexation and decided to be grateful for what had been won.[12] And the army crossed the river, marched south, and made a stab at trying to pen Lee's army up in the Shenandoah Valley. The III Corps had the advance, and the corps was now commanded by bumbling, red-faced General W. H. French, who mishandled his troops so flagrantly that Hooker's and Kearny's veterans sardonically referred to their outfit as "the III Corps as we understand it."[13] The chance was missed and the Confederates got away, and the Army of the Potomac went down to the Rapidan country and went into camp, to rest and refit before taking up the fight again.

So there would be a new campaign, with other campaigns to follow, and in due time the great gloomy Wilderness around Chancellorsville would know gunfire again, and the wild tumult of battle, and the screams of wounded men trapped in burning thickets. It would be the hard fate of this army to fight dreadful battles without glory and without triumph, using itself up so that the victory might be won by other armies on other fields. The army would be ready for it, but it would be a different army henceforth. The ranks were thinner and there was a new name on the regimental flags, and the men were wiser than they had been before. They were beginning to realize that while a great thing had been done they had really done it themselves.[14] Meade was "old Four-Eyes," a general who had won his battle chiefly because his men were incomparably good soldiers. They had fought at Gettysburg with the highest pitch of inspiration, but the inspiration had come from within themselves and had not been fired by anyone at the top, and the staff officers who had felt obliged to hearten the men by spreading the McClellan rumor had simply shown that they themselves did not know what the men were really like. This army was a military instrument at last, and it could be used to the last full measure of its own inexpressible devotion, but from now on it would display enthusiasm for no generals.

A few days after Gettysburg, Meade issued a general order congratulating his troops on their victory, and the order was read in all the regiments at evening parade. The men were very matter-of-fact as they listened. In one regiment the colonel waved his hat and called for three cheers for General Meade, but the cheers were not forthcoming—not, as one of the men explained, because the men disliked Meade, but simply because they did not feel like cheering any more. These soldiers, he pointed out, "with their lights and experiences, could not see the wisdom or the occasion for any such manifestation of enthusiasm"; the army had matured, "its business sense increased with age," and hereafter it would wait and see before it tossed its caps in the air.[15]

It would wait and see, and there would still be a great deal to look at, for half of the price had not yet been paid. Yet the biggest test had been passed. Meade might draw no cheers, but in his own way he had not done too badly. At Gettysburg, for the first time, the Army of the Potomac had not been crippled by the mistakes of its commanding general. It had been given a chance, and the chance had been enough. At that crisis of the war everything had come down to the naked fury of the fighting men, and the fighting men had stood up under it—along Willoughby Run and Seminary Ridge, amid the rocks and bushes by Little Round Top, on the slopes back of the peach orchard and the wheat field, in the smoky twilight around Culp's Hill and the cemetery, and in the dust of the terrible pounding near the little clump of trees. They had won a victory. It might be less of a victory than Mr. Lincoln had hoped for, but it was nevertheless a victory—and, because of it, it was no longer possible for the Confederacy to win the war. The North might still lose it, to be sure, if the soldiers or the people should lose heart, but outright defeat was no longer in the cards. Both the army and the country were in shape to win at last, and from now on it would be a question of courage and endurance.

If the army was not especially enthusiastic, no more was Meade. He was crabbed and dyspeptic, a regular-army officer who had never cared very much for the volunteer system, and less than a year ago he had remarked that most of the men in the army had not the faintest idea of what soldiering really meant. But he paid his tribute, just the same, in one sentence of a letter which he wrote to Mrs. Meade two days after the battle: "The men behaved splendidly; I really think they are becoming soldiers."[16]

If anyone had doubted it, there was still plenty of proof around Gettysburg. An army medical officer was telling no more than the plain truth when he wrote that the ten days immediately after the battle were "the occasion of the greatest amount of human suffering known to this nation since its birth." This country market town of two thousand inhabitants had been presented with some twenty-two thousand wounded men, and the place was swamped with them. They lay on the fields and in ditches, in the woods under trees, in barns and haystacks and homes and churches for miles around.[17] The very fact that the battle had been a victory made the men's lot worse, for instead of remaining on the field where it could care for them the army had marched south in expectation of a new battle and had been able to leave behind it only a fraction of the required number of doctors and hospital attendants.

So appalling was the number of men awaiting attention that the overworked doctors had begun with a grim job of sorting out, separating the men who were bound to die from those whose lives might be saved. In one wood there was a long, pathetic row of semi-conscious men who lay on the ground, moaning and twitching fitfully, completely unattended—men who had been shot through the head and whose wounds, upon hasty inspection, had been pronounced mortal and who had simply been put aside to die as quickly as they might. Not far away there was a long table where for an entire week doctors worked from dawn to twilight cutting off arms and legs, with an army wagon standing by to carry off the wreckage and hurry back for a new load. A young woman who came to Gettysburg to help nurse the wounded entered a church which had been hastily converted into a hospital and found that planks had been laid across the tops of the pews so that the entire auditorium was one vast hard bed, jammed with wounded men lying elbow to elbow: "I seemed to stand breast-high in a sea of anguish." Permeating everything in and near the town was the foul, overpowering stench of the unburied dead—an atmosphere which, as this woman said, "robbed the battlefield of its glory, the survivors of their victory, and the wounded of what little chance of life was left to them."[18]

Little by little order was restored, the army working hand in hand with the Sanitary Commission and the Christian Commission. The one railroad leading into Gettysburg had been broken, but Herman Haupt was on the job almost before the battle ended, and as always he made things happen. He found the railroad totally inadequate, even after its breaks had been made good—a country railroad without experienced officers, with no more sidings, water tanks, turntables, or fuel than were needed for its normal traffic of three or four trains a day. It was necessary now to operate thirty trains a day, and he had locomotives and cars sent up from Alexandria. He improvised water tanks, brought in loads of fuel, got repair crews on the job with pre-fabricated bridges and culverts, and before long he had the railway in shape to move fifteen hundred tons of freight each way every day. The army medical service was telegraphing frantically to Baltimore for immediate shipments of alcohol, creosote, nitric acid, permanganate of potassium, tin cups, buckets, stretchers, bed sacks, and other equipment, and the Sanitary Commission made up a special train of food, tents, clothing, stoves, and bandages which reached the town three days after the battle.[19]

All across the northeast, in the pulpits of hundreds of churches, ministers read appeals for help. Money was needed, and food, and medicines, and the little delicacies sick men need—and, above all, "all females qualified for usefulness in this emergency." Nurses were brought in; regular-army nurses recruited by Miss Dorothea Dix, who sternly refused to accept women who were either young or pretty, considering such persons quite unsuited for work in army hospitals, and women enlisted by the Sanitary Commission, which had agents at railroad stations in the big Eastern cities to interview applicants and organize them into working units. Pennsylvania militia regiments were brought in to guard the place, and as the hospital tents were set up in the groves near the town these soldiers marched all visitors away at four every afternoon so that the nurses might not be exposed to nameless perils. The nurses found themselves far too busy to be in any danger, however. Five days after the battle ambulances were still going about the fields collecting hundreds of men whose wounds had not yet been dressed and who had had nothing to eat except such hardtack as they happened to have in their haversacks.[20]

As these women worked, an ancient tradition quietly died. It had always been supposed that army nursing was strictly a job either for enlisted men or for superannuated trollops who were beyond con- tamination. But here they were, women precisely like the wives and sisters and mothers the soldiers had left behind, up to their elbows in it and taking no harm whatever. One of them quietly wrote: "I have been for weeks the only lady in a camp of seven hundred men, and have never been treated with more deference, respect, and kindness." Uniformly, these women testified that the men they cared for were nothing less than magnificent, and in a letter to her sister a little New Jersey Quaker wrote: "More Christian fortitude was never witnessed than they exhibit, always say—'Help my neighbor first, he is worse.'" After some weeks, when the emergency had passed and one group of women prepared to leave, two army bands turned out to escort them to the railroad station.[21]

As rapidly as the men became well enough to be moved they were sent off to permanent hospitals in Baltimore, Washington, York, and

Harrisburg, and before long six hospital trains were leaving town every day. Until the army got hold of this business the trips were pretty grim. A medical inspector who looked into matters protested with fury that "the railroad companies, who got the only profit of the battle, and who had the greatest opportunities of ameliorating the sufferings of the wounded, alone stood aloof and rendered no aid." He specified: trains were fearfully unclean, there were no attendants for the wounded, there was no water, there was not even straw for the men to lie upon—"absolutely nothing but the bare cars, filthy from the business of transporting cattle and freight." He cracked down hard, and a medical officer was detailed to accompany each train, water coolers and bedpans and medicines and bandages were provided, and at the first junction point agents of the Christian Commission were alerted to meet the trains and provide any help that might be needed. In the end, things were fairly well organized, and in three weeks sixteen thousand men were sent away.[22] The Gettysburg hospitals still contained four thousand more who were too sick to be moved, but the worst of it was over.

So the wounded were taken care of. There were still the dead. Many bodies had never been buried—the gullies and rocky crannies around Devil's Den contained some horrible relics—and the rains had washed the earth away from bodies imperfectly covered, and there were many unmarked graves. Governor Andrew Curtin visited the place and appointed a local businessman as his agent to see to it that the state of Pennsylvania did what was necessary, and toward the end of July, at Curtin's request, this agent got in touch with the governors of all of the Northern states whose men had fought at Gettysburg and proposed that they get together to provide a proper cemetery. There were meetings and an exchange of letters, and by mid-August money had been raised and Pennsylvania had bought seventeen acres of land on Cemetery Hill, and the work of establishing a cemetery was under way.[23]

It would be a project for the states, naturally. They had thought of it first, they were putting up the money, their governors were making the arrangements, and anyway, the national government was busy with other matters. As the lifeless bodies were moved up to Cemetery Hill it was agreed that they should be grouped there by states—one plot for New Yorkers, another for Pennsylvanians, and so on down the list—and if from these honored dead each governor could take increased prestige, with visible proof that his state had done its full share, that would be so much the better, because possibly this battle had really been an affair of the separate states from the beginning.[24] As host, Governor Curtin was the man of the hour, and he invited the famous orator, Edward Everett, to do the talking when the cemetery was formally dedicated. He also asked General Meade to attend if he could.

Everett could come, but he would need more time. A speech commemorating the Gettysburg dead could not be put together overnight, and Everett had certain engagements. The date originally selected was October 23, and it would not be possible for him to complete his preparations by that time: could not there be a postponement? Governor Curtin and the others agreed that there could, and the ceremonies were put off until November 19. General Meade sent his regrets, pointing out that military affairs in the state of Virginia would be taking all of his time.[25]

Settled, then, for the nineteenth of November, and the battlefield could be fairly well policed up by that time. There were still a few wounded men around, but by late November it should be possible to get all of them shipped off, and the air was becoming fit to breathe again. The summer wore away, the burial squads were busy, the hilltop was being nicely landscaped, and down below the Potomac the army was maneuvering back and forth, getting into small fights occasionally, losing a few men here and killing a few Rebels there, sparring the time away until a new campaign could be begun. The drafted men were coming in to fill the ranks—coming in under guard, with a roll call every two hours, because most of them had very little intention of remaining with the army if they could help it—and the veterans looked forward to their arrival with a certain unholy pleasure. Their attitude was pretty well expressed by a diarist in the 15th Massachusetts, which had been consolidated to four companies because of heavy battle losses, who wrote: "I wish the conscripts were out here now. I want to see them. I want to put some of them through the drill. I want to see them live on salt pork and hard bread. I want to see them carry their knapsacks."[26] Admittedly, the draftees were not very good material, but there were men in the army who would see that they became soldiers once they got to camp.

The great day came at last, and there were troops in Gettysburg again, and bands, and special trains bringing distinguished guests, and there was a big parade through the town and up to the hill, with parade marshals in their sashes, horses shying and curvetting

affectedly, much pomp and circumstance, and a famous orator with
an hour-long speech in his hand. There was also Abraham Lincoln,
who had been invited more or less as an afterthought—the invitation
went to him on November 2, suggesting that he might honor the
occasion by his presence—and Mr. Lincoln was to say a few words
after Mr. Everett had made the speech. After the usual fuss and
confusion the procession climbed the hill and the honored guests got
up on the flag-draped speakers' stand, and eventually a certain degree of quiet was restored. A chaplain offered a prayer, and a glee
club sang an ode composed especially for the occasion, and at last
the orator got up to make his speech.

An oration was an oration in those days, and it had to have a
certain style to it—classical allusions, a leisurely approach to the subject matter, a carefully phrased recital of the background and history
of the occasion, the whole working up to a peroration which would
sum everything up in memorable sentences. Mr. Everett was a master
of this art form and had been hard at work for many weeks, and he
stood up now in the center of the field where five thousand men had
died and began his polished cadenced sentences. He recalled how the
ancient Greeks commemorated their heroic dead in the days of
Pericles. . . .

There were many thousands of people at this ceremony, and among
them were certain wounded veterans who had come back to see all
of this, and a knot of these wandered away from the crowd around
the speakers' stand and strolled down along Cemetery Ridge, pausing
when they reached a little clump of trees, and there they looked off
toward the west and talked quietly about what they had seen and
done there.[27]

In front of them was the wide gentle valley of the shadow of death,
brimming now with soft autumn sunlight, and behind them the flags
waved lazily about the speakers' stand and the voice droned on,
building up toward a literary climax. The valley was a mile wide, and
there was the rolling ground where the Rebel guns had been ranked,
and on the crest of this ridge was the space where a girlish artillery
lieutenant had had a sergeant hold him up while he called for the
last round of canister, the ground where file closers had gripped hands
and dug in their heels to hold a wavering line together, the place
where the noise of men desperately fighting had been heard as a great
mournful roar; and the voice went on, and the governors looked

dignified, and the veterans by the trees looked about them and saw again the fury and the smoke and the killing.

This was the valley of dry bones, waiting for the word, which might or might not come in rhythmic prose that began by describing the customs of ancient Athens. The bones had lain there in the sun and the rain, and now they were carefully arranged state by state under the new sod. They were the bones of men who had exulted in their youth, and some of them had been unstained heroes while others had been scamps who pillaged and robbed and ran away when they could, and they had died here, and that was the end of them. They had come here because of angry words and hot passions in which they had not shared. They had come, too, because the drums had rolled and the bands had blared the swinging deceitful tunes that piped men off to battle . . . three cheers for the red white and blue, here's a long look back at the girl I left behind me, John Brown's body lies a-moldering in the grave but we go marching on, and Yankee Doodle on his spotted pony rides off into the eternal smoky mist of war.

Back of these men were innumerable long dusty roads reaching to the main streets of a thousand youthful towns and villages where there had been bright flags overhead and people on the board sidewalks cheering and crying and waving a last good-by. It had seemed once that there was some compelling reason to bring these men here—something so broad that it would encompass all of the terrible contradictory manifestations of the country's pain and bewilderment, the riots and the lynchings, the hysterical conspiracies with their oaths written in blood, the hard hand that had been laid upon the countryside, the scramble for riches and the scheming for high place, and the burdens carried by quiet folk who wanted only to live at peace by the faith they used to have.

Perhaps there was a meaning to all of it somewhere. Perhaps everything that the nation was and meant to be had come to a focus here, beyond the graves and the remembered echoes of the guns and the wreckage of lives that were gone forever. Perhaps the whole of it somehow was greater than the sum of its tragic parts, and perhaps here on this wind-swept hill the thing could be said at last, so that the dry bones of the country's dreams could take on flesh.

The orator finished, and after the applause had died away the tall man in the black frock coat got to his feet, with two little sheets of paper in his hand, and he looked out over the valley and began to speak.

The writer of any book which is concerned with a war that is no longer a part of any living memories incurs many obligations to the helpful people who run libraries. For their kindness in finding and making available needed material, and for their interest and patience, I am indebted to various persons, including Mr. David C. Mearns, chief of the Manuscript Division of the Library of Congress; Colonel Willard Webb, distinguished combat soldier and chief of the Stack and Reader Division of that library; Mr. Legare Obear, chief of the Library's Loan Division; Miss Georgia Cowan and Mr. Walter D. Campbell of the History Division of the District of Columbia Public Library, and Mr. Paul Howard, Librarian of the U. S. Department of the Interior.

Bibliography

A principal reliance in the preparation of this book has of course been the voluminous *War of the Rebellion: A Compilation of the Official Records of the Union and Confederate Armies,* published by the War Department in 1902. Unless otherwise noted, volumes cited in the notes are from Series I of this compilation. Use has also been made of Appleton's *Cyclopedia of American Biography,* published in 1888, and of the more modern *Dictionary of American Biography.* In addition, the following works were consulted:

GENERAL HISTORICAL WORKS AND BOOKS
DEALING WITH THE POLITICAL AND ECONOMIC BACKGROUND
OF THE WAR

Abraham Lincoln and the Fifth Column, by George Fort Milton. New York, 1942.

Abraham Lincoln and Men of War Times, by Alexander K. McClure. Philadelphia, 1892.

Adventures of America, 1857–1900, by John A. Kouwenhoven. New York, 1938.

Annual Report of the Commissioner of Patents for 1864. 2 vols. Washington, 1866.

Centennial History of the City of Washington, D.C., by H. W. Crew. Dayton, 1892.

Discontent in New York City, 1861–65. A dissertation submitted to the Faculty of the Graduate School of Arts and Sciences of the Catholic University of America, by Brother Basil Leo Lee, F.S.C. Washington, 1943.

Experiment in Rebellion, by Clifford Dowdey. New York, 1950.

In French Creek Valley, by John Earle Reynolds. Meadville, Pa., 1938.

The German Soldier in the Wars of the United States, by J. G. Rosengarten. Philadelphia, 1886.

The Growth of the American Republic, by Samuel Eliot Morison and Henry Steele Commager. 2 vols. New York, 1942.

The Hidden Civil War, the Story of the Copperheads, by Wood Gray. New York, 1942.

History of the Administration of President Lincoln, by Henry J. Raymond. New York, 1864.

History of the National Capital, by Wilhelmus Bogart Bryan, 1916.

History of the United States from the Compromise of 1850, by James Ford Rhodes. 9 vols. New York, 1899.

Influence of the War on Our National Prosperity, by William E. Dodge. New York, 1865.

Labor Disturbances in Pennsylvania, 1850–1880. A dissertation submitted to the Faculty of the Graduate School of Arts and Sciences of the Catholic University of America, by J. Walter Coleman. Washington, 1936.

Lincoln and the War Governors, by William B. Hesseltine. New York, 1948.

Lincoln's Daughters of Mercy, by Marjorie Barstow Greenbie. New York, 1944.

Lincoln's War Cabinet, by Burton J. Hendrick. Boston, 1946.

The Long Ships Passing, by Walter Havighurst. New York, 1942.

The Molly Maguires, by Anthony Bimba. New York, 1932.

The Movement for Peace without Victory during the Civil War, by Elbert J. Benton. Cleveland, 1918.

Old-Time Notes of Pennsylvania, by Alexander K. McClure. 2 vols. Philadelphia, 1905.

Photographic History of the Civil War, edited by Francis Trevelyan Miller. 10 vols. New York, 1911.

Pictorial History of the Civil War, by Benson J. Lossing. 3 vols. Philadelphia, 1866.

Political and Social Growth of the American People, by Arthur M. Schlesinger. New York, 1941.

The Rebellion Record: A Diary of American Events, edited by Frank Moore. 12 vols. New York, 1864.

Recollections of War Times, by Albert Gallatin Riddle. New York, 1895.

Social and Industrial Conditions in the North during the Civil War, by Emerson David Fite. New York, 1910.

South after Gettysburg: Letters of Cornelia Hancock from the Army of the Potomac, 1863–65, edited by Henrietta Stratton Jaquette. Philadelphia, 1937.

Speeches, Correspondence and Political Papers of Carl Schurz, selected and edited by Frederic Bancroft. 6 vols. New York, 1913.

A True History of the Reign of Terror in Southern Illinois, by James D. Fox. Aurora, Ill., 1884.

War Government, Federal and State, 1861–1865, by William B. Weeden. Boston, 1906.

AUTOBIOGRAPHIES,
BIOGRAPHICAL STUDIES, MEMOIRS, ETC.

Abraham Lincoln: The War Years, by Carl Sandburg. 4 vols. New York, 1939.

Autobiography of Oliver Otis Howard. 2 vols. New York, 1907.

Charles Francis Adams: An Autobiography. Boston, 1906.

Dan Sickles, Hero of Gettysburg and "Yankee King of Spain," by Edgcumb Pinchon. New York, 1945.

Days and Events: 1860–1866, by Colonel Thomas L. Livermore. Boston, 1920.

A Diary from Dixie, by Mary Boykin Chesnut, edited by Ben Ames Williams. Cambridge, 1949.

Diary of Gideon Welles, with an introduction by John T. Morse, Jr. 3 vols. Boston, 1911.

Fighting Joe Hooker, by Walter H. Hebert. Indianapolis, 1944

General Hancock, by General Francis A. Walker. New York, 1894.

Gouverneur Kemble Warren: The Life and Letters of an American Soldier, by Emerson Gifford Taylor. Boston, 1932.

Jeb Stuart, by John W. Thomason, Jr. New York, 1930.

Jefferson Davis: The Unreal and the Real, by Robert McElroy. 2 vols. New York, 1937.

Lee's Lieutenants, by Douglas Southall Freeman. 3 vols. New York, 1942.

The Life and Letters of George Gordon Meade, by Colonel George Meade. 2 vols. New York, 1913.

Life and Letters of Henry Lee Higginson, by Bliss Perry. Boston, 1921.

The Life and Public Services of Salmon Portland Chase, by J. W. Schuckers. New York, 1874.

The Life and Services of Ambrose E. Burnside: Soldier—Citizen—Statesman, by Ben Perley Poore. Providence, 1882.

Life of Oliver P. Morton, by William Dudley Foulke. 2 vols. Indianapolis, 1899.

Lincoln and the Episodes of the Civil War, by Brevet Brigadier General William E. Doster. New York, 1915.

Major General Hiram G. Berry, by Edward K. Gould. Rockland, Me., 1899.

The Military Services of Gen. Ambrose E. Burnside in the Civil War, by Daniel R. Ballou. Providence, 1914.

Old Thad Stevens: A Story of Ambition, by Richard Nelson Current. Madison, 1942.

Personal Recollections of the Civil War, by Brigadier General John Gibbon. New York, 1928.

Personal Recollections of Distinguished Generals, by William F. G. Shanks. New York, 1866.

Political Recollections, by George W. Julian. Chicago, 1884.

Ranger Mosby, by Virgil Carrington Jones. Chapel Hill, 1944.

A Rebel War Clerk's Diary, by J. B. Jones, edited by Howard Swiggett. 2 vols. New York, 1935.

Recollections of Half a Century, by Alexander K. McClure. Salem, Mass., 1902.

R. E. Lee: A Biography, by Douglas Southall Freeman. 4 vols. New York, 1934.

Reminiscences of the Civil War, by General John B. Gordon. New York, 1903.

Reminiscences of Winfield Scott Hancock, by His Wife. New York, 1887.

Robert E. Lee, the Soldier, by Major General Sir Frederick Maurice. Boston, 1925.

Sketch of the Life, Character and Public Services of Oliver P. Morton, prepared for the Indianapolis *Journal* by Charles M. Walker. Indianapolis, 1878.

Stonewall Jackson and the American Civil War, by Colonel G. F. R. Henderson. London and New York, 1936.

The Tall Sycamore of the Wabash: Daniel Wolsey Voorhees, by Leonard S. Kenworthy. Boston, 1936.

Three Wisconsin Cushings, by Theron Wilber Haight. Madison, 1910.

Touched with Fire: Civil War Letters and Diary of Oliver Wendell Holmes, Jr., edited by Mark De Wolfe Howe. Cambridge, 1946.

MILITARY HISTORIES AND BOOKS
DEALING WITH SPECIFIC BATTLES OR CAMPAIGNS

The Antietam and Fredericksburg, by Francis Winthrop Palfrey. New York, 1882.

The Army of Tennessee, by Stanley F. Horn. Indianapolis, 1941.

The Battle of Chancellorsville, by Augustus Choate Hamlin. Bangor, Me., 1896.

The Battle of Chancellorsville and the Eleventh Army Corps. Reprints of speeches at a mass meeting in the Cooper Institute, New York, June 2, 1863.

The Battle of Gettysburg, by Colonel Frank Aretas Haskell. Madison, 1908.

The Battle of Gettysburg, by the Comte de Paris. Philadelphia, 1886.

Battles and Leaders of the Civil War. Grant-Lee edition. 4 vols. New York, 1884.

"From Burnside to Hooker" and "The Army of the Potomac under Hooker": articles by William Howard Mills in the *Magazine of American History,* Vol. XV.

Camp and Outpost Duty for Infantry, by Brigadier General Daniel Butterfield. New York, 1862.

The Campaign of Chancellorsville, by John Bigelow, Jr. New Haven, 1910.

Campaigns of the Army of the Potomac, by William Swinton. New York, 1866.

The Celebrated Case of Fitz-John Porter, by Otto Eisenschiml. Indianapolis, 1950.

Chancellorsville and Gettysburg, by Major General Abner Doubleday. New York, 1882.

The Charge of the 8th Pennsylvania Cavalry at Chancellorsville, by Pennock Huey. Philadelphia, 1884.

The Crisis of the Confederacy, by Cecil Battine. London and New York, 1905.

Fredericksburg: A Study in War, by Major G. W. Redway. New York, 1906.

General Halleck and General Burnside: a reprint, with additions, of two articles originally communicated to the Providence *Journal* by "W." Boston, 1864.

Gettysburg and Lincoln: The Battle, the Cemetery and the National Park, by Henry Sweetser Burrage. New York, 1906.

History of the Army of the Potomac, by J. H. Stine. Philadelphia, 1892.

History of the Second Massachusetts Regiment of Infantry: Gettysburg, by Colonel Charles F. Morse. Boston, 1882.

The Iron Brigade at Gettysburg, anonymous. Cincinnati, 1879.

Lincoln Finds a General, by Kenneth P. Williams. 2 vols. New York, 1950.

The Long Arm of Lee, by Jennings Wise. 2 vols. Lynchburg, Va., 1915.

Maine in the War for the Union, by William E. S. Whitman and Charles H. True. Lewiston, Me., 1865.

The Military Genius of Abraham Lincoln, by Brigadier General Colin R. Ballard. London, 1926.

The Military Policy of the United States, by Brevet Major General Emory Upton. Washington, 1916.

New Jersey and the Rebellion, by John Y. Foster. Newark, 1868.

New Jersey Troops in the Gettysburg Campaign, by Samuel Toombs. Orange, N.J., 1888.

Our Campaign around Gettysburg, by John Lockwood. Brooklyn, 1864.

Papers of the Military Historical Society of Massachusetts, edited by Theodore Dwight. 10 vols. Boston, 1895.

The Second Massachusetts Infantry and the Campaign of Chancellorsville, by George A. Thayer. Boston, 1882.

The 17th Connecticut Volunteers at Gettysburg. Pamphlet. Bridgeport, 1884.

Strong Vincent and His Brigade at Gettysburg, by Oliver W. Norton. Chicago, 1909.

REGIMENTAL HISTORIES,
SOLDIERS' REMINISCENCES, ETC.

Army Letters, 1861–1865, by Oliver Willcox Norton. Chicago, 1903.

Army Life: A Private's Reminiscences of the Civil War, by the Rev. Theodore Gerrish. Portland, Me., 1882.

Berdan's United States Sharpshooters in the Army of the Potomac, by Captain C. A. Stevens. St. Paul, 1892.

The Bivouac and the Battlefield, by Captain George F. Noyes. New York, 1863.

Camp, March and Battlefield; or, Three Years and a Half with the Army of the Potomac, by the Rev. A. M. Stewart, chaplain of the 102nd Pennsylvania. Philadelphia, 1865.

Campaigning with the 6th Maine, by Brevet Lieutenant Colonel Charles A. Clark. Des Moines, 1897.

Campaigns of the 146th Regiment New York State Volunteers, compiled by Mary Genevie Green Brainard. New York, 1915.

Civil War Diary of James T. Ayres, edited by John Hope Franklin. Springfield, Ill., 1947.

Deeds of Daring; or, History of the 8th New York Volunteer Cavalry, by Henry Norton. Norwich, N.Y., 1889.

The Diary of a Young Officer, by Josiah M. Favill. Chicago, 1909.

The Dutchess County Regiment, edited by S. G. Cook and Charles E. Benton. Danbury, Conn., 1907.

A Famous Battery and Its Campaigns, 1861–64, by Captain James E. Smith. Washington, 1892.

The Fifth Regiment Connecticut Volunteers: A History, by Edwin E. Marvin. Hartford, 1889.

The 48th in the War: being a Narrative of the Campaigns of the 48th Regiment, Infantry, Pennsylvania Veteran Volunteers, during the War of the Rebellion, by Oliver Christian Bosbyshell. Philadelphia, 1895.

Four Years Campaigning in the Army of the Potomac, by D. G. Crotty. Grand Rapids, 1874.

Four Years in the Army of the Potomac: A Soldier's Recollections, by Major Evan Rowland Jones. London, 1881.

Four Years with the Army of the Potomac, by Regis de Trobriand, translated by George K. Dauchy. Boston, 1889.

Henry Wilson's Regiment: History of the 22nd Massachusetts Infantry, by John L. Parker. Boston, 1887.

History and Honorary Roll of the 12th Regiment, Infantry, N.G.S.N.Y., by M. Francis Dowley. New York, 1869.

History of a Cavalry Company: A Complete Record of Company A, 4th Pennsylvania Cavalry, by Captain William Hyndman. Philadelphia, 1870.

History of the Corn Exchange Regiment, 118th Pennsylvania Volunteers, by the Survivors Association. Philadelphia, 1888.

History of the 8th Cavalry Regiment, Illinois Volunteers, by Abner Hard. Aurora, Ill., 1868.

History of the 87th Pennsylvania Volunteers, by George R. Prowell. York, Pa., 1903.

A History of the First Regiment of Massachusetts Cavalry Volunteers, by Major Benjamin W. Crowninshield. Boston, 1891.

History of the First Regiment Minnesota Volunteer Infantry, by R. I. Holcombe. Stillwater, Minn., 1916.

The History of the 9th Regiment Massachusetts Volunteer Infantry, by Daniel George MacNamara. Boston, 1899.

History of the Philadelphia Brigade, by Charles H. Banes. Philadelphia, 1876.

History of the Sauk County Riflemen, by Philip Cheek and Mair Pointon. Privately printed, 1909.

History of the Second Army Corps in the Army of the Potomac, by Brevet Brigadier General Francis A. Walker. New York, 1886.

History of the Tenth Massachusetts Battery, by John D. Billings. Boston, 1881.

History of the Third Indiana Cavalry, by W. N. Pickerill. Indianapolis, 1906.

History of the 12th Regiment New Hampshire Volunteers in the War of the Rebellion, by Captain A. W. Bartlett. Concord, N.H., 1897.

History of the 21st Regiment Ohio Volunteer Infantry in the War of the Rebellion, by Captain S. S. Canfield. Toledo, 1893.

History of the 24th Michigan of the Iron Brigade, by O. B. Curtis. Detroit, 1891.

I Rode with Stonewall, by Henry Kyd Douglas. Chapel Hill, 1940.

Journal History of the 29th Ohio Veteran Volunteers, by J. Hamp Se Cheverell. Cleveland, 1883.

Letters from a Surgeon of the Civil War, compiled by Martha Derby Perry. Boston, 1906.

Life in Camp: A History of the Nine Months' Service of the 14th Vermont Regiment, by J. C. Williams. Claremont, N.H., 1864.

A Military History of the 8th Regiment Ohio Volunteer Infantry, by Lieutenant Colonel Franklin Sawyer. Cleveland, 1881.

A Narrative of the Formation and Services of the Eleventh Massachusetts Volunteers, by Gustavus B. Hutchinson. Boston, 1893.

Nineteenth Indiana Volunteer Infantry: taken from *Indiana at Antietam.* Report of the Indiana Antietam Monument Commission. Indianapolis, 1911.

The 95th Pennsylvania Volunteers, by G. Norton Galloway. Philadelphia, 1884.

The Ninth Ohio Volunteers, by Carl Wittke. Columbus, 1926.

The Old Fourth Michigan Infantry, by O. S. Barrett. Detroit, 1888.

On the Parallels; or, Chapters of Inner History, by Benjamin Borton. Woodstown, N.J., 1903.

Recollections of a Confederate Staff Officer, by General G. Moxley Sorrel. New York, 1905.

Recollections of a Private, by Warren Lee Goss. New York, 1890.

Recollections of a Private Soldier in the Army of the Potomac, by Frank Wilkeson. New York, 1887.

Recollections of the Civil War, by Mason Whiting Tyler. New York, 1912.

Record of the 33rd Massachusetts Volunteer Infantry, by Andrew J. Boies. Fitchburg, Mass., 1880.

Red-Tape and Pigeon-Hole Generals; as Seen from the Ranks during a Campaign in the Army of the Potomac, by a Citizen-Soldier. New York, 1864.

Regimental History of the First New York Dragoons, by the Rev. J. R. Bowen. Lyons, Mich., 1900.

Reminiscences and Record of the 6th New York Veteran Volunteer Cavalry, by Alonzo Foster. Privately printed, 1892.

Reminiscences of General Herman Haupt. Milwaukee, 1901.

Reminiscences of the 19th Massachusetts Regiment, by Captain John G. B. Adams. Boston, 1899.

The Road to Richmond: The Civil War Memoirs of Major Abner Small, of the 16th Maine Volunteers, edited by Harold Adams Small. Berkeley, Calif., 1939.

Service with the Sixth Wisconsin Volunteers, by Rufus R. Dawes. Marietta, O., 1890.

The 61st Ohio Volunteers, 1861–1865, by Frederick Stephen Wallace. Marysville, O., 1902.

A Soldier's Diary: The Story of a Volunteer, by David Lane. Privately printed, 1905.

Some Personal Reminiscences of Service in the Cavalry of the Army of the Potomac, by Colonel Hampton S. Thomas. Philadelphia, 1889.

The Story of a Thousand: being a History of the Service of the 105th Ohio Volunteer Infantry, by Albion W. Tourgee. Buffalo, 1896.

The Story of the 15th Regiment Massachusetts Volunteer Infantry, by Andrew E. Ford. Clinton, Mass., 1898.

The Story of the 48th, by Joseph Gould. Philadelphia, 1908.

Three Years Campaign of the 9th N.Y.S.M. during the Southern Rebellion, by John W. Jaques. New York, 1865.

Three Years in the Army of the Potomac, by Henry N. Blake. Boston, 1865.

Three Years in the Field Hospitals of the Army of the Potomac, by Mrs. William H. Holstein. Philadelphia, 1867.

The Three Years Service of the 33rd Massachusetts Infantry Regiment, 1862–65, by Adin B. Underwood. Boston, 1881.

Trials and Triumphs: The Record of the 55th Ohio Volunteer Infantry, by Captain Hartwell Osborn and Others. Chicago, 1904.

The Twentieth Connecticut: A Regimental History, by John W. Storrs. Ansonia, Conn., 1886.

The 25th Ohio Veteran Volunteer Infantry in the War for the Union, by Edward C. Culp. Topeka, Kans., 1885.

The Ulster Guard and the War of the Rebellion, by Colonel Theodore B. Gates. New York, 1879.

Under the Maltese Cross: Antietam to Appomattox: Campaigns of the 155th Pennsylvania Regiment, narrated by the Rank and File. Pittsburgh, 1910.

Under the Red Patch: The Story of the 63rd Regiment Pennsylvania Volunteers, compiled by Gilbert Adams Hays. Pittsburgh, 1908.

War Letters of William Thompson Lusk. Privately printed, New York, 1911.

War Years with Jeb Stuart, by Lieutenant Colonel W. W. Blackford. New York, 1945.

Notes

CHAPTER ONE: DEEP RIVER

FOR WHAT THERE WAS IN IT

1. *Camp, March and Battlefield*, by the Rev. A. M. Stewart, p. 248.

2. *The Rebellion Record*, edited by Frank Moore, Vol. VI, Part 2, p. 4; *The Hidden Civil War*, by Wood Gray, p. 111.

3. For the Democrats' conversations with the British Minister, see Lord Lyons's dispatch, quoted in *Pictorial History of the Civil War*, by Benson J. Lossing, Vol. III, p. 47.

4. Chase's visits with Hooker and what came of them are related in *Fighting Joe Hooker*, by Walter H. Hebert, p. 147. The National Insane Asylum, now St. Elizabeth's Hospital, was built in the mid-1850s on what was then a rural estate not far from the Anacostia River, and was designed to care for mental patients from the District of Columbia and the armed services. (*Centennial History of the City of Washington, D.C.*, by H. W. Crew; *History of the National Capital*, by Wilhelmus Bogart Bryan.) During the Civil War the hospital offered a pleasant place in which a high-ranking general might recuperate from a light wound.

5. The visit of Hamlin, Berry, and Hooker is described by General Charles Hamlin, son of the Vice-President, in E. K. Gould's *Major General Hiram G. Berry*, p. 229. It might be noted that at this time Hooker's sardonic brother officer, George Gordon Meade, was writing to his wife: "Hooker is a Democrat and anti-abolitionist—that is to say, he was. What he will be, when the command of the army is held out to him, is more than anyone can tell, because I fear he is open to temptation and liable to be seduced by flattery." (*Life and Letters of George Gordon Meade*, Vol. I, p. 319.)

6. As distinguished a soldier as John Gibbon, who closed the war as a major general commanding an army corps, became a captain again in 1866. This cataclysmic descent is recalled in Gibbon's *Personal Recollections of the Civil War*, pp. 370–71.

7. Buell's account of his difficulties with Morton, the killing of Nelson, and the failure of all efforts to bring Davis to trial appears in *Battles and Leaders of*

the Civil War, Vol. III, pp. 42–44. From a very different point of view, the same topics are also discussed extensively in William Dudley Foulke's *Life of Oliver P. Morton*, Vol. I, pp. 187–95, and in *Sketch of the Life, Character and Public Services of Oliver P. Morton*, by Charles M. Walker, pp. 70, 73, 79. An interesting picture of the breezy Nelson as his troops saw him in battle appears in *History of the 21st Regiment Ohio Volunteer Infantry in the War of the Rebellion*, by Captain S. S. Canfield, pp. 32–33. Colonel R. M. Kelly describes Nelson vividly in *Battles and Leaders*, Vol. I, p. 375 ff., and another picture of the man is found in *The Story of a Thousand*, by Albion W. Tourgee, p. 70 ff. There is a brief sketch of the slightly satanic General Davis in Vol. 2 of Appleton's *Cyclopedia of American Biography*. Union defeats during the Bragg invasion are well described in Stanley F. Horn's *The Army of Tennessee*, pp. 164, 168–69.

8. General Gibbon's indignant account of the Meredith-Hooker deal and his caustic verdict on both men, in all of which Meredith is never mentioned by name, appear in his *Personal Recollections*, pp. 107–9. Unfortunately there is no full-length history of the 19th Indiana. A sketch of the regiment's career is printed in *Indiana at Antietam*, pp. 107–23; it remarks that the 19th was "a pet regiment" of Governor Morton's, emphasizes the close tie between Meredith and Morton, and is notably reserved about Meredith's promotion. Meredith is briefly described in Appleton's *Cyclopedia*. Foulke's *Oliver P. Morton* (pp. 152–53, Vol. I) reveals that Morton incurred a good deal of criticism in Indiana by giving Meredith his colonelcy in the first place. In the early spring of 1861 Morton was employing Meredith as a special emissary to the War Department (*Official Records*, Series III, Vol. I, p. 243.)

9. This allegation is discussed by two enlisted veterans of the Iron Brigade in *Battles and Leaders*, Vol. III, p. 142.

10. *History of the 24th Michigan*, by O. B. Curtis, p. 65. The early portion of Curtis's book has been drawn on extensively for material on the regiment's organization, background, and general personality. For glimpses of the ceremony at which the 24th was received (if not welcomed) into the Iron Brigade, see Gibbon's *Personal Recollections*, p. 92, and *Service with the 6th Wisconsin Volunteers*, by Rufus R. Dawes, p. 101.

11. *History of the 24th Michigan*, p. 69; *Service with the 6th Wisconsin Volunteers*, p. 105.

12. *History of the 24th Michigan*, p. 84.

JORDAN WATER, RISE OVER ME

1. Haupt to Burnside, *Official Records*, Vol. XXI, p. 850; *Rebellion Record*, Vol. VI, Part 2, pp. 94–100; *Camp, March and Battlefield*, p. 250.

2. *History of the Sauk County Riflemen*, by Philip Cheek and Mair Pointon, p. 215; *Days and Events*, by Colonel Thomas L. Livermore, p. 156. The technique of beehive stealing is described by Frederick Stephen Wallace in *The 61st Ohio Volunteers*, pp. 10–11.

3. *Under the Maltese Cross . . . Campaigns of the 155th Pennsylvania Regiment*, narrated by the Rank and File, pp. 87–88.

4. *The Life and Public Services of Ambrose E. Burnside,* by Ben Perley Poore, pp. 26–34, 50–52, 57, 73–74.

5. For these tributes, see *The 48th in the War,* by Oliver Christian Bosbyshell, p. 47, and *Red-Tape and Pigeon-Hole Generals,* by a Citizen-Soldier, p. 226. Bosbyshell, recalling the Carolina junket, rhapsodized: "Constant were the visits of General Burnside through the camps of the various regiments, and frequent his interviews with the company cooks."

6. A British soldier who wrote a study of Fredericksburg several years before World War I remarked: "The general in command of the Army of the Potomac at this period, whoever he might be, had need of tremendous force of character, of an indomitable will, and of absolute authority, to accomplish the task he had been set." (*Fredericksburg: A Study in War,* by Major G. W. Redway, p. 22.)

7. Burnside's explanation of all of this is found in his report on Fredericksburg, *Official Records,* Vol. XXI, pp. 82–97. Major Redway remarks that Burnside's original plan was not bad, but that the man seems to have underestimated the time that would be required to set up a new base of supplies and get his army properly established on the Rappahannock. There is a good, if highly partisan, discussion of Burnside's plan and the effect upon it of the non-arrival of the pontoons in *General Halleck and General Burnside,* by "W."

8. *Official Records,* Vol. XXI, pp. 790–91.

9. Ibid., p. 794.

10. A detailed account of this fantastic operation, written by Brigadier General Rufus Ingalls, chief quartermaster of the Army of the Potomac, can be found in the *Official Records,* Vol. XXI, pp. 148–51. Interestingly enough, though probably inaccurately, General Howard suggests that Halleck purposely delayed the arrival of the pontoons in order that Burnside would have to go into winter quarters, thus postponing a battle until spring. (*Autobiography of Oliver Otis Howard,* Vol. I, p. 318.)

11. *Official Records,* Vol. XXI, p. 832.

12. For the invention and operation of the car floats, see *Reminiscences of General Herman Haupt,* pp. 165–66, 179–80. His tribute to Burnside appears on p. 179.

13. In February 1865, Lieutenant Colonel F. W. Sims, C.S.A., reported to the Superintendent of Railway Transportation, Confederate States Quartermaster Department, that railroad lines could be maintained only by taking rails from sidings and branch lines: "Not a single bar of railroad iron has been rolled in the Confederacy since the war, nor can we hope to do any better during the continuance." (*Official Records,* Series IV, Vol. III, p. 1092.) Haupt's promise to buy an extra ten miles of rail appears in *Official Records,* Vol. XXI, p. 832.

14. *Official Records,* Vol. XXI, pp. 773–74.

15. William B. Weeden in *War Government, Federal and State, 1861–1865,* p. 95.

16. *History of the 9th Regiment Massachusetts Volunteer Infantry,* by David George MacNamara, p. 241; *Henry Wilson's Regiment: History of the 22nd*

Massachusetts Infantry, by John L. Parker, p. 219; *Campaigns of the 146th Regiment New York State Volunteers,* compiled by Mary Genevie Green Brainard, p. 22; *Under the Maltese Cross,* p. 85.

17. *War Letters of William Thompson Lusk,* p. 241.

18. *Touched with Fire: Civil War Letters and Diary of Oliver Wendell Holmes, Jr.,* edited by Mark De Wolfe Howe, p. 73.

19. *The 48th in the War,* p. 93.

20. Correspondence of the Cincinnati *Commercial,* reprinted in Moore's *Rebellion Record,* Vol. VI, Part 2, p. 94 ff.

21. Ibid., p. 96.

22. *The Road to Richmond,* by Major Abner R. Small, p. 59.

BIG STARS ARE BUSTING

1. A detailed account of the attempt to lay the bridges appears in Major Spaulding's report, *Official Records,* Vol. XXI, pp. 175–77.

2. Ibid., pp. 827–28.

3. *Rebellion Record,* Vol. VI, Part 2, pp. 94–100; *Days and Events,* pp. 167–68.

4. Graphic accounts of the bombardment of the town and the fight over the bridges appear in *Battles and Leaders,* Vol. III, pp. 75, 86–89, 108, 121–22. General Hunt's remarks on the artillery's inability to silence the river-front riflemen are in *Official Records,* Vol. XXI, p. 183. See also, in that same volume, General Couch's report, p. 221, and Colonel Hall's, pp. 282–85.

5. *Touched with Fire,* p. 90; *History of the Second Army Corps,* by Brevet Brigadier General Francis A. Walker, p. 150.

6. *Rebellion Record,* Vol. VI, Part 2, p. 92.

7. Ibid., p. 98.

8. *Battles and Leaders,* Vol. III, p. 142.

9. Ibid., pp. 79, 81.

10. *Service with the 6th Wisconsin Volunteers,* p. 110.

11. Ibid., p. 111; *Major General Hiram G. Berry,* p. 219; *Camp, March and Battlefield,* p. 281.

12. *The Road to Richmond,* p. 65.

13. *Letters from a Surgeon of the Civil War,* compiled by Martha Derby Perry, p. 38; *History of the Sauk County Riflemen,* p. 39. See also *Four Years Campaigning in the Army of the Potomac,* by D. G. Crotty, p. 74.

14. *History of the 24th Michigan,* pp. 100–2, 203; *Battles and Leaders,* Vol. III, p. 142; *Service with the 6th Wisconsin Volunteers,* p. 112. General Double-

day's report, which praises the 24th's conduct, is in Vol. XXI of the *Official Records*, pp. 461–65. Note that Meredith's suspension was temporary; he was reinstated in brigade command after the battle.

BURNISHED ROWS OF STEEL

1. *History of the Second Army Corps*, p. 152.

2. *History of the Corn Exchange Regiment*, by the Survivors Association, p. 114.

3. *On the Parallels; or, Chapters of Inner History*, by Benjamin Borton, p. 65. Good accounts of the ground to be covered and of the difficulties of the approach are in *History of the Second Army Corps*, pp. 159–64, and in General Walker's *General Hancock*, pp. 64–68. See also General Orlando Willcox's report, *Official Records*, Vol. XXI, p. 310 ff.; *History of the Philadelphia Brigade*, by Charles H. Banes, p. 141, and Palfrey's *The Antietam and Fredericksburg*, pp. 161–62, 167.

4. Complaints about defective shell may be found in General Hunt's report, *Official Records*, Vol. XXI, p. 189, and in the reports of various subordinate gunners, pp. 192, 195, and 200 of the same volume.

5. *On the Parallels*, pp. 68–69; *Autobiography of Oliver Otis Howard*, Vol. I, p. 341.

6. *The 48th in the War*, p. 96; Meagher's report, *Official Records*, Vol. XXI, pp. 240–46.

7. Ibid., pp. 249–50.

8. Ibid., pp. 277–80.

9. Ibid., pp. 233, 236–38.

10. *Battles and Leaders*, Vol. III, p. 113.

11. I am indebted to Francis Wilshin, historian of the Fredericksburg and Spotsylvania Courthouse National Military Park, for calling my attention to the existence and importance of this generally neglected feature of the terrain, and for producing a map of Fredericksburg, dated 1867, which shows where the slough was. It is also referred to by Captain John Bigelow, Jr., in the *Papers of the Military Historical Society of Massachusetts*, Vol. III, pp. 244–45. Couch's official report, describing the canal and the open ground beyond and telling of his orders to Howard to try to turn the Confederate left, is in the *Official Records*, Vol. XXI, pp. 221–25.

12. *Autobiography of Oliver Otis Howard*, Vol. I, p. 344.

13. *History of the 9th Massachusetts*, p. 257; *Under the Maltese Cross*, p. 102.

14. *Henry Wilson's Regiment*, p. 228.

15. *History of the 9th Massachusetts*, p. 256; *Official Records*, Vol. XXI, p. 233.

16. Ibid., pp. 262–65, 267–68; *History of the Second Army Corps*, pp. 177–78.

17. *Battles and Leaders*, Vol. III, pp. 115–16; *History of the Second Army Corps*, p. 180.

18. *History of the 9th Massachusetts*, p. 256; *Official Records*, Vol. XXI, pp. 430–34; *The Antietam and Fredericksburg*, p. 172; *Red-Tape and Pigeon-Hole Generals*, p. 241. For Humphreys's roundup of the young soldiers who had been detailed to stay in the rear, see *Under the Maltese Cross*, p. 97.

19. *Rebellion Record*, Vol. VI, Part 2, p. 84; *Official Records*, Vol. XXI, pp. 335–36, 338–43; *War Letters of William Thompson Lusk*, p. 246.

20. *History of the First Regiment Minnesota Volunteer Infantry*, by R. I. Holcombe, p. 269; *Official Records*, Vol. XXI, pp. 425–26. For a particularly vivid account of the trials of these helpless regiments, see *Battles and Leaders*, Vol. III, pp. 122–25.

21. *On the Parallels*, p. 90.

22. *Under the Maltese Cross*, p. 99; *Rebellion Record*, Vol. VI, Part 2, p. 100.

CHAPTER TWO: ALL PLAYED OUT

A LONG TALK WITH ROBERT

1. *Diary of Gideon Welles*, with an introduction by John T. Morse, Vol. I, p. 192.

2. *Life of Oliver P. Morton*, Vol. I, p. 198.

3. *Battles and Leaders*, Vol. III, pp. 117, 127.

4. Major Redway, the British critic, suggests in his *Fredericksburg: A Study in War*, that the attack on the Union left need not have been as hopeless as it now appears to have been. General Meade, who was well qualified to judge, wrote shortly after the battle that he believed the attack there would have succeeded if Franklin had put in all of his men. He added, however, that Burnside's orders were far from clear. (*Life and Letters of George Gordon Meade*, Vol. I, pp. 359–60, 361–62, 365–66, 367.)

5. *History of the Corn Exchange Regiment*, p. 122; *Under the Maltese Cross*, p. 105.

6. *History of the First Regiment Minnesota Volunteer Infantry*, pp. 266–68. This writer appears to have borrowed his combined justification and expression of regret verbatim from Walker's *History of the Second Army Corps*, p. 153.

7. *On the Parallels*, pp. 39–40.

8. *War Letters of William Thompson Lusk*, pp. 231–32.

9. *Life in Camp: A History of the Nine Months' Service of the 14th Vermont Regiment*, by J. C. Williams, p. 7; *Record of the 33rd Massachusetts Volunteer Infantry*, by Andrew J. Boies, p. 17.

10. *The 48th in the War*, p. 100.

11. *Political Recollections*, by George W. Julian, p. 225; *Four Years in the Army of the Potomac: A Soldier's Recollections*, by Major Evan Rowland Jones, p. 104.

12. Julian's *Political Recollections*, p. 235.

13. *On the Parallels*, pp. 122–25. The regimental history of the 1st Minnesota also describes the making and sailing of miniature cargo carriers.

14. *Reminiscences of the Civil War*, by General John B. Gordon, pp. 111–12.

15. Report of Dr. J. H. Douglas, of the Sanitary Commission, in *Rebellion Record*, Vol. VI, Part 2, pp. 90–92; Walker's *General Hancock*, p. 69.

16. *History of a Cavalry Company: A Complete Record of Company A, 4th Pennsylvania Cavalry*, by Captain William Hyndman, p. 74. There is an excellent account of the training, organization, equipment, and use of Federal cavalry, and a comparison with the same features of the Confederate service, in Major Benjamin W. Crowninshield's *History of the 1st Regiment of Massachusetts Cavalry Volunteers*, pp. 3–39. There is also a good description of the training undergone by green cavalrymen in *Regimental History of the First New York Dragoons*, by the Rev. J. R. Bowen, pp. 96–98.

17. *History of the 9th Massachusetts*, p. 227.

18. Major Higginson's remarks on the expedition can be found in *Life and Letters of Henry Lee Higginson*, by Bliss Perry, p. 176. For a formal statement of the projected venture, see *Official Records*, Vol. XXI, pp. 895–96.

19. An exhaustive treatment of this whole affair is William Howard Mills's "From Burnside to Hooker," *Magazine of American History*, Vol. XV, pp. 44–56. There is also a good account in Sandburg's *Abraham Lincoln: The War Years*, Vol. I, pp. 632–37.

20. Burnside wrote to Lincoln on January 1, 1863, saying that he was putting on paper a résumé of the remarks which he had just made to the President in person, so that Lincoln could have a formal record if he wished one. See *Official Records*, Vol. XXI, pp. 941–42.

21. This series of letters—Lincoln to Halleck, Halleck to Stanton, Burnside to Lincoln, Halleck to Burnside, and so on—is in Vol. XXI of the *Official Records*, pp. 940, 944–45, 953–54.

22. Letter of General W. F. Smith in *Magazine of American History*, Vol. XV, pp. 197–201. According to Poore's *Life and Services of Ambrose E. Burnside*, pp. 136–37, Robert was captured by the Confederates at the first battle of Bull Run; months later Burnside got him back by arranging an exchange for a Confederate captured on Roanoke Island.

THE FOOLS THAT BRING DISASTER

1. *A Soldier's Diary: The Story of a Volunteer,* by David Lane, p. 29.

2. *History of the Sauk County Riflemen,* p. 28.

3. There is a graphic picture of the sprawling log-and-canvas military city and a detailed description of the construction and furnishing of a typical hut in Colonel Livermore's *Days and Events,* p. 160. Other details are from *Under the Maltese Cross,* p. 119, and *Campaigns of the 146th Regiment New York State Volunteers,* pp. 51–52.

4. *Four Years Campaigning in the Army of the Potomac,* p. 75.

5. *Camp, March and Battlefield,* p. 280.

6. *Life and Letters of Henry Lee Higginson,* pp. 176–77; *The Three Years Service of the 33rd Massachusetts Infantry Regiment,* by Adin B. Underwood, p. 15; *Service with the 6th Wisconsin Volunteers,* p. 115.

7. *War Letters of William Thompson Lusk,* pp. 244–45, 256.

8. *Official Records,* Vol. XXI, pp. 916–18.

9. *Reminiscences of the 19th Massachusetts Regiment,* by Captain John G. B. Adams, pp. 60–61.

10. *Official Records,* Vol. XXI, p. 127; *Record of the 33rd Massachusetts Volunteer Infantry,* p. 20.

11. The normal routine for breaking camp and taking to the road, as prescribed in General Daniel Butterfield's *Camp and Outpost Duty for Infantry.*

12. *Diary of Gideon Welles,* Vol. I, p. 225.

13. *Four Years Campaigning in the Army of the Potomac,* p. 80.

14. The New York *Times* article from which this quotation comes is the best description of the mud march which this writer has encountered. It has been drawn on liberally in the preparation of this chapter and is printed in full in Moore's *Rebellion Record,* Vol. VI, Part 2, pp. 396–400.

15. *Ibid.,* p. 398.

16. *Official Records,* Vol. XXI, pp. 1000–1; *The Bivouac and the Battlefield,* by Captain George F. Noyes, pp. 325–28; *History of a Cavalry Company,* p. 85; *History of the Corn Exchange Regiment,* pp. 160–64; *Recollections of a Private,* by Warren Lee Goss, pp. 136–39; *Four Years with the Army of the Potomac,* by Regis de Trobriand, pp. 407–9.

17. *Recollections of the Civil War,* by Mason Whiting Tyler, p. 71.

18. *Rebellion Record,* Vol. VI, Part 2, p. 398.

19. *Campaigns of the 146th Regiment New York State Volunteers,* p. 58.

20. *Recollections of a Private,* p. 136.

21. *Under the Red Patch: The Story of the 63rd Regiment Pennsylvania Volunteers,* compiled by Gilbert Adams Hays, p. 169. It was at this time that an engineer officer, making out a requisition for a detail to work on some of the stalled equipment, wrote an order calling for "50 men, 25 feet high, to work in mud 18 feet deep." (*Berdan's United States Sharpshooters in the Army of the Potomac,* by Captain C. A. Stevens, p. 231.)

22. *Recollections of a Private,* p. 138; *Service with the 6th Wisconsin Volunteers,* p. 116.

23. *Official Records,* Vol. XXI, pp. 989–90.

24. *Rebellion Record,* Vol. VI, Part 2, p. 399; *History of the 24th Michigan,* p. 112.

25. *Henry Wilson's Regiment,* pp. 244–45. Memories appear to have been hazy regarding this fight; the historian of the 118th Pennsylvania recalls the whisky ration and the ensuing fisticuffs but remembers a different origin. (*History of the Corn Exchange Regiment,* p. 162.)

26. *History of the 9th Massachusetts,* p. 271; *Service with the 6th Wisconsin Volunteers,* p. 117; *The Road to Richmond,* p. 77.

27. *History of the 24th Michigan,* p. 113.

28. *Four Years Campaigning in the Army of the Potomac,* p. 80.

29. The book referred to is *Campaigns of the 146th Regiment New York State Volunteers,* pp. 311–418.

30. *History of the Second Army Corps,* p. 200.

THE THIRD THAT REMAINED

1. *Official Records,* Vol. XXI, p. 67; *Recollections of Half a Century,* by A. K. McClure, p. 346.

2. *Battles and Leaders,* Vol. III, p. 138.

3. This luncheon party and Burnside's bewildering outburst are presented in detail by General Smith in *Magazine of American History,* Vol. XV, pp. 197–201.

4. General Orders No. 8 is found in *Official Records,* Vol. XXI, pp. 998–99. Burnside's explanation of the mistake regarding General Ferrero appears in the same volume, p. 1123. A little later, when Burnside had been assigned to duty in Ohio, he specifically asked that Ferrero be assigned to serve there with him. (*Official Records,* Vol. XXV, Part 2, p. 503.)

5. *Fighting Joe Hooker,* p. 164; *Autobiography of Oliver Otis Howard,* Vol. I, p. 348.

6. *Speeches, Correspondence and Political Papers of Carl Schurz,* selected and edited by Frederic Bancroft, Vol. I, p. 221.

7. *History of the Second Army Corps,* p. 198.

8. *History of the 24th Michigan,* p. 113; "The Army of the Potomac under Hooker," by William Howard Mills, *Magazine of American History,* Vol. XV, p. 185; *Official Records,* Vol. XXV, Part 2, p. 73.

9. Details about the measures taken to catch deserters around Washington and Baltimore are in *Lincoln and the Episodes of the Civil War,* by General W. E. Doster, pp. 68–73, 99. See also *Official Records,* Vol. XXV, Part 2, p. 123.

10. *Four Years Campaigning in the Army of the Potomac,* pp. 77–78.

11. Ibid., p. 81; *Official Records,* Series II, Vol. V, p. 194.

12. Ibid., p. 169. For other abuses of the parole system, see *Official Records,* Series II, Vol. IV, pp. 449, 546, 562.

13. *Lincoln and the Episodes of the Civil War,* pp. 99–101.

14. *Official Records,* Vol. XXI, p. 985; Vol. XXV, Part 2, p. 86.

15. Ibid., pp. 36–37, 43.

16. Ibid., pp. 1112–15, report of Colonel Henry A. Morrow, 24th Michigan. For other reports on attempts to break up the transit of contraband goods and persons, see that same volume, pp. 13–17. A good account of cavalry's part in these forays is in *History of the 8th Cavalry Regiment, Illinois Volunteers,* by Abner Hard, pp. 238–41. For the argument between army and navy regarding their mutual sins and responsibilities, see *Official Records,* Vol. XXV, Part 2, pp. 124–27.

17. Hooker's report to J. C. Kelton, assistant adjutant general, dated February 15, 1863.

18. An extremely readable account of the way the women of America, aided and financed by a few men, forced a revolution in the War Department's method of caring for wounded men is contained in Marjorie Barstow Greenbie's excellent book, *Lincoln's Daughters of Mercy.* There is also an interesting picture of the way women worked with the Sanitary Commission, through Ladies' Aid Societies and otherwise, in *Three Years in Field Hospitals of the Army of the Potomac,* by Mrs. William H. Holstein, pp. 12, 26–27, 41–57.

19. *The Military Policy of the United States,* by Brevet Major General Emory Upton, pp. 402–4, 406, 409.

20. Ibid., p. 409; *Official Records,* Series III, Vol. V, p. 543 ff.

21. *Military Policy of the United States,* pp. 407, 412.

22. *Official Records,* Series III, Vol. V, p. 752.

23. Ibid., p. 678.

24. Ibid., Series II, Vol. IV, pp. 594–95.

25. Ibid., Series III, Vol. V, p. 840.

26. Report of Thomas F. Perley, medical inspector general, dated January 8, 1863: *Official Records*, Vol. XXI, pp. 957–59.

27. *Charles Francis Adams: An Autobiography*, p. 163.

28. *Official Records*, Vol. XXI, p. 1008.

29. *On the Parallels*, p. 134.

CHAPTER THREE: REVIVAL

MEN WHO ARE GREATLY IN EARNEST

1. *Life of Oliver P. Morton*, by William Dudley Foulke, Vol. I, pp. 23–25, 51. The early pages of this book have been followed in this sketch of Morton's boyhood and youth.

2. Ibid., p. 28.

3. Ibid., p. 67.

4. Ibid., pp. 92, 102.

5. *Battles and Leaders*, Vol. I, p. 86.

6. *Sketch of the Life, Character and Public Services of Oliver P. Morton*, by Charles M. Walker, p. 70.

7. Foulke's *Life of Oliver P. Morton*, Vol. I, p. 148.

8. *The Tall Sycamore of the Wabash: Daniel Wolsey Voorhees*, by Leonard S. Kenworthy, pp. 55–56; *War Government, Federal and State, 1861–1865*, p. 143.

9. Foulke's *Life of Oliver P. Morton*, Vol. I, pp. 163–67, 179.

10. Ibid., pp. 187–88, 196–97.

11. Ibid., p. 213 ff.

12. Ibid., p. 209; *The Hidden Civil War*, pp. 63–70.

13. For a good discussion of this point, see the introduction to *War Government, Federal and State, 1861–1865*, p. xiv ff. An excellent analysis of the development of the "peace Democrats" during the war years is also to be found in Elbert J. Benton's *The Movement for Peace without Victory during the Civil War*.

14. Judge Advocate General Holt's extensive and somewhat wide-eyed report on this order is printed in *Official Records*, Series II, Vol. VII, pp. 930–53.

15. *A Rebel War Clerk's Diary*, by J. B. Jones, edited by Howard Swiggett, Vol. I, pp. 253, 259.

16. Most of these details as to countersigns, shameful deaths, and what not are drawn from Holt's report. See also *Official Records*, Series II, Vol. VII, pp. 629–31, 643–44, 657.

17. Foulke's *Life of Oliver P. Morton*, Vol. I, pp. 238–39.

18. *Sketch of the Life, Character and Public Services of Oliver P. Morton*, pp. 100–1; *Lincoln and the War Governors*, by William B. Hesseltine, pp. 311–15.

19. *Recollections of War Times*, by Albert Gallatin Riddle, p. 321.

THE IMPERATIVES OF WAR

1. *History of the 9th Massachusetts*, p. 280.

2. *History of the Philadelphia Brigade*, p. 155; *The Diary of a Young Officer*, by Josiah M. Favill, p. 225.

3. *History of the 9th Massachusetts*, p. 259.

4. *A History of the 1st Regiment of Massachusetts Cavalry Volunteers*, p. 298; *Four Years with the Army of the Potomac*, by Regis de Trobriand, p. 399; *Days and Events*, p. 183.

5. *History of the Corn Exchange Regiment*, p. 215.

6. *History of the Philadelphia Brigade*, p. 157; *History of the 12th Regiment New Hampshire Volunteers in the War of the Rebellion*, by Captain A. W. Bartlett, p. 19.

7. *Official Records*, Vol. XXV, Part 2, pp. 217–19.

8. Ibid., p. 219. For a good sketch of General Patrick, see *The Ulster Guard and the War of the Rebellion*, by Colonel Theodore B. Gates, pp. 191, 192, 198, 199.

9. *Official Records*, Series III, Vol. III, pp. 35–36, 62–63, 69–71, 116, 324.

10. *The Celebrated Case of Fitz-John Porter*, by Otto Eisenschiml, p. 17.

11. *Recollections of Half a Century*, by A. K. McClure, pp. 435–36.

12. *Old Thad Stevens: A Story of Ambition*, by Richard Nelson Current, p. 174.

13. Gideon Welles did not care greatly for Stanton and referred to him acidly a number of times; he gives a caustic opinion on the War Secretary's stamina, or lack of it, in Vol. I of his famous *Diary*, pp. 67–68.

14. *Lincoln and the Episodes of the Civil War*, pp. 124–25.

15. *Service with the 6th Wisconsin Volunteers*, p. 125.

16. *Life and Letters of Henry Lee Higginson*, pp. 179–80.

17. *Lincoln and the War Governors*, p. 281. For the decline in recruiting in 1863, see *Official Records*, Series III, Vol. V, pp. 599, 601, 612, 618–19. Hooker's belief that few of his short-term men would re-enlist is in Vol. XXV, Part 2, p. 243.

18. *War Government, Federal and State, 1861–1865*, p. 219.

19. *Official Records*, Series IV, Vol. I, p. 1162.

20. For the Davis-Brown exchange, see Ibid., pp. 1133–38, 1156–69. There is a first-rate dissection of Brown and his unrealistic opposition to conscription in Clifford Dowdey's *Experiment in Rebellion*, pp. 165–67.

21. *The Military Policy of the United States*, p. 234.

22. *Lincoln and the War Governors*, p. 289.

23. A glimpse of the men and methods employed in recruiting ex-slaves is provided in *Civil War Diary of James T. Ayres*, edited by John Hope Franklin. Ayres, who referred to his work as *Gathering Up Sambo*, could write reflections such as: "No niggers enlisted yet. . . . Pore ignorant devils, they would Rather Stay behind and geather up Boxes, oald shoes and oald shirts and Pants our Boys have left than be Soldiers." He also wrote that he had told a colored woman: "I want your man. You ought to be a slave as long as you live and him too if he is so mean as not to help get his liberty but sneak around our camps to live on the rags we throw away when he might do better."

SOLDIERS' BARGAIN

1. *Recollections of Half a Century*, p. 347; *Service with the 6th Wisconsin*, p. 132; *Fighting Joe Hooker*, p. 154; *Personal Recollections of Distinguished Generals*, by William F. G. Shanks, pp. 190–91.

2. *On the Parallels*, p. 132; *Four Years Campaigning in the Army of the Potomac*, pp. 80–81.

3. *Official Records*, Vol. XXV, Part 2, pp. 855–56.

4. *Recollections of Half a Century*, p. 348.

5. The little song about Joe Hooker, which touches on many other matters as well, is printed in *History of the Corn Exchange Regiment*, pp. 166–67.

6. *History of the 9th Massachusetts*, p. 276.

7. *Official Records*, Vol. XXV, Part 2, p. 57.

8. *History of the 12th Regiment New Hampshire Volunteers*, p. 58.

9. Report to Hooker from Dr. Jonathan Letterman: *Official Records*, Vol. XXV, Part 2, p. 239.

10. Ibid., pp. 491–92; *Berdan's United States Sharpshooters*, p. 235.

11. *History of the 9th Massachusetts*, p. 276; *Recollections of the Civil War*, p. 76; *Henry Wilson's Regiment*, p. 248.

12. *The Three Years Service of the 33rd Massachusetts Infantry Regiment*, p. 18; *Henry Wilson's Regiment*, p. 248. For a good general discussion of the improvement brought about under Hooker, see De Trobriand's *Four Years with the Army of the Potomac*, pp. 413–17.

13. *History of the Corn Exchange Regiment*, p. 165; *Official Records*, Vol. XXV, Part 2, pp. 73, 74, 84, 86; *Lincoln and the Episodes of the Civil War*, pp. 141–42.

14. *Recollections of the Civil War*, p. 76; *The Campaign of Chancellorsville*, by John Bigelow, Jr., pp. 50–52; *History of the 9th Massachusetts*, pp. 283–84; *Road to Richmond*, p. 81; "The Army of the Potomac under Hooker," by William Howard Mills, pp. 185–95 of the *Magazine of American History*, Vol. XV.

15. *Fighting Joe Hooker*, p. 182. For Lincoln's dismay at Hooker's boasts, see *Abraham Lincoln: The War Years*, Vol. II, p. 80.

16. *Official Records*, Vol. XXV, Part 2, p. 52. The remark would seem to have been something of an overstatement.

17. *History of the First Regiment Minnesota Volunteer Infantry*, p. 227. For Sumner's criticism of army "croaking," see *The Military Services of Major General Ambrose Everett Burnside in the Civil War*, by Daniel R. Ballou, Part 2, p. 44.

18. *Battles and Leaders*, Vol. III, p. 154.

19. *Army Letters, 1861–65*, by O. W. Norton, pp. 327–28. There is a sketch of Butterfield in the *Dictionary of American Biography*, Vol. III, pp. 372–74, and he appears sporadically in M. Francis Dowley's *History and Honorary Roll of the 12th Regiment, Infantry, N.G.S.N.Y.*, of which he used to be colonel.

20. *Charles Francis Adams: An Autobiography*, p. 161.

21. *Life and Letters of George Gordon Meade*, Vol. I, pp. 351, 354.

22. This material on Sickles follows the account in *Dan Sickles, Hero of Gettysburg and "Yankee King of Spain,"* by Edgcumb Pinchon.

23. *A Diary from Dixie*, by Mary Boykin Chesnut, edited by Ben Ames Williams, p. 247; Pinchon's *Dan Sickles*, pp. 136–37.

24. *Fighting Joe Hooker*, p. 173 ff.

25. For the difficulties of outpost duty that winter, see *History of the First Regiment of Massachusetts Cavalry Volunteers*, p. 33; *Deeds of Daring; or, History of the 8th New York Volunteer Cavalry*, by Henry Norton, pp. 56–58; *The Campaign of Chancellorsville*, pp. 60, 72.

26. *Official Records*, Vol. XXV, Part 2, p. 197.

27. *The Campaign of Chancellorsville*, pp. 73–74. This apparently is the origin of the belief—widely held during the war—that it was Hooker who originated the common wisecrack, "Whoever saw a dead cavalryman?" (In the Confederacy, the remark was generally attributed to acid-tongued D. H. Hill.)

28. This cavalry fight and Hooker's reaction to it are detailed in *The Campaign of Chancellorsville*, pp. 89, 98–102, 105. Good descriptions of the fight occur in J. H. Stine's *History of the Army of the Potomac*, pp. 319–22, and in John W. Thomason's *Jeb Stuart*, pp. 355–61.

29. *Fighting Joe Hooker*, p. 182.

MAY DAY IN THE WILDERNESS

1. *R. E. Lee,* by Douglas Southall Freeman, Vol. II, p. 480.

2. *Diary of Gideon Welles,* Vol. I, p. 336; *Recollections of Half a Century,* p. 348; *The Campaign of Chancellorsville,* p. 108.

3. Stoneman is sketched briefly in the *Dictionary of American Biography,* Vol. XVIII, p. 92.

4. *The Campaign of Chancellorsville,* p. 110 ff.; *Official Records,* Vol. XXV, Part 2, pp. 199–200.

5. Ibid., pp. 199–200; *Battles and Leaders,* Vol. III, p. 155.

6. Stine's *History of the Army of the Potomac,* footnote, pp. 324–35.

7. Stoneman's abortive attempt to cross the river is discussed in *Jeb Stuart,* pp. 364–66, and in *The Campaign of Chancellorsville,* pp. 148–58.

8. For the exchange of letters between Hooker and Lincoln, and between Hooker and Stoneman, see *Official Records,* Vol. XXV, Part 2, pp. 213–14, 220–21.

9. Testimony before the Committee on the Conduct of the War, cited in *The Campaign of Chancellorsville,* p. 166.

10. *The 95th Pennsylvania Volunteers,* by G. Norton Galloway, p. 48; *Official Records,* Vol. XXV, Part 2, p. 488.

11. *History of the 12th Regiment New Hampshire Volunteers,* p. 65; *The Second Massachusetts Infantry and the Campaign of Chancellorsville,* by George A. Thayer, p. 10; *Life and Letters of Henry Lee Higginson,* p. 182.

12. *History of the 12th Regiment New Hampshire Volunteers,* p. 68.

13. Ibid., p. 68.

14. *History of the 9th Massachusetts,* pp. 296–97; *History of the Corn Exchange Regiment,* p. 169; *The Campaign of Chancellorsville,* pp. 197–200.

15. Ibid., p. 221.

16. *Battles and Leaders,* Vol. III, pp. 175–77; *Jeb Stuart,* pp. 368–71.

17. *Battles and Leaders,* Vol. III, p. 224.

18. *History of the Corn Exchange Regiment,* pp. 169–70; *Battles and Leaders,* Vol. III, p. 157; *Days and Events,* p. 190; *The Fifth Regiment Connecticut Volunteers: A History,* by Edwin E. Marvin, p. 251.

19. The best account of this fruitless operation is in *The Campaign of Chancellorsville,* pp. 243–54.

20. *History of the Second Army Corps,* p. 224.

21. Ibid., p. 223.

22. *Battles and Leaders,* Vol. III, p. 161.

23. *The Campaign of Chancellorsville,* pp. 236–37. For the circular which expresses the confidence that the Rebels will be bold enough to attack, see *Official Records,* Vol. XXV, Part 2, p. 328.

CHAPTER FOUR: ON THE OTHER SIDE OF THE RIVER

SOME OF US WILL NOT SEE ANOTHER SUNRISE

1. An exceptionally good discussion of this point is contained in *The Ninth Ohio Volunteers,* by Carl Wittke, a booklet which is not so much a history of the regiment as a study of its background. See also *The German Soldier in the Wars of the United States,* by J. G. Rosengarten, pp. 92–93, 95.

2. *Official Records,* Vol. XXV, Part 1, pp. 660–61.

3. Blenker is sketched in Appleton's *Cyclopedia of American Biography.* References to his work as a recruiter are in *Official Records,* Series III, Vol. I, pp. 534, 623.

4. *Official Records,* Vol. XII, Part 3, pp. 81, 82, 86, 92, 96, 99, 186–87; also Vol. XII, Part 1, pp. 27–28. There is an account of some of the trials of Blenker's men in *Trials and Triumphs: The Record of the 55th Ohio Infantry,* by Captain Hartwell Osborn and Others, pp. 25–26.

5. *The Three Years Service of the 33rd Massachusetts Infantry Regiment,* p. 11; *Trials and Triumphs,* p. 29.

6. Frémont's report is in the *Official Records,* Vol. XII, Part 1, pp. 3–13. See also p. 30 for his medical director's report, and p. 647 for Frémont's account of the straggling. Carl Schurz to Lincoln is in Vol. XII, Part 3, pp. 397–401.

7. *The Campaign of Chancellorsville,* pp. 39–42.

8. *The Road to Richmond,* p. 9; *Three Years Service of the 33rd Massachusetts,* p. 96; *The Battle of Chancellorsville,* by Augustus Choate Hamlin, p. 34; *Trials and Triumphs,* p. 61; *The 25th Ohio Veteran Volunteer Infantry in the War for the Union,* by Howard C. Culp, p. 59; *Autobiography of Oliver Otis Howard,* Vol. I, p. 349.

9. For references to the XI Corps' status as a pariah, see *History of the Second Army Corps,* pp. 229–30; *The Battle of Chancellorsville,* pp. 23–24; Walker's *General Hancock,* p. 84.

10. *Battles and Leaders,* Vol. III, p. 195.

11. *Four Years Campaigning in the Army of the Potomac,* p. 82.

12. *Battles and Leaders,* Vol. III, p. 163.

13. *History of the 12th Regiment New Hampshire Volunteers*, pp. 71–72.

14. *Berdan's United States Sharpshooters*, pp. 2–7, 16, 20–21, 235–37, 244–45.

15. Ibid., p. 251.

16. *History of the 12th Regiment New Hampshire Volunteers*, p. 448; *Battles and Leaders*, Vol. III, p. 183. There is a detailed examination of the XI Corps' arrangements in Bigelow's *The Campaign of Chancellorsville*, pp. 284–86. Even more exhaustive is the account in Hamlin's *The Battle of Chancellorsville*, pp. 34–47, 55–58–a book which devotes itself with a good deal of success to the thesis that this corps was much more sinned against than sinning.

17. *Trials and Triumphs*, pp. 68–69; *The 25th Ohio Veteran Volunteer Infantry*, pp. 61–64; *The Campaign of Chancellorsville*, p. 287.

18. Ibid., pp. 288–89; *Trials and Triumphs*, pp. 69–70; *Official Records*, Vol. XXV, Part 1, pp. 652–53.

19. *The Battle of Chancellorsville*, p. 62.

20. *Trials and Triumphs*, p. 80; *The Three Years Service of the 33rd Massachusetts Infantry Regiment*, pp. 41, 97; *The 25th Ohio Veteran Volunteer Infantry*, pp. 64–65.

21. *Official Records*, Vol. XXV, Part 1, pp. 632–37, 640–46; *The Campaign of Chancellorsville*, pp. 296–97.

22. *Official Records*, Vol. XXV, Part 1, p. 643.

23. *The 25th Ohio Veteran Volunteer Infantry*, pp. 65–66; *The 61st Ohio Volunteers, 1861–1865*, by Frederick Stephen Wallace, pp. 13–14.

24. *Official Records*, Vol. XXV, Part 1, pp. 655–56.

25. Ibid., p. 657; *The Campaign of Chancellorsville*, p. 297; *The Battle of Chancellorsville*, p. 76; *Battles and Leaders*, Vol. III, pp. 200–1.

26. *The Campaign of Chancellorsville*, p. 306.

27. *The Charge of the 8th Pennsylvania Cavalry at Chancellorsville*, by Pennock Huey, a little booklet which is an excellent corrective to General Pleasonton's imaginative and dramatic story in *Battles and Leaders*, Vol. III, pp. 179–81.

HELL ISN'T HALF A MILE OFF

1. *Berdan's United States Sharpshooters*, pp. 275–76.

2. *Four Years Campaigning in the Army of the Potomac*, p. 82; *History of the 12th Regiment New Hampshire Volunteers*, p. 72 ff.; *Official Records*, Vol. XXV, Part 1, p. 487.

3. *The Battle of Chancellorsville*, pp. 93–100; *Battles and Leaders*, Vol. III, pp. 179–82, 188. See also "The Romances of Chancellorsville," by Lieutenant

Colonel Theodore Dodge, *Papers of the Military Historical Society of Massachusetts*, Vol. III, pp. 202–17.

4. *Official Records*, Vol. XXV, Part 1, pp. 483–84, 657, 885.

5. *Campaigns of the 146th Regiment New York State Volunteers*, p. 84; *History of the Corn Exchange Regiment*, pp. 182–83; *Days and Events*, p. 203; *The Campaign of Chancellorsville*, p. 303.

6. Ibid., pp. 324–25.

7. *Official Records*, Vol. XXV, Part 1, p. 437.

8. *Four Years Campaigning in the Army of the Potomac*, p. 84; *Under the Red Patch*, p. 181.

9. *The Fifth Regiment Connecticut Volunteers: A History*, by Edwin E. Marvin, p. 253; *Four Years with the Army of the Potomac*, pp. 447–55.

10. *The Campaign of Chancellorsville*, p. 327; *Official Records*, Vol. XXV, Part 1, p. 670; *The Three Years Service of the 33rd Massachusetts Infantry Regiment*, p. 67.

11. *Lincoln and the Episodes of the Civil War*, p. 195.

12. *Berdan's United States Sharpshooters*, p. 259; *History of the 12th Regiment New Hampshire Volunteers*, p. 76; *The Road to Richmond*, p. 86; *Journal History of the 29th Ohio Veteran Volunteers*, by J. Hamp Se Cheverell, pp. 64–65.

13. For an appreciation of the tactical opportunities open to Hooker that morning, see *The Military Genius of Abraham Lincoln*, by Brigadier General Colin R. Ballard, pp. 157–58.

14. *Official Records*, Vol. XXV, Part 1, pp. 724, 726, 729, 754–56, 764. For a standard method of making an abatis of felled trees, see *The Diary of a Young Officer*, p. 127.

15. *The Three Years Service of the 33rd Massachusetts Infantry Regiment*, p. 69.

16. *Official Records*, Vol. XXV, Part 1, pp. 684–89.

17. *The 20th Connecticut: A Regimental History*, by John W. Storrs, p. 57.

18. *Official Records*, Vol. XXV, Part 1, p. 731.

19. Ibid., p. 711; *The Three Years Service of the 33rd Massachusetts Infantry Regiment*, pp. 73–74; *The Second Massachusetts Infantry and the Campaign of Chancellorsville*.

20. *History of the 12th Regiment New Hampshire Volunteers*, pp. 81–86.

21. *The Long Arm of Lee*, by Jennings Cropper Wise, Vol. II, pp. 507–11; *The Crisis of the Confederacy*, by Cecil Battine, p. 80.

22. *A Military History of the 8th Regiment Ohio Volunteer Infantry*, by Lieutenant Colonel Franklin Sawyer, p. 114; *History of a Cavalry Company*, p. 93.

23. *Under the Red Patch*, pp. 185–86. There is a glimpse of Annie minister-
ing to wounded men on the firing line in *Henry Wilson's Regiment*, p. 294. For
an appealing sketch of this remarkable young woman, see *Lincoln's Daughters
of Mercy*, p. 135.

24. *Battles and Leaders*, Vol. III, p. 221; *Official Records*, Vol. XXV, Part 1,
pp. 314, 399–403, 714; *The 20th Connecticut*, p. 53.

25. *Battles and Leaders*, Vol. III, pp. 169–70.

26. Walker's *General Hancock*, p. 83.

27. *Days and Events*, pp. 202, 205–6.

28. Ibid., p. 196.

29. *Official Records*, Vol. XXV, Part 1, pp. 284–85, 307, 314; *History of the
Second Army Corps*, pp. 245–46; Walker's *General Hancock*, pp. 90–91.

30. *Official Records*, Vol. XXV, Part 1, p. 917; *Berdan's United States Sharpshooters*, pp. 264–65.

31. *Days and Events*, p. 206. For the removal of the guns, see *History of
the Second Army Corps*, p. 247; *Official Records*, Vol. XXV, Part 1, pp. 328–29.

32. *History of the Corn Exchange Regiment*, p. 187.

33. *The Campaign of Chancellorsville*, p. 381.

GO BOIL YOUR SHIRT

1. *Official Records*, Vol. XXV, Part 1, pp. 749, 751; *Reminiscences of Winfield Scott Hancock*, by His Wife, pp. 93–94; *Three Years Campaign of the
9th N.Y.S.M. during the Southern Rebellion*, by John W. Jaques, p. 141; *History
of the Corn Exchange Regiment*, p. 201.

2. "The Battle of Marye's Heights and Salem Church," by Captain John W.
Bigelow, Jr., *Papers of the Military Historical Society of Massachusetts*, Vol.
III, p. 255.

3. One of the Federals who stormed the wall wrote: "It is not true that
bayonets were never crossed during the war. They were used at the stone wall
by our men, and after the battle it was found, by actual count, that 40 of the
enemy had been bayoneted there." (*Campaigning with the 6th Maine*, by Lieutenant Colonel Charles A. Clark, p. 33.)

4. *Army Life: A Private's Reminiscences of the Civil War*, by the Rev.
Theodore Gerrish, pp. 340–41.

5. *The 95th Pennsylvania Volunteers*, p. 74.

6. General Couch's account of this meeting is in *Battles and Leaders*, Vol.
III, p. 171. See also *Gouverneur Kemble Warren: The Life and Letters of an
American Soldier*, by Emerson Gifford Taylor, p. 110; *History of the Second
Army Corps*, pp. 250–51.

7. *History of the 12th Regiment New Hampshire Volunteers*, p. 92; *Battles and Leaders*, Vol. III, p. 171. For a good picture of the miseries of the rear-guard details on that rainy night, see *History of the Corn Exchange Regiment*, pp. 203–5.

8. Report of Provost Marshal General Patrick, *Official Records*, Vol. XXV, Part 2, pp. 476–77.

9. *History of the 12th Regiment New Hampshire Volunteers*, p. 93; *Army Letters, 1861–65*, pp. 150–51.

10. General Patrick's report, cited in Note 8.

11. *The Campaign of Chancellorsville*, p. 444.

12. Ibid., p. 458.

13. *Some Personal Reminiscences of Service in the Cavalry of the Army of the Potomac*, by Colonel Hampton S. Thomas, p. 9; *Lincoln and the Episodes of the Civil War*, p. 202; *The Campaign of Chancellorsville*, pp. 458–59.

14. Ibid., pp. 378, 482.

15. *Diary of Gideon Welles*, Vol. I, pp. 291, 293; *Abraham Lincoln: The War Years*, Vol. II, p. 97.

16. *History of the Philadelphia Brigade*, pp. 164–65.

17. *Official Records*, Vol. XXV, Part 1, pp. 631, 658.

18. Ibid., p. 622; *The Battle of Chancellorsville and the Eleventh Army Corps*, p. 48.

19. *Life and Letters of George Gordon Meade*, Vol. I, pp. 373, 377, 379; *Personal Recollections of the Civil War*, p. 120; *Gouverneur Kemble Warren*, p. 111; *History of the Second Army Corps*, pp. 155–56; *Reminiscences of Winfield Scott Hancock*, pp. 94–95.

20. *History of the 12th Regiment New Hampshire Volunteers*, p. 90.

21. *History of the Philadelphia Brigade*, p. 166; *Letters from a Surgeon of the Civil War*, p. 41. A Massachusetts soldier asserted: "The morale of the Army of the Potomac was better in June than it had been in January. . . . The diaries and letters of the members of the 15th show nothing of that spirit of insubordination and despondency . . . which had prevailed in the middle of the winter." (*The Story of the 15th Regiment Massachusetts Volunteer Infantry*, by Andrew E. Ford, p. 253.)

22. *Under the Red Patch*, p. 186; *History of the 24th Michigan*, p. 142.

23. *The 95th Pennsylvania Volunteers*, p. 56; *Army Letters, 1861–65*, p. 156; *The Campaign of Chancellorsville*, p. 488.

24. *History of the Corn Exchange Regiment*, p. 147; *History of the 12th Regiment New Hampshire Volunteers*, p. 94.

25. *History of the 24th Michigan*, p. 138.

26. *Berdan's United States Sharpshooters,* p. 277.

27. *The Battle of Gettysburg,* by Colonel Frank Aretas Haskell, pp. 3–4.

28. *Berdan's United States Sharpshooters,* pp. 277–78.

CHAPTER FIVE: LINCOLN COMIN' WID HIS CHARIOT

THE GRAPES OF WRATH

1. *Army Letters, 1861–65,* p. 281.

2. *Diary of Gideon Welles,* Vol. I, pp. 251, 259.

3. *Abraham Lincoln: The War Years,* Vol. II, pp. 172–74.

4. *The Molly Maguires,* by Anthony Bimba, pp. 11–28; *Labor Disturbances in Pennsylvania, 1850–1880,* by J. Walter Coleman, pp. 3, 10, 17.

5. Ibid., p. 23.

6. In the spring of 1864, when the 48th Pennsylvania "veteranized"—i.e., re-enlisted as a regiment for three more years—and returned to Schuylkill County to recruit, it had no trouble getting men, and its historian noted that it quickly got more recruits than the regulations required. (*The Story of the 48th,* by Joseph Gould, p. 160.)

7. *Labor Disturbances in Pennsylvania,* p. 42.

8. Ibid., pp. 40–69; *The Molly Maguires,* p. 11; *Discontent in New York City, 1861–65,* by Brother Basil Leo Lee, F.S.C., pp. 175–76; *Official Records,* Series III, Vol. III, pp. 1008–9.

9. Ibid., p. 629.

10. See the chapter on the 10th New Jersey in *New Jersey and the Rebellion,* by John W. Foster.

11. McClure's account of all of this is in his *Old-Time Notes of Pennsylvania,* Vol. I, pp. 542–49.

12. Ibid., p. 550.

13. *Old Thad Stevens: A Story of Ambition,* pp. 53–54.

14. *The Hidden Civil War,* p. 110.

15. *A True History of the Reign of Terror in Southern Illinois,* by James D. Fox, pp. 13–14.

16. *History of the United States from the Compromise of 1850,* by James Ford Rhodes, Vol. IV, pp. 226–27.

17. *The Life and Public Services of Ambrose E. Burnside,* pp. 206–7.

18. Rhodes's *History of the United States,* Vol. IV, p. 247.

19. Ibid., p. 248; *Abraham Lincoln: The War Years,* Vol. II, p. 162.

20. *A Rebel War Clerk's Diary,* Vol. I, p. 357.

21. *History of the Administration of President Lincoln,* by Henry J. Raymond, p. 359.

22. *Army Life: A Private's Reminiscences of the Civil War,* pp. 124–28.

GLORY! GLORY! HALLELUJAH!

1. *In French Creek Valley,* by John Earle Reynolds, p. 304 ff.

2. *Social and Industrial Conditions in the North during the Civil War,* by Emerson David Fite, pp. 11, 32–41.

3. Ibid., p. 23.

4. Ibid., p. 32 ff.; *The Long Ships Passing,* by Walter Havighurst, pp. 140–41, 184 ff.

5. Among the bewildering list of patents in the *Annual Report of the Commissioner of Patents, 1864,* is one for a device (pictured in Vol. II, p. 306) which appears to be a fair approximation of the modern strapless bra.

6. *Influence of the War on Our National Prosperity,* by William E. Dodge, pp. 9, 11, 13; *The Growth of the American Republic,* by Samuel Eliot Morison and Henry Steele Commager, Vol. I, p. 703.

7. *I Rode with Stonewall,* by Henry Kyd Douglas, p. 251. Wesley Culp moved to Virginia before the war and enlisted in 1861 in the 2nd Virginia, of the famous Stonewall Brigade. He was killed in the assault on Culp's Hill within sight of the house where he had been born.

8. *Influence of the War on Our National Prosperity,* pp. 15–16.

9. *The Bivouac and the Battlefield,* p. 338.

10. *Social and Industrial Conditions in the North,* pp. 85–91; *Adventures of America, 1857–1900,* by John A. Kouwenhoven, Section 90; *Political and Social Growth of the American People,* by Arthur M. Schlesinger, pp. 40–41; *The Growth of the American Republic,* Vol. I, p. 704 ff.

11. *Official Records,* Series IV, Vol. III, p. 677.

12. *Berdan's United States Sharpshooters,* p. 237.

13. For Pleasonton, see Haskell's *The Battle of Gettysburg,* p. 70, and *Lincoln and the Episodes of the Civil War,* p. 232. Wyndham was a fabulous character who had served in the British, French, Austrian, and Italian armies and in the French Navy as well. He survived the Civil War, edited a comic magazine in Calcutta, undertook cotton and timber speculations in Mandalay and Burma, and finally lost his life in the explosion of a balloon in which he was giving aeronautical exhibitions in India. He is sketched in *New Jersey Troops in the Gettysburg Campaign,* by Samuel Coombs, pp. 402–6.

14. *Deeds of Daring; or, History of the 8th New York Cavalry*, pp. 66–67. This delightfully unsophisticated little book, one of the pleasantest of the regimental histories, contains fascinating glimpses of the way Grimes Davis turned a collection of rookies into a crack cavalry outfit. See also *Some Personal Reminiscences of Service in the Cavalry of the Army of the Potomac*, pp. 9–10; *History of the 8th Cavalry Regiment, Illinois Volunteers*, pp. 243–47; *A History of the First Regiment of Massachusetts Cavalry Volunteers*, pp. 18, 140.

15. Ibid., p. 296; *Reminiscences and Record of the 6th New York Veteran Volunteer Cavalry*, p. 67.

16. *History of the Third Indiana Cavalry*, by W. N. Pickerill, p. 12.

17. *History of the 8th Cavalry Regiment, Illinois Volunteers*, pp. 202–3; *History of the First Regiment of Massachusetts Cavalry Volunteers*, pp. 291, 294–95.

18. Ibid., p. 159.

19. *Reminiscences of General Herman Haupt*, p. 205.

20. *Three Years in the Field Hospitals of the Army of the Potomac*, pp. 34–35; *Military History of the 8th Regiment Ohio Volunteer Infantry*, p. 119; *Three Years Campaign of the 9th N.Y.S.M.*, p. 149; *History of the 12th Regiment New Hampshire Volunteers*, p. 114.

21. *The Story of the 15th Regiment Massachusetts Volunteer Infantry*, by Andrew E. Ford, p. 256. See also *The 20th Connecticut: A Regimental History*, p. 70; *History of the Philadelphia Brigade*, p. 172; *New Jersey Troops in the Gettysburg Campaign*, pp. 104–5.

22. *Military History of the 8th Regiment Ohio Volunteer Infantry*, p. 122.

23. *The Road to Richmond*, pp. 95–96, with the spelling very slightly modernized.

24. *New Jersey Troops in the Gettysburg Campaign*, pp. 92–93.

WHITE ROAD IN THE MOONLIGHT

1. *Rebellion Record*, Vol. VII, Part 2, pp. 194–95, 197.

2. *Our Campaign around Gettysburg*, by John Lockwood, pp. 35–58; *Rebellion Record*, Vol. VII, Part 2, p. 10.

3. *New Jersey Troops in the Gettysburg Campaign*, pp. 126–27.

4. *Lincoln and the Episodes of the Civil War*, p. 213. Duffié's report on the fight is in *Official Records*, Vol. XXVII, Part 1, pp. 963–64. There are some good glimpses of this cavalry fighting in *History of the 8th Cavalry Regiment, Illinois Volunteers*, pp. 251–54, and there is Confederate testimony to the improvement in Federal cavalry in *War Years with Jeb Stuart*, by Lieutenant Colonel W. W. Blackford, p. 221.

5. The most detailed recent study of Stuart's moves is Freeman's, in *Lee's Lieutenants*, Vol. III, pp. 51–72. See also Thomason's account in *Jeb Stuart*, pp. 420–29, and *Ranger Mosby*, by Virgil Carrington Jones, pp. 145–50.

6. This anecdote is from Current's *Old Thad Stevens*.

7. *Official Records*, Vol. XXVII, Part 1, p. 151; abstract from returns of the Army of the Potomac, June 20, 1863.

8. The most generally accepted account of the reasons for Hooker's removal is Charles F. Benjamin's in *Battles and Leaders*, Vol. III, pp. 239–43. The British critic, General Ballard, remarks that Hooker simply quit in a fit of petulance. (*The Military Genius of Abraham Lincoln*, pp. 163–64.) Writing in 1879, Colonel Theodore Gates of the 80th New York suggested that Hooker quit because he was afraid to command the army against Lee in another battle. (*The Ulster Guard and the War of the Rebellion*, p. 404.)

9. *Life and Letters of George Gordon Meade*, Vol. I, pp. 388–89.

10. Ibid., pp. 19, 30–32, 34–35, 37–38, 161 ff., 241, 243.

11. Ibid., pp. 214–15.

12. *Battles and Leaders*, Vol. III, p. 243; *Gouverneur Kemble Warren*, p. 119.

13. *The Battle of Gettysburg*, by the Comte de Paris.

14. *New Jersey Troops in the Gettysburg Campaign*, p. 134; *History of the 12th Regiment New Hampshire Volunteers*, pp. 116–17. There is a good sketch of Humphreys by Major General James H. Wilson in *Papers of the Military Historical Society of Massachusetts*, Vol. X, pp. 71–96.

15. *The 48th in the War*, p. 88.

16. *History of the 2nd Massachusetts Regiment of Infantry: Gettysburg*, by Colonel Charles F. Morse, p. 4.

17. Ibid., p. 5.

18. *Four Years Campaigning in the Army of the Potomac*, p. 88; *The History of the 9th Regiment Massachusetts Volunteer Infantry*, p. 312; *Army Life: A Private's Reminiscences of the Civil War*, p. 99.

19. References to the soldiers' deep disappointment at Hooker's removal are innumerable, and it is clear that if the higher officers had lost confidence in him the enlisted man had not. See *Four Years in the Army of the Potomac*, p. 106; *New Jersey Troops in the Gettysburg Campaign*, pp. 128–29; *The Story of the 15th Regiment Massachusetts Volunteer Infantry*, p. 260; *History of the 12th Regiment New Hampshire Volunteers*, pp. 118, 130; *Army Life: A Private's Reminiscences*, p. 100; *Military History of the 8th Regiment Ohio Volunteer Infantry*, p. 123; *The 20th Connecticut: A Regimental History*, p. 73; *The Three Years Service of the 33rd Massachusetts Infantry Regiment*, p. 110.

20. *Rebellion Record*, Vol. VII, Part 2, pp. 20–21.

21. Ibid., pp. 86–87.

22. See Josiah M. Favill's *Diary of a Young Officer*, p. 218: "The aim of the government would seem to be to encourage officers to keep their commands out of dangerous places, for their chances of promotion are lessened in exact proportion as they lose their men by fighting." For a similar complaint by Rufus Dawes, see *Service with the 6th Wisconsin Volunteers*, p. 188.

23. *Days and Events*, p. 234; *History of the First Regiment Minnesota Volunteer Infantry*, p. 347.

24. *The 20th Connecticut: A Regimental History*, p. 75; *Our Campaign around Gettysburg*, pp. 121–22.

25. *Rebellion Record*, Vol. VII, Part 2, p. 122.

26. *The Ulster Guard and the War of the Rebellion*, p. 422.

27. *Henry Wilson's Regiment*, p. 331; *Army Life: A Private's Reminiscences*, p. 101; *The Old Fourth Michigan Infantry*, pp. 21–22; *History of the 9th Regiment Massachusetts Volunteer Infantry*, p. 312; *History of the Sauk County Riflemen*, p. 70; *Battles and Leaders*, Vol. III, p. 301. In most cases the report seems to have been formally announced to the troops by mounted staff officers, which is not the way the spontaneous army rumor circulates.

28. *Army Letters, 1861–65*, p. 322.

CHAPTER SIX: END AND BEGINNING

THE ECONOMICS OF EIGHTY PER CENT

1. *Battles and Leaders*, Vol. III, pp. 274–75; *History of the 8th Cavalry Regiment, Illinois Volunteers*, pp. 256–57.

2. Stine's *History of the Army of the Potomac*, pp. 453–54.

3. Wadsworth is affectionately sketched in *The Ulster Guard and the War of the Rebellion*, pp. 153–54, and in *Lincoln and the Episodes of the Civil War*, pp. 49–54.

4. *History of the Sauk County Riflemen*, p. 71; *History of the 24th Michigan*, p. 142.

5. *History of the Army of the Potomac*, p. 462–63.

6. *Official Records*, Vol. XXVII, Part 1, pp. 359–60.

7. *History of the Sauk County Riflemen*, p. 73; *History of the 24th Michigan*, p. 160; Doubleday's report, *Official Records*, Vol. XXVII, Part 1, p. 244.

8. *History of the Army of the Potomac*, pp. 466–67; *Service with the 6th Wisconsin Volunteers*, pp. 168–69; *Official Records*, Vol. XXVII, Part 1, p. 281 ff.

9. *Battles and Leaders*, Vol. III, p. 285.

10. *Official Records*, Vol. XXVII, Part 1, p. 360.

11. *The Road to Richmond,* p. 80.

12. *Official Records,* Vol. XXVII, Part 1, p. 723.

13. *Trials and Triumphs,* p. 96.

14. *Official Records,* Vol. XXVII, Part 1, pp. 229, 752, 754.

15. Ibid., pp. 727–28, 756; *Battles and Leaders,* Vol. III, p. 281. Battine's *Crisis of the Confederacy,* pp. 195–99, has an excellent account of the XI Corps' fight and its relation to the fighting west of town. There is a very detailed story of the first day at Gettysburg in Stine's *History of the Army of the Potomac,* pp. 452–93.

16. *Official Records,* Vol. XXVII, Part 1, p. 753.

17. *The Road to Richmond,* pp. 99–102—an exceptionally good description of this part of the battle.

18. *Official Records,* Vol. XXVII, Part 1, pp. 291, 330–31.

19. Ibid., p. 284.

20. Colonel Morrow's report, Ibid., pp. 267–73; *History of the 24th Michigan,* p. 165.

21. *Official Records,* Vol. XXVII, Part 1, p. 280.

22. Ibid., pp. 356–57, 360; *History of the 24th Michigan,* p. 121.

23. *The Three Years Service of the 33rd Massachusetts Infantry Regiment,* p. 118.

24. *Official Records,* Vol. XXVII, Part 1, pp. 286, 716, 729, 735, 742, 755; *Service with the 6th Wisconsin Volunteers,* pp. 176–78.

25. Captain Edward N. Whittier in Vol. III, *Papers of the Military Historical Society of Massachusetts,* p. 315; *Official Records,* Vol. XXVII, Part 1, p. 281; *The Iron Brigade at Gettysburg,* p. 15; *History of the 24th Michigan,* p. 184.

26. *Reminiscences of Winfield Scott Hancock,* p. 189.

27. Ibid., p. 190. For the encounter between Hancock and Howard, see *Battles and Leaders,* Vol. III, pp. 285–86.

ALL THE TRUMPETS SOUNDED

1. De Trobriand's engaging account of the stay at Emmitsburg is in his *Four Years with the Army of the Potomac,* pp. 486–87. See also Crotty's *Four Years Campaigning in the Army of the Potomac,* p. 89.

2. *Days and Events,* pp. 240, 247.

3. *Battles and Leaders,* Vol. III, pp. 295–96, 301–3; *Life and Letters of George Gordon Meade,* Vol. II, pp. 66, 71, 74; *Four Years with the Army of the Potomac,* p. 494.

4. *Reminiscences of Winfield Scott Hancock,* p. 193.

5. *Berdan's United States Sharpshooters,* pp. 303–11.

6. *Battles and Leaders,* Vol. III, p. 303; Gibbon's *Personal Recollections of the Civil War,* pp. 135–36; *Life and Letters of George Gordon Meade,* Vol. II, pp. 72–73; *The Long Arm of Lee,* Vol. II, p. 644.

7. *Trials and Triumphs,* pp. 101, 249; *Official Records,* Vol. XXVII, Part 1, p. 358; *The Three Years Service of the 33rd Massachusetts Infantry Regiment,* p. 123; *The Long Arm of Lee,* Vol. II, p. 652; *Papers of the Military Historical Society of Massachusetts,* Vol. III, p. 320.

8. *Official Records,* Vol. XXVII, Part 1, pp. 881, 900.

9. *Four Years with the Army of the Potomac,* pp. 497–500. For a good account of the artillery in Devil's Den, see *A Famous Battery and Its Campaigns,* by Captain James E. Smith, pp. 101–12.

10. *Strong Vincent and His Brigade at Gettysburg,* by Oliver W. Norton, p. 8. Sykes is sketched from Haskell's *Battle of Gettysburg,* p. 69.

11. An uncommonly vivid description of this fighting is in *Army Life: A Private's Reminiscences of the Civil War,* pp. 107–11. Almost equally good is Colonel Chamberlain's report, *Official Records,* Vol. XXVII, Part 1, pp. 623–25.

12. *Strong Vincent and His Brigade at Gettysburg,* pp. 8–17; *Official Records,* Vol. XXVII, Part 1, pp. 616–17; *Campaigns of the 146th Regiment New York State Volunteers,* pp. 116–19; *Gouverneur Kemble Warren,* p. 128.

13. *Official Records,* Vol. XXVII, Part 1, p. 611; *The Old Fourth Michigan Infantry,* p. 23.

14. *Official Records,* Vol. XXVII, Part 1, p. 612.

15. Ibid., pp. 623, 640–41, 646, 650.

16. Ibid., p. 882; *Papers of the Military Historical Society of Massachusetts,* Vol. X, pp. 84–85.

17. *New Jersey Troops in the Gettysburg Campaign,* pp. 223–24, 239–40.

18. *The Story of the 15th Regiment Massachusetts Volunteer Infantry,* pp. 267–69, 280; *History of the 12th Regiment New Hampshire Volunteers,* pp. 123–25; *Days and Events,* pp. 251–52.

19. *Three Years Service of the 33rd Massachusetts,* p. 126; *Official Records,* Vol. XXVII, Part 1, p. 886; *History of the Corn Exchange Regiment,* p. 267. According to this latter book (pp. 287–88) Bigelow's 9th Massachusetts battery would not have been at Gettysburg at all except for a freak of chance. With other new batteries, it put in at Centreville, Va., in the spring of 1863. When the Army of the Potomac marched north, the Keystone Battery of Philadelphia was ordered to leave the reserve at Centreville and join up with the army. It delayed in order to accommodate a general of the II Corps in the matter of transporting some of his personal effects in a battery wagon. The delay irked General Hunt, the army's chief of artillery, and he canceled the Keystone's orders and called up the Massachusetts battery in its place.

20. *Official Records,* Vol. XXVII, Part 1, pp. 882–83, 897–98.

21. *Reminiscences of Winfield Scott Hancock,* p. 199; *History of the First Regiment Minnesota Volunteer Infantry,* p. 344 ff. Hancock gave the 1st Minnesota credit for capturing the flag, but the regimental historian insisted that this was not so; the flag the regiment got, he said, was taken in the repulse of Pickett's charge next day.

22. *Life and Letters of George Gordon Meade,* Vol. II, p. 89.

23. *History of the Second Massachusetts Regiment of Infantry: Gettysburg,* pp. 8–9.

24. Probably the best description of this attack and its repulse is Captain Whittier's in Vol. III, *Papers of the Military Historical Society of Massachusetts,* pp. 326–31. Another good narrative is in *The Three Years Service of the 33rd Massachusetts Infantry Regiment,* pp. 129–30. See also *Official Records,* Vol. XXVII, Part 1, pp. 360–61, 894.

AND IT MAY BE FOREVER

1. *The 20th Connecticut: A Regimental History,* pp. 88–91.

2. *Journal History of the 29th Ohio Veteran Volunteers,* p. 70; *Four Years Campaigning in the Army of the Potomac,* p. 91.

3. *The Diary of a Young Officer,* pp. 246–47.

4. *Pictorial History of the Civil War,* Vol. III, p. 67; *Days and Events,* pp. 255–56.

5. *Personal Recollections of the Civil War,* pp. 141–45.

6. *The 20th Connecticut: A Regimental History,* p. 194.

7. *Papers of the Military Historical Society of Massachusetts,* Vol. III, pp. 346–47; *Official Records,* Vol. XXVII, Part 1, pp. 781, 813–15.

8. Ibid., p. 841; *The Dutchess County Regiment in the Civil War,* p. 36.

9. *New Jersey Troops in the Gettysburg Campaign,* p. 290.

10. *Life in Camp: A History of the Nine Months' Service of the 14th Vermont Regiment,* an unassuming little record which is pure Vermont.

11. *The 20th Connecticut: A Regimental History,* pp. 104–5.

12. The story of the lunch party and the way the bombardment scattered it is from Gibbon's *Personal Recollections,* pp. 146–47; *Reminiscences of Winfield Scott Hancock,* p. 207; Haskell's *Battle of Gettysburg,* pp. 95–96.

13. *Papers of the Military Historical Society of Massachusetts,* Vol. III, p. 353; *The Road to Richmond,* p. 105; *History of the First Regiment Minnesota Volunteer Infantry,* p. 366; *History of the Corn Exchange Regiment,* p. 259.

14. *Personal Recollections of the Civil War,* pp. 147–48.

15. *The 20th Connecticut: A Regimental History,* pp. 95–96; *Official Records,* Vol. XXVII, Part 1, p. 902.

16. *Rebellion Record,* Vol. VII, Part 2, p. 101; *Life and Letters of George Gordon Meade,* Vol. II, pp. 106–7.

17. Mrs. Hancock tells about this farewell party in *Reminiscences of Winfield Scott Hancock,* pp. 69–70.

18. An unforgettable picture of Cushing and his battery on Cemetery Ridge is given in *Three Wisconsin Cushings,* by Theron Wilber Haight, pp. 47–50, 53, 57.

19. Haskell's *Battle of Gettysburg,* pp. 124–25; *Battles and Leaders,* Vol. III, pp. 388–89.

20. *Military History of the 8th Regiment Ohio Volunteer Infantry,* p. 131.

21. *Three Wisconsin Cushings,* p. 54.

22. *The Road to Richmond,* p. 106; *Days and Events,* p. 262.

23. *The Story of the 15th Regiment Massachusetts Volunteer Infantry,* pp. 275–76. See also *Days and Events,* p. 262, and Haskell's *Battle of Gettysburg,* p. 127.

24. *Reminiscences of Winfield Scott Hancock,* pp. 215–16.

25. *The Road to Richmond,* p. 107.

VALLEY OF DRY BONES

1. *Battles and Leaders,* Vol. III, p. 424.

2. The Comte de Paris's *Battle of Gettysburg; Official Records,* Vol. XXVII, Part 1, pp. 153, 187, 193; *Battles and Leaders,* Vol. III, p. 440.

3. *Four Years with the Army of the Potomac,* pp. 512, 514; *Days and Events,* p. 266.

4. *Lincoln and the Episodes of the Civil War,* p. 221.

5. Ibid., p. 222; *War Years with Jeb Stuart,* p. 231; *History of the 87th Regiment Pennsylvania Volunteers,* p. 84.

6. *New Jersey Troops in the Gettysburg Campaign,* p. 320; *Henry Wilson's Regiment,* p. 345.

7. *The Story of the 15th Regiment Massachusetts Volunteer Infantry,* p. 286; *Three Wisconsin Cushings,* pp. 50–51; *Journal History of the 29th Ohio Veteran Volunteers,* p. 72.

8. *Official Records,* Vol. XXVII, Part 1, p. 25; *New Jersey Troops in the Gettysburg Campaign,* p. 327; *Reminiscences of the 19th Massachusetts Regiment,* p. 71.

9. *History of the Corn Exchange Regiment,* pp. 274–75.

10. *Official Records,* Vol. XXVII, Part 1, p. 626.

11. *History of the 9th Regiment Massachusetts Volunteer Infantry*, p. 333.

12. The Meade-Halleck interchange can be found in *Battles and Leaders*, Vol. III, pp. 383–84. For the letter Lincoln wrote but did not send, see *Abraham Lincoln: The War Years*, Vol. II, pp. 353–54.

13. *Four Years with the Army of the Potomac*, p. 517.

14. For the enlisted man's point of view on this, see *Henry Wilson's Regiment*, p. 339: "If there ever was a battle won through the indomitable courage and intelligence of the rank and file of the Army of the Potomac, without planning strategical movement, or audible commands from their superior officers, it was Gettysburg."

15. *History of the Corn Exchange Regiment*, p. 269.

16. *Life and Letters of George Gordon Meade*, Vol. II, p. 125.

17. *Official Records*, Vol. XXVII, Part 1, p. 28; *Lincoln's Daughters of Mercy*, p. 169.

18. *South after Gettysburg: Letters of Cornelia Hancock*, edited by Henrietta Stratton Jaquette, pp. 4–5.

19. *Official Records*, Vol. XXVII, Part 1, pp. 22–23.

20. *Lincoln's Daughters of Mercy*, pp. 169–72.

21. *Three Years in the Field Hospitals of the Army of the Potomac*, p. 55; *South after Gettysburg*, p. 9; *Lincoln's Daughters of Mercy*, p. 173.

22. *Official Records*, Vol. XXVII, Part 1, pp. 26–28.

23. *Gettysburg and Lincoln: The Battle, the Cemetery and the National Park*, by Henry Sweetser Burrage, pp. 81–86.

24. For the indignation which this burial-by-states aroused in a fighting man, see Haskell's *Battle of Gettysburg*, p. 183: "If it be not one of the lessons that the war teaches, that we have a country paramount over faction, and party, and state, then was the blood of 50,000 citizens shed upon this field in vain." It might be noted that Colonel Haskell wrote his invaluable account of the battle while the war was still on. He was killed at Cold Harbor.

25. *Gettysburg and Lincoln*, pp. 87–90.

26. *The Story of the 15th Regiment Massachusetts Volunteer Infantry*, pp. 288, 290.

27. Gibbon's *Personal Recollections*, p. 184.

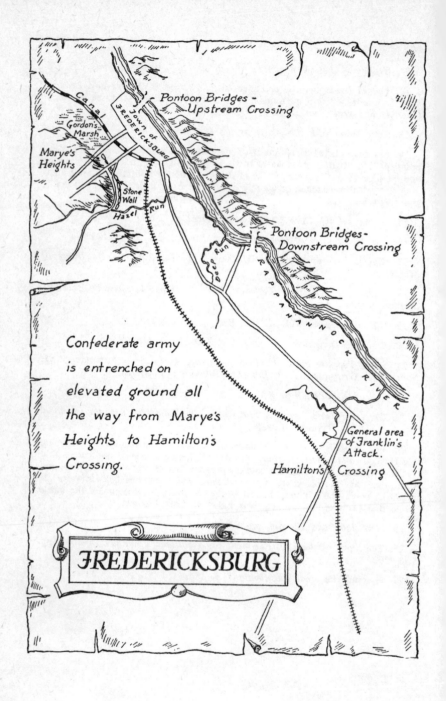

Pontoon Bridges -
Upstream Crossing

Canal

Gordon's Marsh

Marye's Heights

Town of FREDERICKSBURG

Stone Wall

Hazel Run

Pontoon Bridges-
Downstream Crossing

Deep Run

RAPPAHANNOCK RIVER

Confederate army is entrenched on elevated ground all the way from Marye's Heights to Hamilton's Crossing.

General area of Franklin's Attack.

Hamilton's Crossing

FREDERICKSBURG

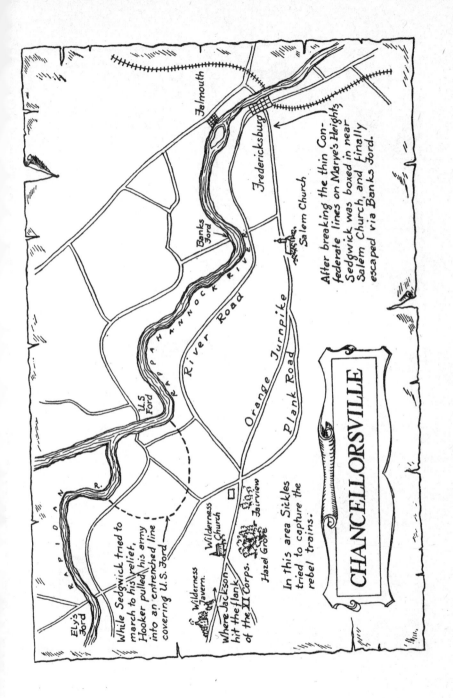

CHANCELLORSVILLE

Ely's Ford

RAPIDAN R.

While Sedgwick tried to march to his relief, Hooker pulled his army into an entrenched line covering U.S. Ford.

Wilderness Tavern

Where Jackson hit the flank of the XI Corps.

Wilderness Church

Hazel Grove

Fairview

In this area Sickles tried to capture the rebel trains.

U.S. Ford

RAPPAHANNOCK RIVER

Banks Ford

River Road

Orange Turnpike

Plank Road

Salem Church

Falmouth

Fredericksburg

After breaking the thin Confederate lines on Marye's Heights Sedgwick was boxed in near Salem Church, and finally escaped via Banks Ford.

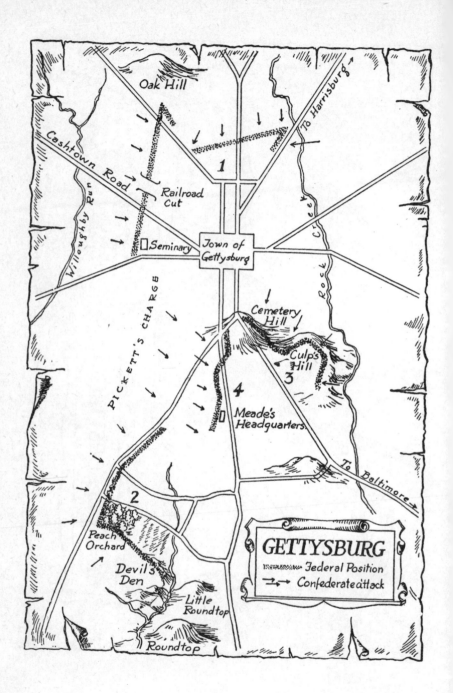

Oak Hill

Cashtown Road

Willoughby Run

To Harrisburg

Rock Creek

Railroad Cut

1

Seminary

Town of Gettysburg

PICKETT'S CHARGE

Cemetery Hill

Culp's Hill

3

4

Meade's Headquarters

To Baltimore

2

Peach Orchard

Devil's Den

Little Roundtop

Roundtop

GETTYSBURG

Federal Position

Confederate attack

Index